.remote.

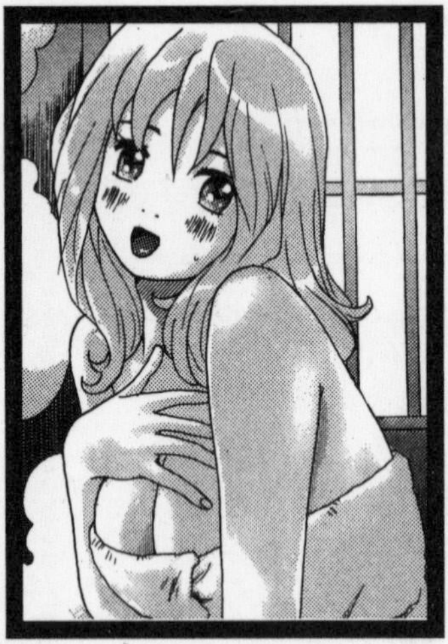

INSPECTOR
KOZABURO HIMURO

Kozaburo Himuro is the reclusive head of Special Unit A (aka the Crypt). From within his secluded headquarters, Himuro uses his genius intellect and understanding of the criminal mind to help solve the most heinous and bizarre cases. Due to mysterious events in his past, he is incapable of leaving the Crypt to face the world and his own personal demons.

DETECTIVE
KURUMI AYAKI

As Inspector Himuro's eyes and ears outside the Crypt, Kurumi Ayaki helps investigate the gruesome crimes assigned to Special Unit A. Although completely out of her element, Ayaki's heart and determination help compensate for her lack of practical experience. It is Ayaki's emotional tenacity combined with Himuro's cold logic that may be the team's greatest asset.

Previously in REMOTE...

Former meter maid Kurumi Ayaki's stint with the Metropolitan Police Department's Special Unit A has proven to be anything but dull. Working directly under the reclusive Inspector Himuro Kozaburo, Ayaki aids him in his efforts to solve the city's most heinous crimes. From killer clowns to mad bombers to lethal stalkers, no crime is too bizarre, no criminal too crafty.

But, recently, the line between Kurumi's professional and personal life has begun to blur. First, there was the stalker of Shingo's ex-girlfriend who was brutally murdered at the beach resort. Then, an old high school friend of Kurumi's was horribly murdered after a sordid career as a Fuzoku girl in Japan's sex industry. And immediately after, as Shingo and Kurumi were on their way to relax at a mountain spa, a random flat tire embroils the couple in yet another murder! Finally, the two arrive at the serenity of the spa—but can trouble be far behind?

Remote Vol. 8
written by Seimaru Amagi
illustrated by Tetsuya Koshiba

Translation - Haruko Furukawa
English Adaptation - Aaron Sparrow
Copy Editor - Peter Ahlstrom
Retouch and Lettering - Bowen Park
Production Artist - Bowen Park
Cover Artist - Raymond Makowski

Editor - Bryce P. Coleman
Digital Imaging Manager - Chris Buford
Production Managers - Jennifer Miller and Mutsumi Miyazaki
Managing Editor - Lindsey Johnston
VP of Production - Ron Klamert
Publisher and Editor-In-Chief - Mike Kiley
President and C.O.O. - John Parker
C.E.O. - Stuart Levy

A  Manga

TOKYOPOP Inc.
5900 Wilshire Blvd. Suite 2000
Los Angeles, CA 90036

E-mail: info@TOKYOPOP.com
Come visit us online at www.TOKYOPOP.com

ISBN: 1-59532-811-4
First TOKYOPOP printing: January 2006
10 9 8 7 6 5 4 3 2 1
Printed in Canada

.remote.

VOLUME 8
WRITER – SEIMARU AMAGI
ARTIST – TETSUYA KOSHIBA

HAMBURG // LONDON // LOS ANGELES // TOKYO

.remote.

VOL. 8
CONTENTS:

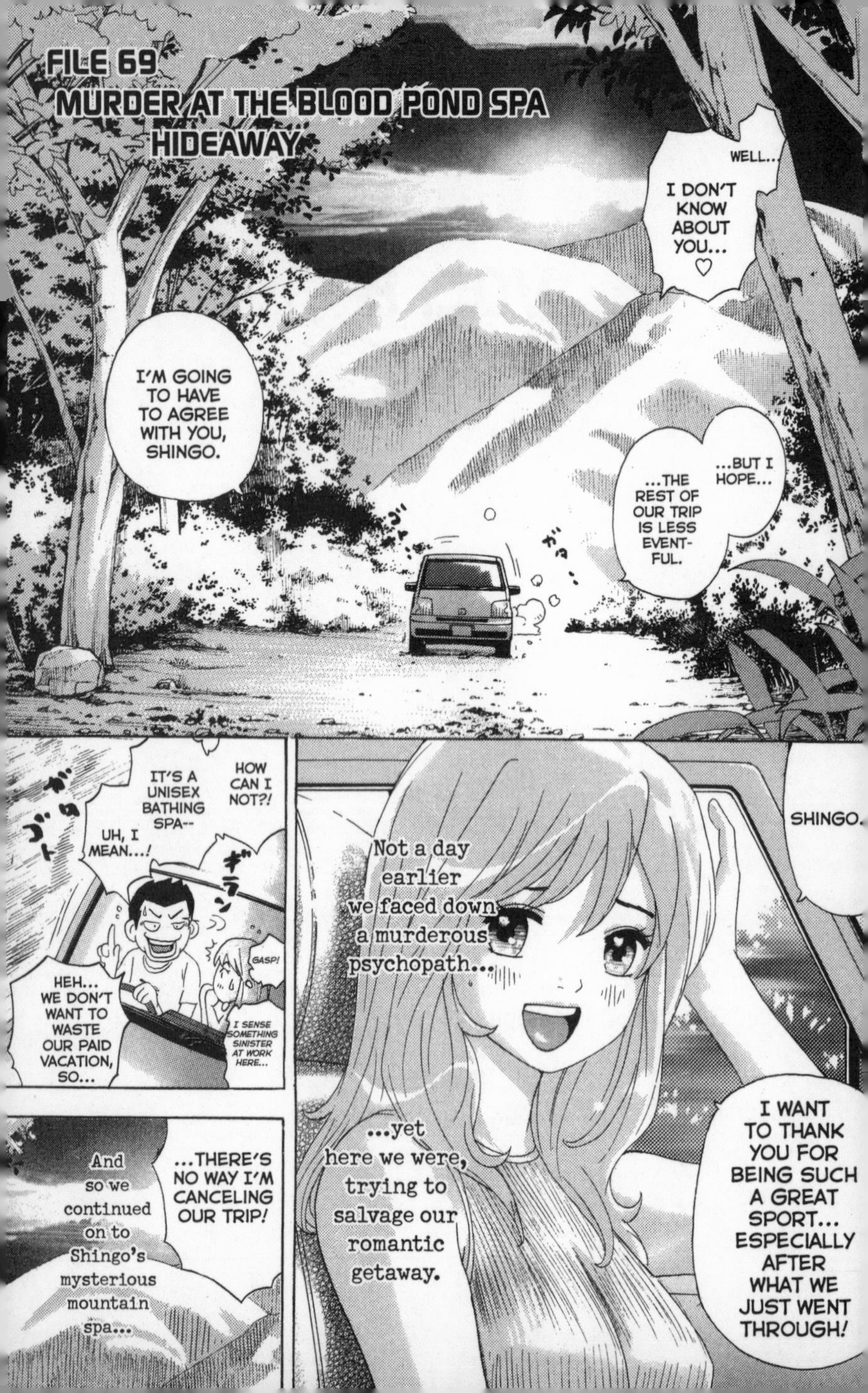
FILE 69
MURDER AT THE BLOOD POND SPA HIDEAWAY
WELL... I DON'T KNOW ABOUT YOU... ♡
...BUT I HOPE...
...THE REST OF OUR TRIP IS LESS EVENT-FUL.
I'M GOING TO HAVE TO AGREE WITH YOU, SHINGO.
SHINGO.
Not a day earlier we faced down a murderous psychopath...
I WANT TO THANK YOU FOR BEING SUCH A GREAT SPORT... ESPECIALLY AFTER WHAT WE JUST WENT THROUGH!
...yet here we were, trying to salvage our romantic getaway.
HOW CAN I NOT?!
IT'S A UNISEX BATHING SPA--
UH, I MEAN...!
GASP!
HEH... WE DON'T WANT TO WASTE OUR PAID VACATION, SO...
I SENSE SOMETHING SINISTER AT WORK HERE...
...THERE'S NO WAY I'M CANCELING OUR TRIP!
And so we continued on to Shingo's mysterious mountain spa...

Chapter 8
Murder at the Blood Pond Spa

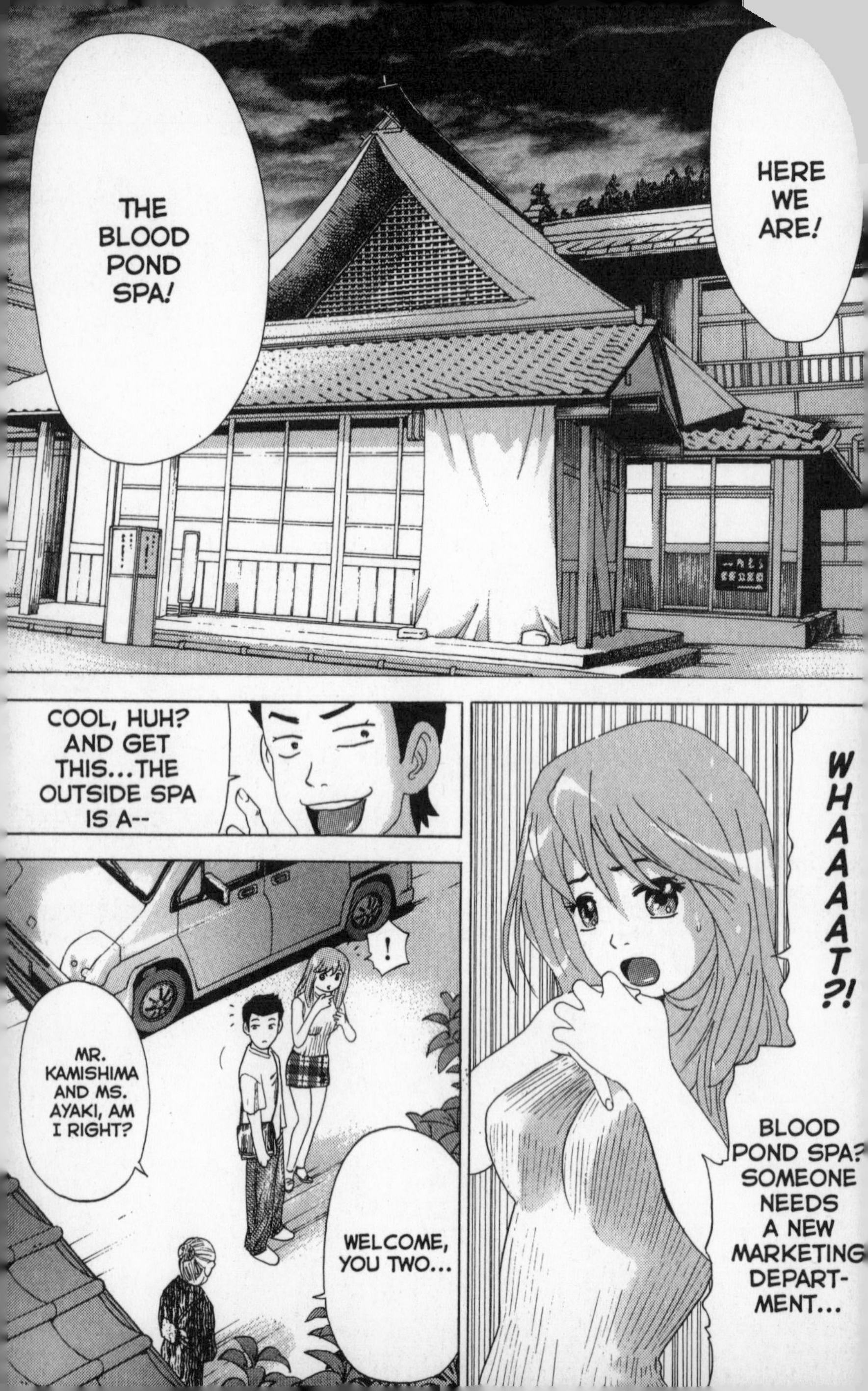
HERE WE ARE!
THE BLOOD POND SPA!
WHAAAAAT?!
BLOOD POND SPA? SOMEONE NEEDS A NEW MARKETING DEPART-MENT...
COOL, HUH? AND GET THIS...THE OUTSIDE SPA IS A--
!
WELCOME, YOU TWO...
MR. KAMISHIMA AND MS. AYAKI, AM I RIGHT?

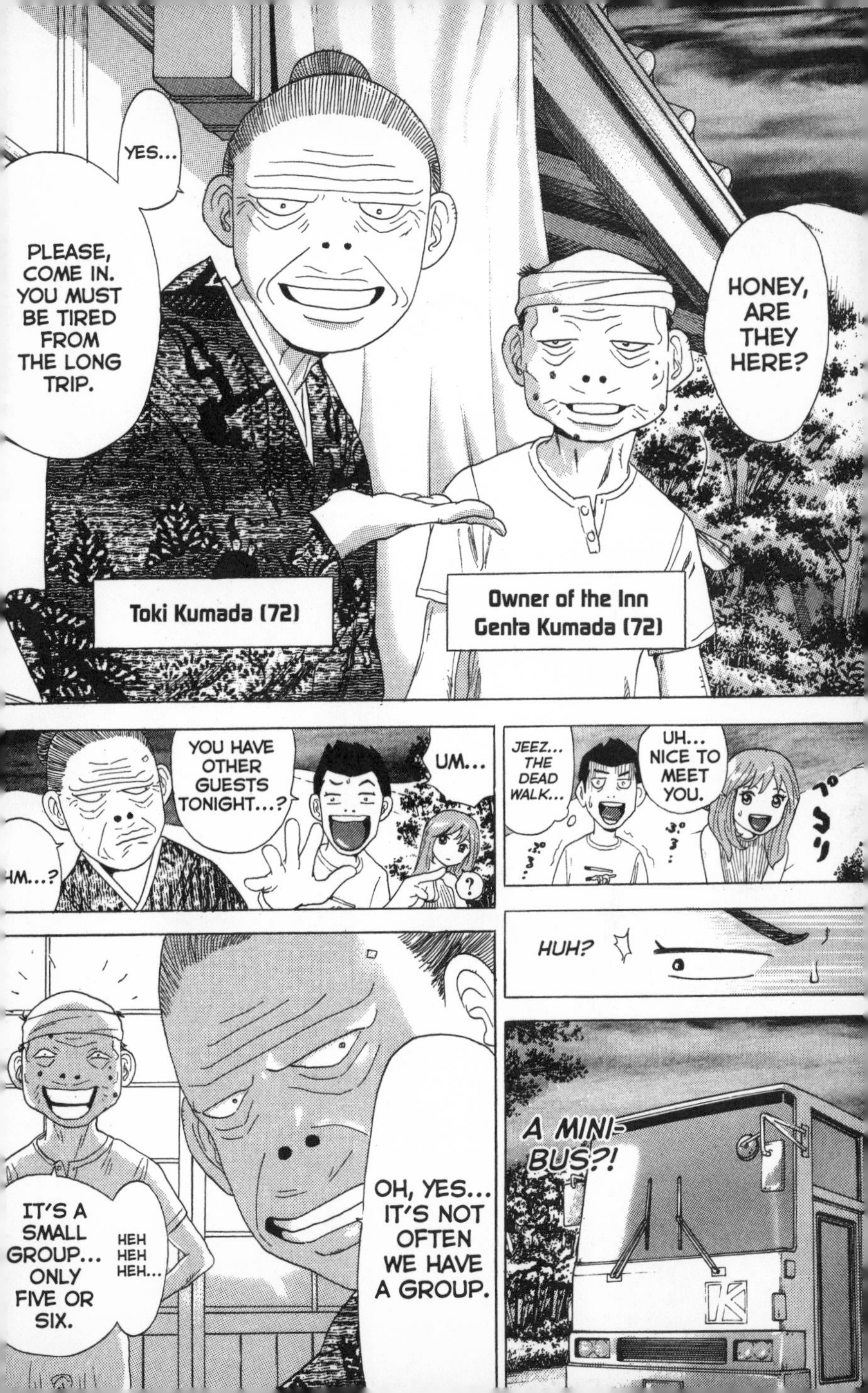
HONEY, ARE THEY HERE?
YES...
PLEASE, COME IN. YOU MUST BE TIRED FROM THE LONG TRIP.
Owner of the Inn Genta Kumada (72)
Toki Kumada (72)
UH... NICE TO MEET YOU.
JEEZ... THE DEAD WALK...
UM...
YOU HAVE OTHER GUESTS TONIGHT...?
HM...?
HUH?
A MINI-BUS?!
OH, YES... IT'S NOT OFTEN WE HAVE A GROUP.
IT'S A SMALL GROUP... ONLY FIVE OR SIX.
HEH HEH HEH...

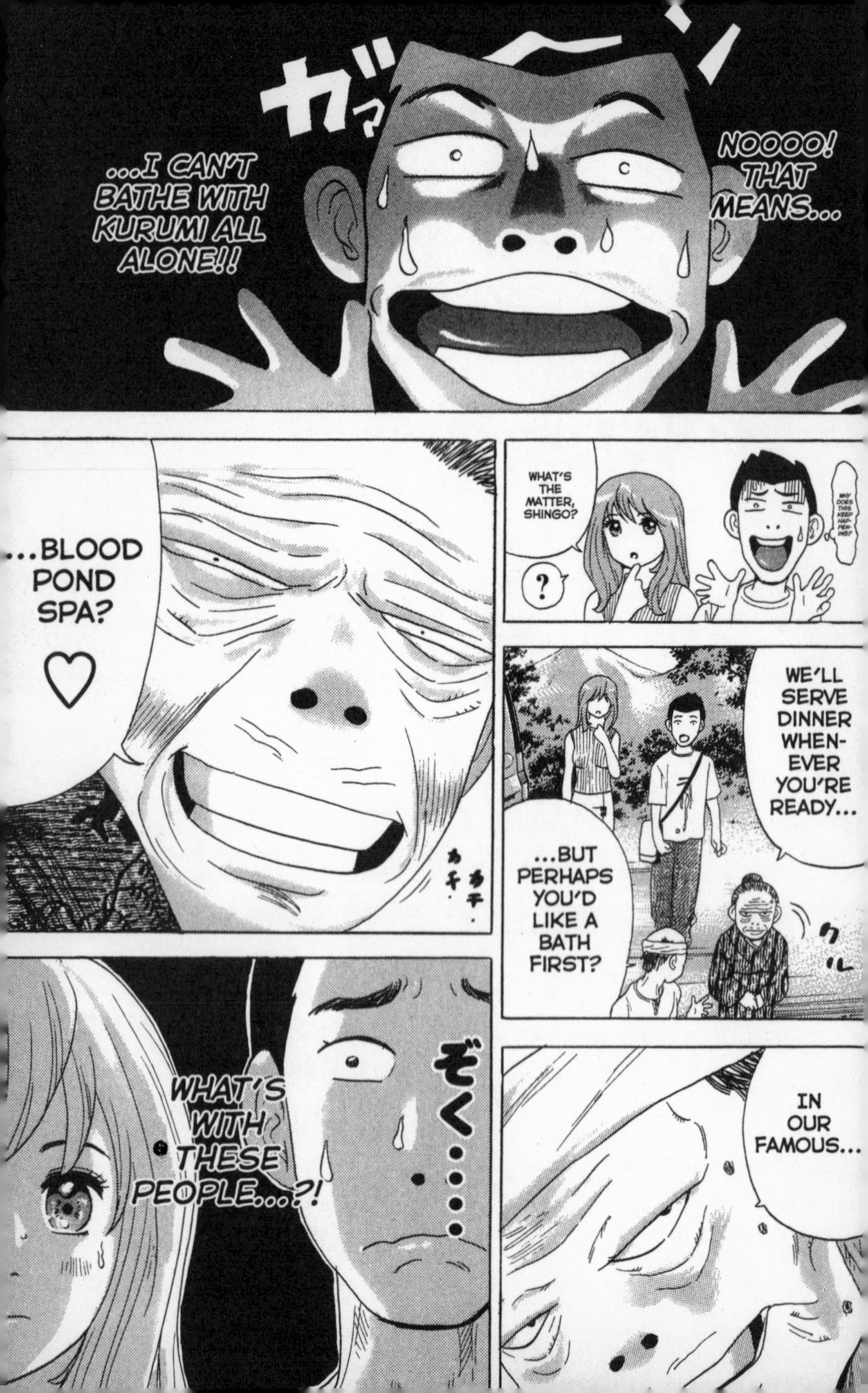
NOOOO! THAT MEANS...
...I CAN'T BATHE WITH KURUMI ALL ALONE!!
WHAT'S THE MATTER, SHINGO?
WHY DOES THIS KEEP HAPPENING?
?
WE'LL SERVE DINNER WHENEVER YOU'RE READY...
...BUT PERHAPS YOU'D LIKE A BATH FIRST?
IN OUR FAMOUS...
...BLOOD POND SPA?
♡
WHAT'S WITH THESE PEOPLE...?!

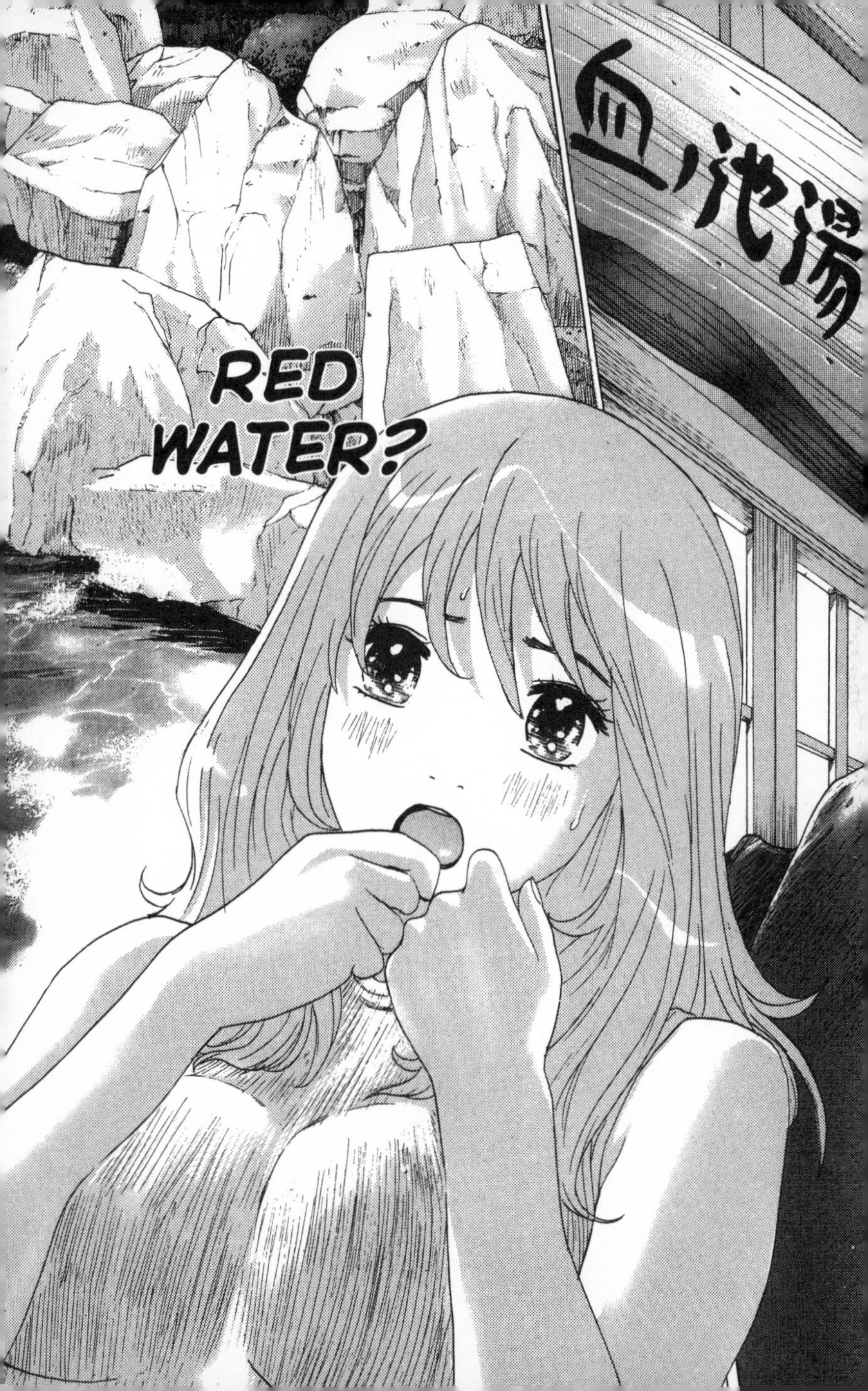
血ノ池湯
RED WATER?

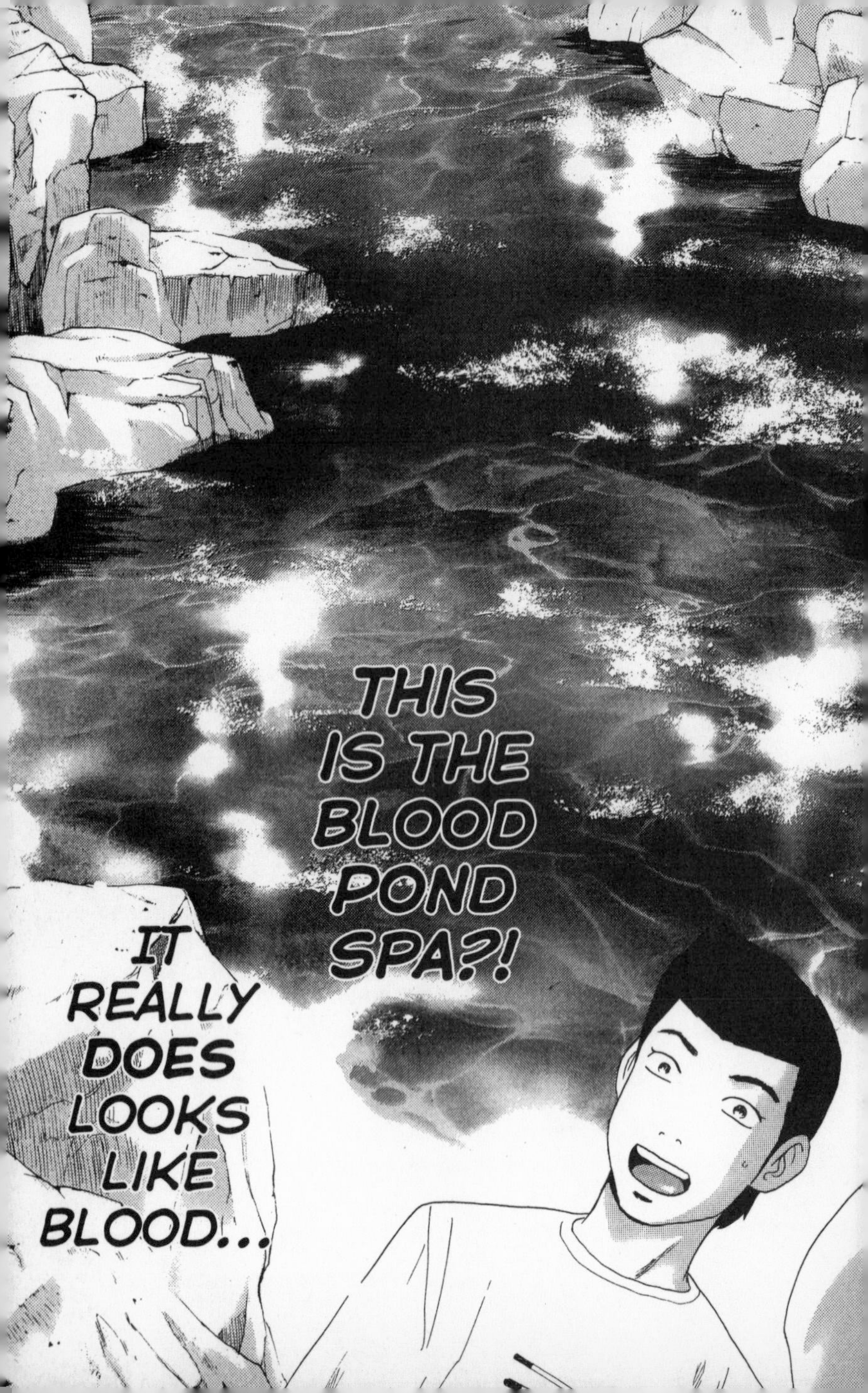
THIS IS THE BLOOD POND SPA?!
IT REALLY DOES LOOKS LIKE BLOOD...

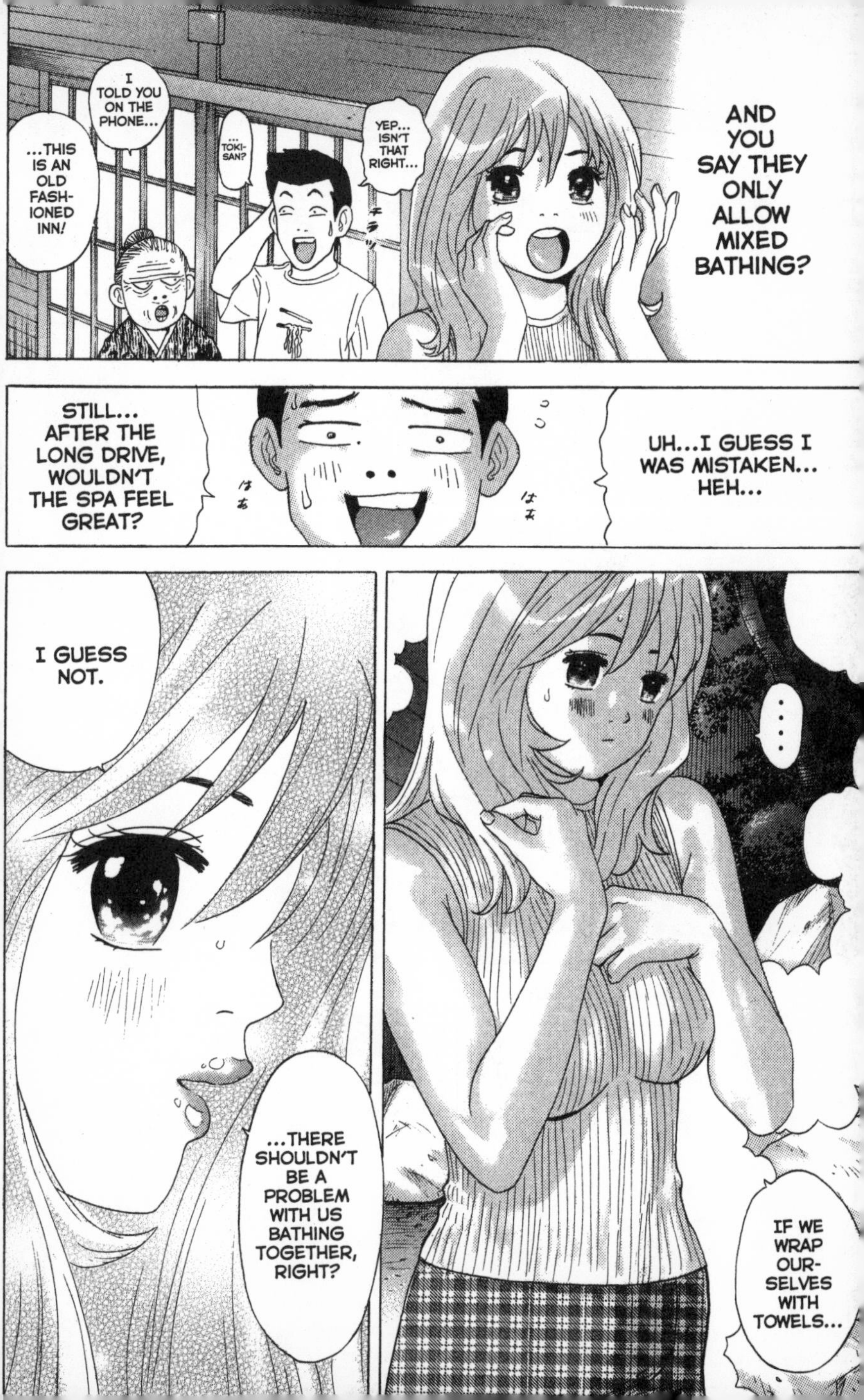
AND YOU SAY THEY ONLY ALLOW MIXED BATHING?
YEP... ISN'T THAT RIGHT...
...TOKI-SAN?
I TOLD YOU ON THE PHONE...
...THIS IS AN OLD FASHIONED INN!
UH...I GUESS I WAS MISTAKEN... HEH...
STILL... AFTER THE LONG DRIVE, WOULDN'T THE SPA FEEL GREAT?
....
IF WE WRAP OURSELVES WITH TOWELS...
...THERE SHOULDN'T BE A PROBLEM WITH US BATHING TOGETHER, RIGHT?
I GUESS NOT.

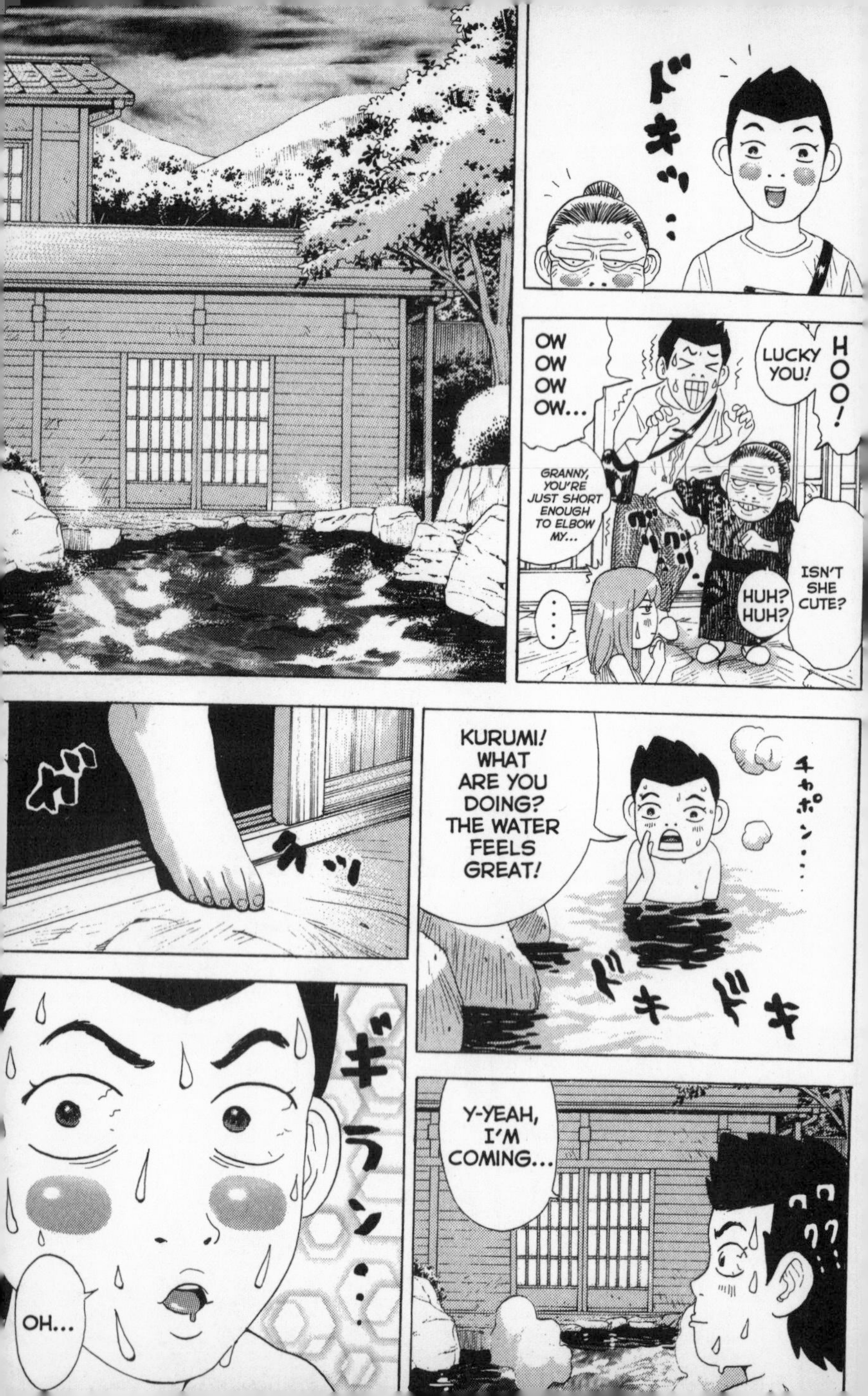
ドキッ…
HOO!
LUCKY YOU!
OW OW OW OW...
GRANNY, YOU'RE JUST SHORT ENOUGH TO ELBOW MY...
ISN'T SHE CUTE?
HUH? HUH?
...
チャポン…
KURUMI! WHAT ARE YOU DOING? THE WATER FEELS GREAT!
ドキ ドキ
Y-YEAH, I'M COMING...
ギラン…
OH...

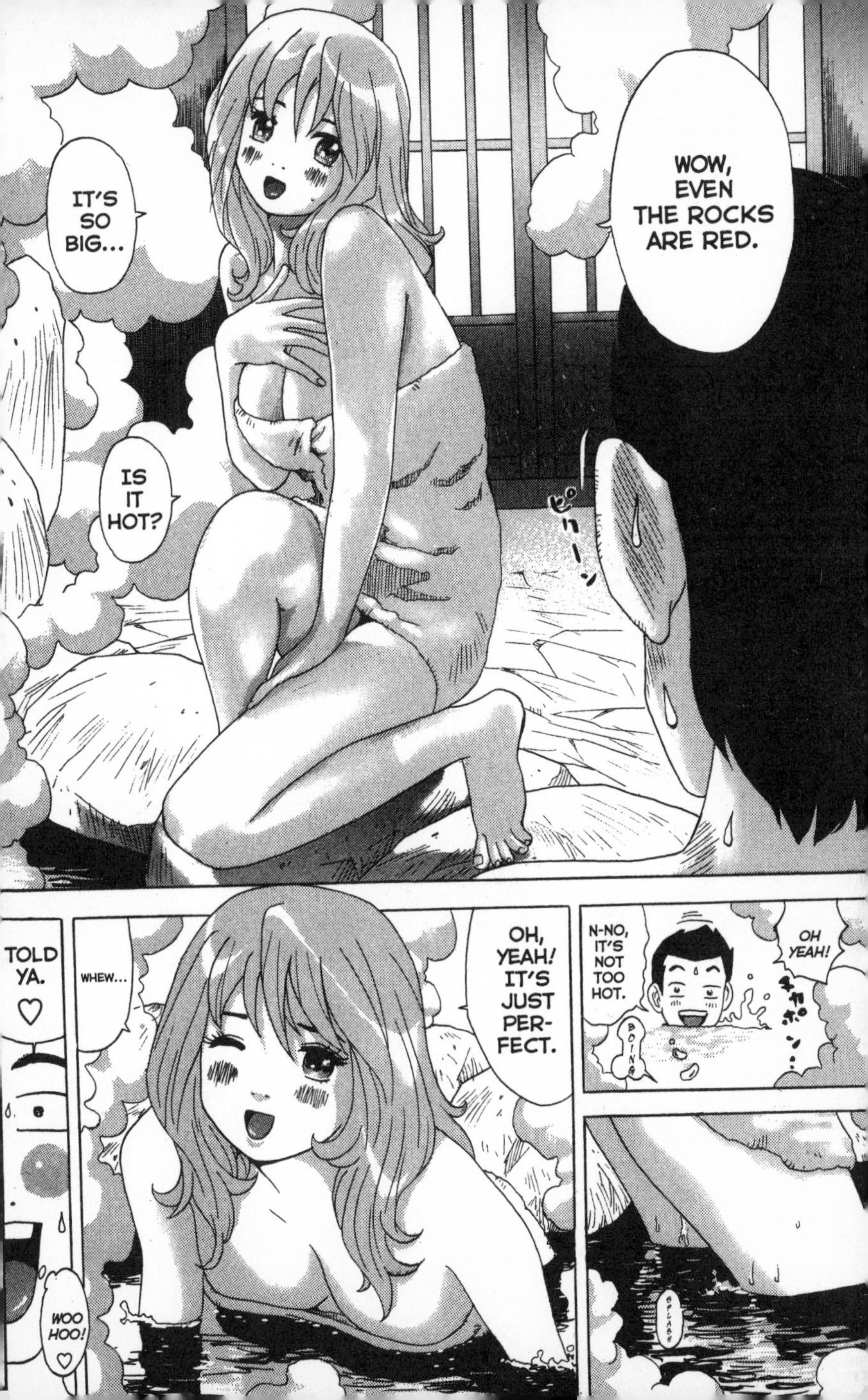
WOW, EVEN THE ROCKS ARE RED.
IT'S SO BIG...
IS IT HOT?
OH YEAH!
N-NO, IT'S NOT TOO HOT.
BOING
OH, YEAH! IT'S JUST PER-FECT.
WHEW...
TOLD YA. ♡
WOO HOO! ♡
SPLASH

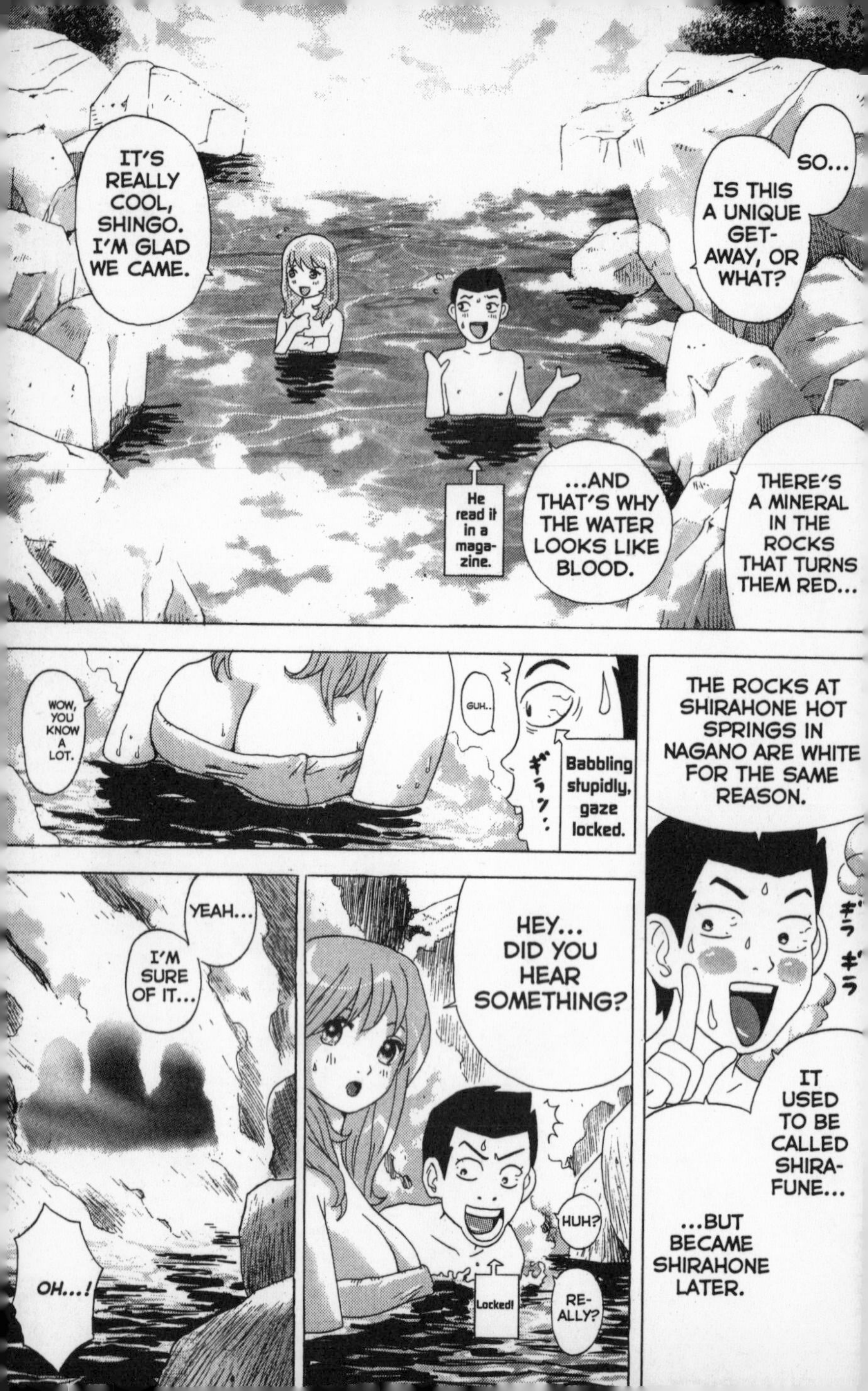
SO... IS THIS A UNIQUE GET-AWAY, OR WHAT?
IT'S REALLY COOL, SHINGO. I'M GLAD WE CAME.
THERE'S A MINERAL IN THE ROCKS THAT TURNS THEM RED...
...AND THAT'S WHY THE WATER LOOKS LIKE BLOOD.
He read it in a maga-zine.
THE ROCKS AT SHIRAHONE HOT SPRINGS IN NAGANO ARE WHITE FOR THE SAME REASON.
ギラ ギラ
IT USED TO BE CALLED SHIRA-FUNE...
...BUT BECAME SHIRAHONE LATER.
GUH..
Babbling stupidly, gaze locked.
ギラッ..
WOW, YOU KNOW A LOT.
HEY... DID YOU HEAR SOMETHING?
HUH?
Locked!
RE-ALLY?
YEAH...
I'M SURE OF IT...
OH...!

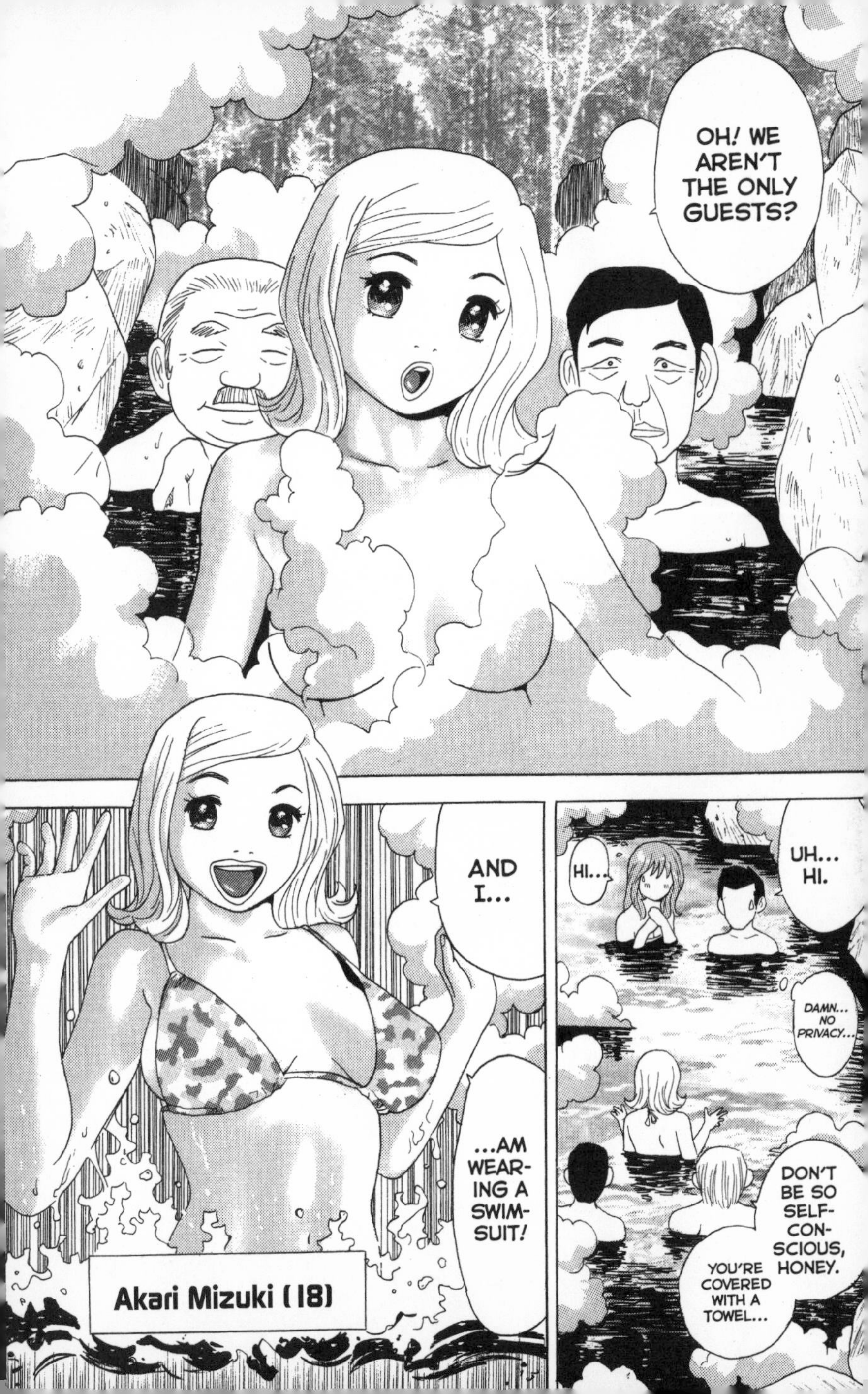
OH! WE AREN'T THE ONLY GUESTS?
UH... HI.
HI...
DAMN... NO PRIVACY...
DON'T BE SO SELF-CONSCIOUS, HONEY.
YOU'RE COVERED WITH A TOWEL...
AND I...
...AM WEARING A SWIMSUIT!
Akari Mizuki (18)

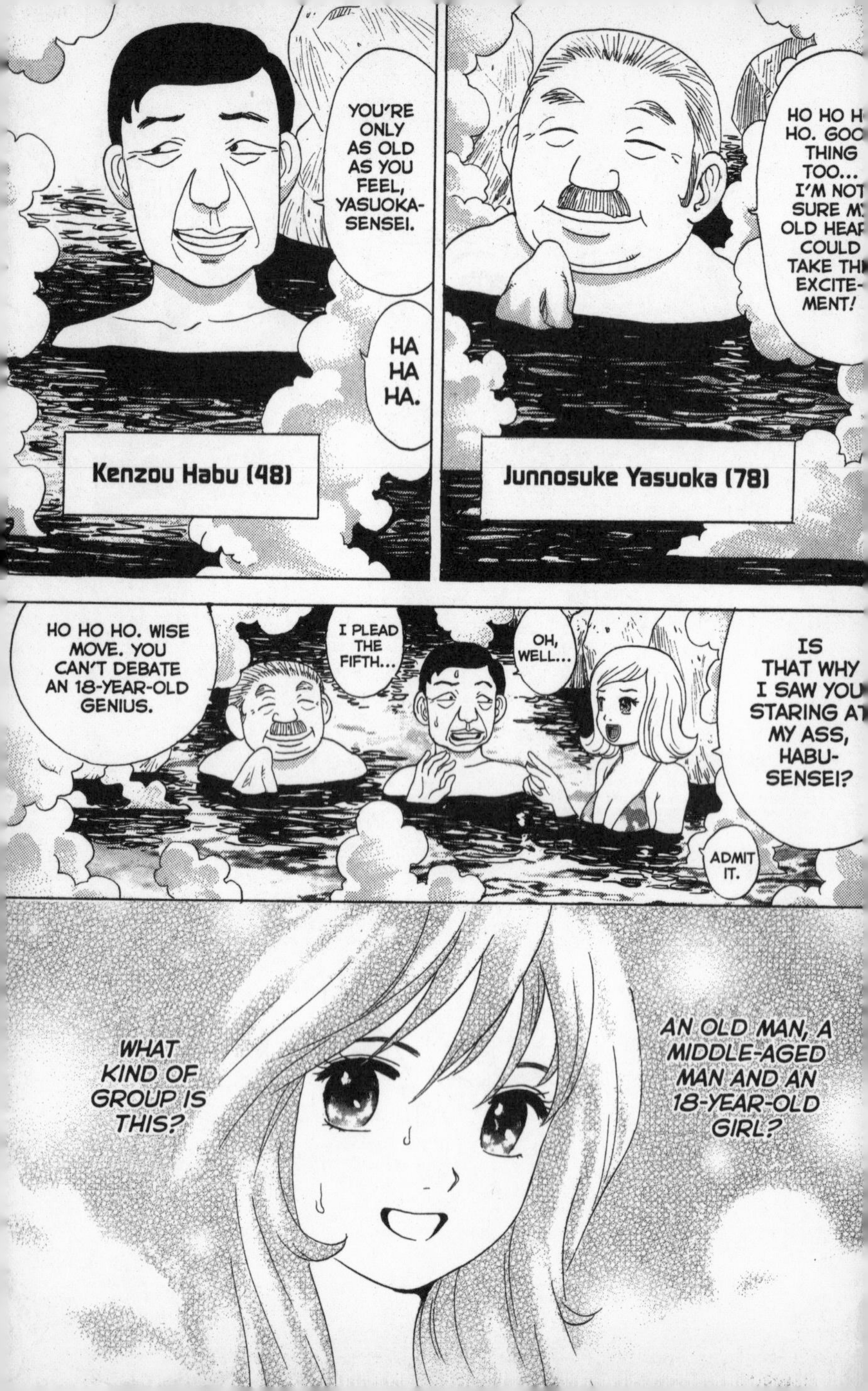
HO HO H HO. GOO THING TOO... I'M NOT SURE M OLD HEAR COULD TAKE TH EXCITE-MENT!
Junnosuke Yasuoka (78)
YOU'RE ONLY AS OLD AS YOU FEEL, YASUOKA-SENSEI.
HA HA HA.
Kenzou Habu (48)
IS THAT WHY I SAW YOU STARING AT MY ASS, HABU-SENSEI?
ADMIT IT.
OH, WELL...
I PLEAD THE FIFTH...
HO HO HO. WISE MOVE. YOU CAN'T DEBATE AN 18-YEAR-OLD GENIUS.
AN OLD MAN, A MIDDLE-AGED MAN AND AN 18-YEAR-OLD GIRL?
WHAT KIND OF GROUP IS THIS?

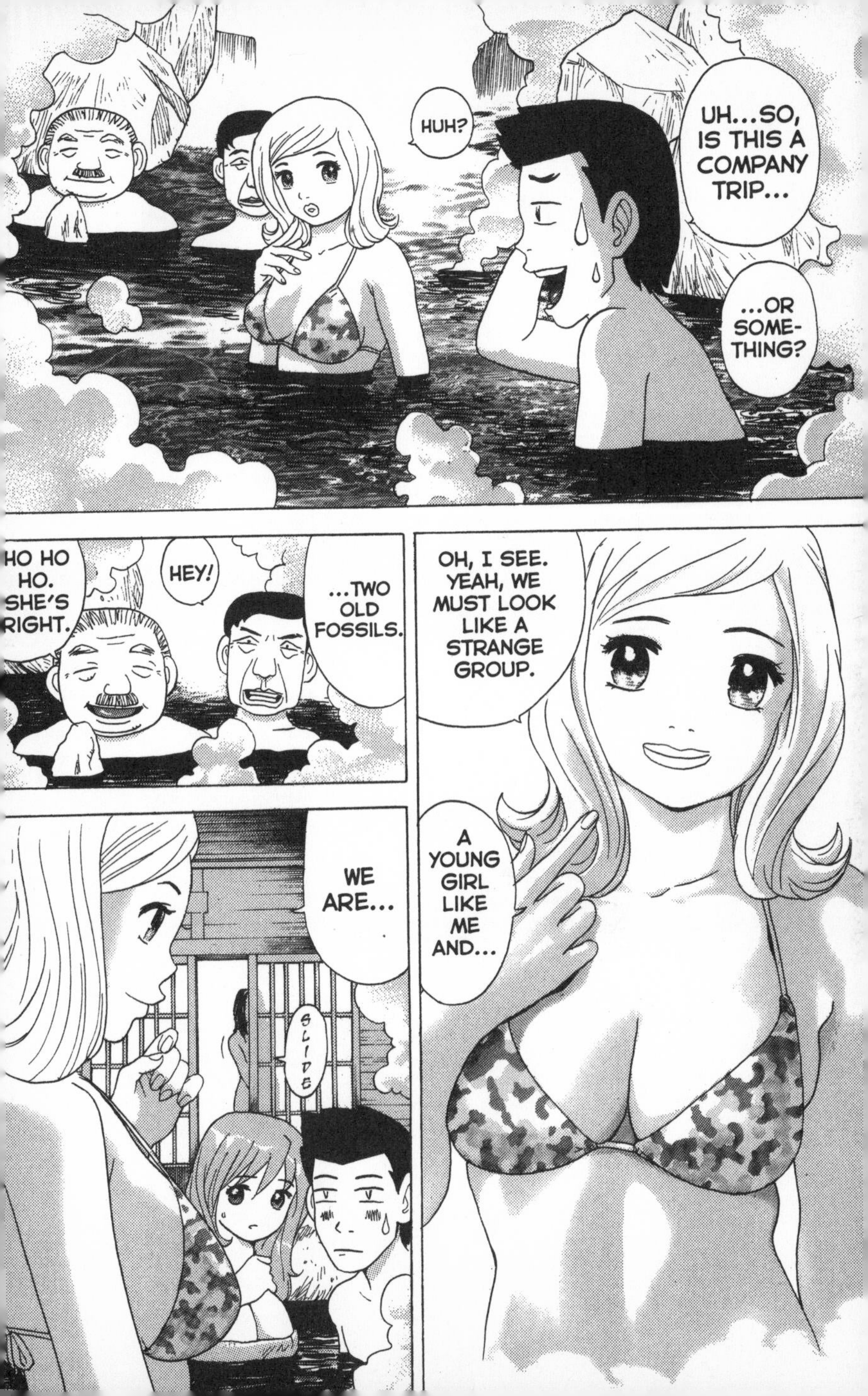
UH...SO, IS THIS A COMPANY TRIP...
...OR SOME-THING?
HUH?
OH, I SEE. YEAH, WE MUST LOOK LIKE A STRANGE GROUP.
A YOUNG GIRL LIKE ME AND...
...TWO OLD FOSSILS.
HEY!
HO HO HO. SHE'S RIGHT.
WE ARE...
SLIDE

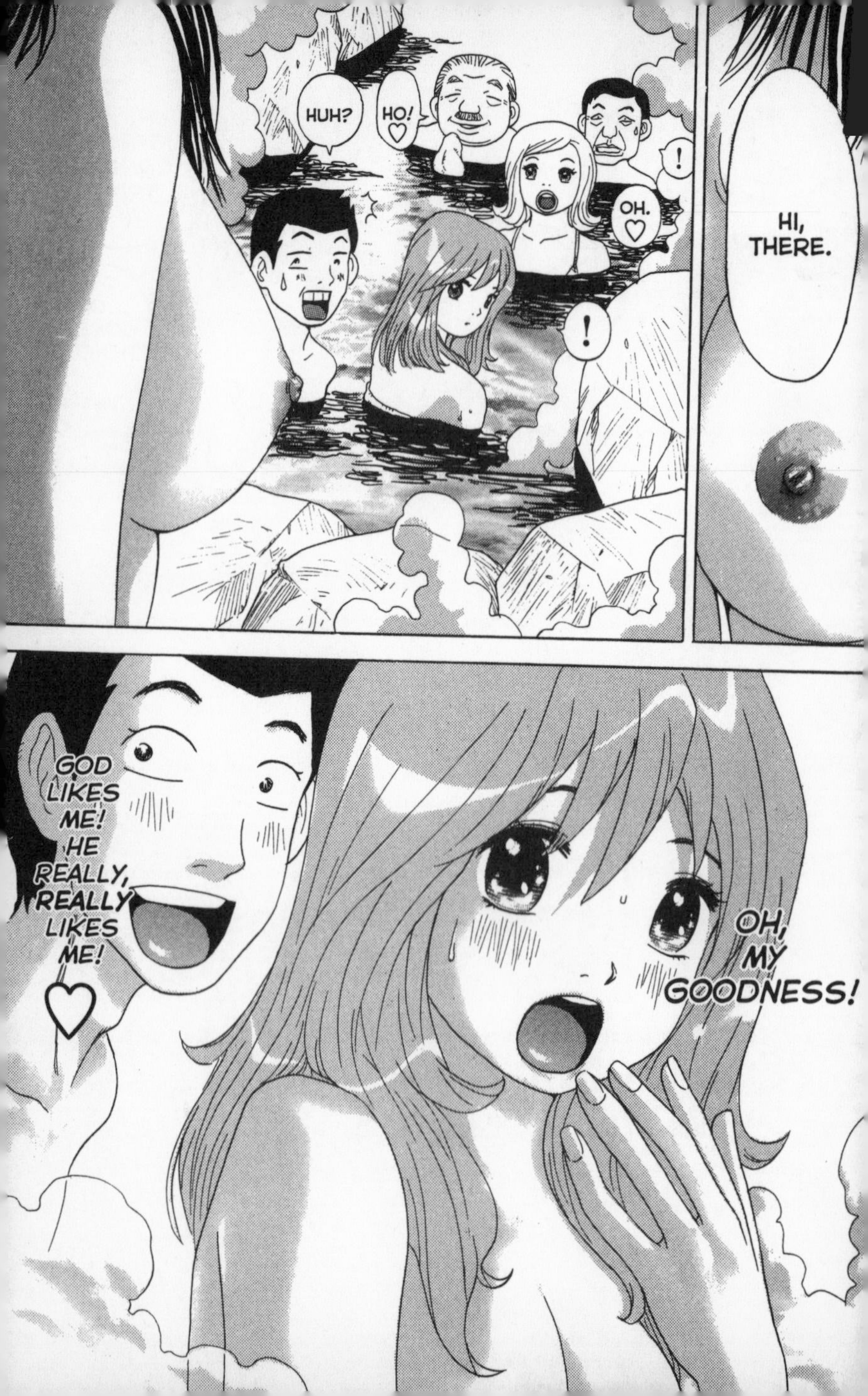
HI, THERE.
!
HO! ♡
HUH?
OH. ♡
!
OH, MY GOODNESS!
GOD LIKES ME! HE REALLY, REALLY LIKES ME! ♡

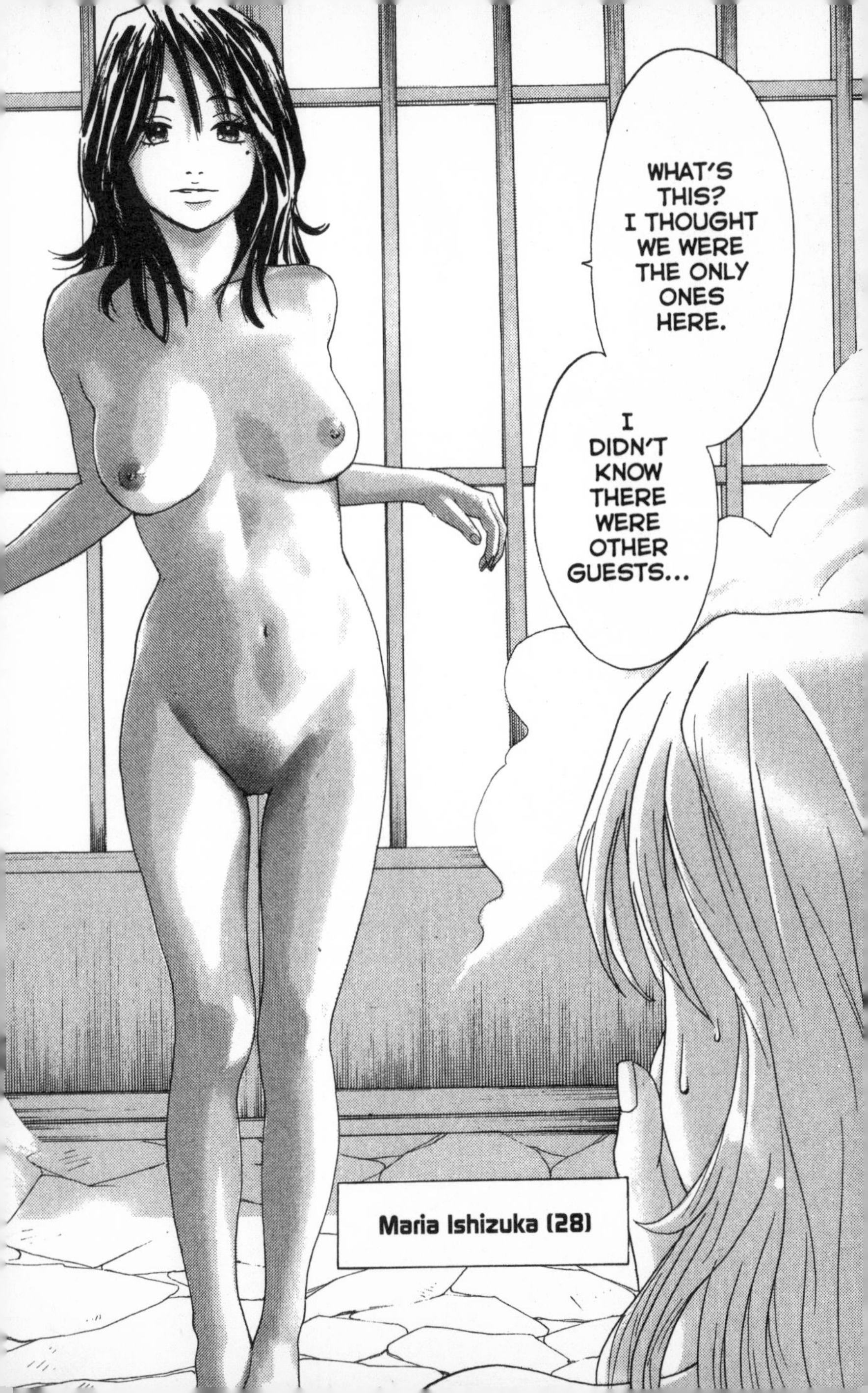
WHAT'S THIS? I THOUGHT WE WERE THE ONLY ONES HERE.
I DIDN'T KNOW THERE WERE OTHER GUESTS...
Maria Ishizuka (28)

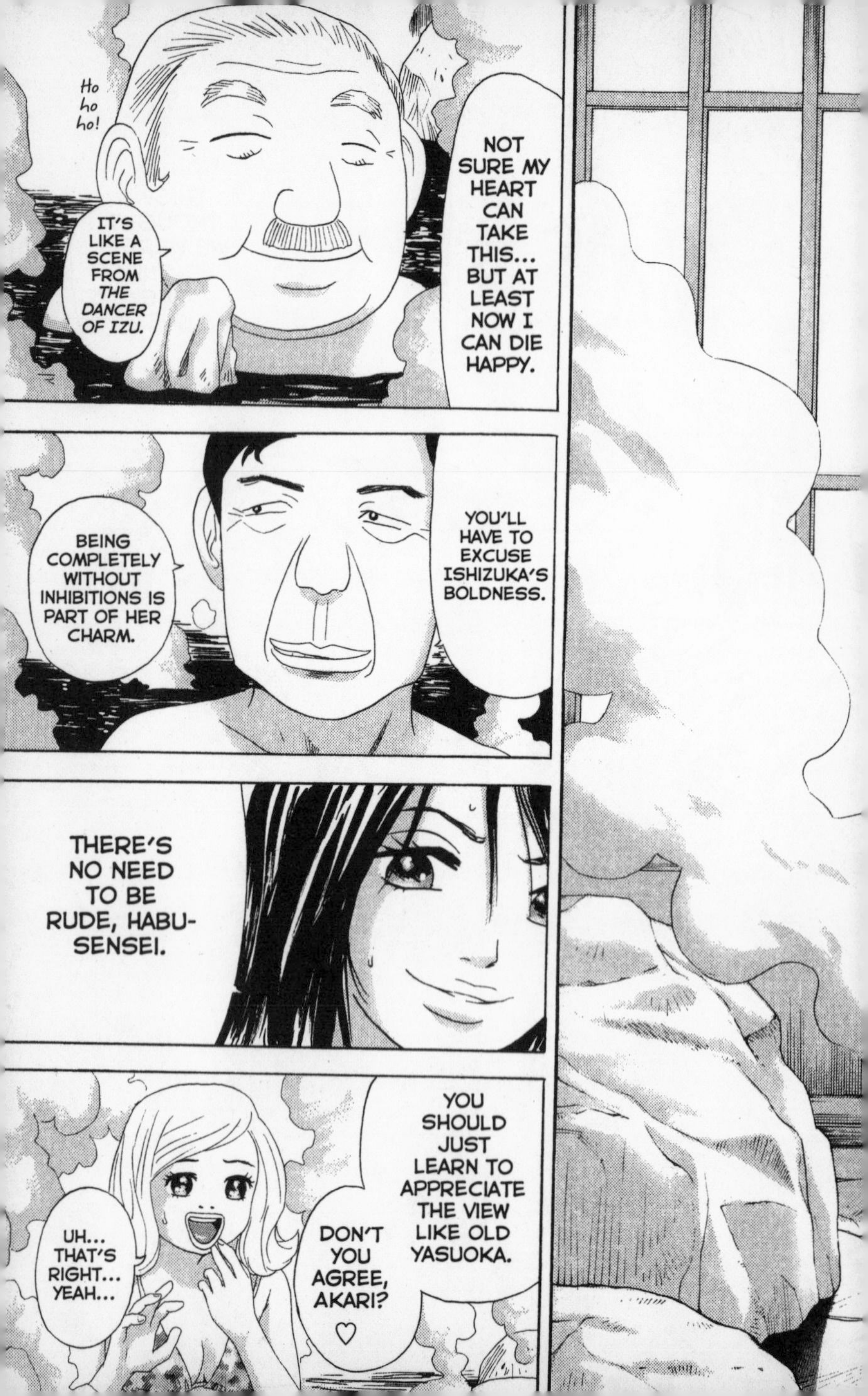
NOT SURE MY HEART CAN TAKE THIS... BUT AT LEAST NOW I CAN DIE HAPPY.
Ho ho ho!
IT'S LIKE A SCENE FROM *THE DANCER OF IZU.*
YOU'LL HAVE TO EXCUSE ISHIZUKA'S BOLDNESS.
BEING COMPLETELY WITHOUT INHIBITIONS IS PART OF HER CHARM.
THERE'S NO NEED TO BE RUDE, HABU-SENSEI.
YOU SHOULD JUST LEARN TO APPRECIATE THE VIEW LIKE OLD YASUOKA.
DON'T YOU AGREE, AKARI? ♡
UH... THAT'S RIGHT... YEAH...

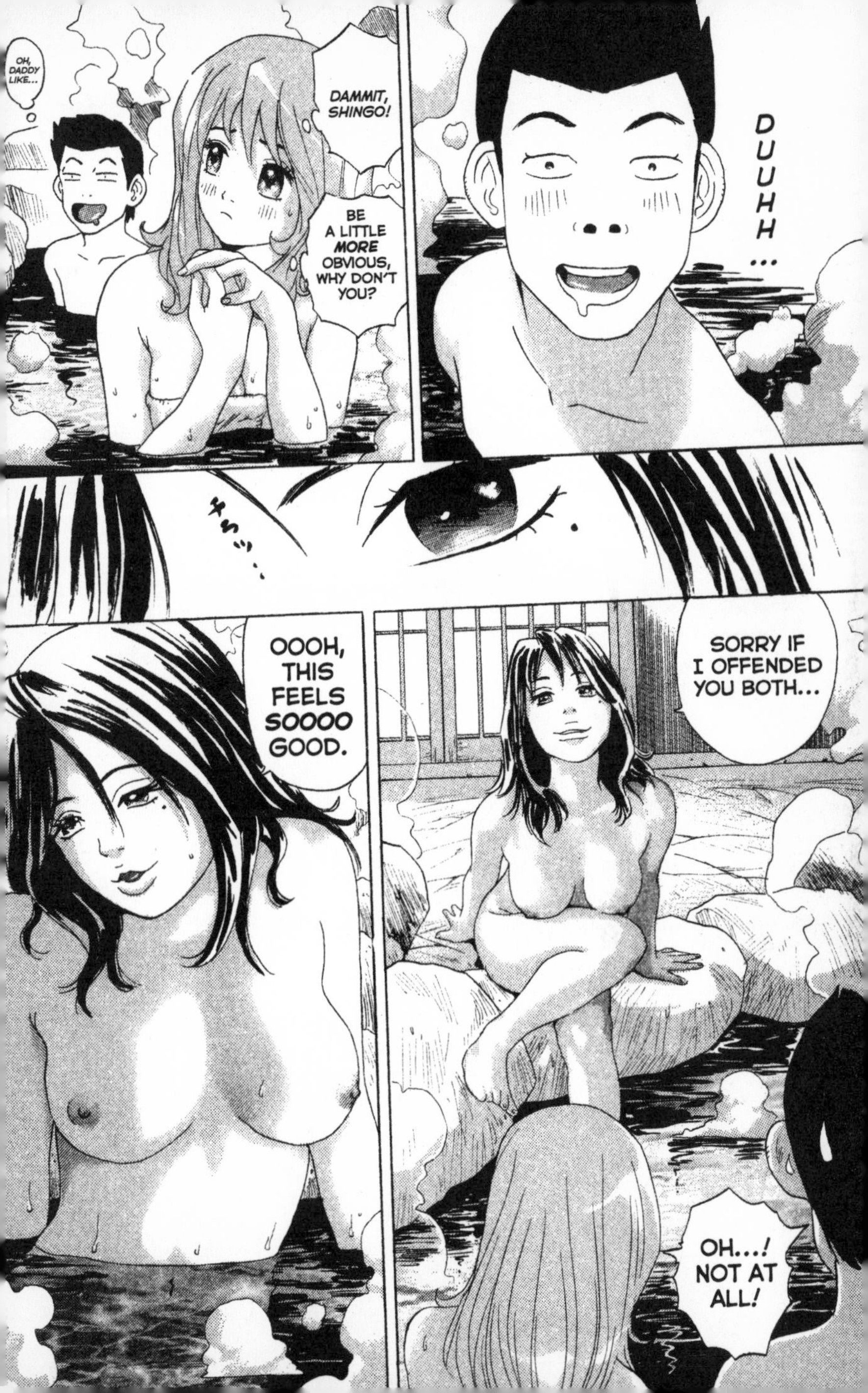
DUUHH...
DAMMIT, SHINGO!
OH, DADDY LIKE...
BE A LITTLE MORE OBVIOUS, WHY DON'T YOU?
SORRY IF I OFFENDED YOU BOTH...
OH...! NOT AT ALL!
OOOH, THIS FEELS SOOOO GOOD.

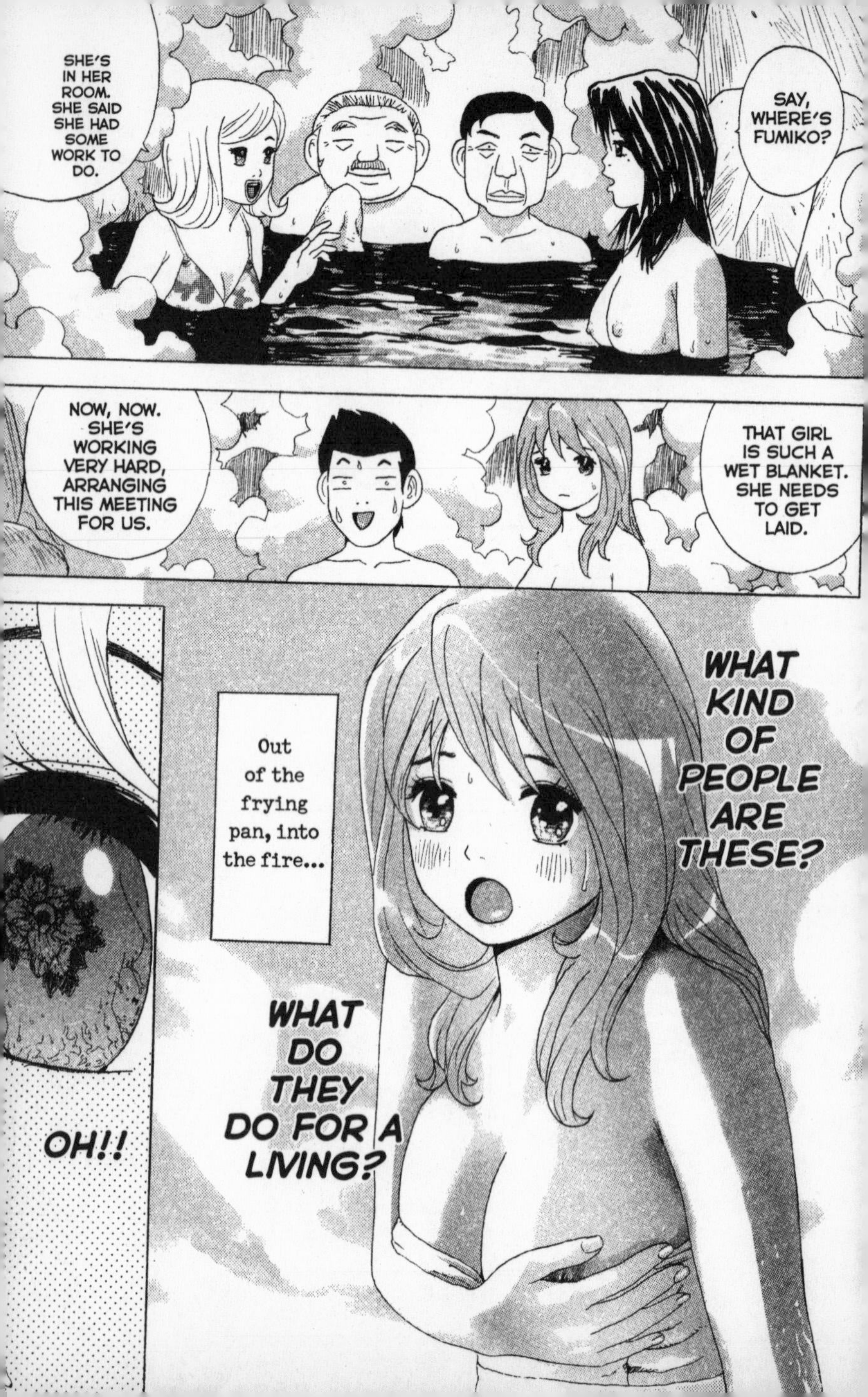
SAY, WHERE'S FUMIKO?
SHE'S IN HER ROOM. SHE SAID SHE HAD SOME WORK TO DO.
THAT GIRL IS SUCH A WET BLANKET. SHE NEEDS TO GET LAID.
NOW, NOW. SHE'S WORKING VERY HARD, ARRANGING THIS MEETING FOR US.
WHAT KIND OF PEOPLE ARE THESE?
Out of the frying pan, into the fire...
WHAT DO THEY DO FOR A LIVING?
OH!!

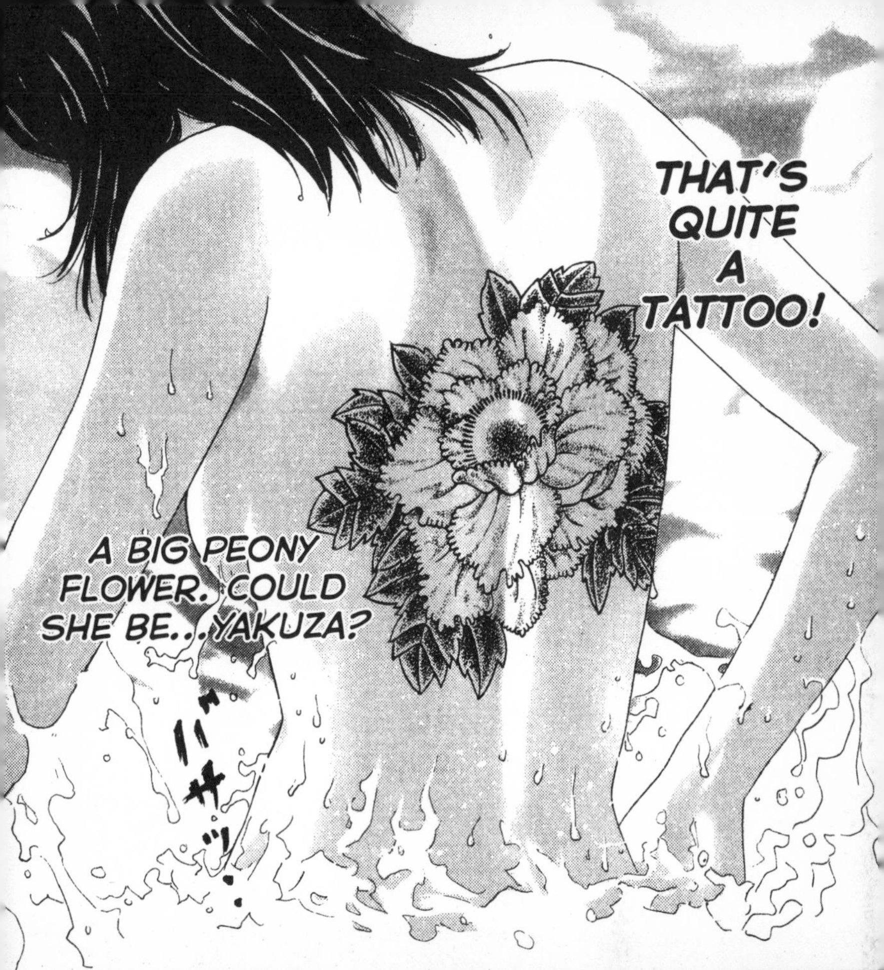
THAT'S QUITE A TATTOO!
A BIG PEONY FLOWER. COULD SHE BE...YAKUZA?
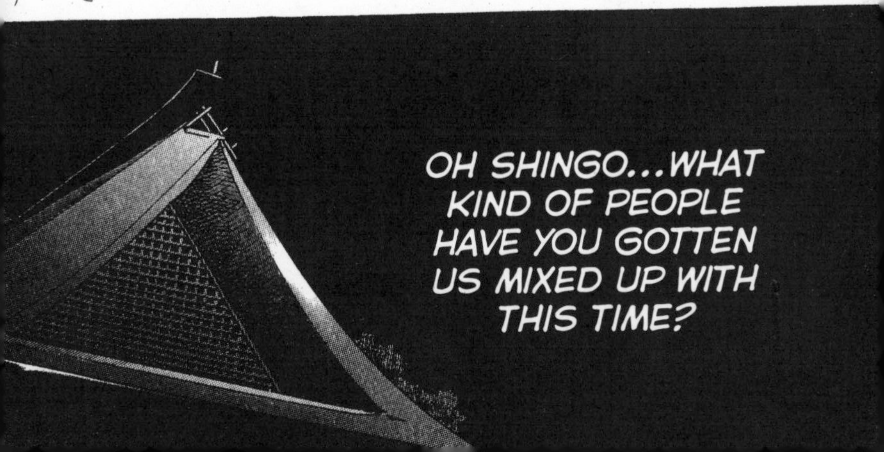
OH SHINGO...WHAT KIND OF PEOPLE HAVE YOU GOTTEN US MIXED UP WITH THIS TIME?

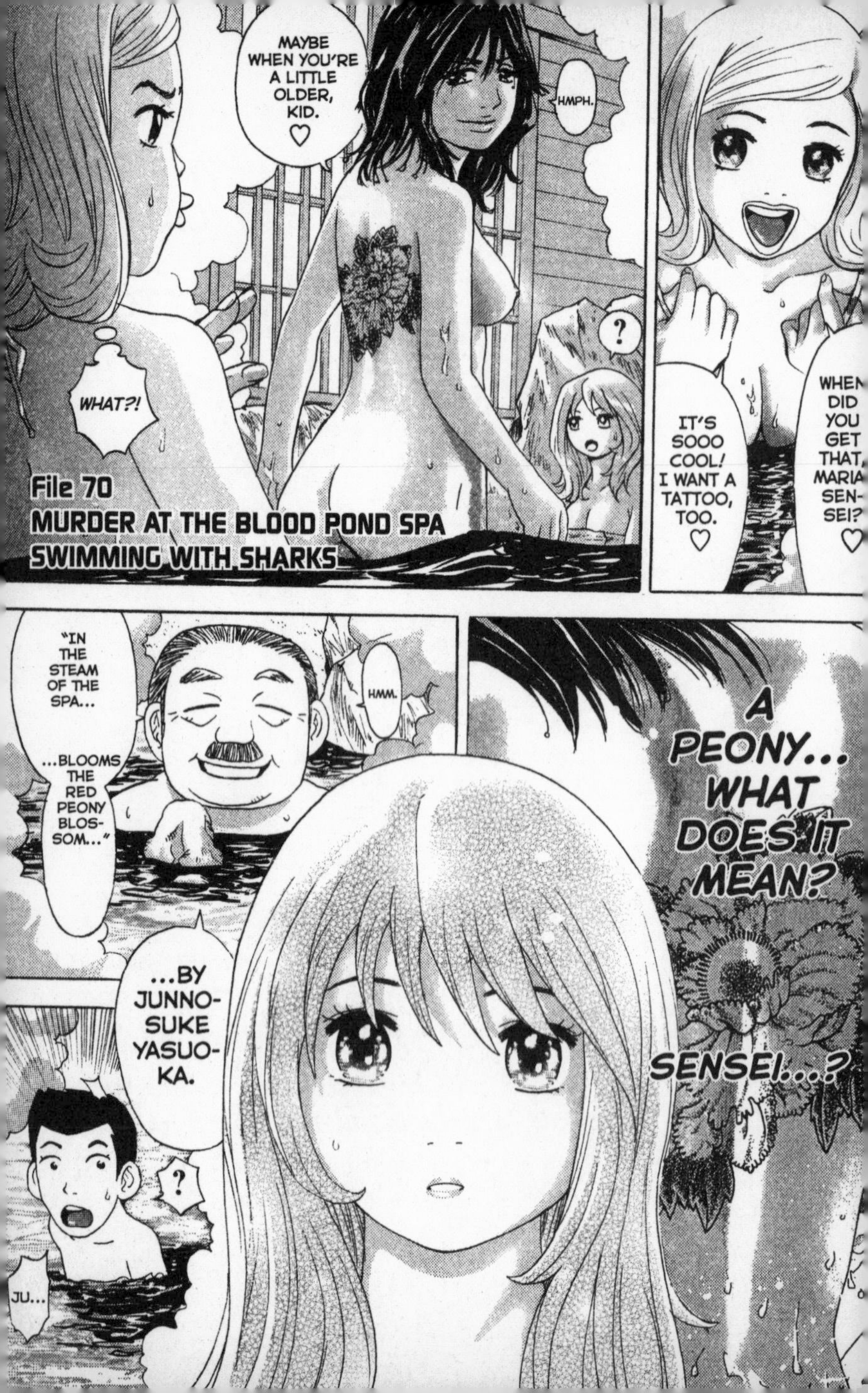
WHEN DID YOU GET THAT, MARIA SENSEI? ♡
IT'S SOOO COOL! I WANT A TATTOO, TOO. ♡
?
HMPH.
MAYBE WHEN YOU'RE A LITTLE OLDER, KID. ♡
WHAT?!
File 70
MURDER AT THE BLOOD POND SPA
SWIMMING WITH SHARKS
A PEONY... WHAT DOES IT MEAN?
SENSEI...?
HMM.
"IN THE STEAM OF THE SPA...
...BLOOMS THE RED PEONY BLOS-SOM..."
...BY JUNNO-SUKE YASUOKA.
?
JU...

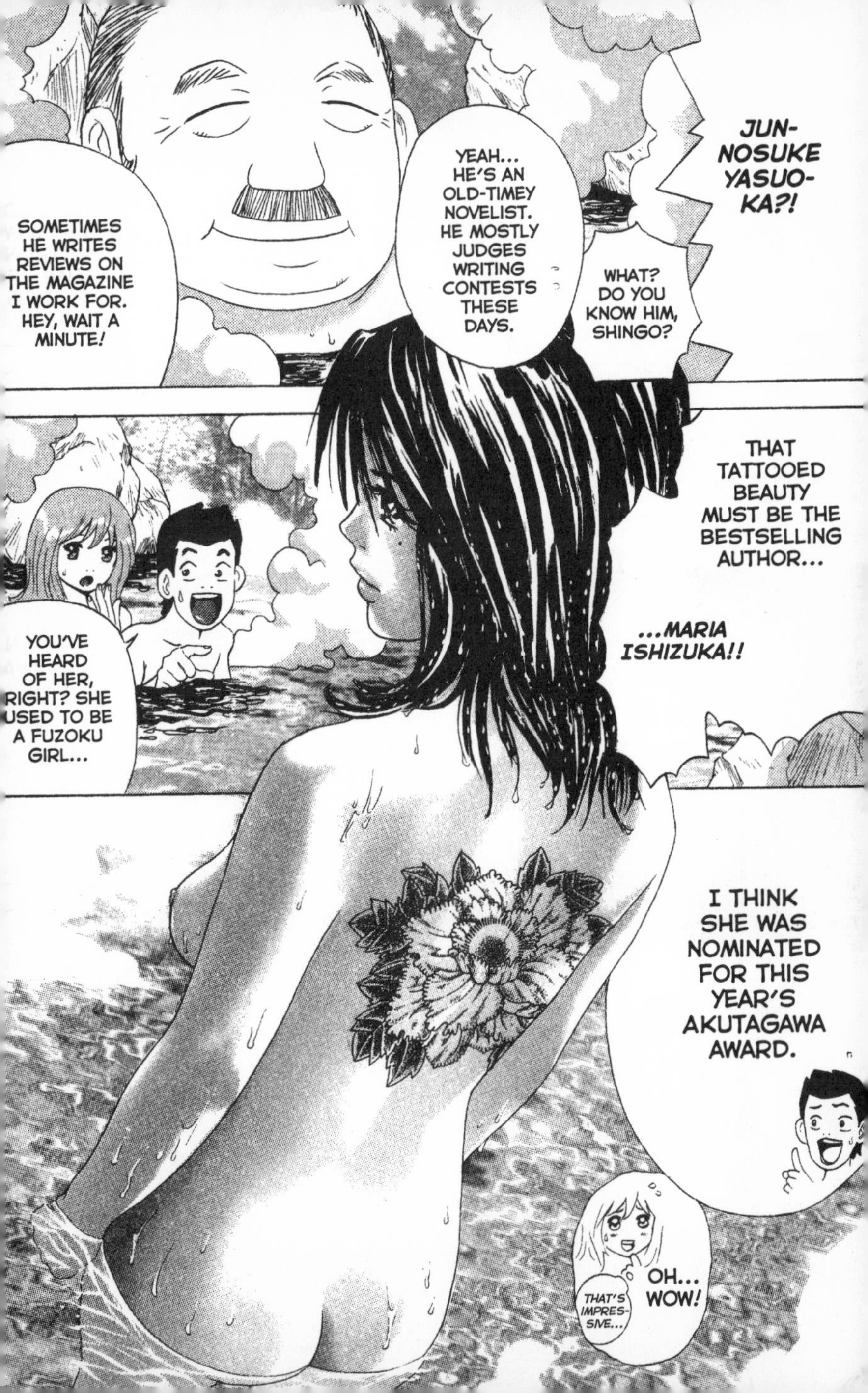
JUN-NOSUKE YASUO-KA?!
WHAT? DO YOU KNOW HIM, SHINGO?
YEAH... HE'S AN OLD-TIMEY NOVELIST. HE MOSTLY JUDGES WRITING CONTESTS THESE DAYS.
SOMETIMES HE WRITES REVIEWS ON THE MAGAZINE I WORK FOR. HEY, WAIT A MINUTE!
THAT TATTOOED BEAUTY MUST BE THE BESTSELLING AUTHOR...
...MARIA ISHIZUKA!!
YOU'VE HEARD OF HER, RIGHT? SHE USED TO BE A FUZOKU GIRL...
I THINK SHE WAS NOMINATED FOR THIS YEAR'S AKUTAGAWA AWARD.
OH... WOW!
THAT'S IMPRES-SIVE...

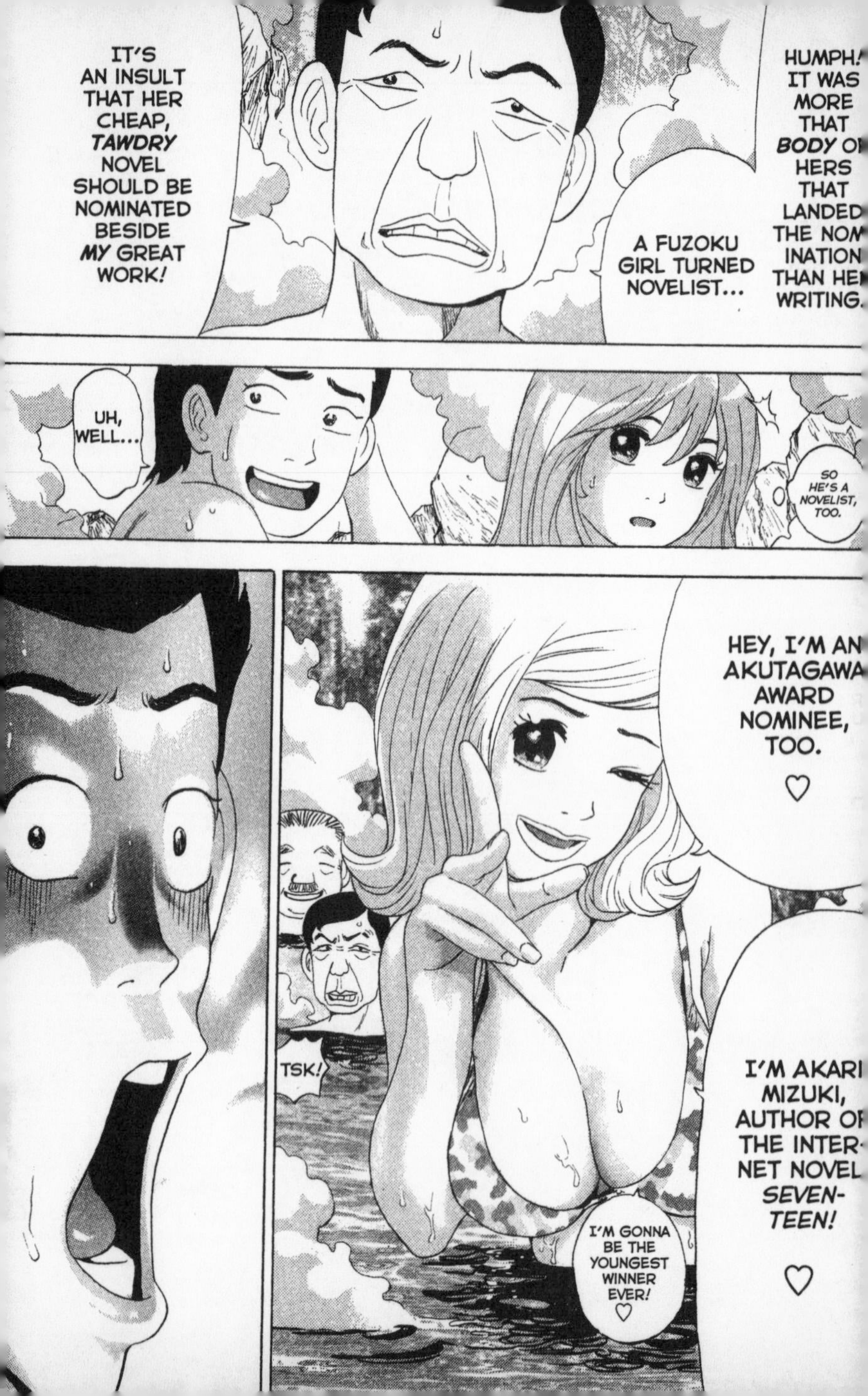
HUMPH! IT WAS MORE THAT *BODY* OF HERS THAT LANDED THE NOMINATION THAN HER WRITING.
A FUZOKU GIRL TURNED NOVELIST...
IT'S AN INSULT THAT HER CHEAP, *TAWDRY* NOVEL SHOULD BE NOMINATED BESIDE *MY* GREAT WORK!
SO HE'S A NOVELIST, TOO.
UH, WELL...
HEY, I'M AN AKUTAGAWA AWARD NOMINEE, TOO. ♡
I'M AKARI MIZUKI, AUTHOR OF THE INTERNET NOVEL *SEVENTEEN!* ♡
I'M GONNA BE THE YOUNGEST WINNER EVER! ♡
TSK!

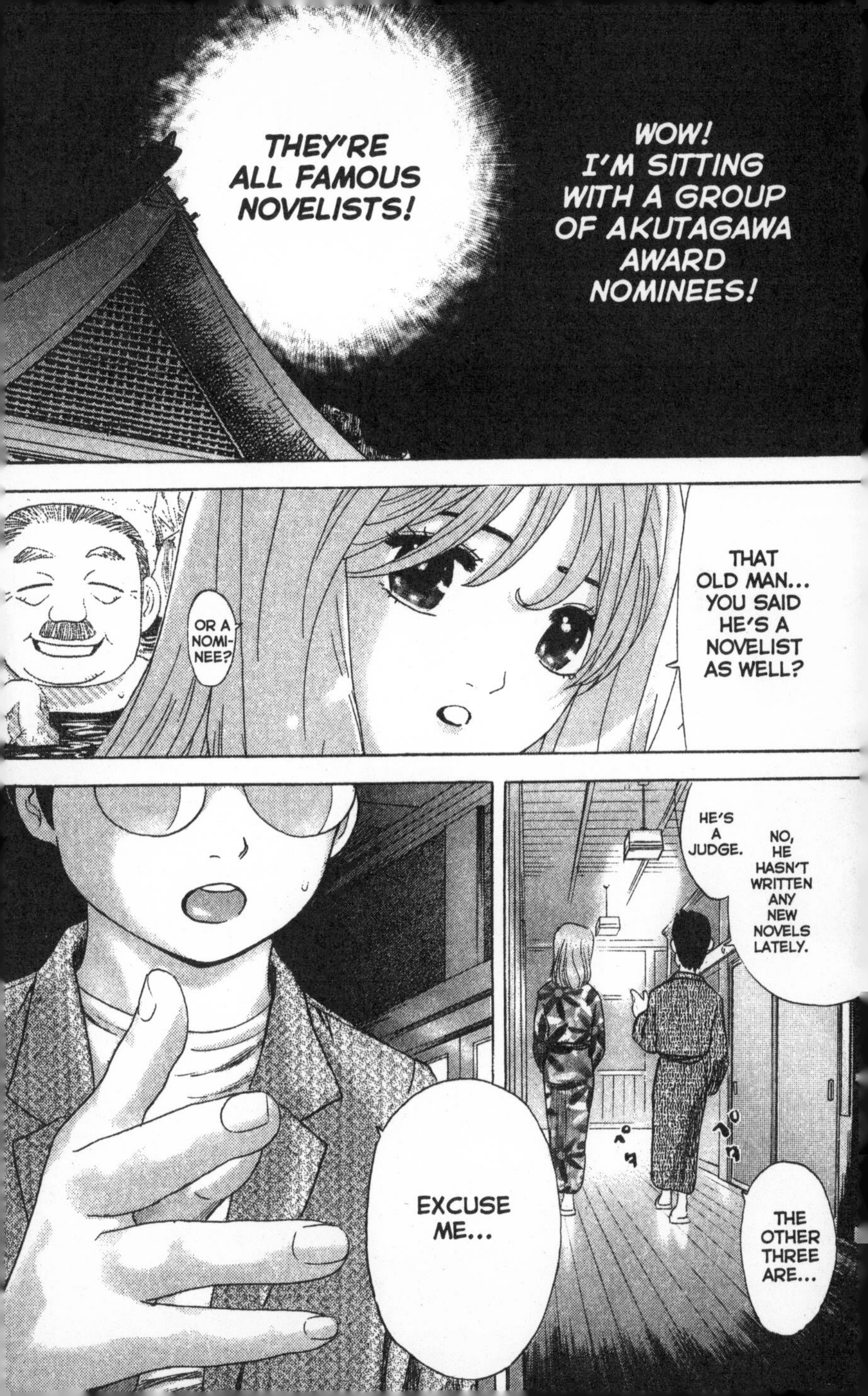
WOW! I'M SITTING WITH A GROUP OF AKUTAGAWA AWARD NOMINEES!
THEY'RE ALL FAMOUS NOVELISTS!
THAT OLD MAN... YOU SAID HE'S A NOVELIST AS WELL?
OR A NOMINEE?
NO, HE HASN'T WRITTEN ANY NEW NOVELS LATELY.
HE'S A JUDGE.
THE OTHER THREE ARE...
EXCUSE ME...

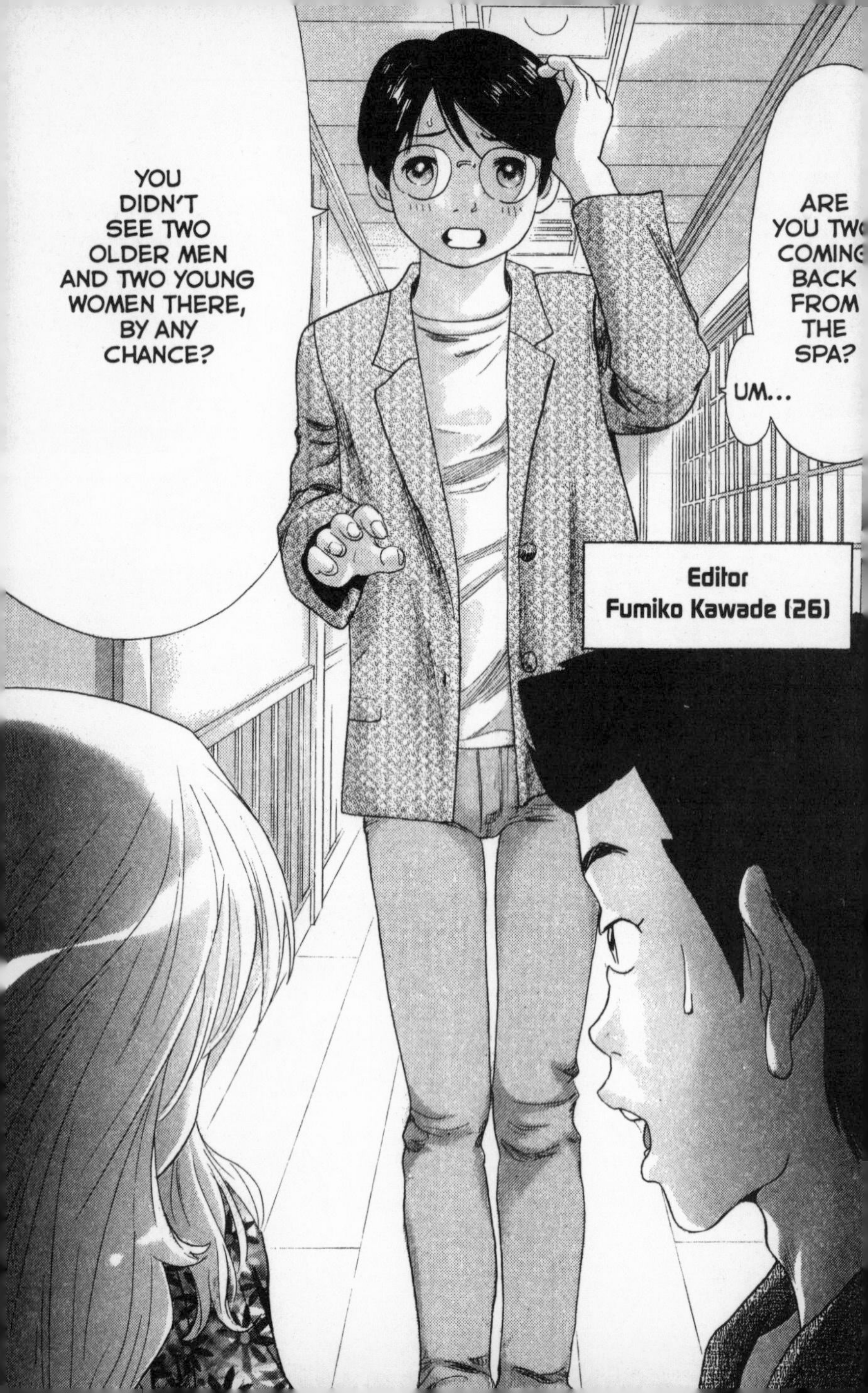
ARE YOU TWO COMING BACK FROM THE SPA?
YOU DIDN'T SEE TWO OLDER MEN AND TWO YOUNG WOMEN THERE, BY ANY CHANCE?
UM...
Editor
Fumiko Kawade (26)

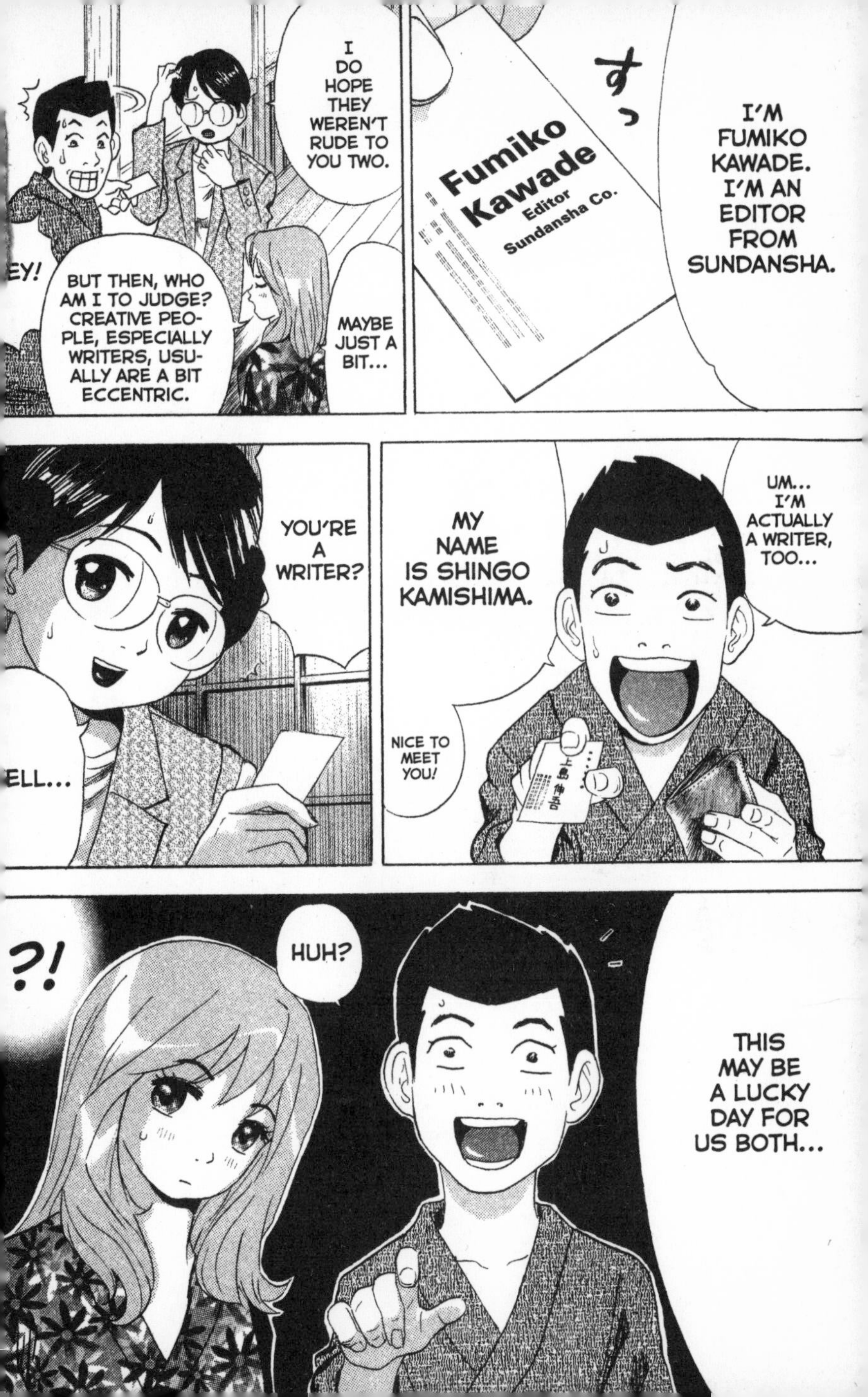
すっ
Fumiko Kawade
Editor
Sundansha Co.
I'M FUMIKO KAWADE. I'M AN EDITOR FROM SUNDANSHA.
I DO HOPE THEY WEREN'T RUDE TO YOU TWO.
MAYBE JUST A BIT...
BUT THEN, WHO AM I TO JUDGE? CREATIVE PEOPLE, ESPECIALLY WRITERS, USUALLY ARE A BIT ECCENTRIC.
EY!
UM... I'M ACTUALLY A WRITER, TOO...
MY NAME IS SHINGO KAMISHIMA.
NICE TO MEET YOU!
YOU'RE A WRITER?
ELL...
THIS MAY BE A LUCKY DAY FOR US BOTH...
HUH?
?!

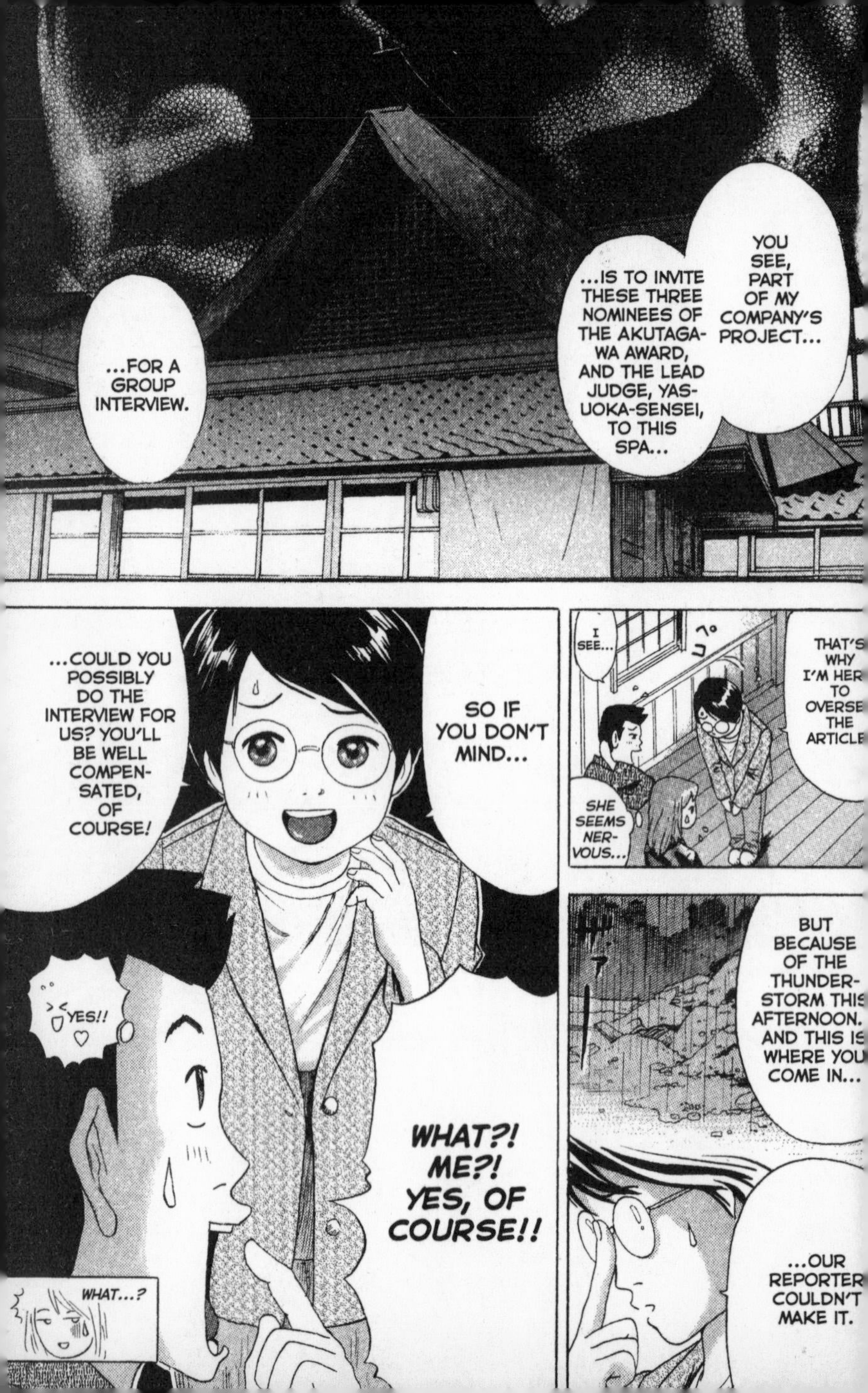
YOU SEE, PART OF MY COMPANY'S PROJECT...
...IS TO INVITE THESE THREE NOMINEES OF THE AKUTAGAWA AWARD, AND THE LEAD JUDGE, YASUOKA-SENSEI, TO THIS SPA...
...FOR A GROUP INTERVIEW.
THAT'S WHY I'M HER TO OVERSE THE ARTICLE
I SEE...
SHE SEEMS NERVOUS...
BUT BECAUSE OF THE THUNDERSTORM THIS AFTERNOON. AND THIS IS WHERE YOU COME IN...
...OUR REPORTER COULDN'T MAKE IT.
SO IF YOU DON'T MIND...
...COULD YOU POSSIBLY DO THE INTERVIEW FOR US? YOU'LL BE WELL COMPENSATED, OF COURSE!
WHAT?! ME?! YES, OF COURSE!!
YES!!
WHAT...?

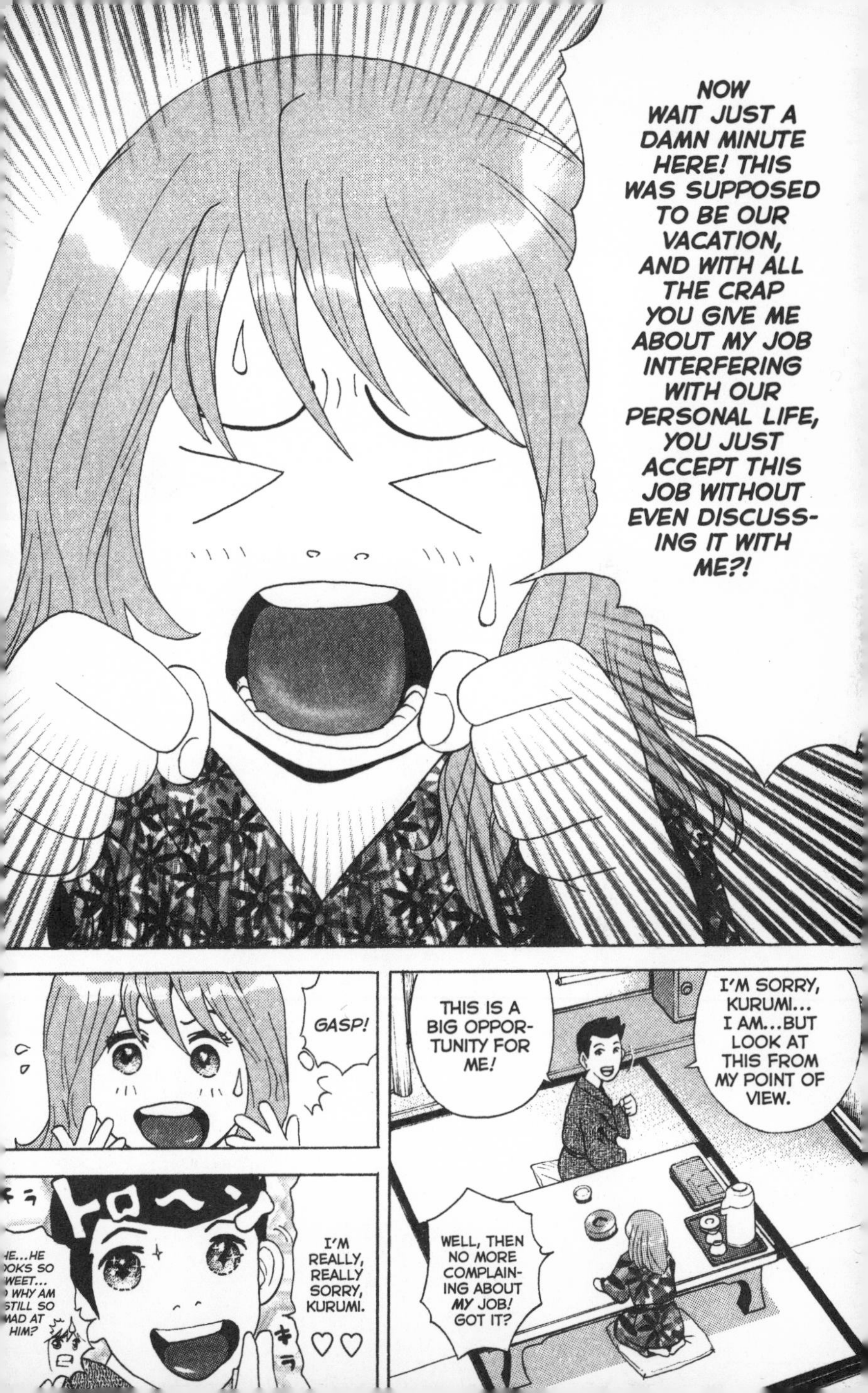
NOW WAIT JUST A DAMN MINUTE HERE! THIS WAS SUPPOSED TO BE OUR VACATION, AND WITH ALL THE CRAP YOU GIVE ME ABOUT MY JOB INTERFERING WITH OUR PERSONAL LIFE, YOU JUST ACCEPT THIS JOB WITHOUT EVEN DISCUSSING IT WITH ME?!
I'M SORRY, KURUMI... I AM...BUT LOOK AT THIS FROM MY POINT OF VIEW.
THIS IS A BIG OPPORTUNITY FOR ME!
WELL, THEN NO MORE COMPLAINING ABOUT *MY* JOB! GOT IT?
GASP!
I'M REALLY, REALLY SORRY, KURUMI.
♡♡
キラ
キラ
STILL SO MAD AT HIM?

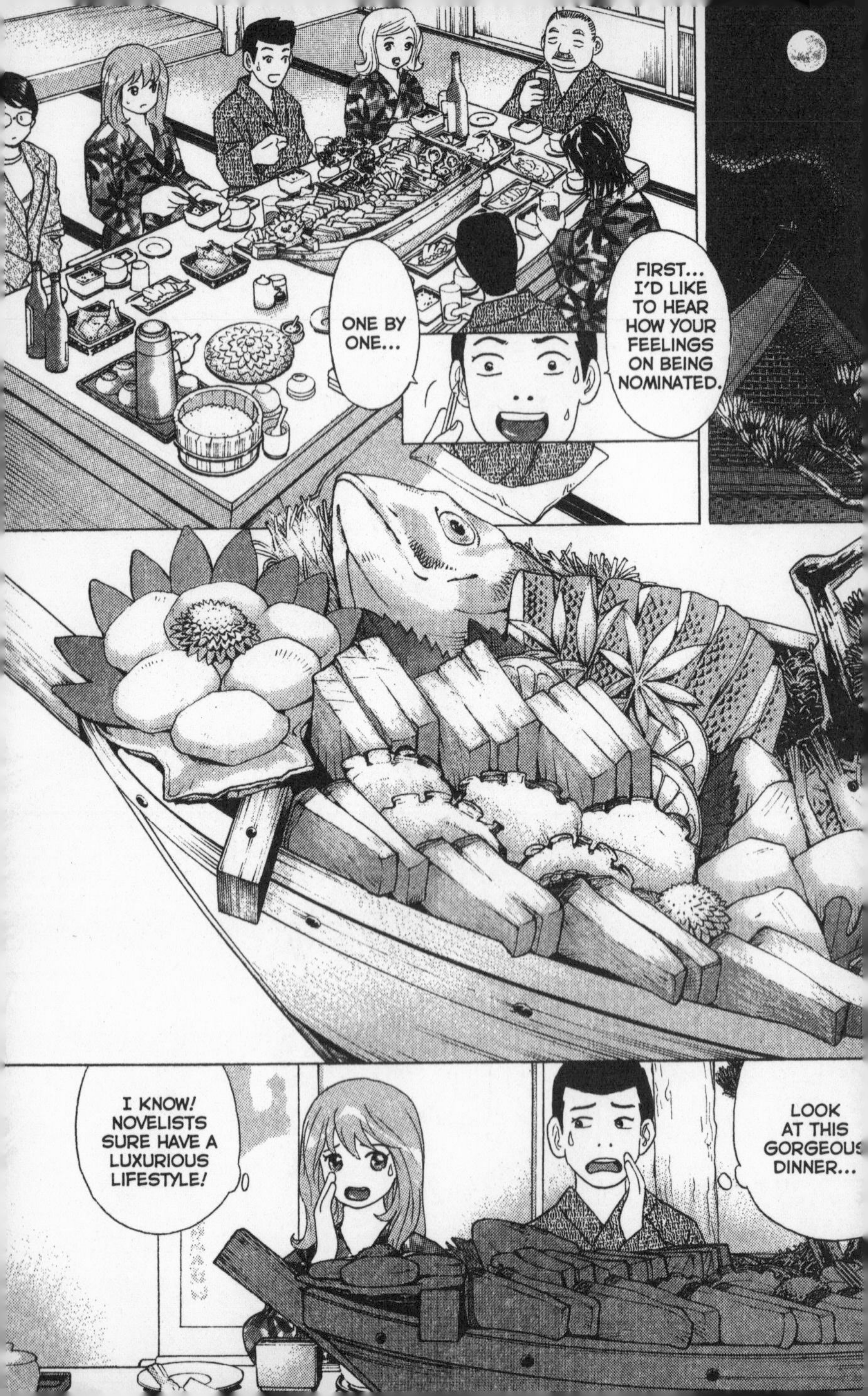
FIRST... I'D LIKE TO HEAR HOW YOUR FEELINGS ON BEING NOMINATED.
ONE BY ONE...
LOOK AT THIS GORGEOUS DINNER...
I KNOW! NOVELISTS SURE HAVE A LUXURIOUS LIFESTYLE!

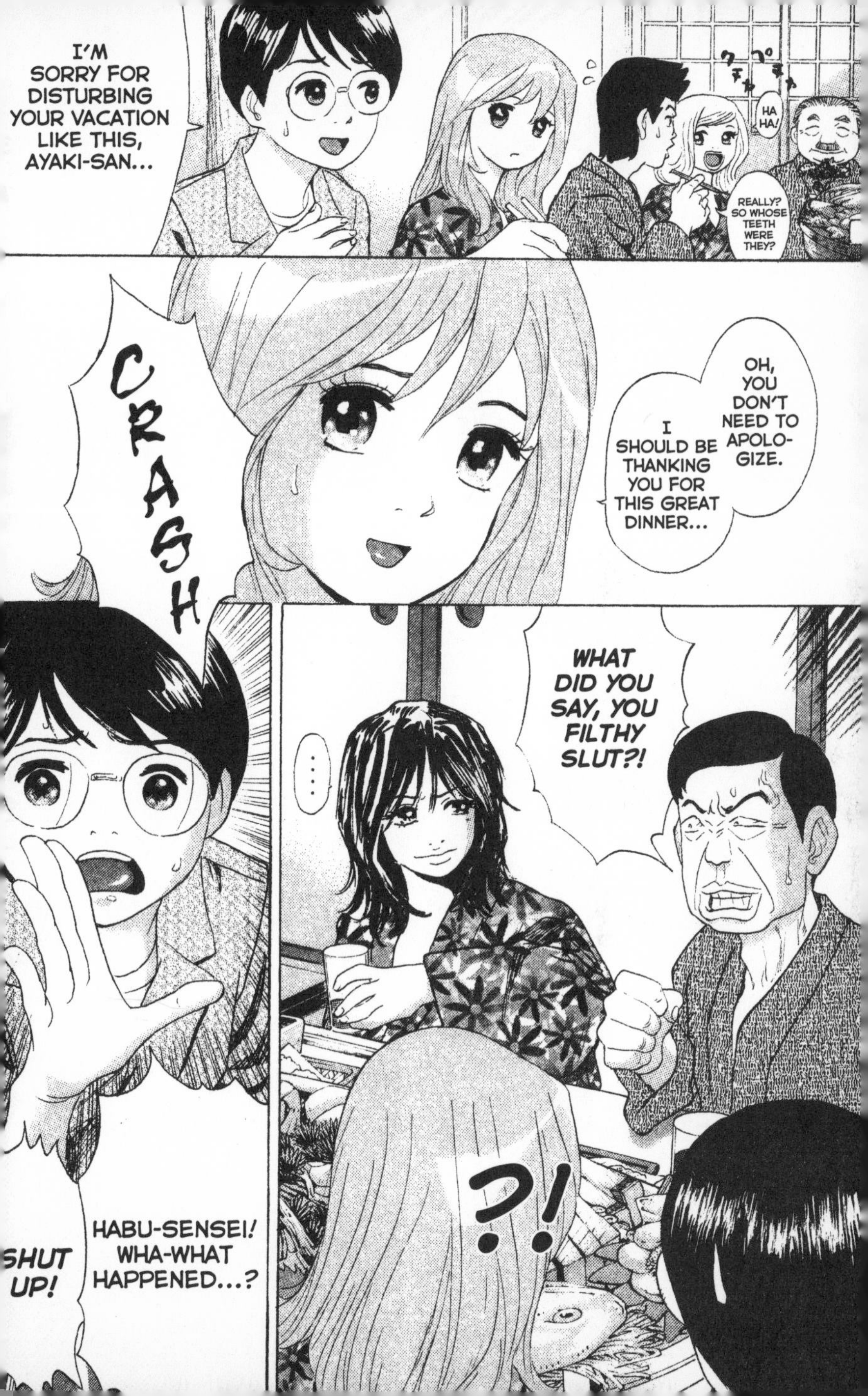
HA HA!
REALLY? SO WHOSE TEETH WERE THEY?
I'M SORRY FOR DISTURBING YOUR VACATION LIKE THIS, AYAKI-SAN...
OH, YOU DON'T NEED TO APOLO-GIZE.
I SHOULD BE THANKING YOU FOR THIS GREAT DINNER...
CRASH
WHAT DID YOU SAY, YOU FILTHY SLUT?!
.....
?!
HABU-SENSEI! WHA-WHAT HAPPENED...?
SHUT UP!

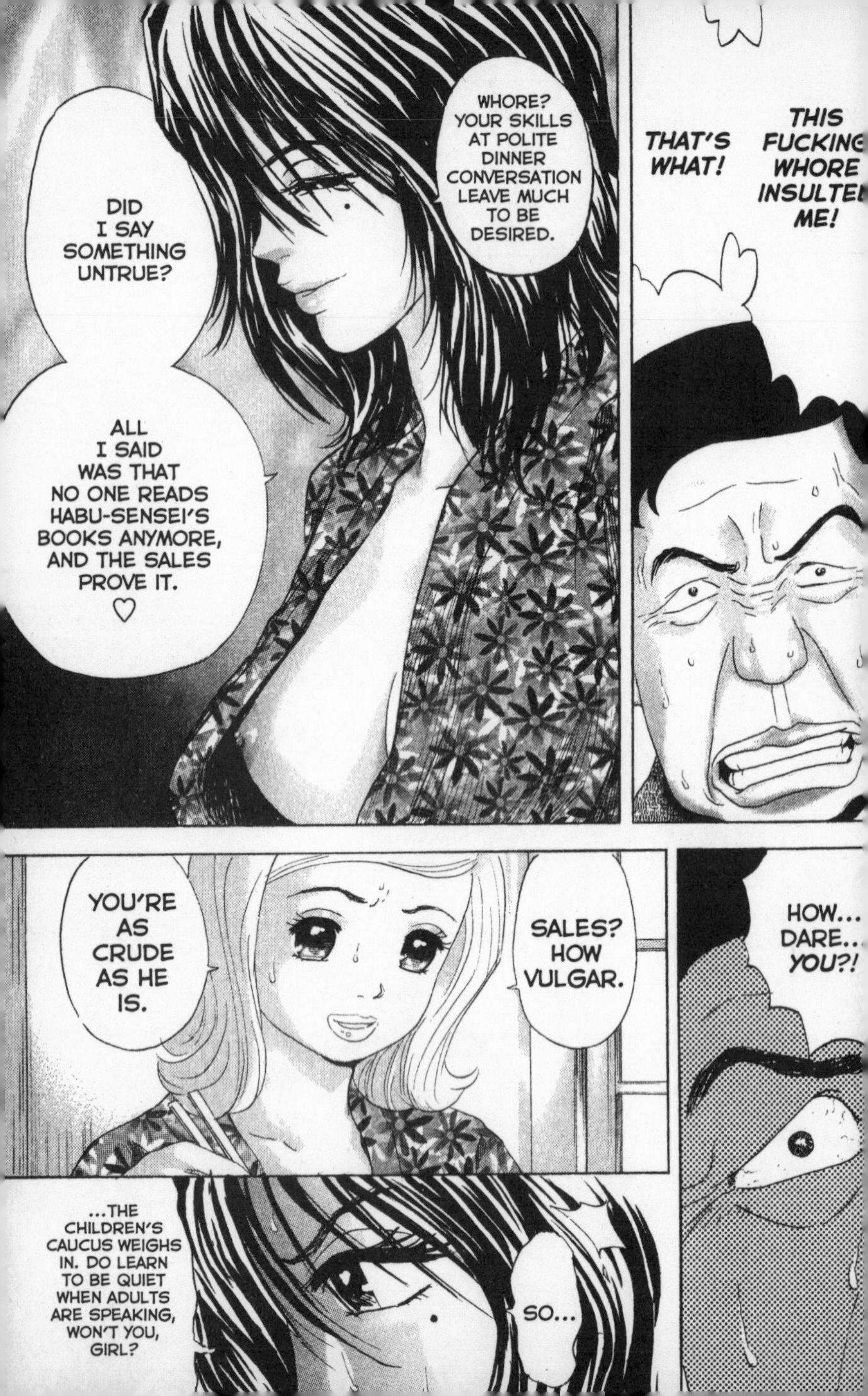

THIS FUCKING WHORE INSULTED ME!
THAT'S WHAT!
WHORE? YOUR SKILLS AT POLITE DINNER CONVERSATION LEAVE MUCH TO BE DESIRED.
DID I SAY SOMETHING UNTRUE?
ALL I SAID WAS THAT NO ONE READS HABU-SENSEI'S BOOKS ANYMORE, AND THE SALES PROVE IT. ♡
HOW... DARE... YOU?!
SALES? HOW VULGAR.
YOU'RE AS CRUDE AS HE IS.
SO...
...THE CHILDREN'S CAUCUS WEIGHS IN. DO LEARN TO BE QUIET WHEN ADULTS ARE SPEAKING, WON'T YOU, GIRL?

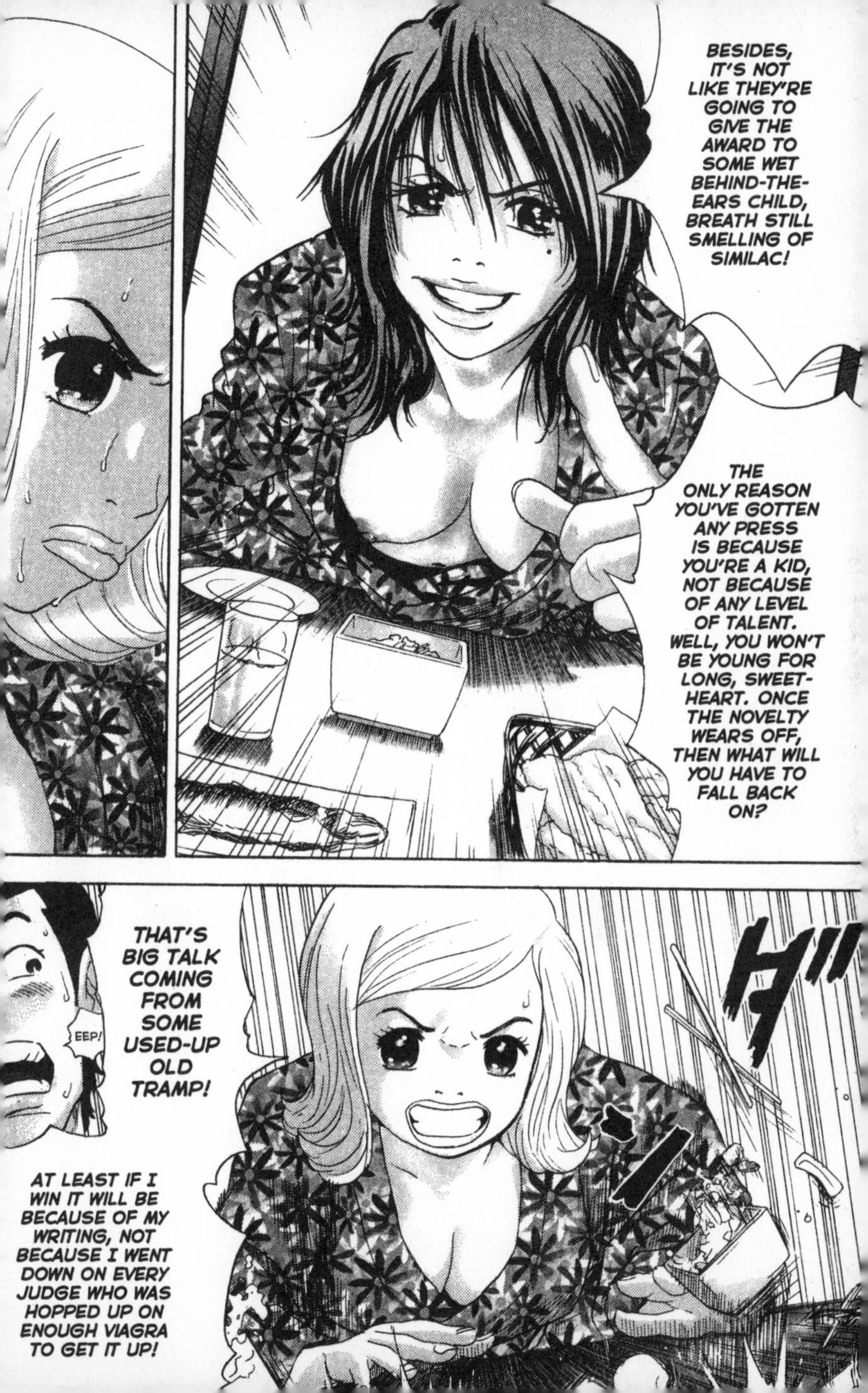
BESIDES, IT'S NOT LIKE THEY'RE GOING TO GIVE THE AWARD TO SOME WET BEHIND-THE-EARS CHILD, BREATH STILL SMELLING OF SIMILAC!
THE ONLY REASON YOU'VE GOTTEN ANY PRESS IS BECAUSE YOU'RE A KID, NOT BECAUSE OF ANY LEVEL OF TALENT. WELL, YOU WON'T BE YOUNG FOR LONG, SWEET-HEART. ONCE THE NOVELTY WEARS OFF, THEN WHAT WILL YOU HAVE TO FALL BACK ON?
THAT'S BIG TALK COMING FROM SOME USED-UP OLD TRAMP!
AT LEAST IF I WIN IT WILL BE BECAUSE OF MY WRITING, NOT BECAUSE I WENT DOWN ON EVERY JUDGE WHO WAS HOPPED UP ON ENOUGH VIAGRA TO GET IT UP!
EEP!

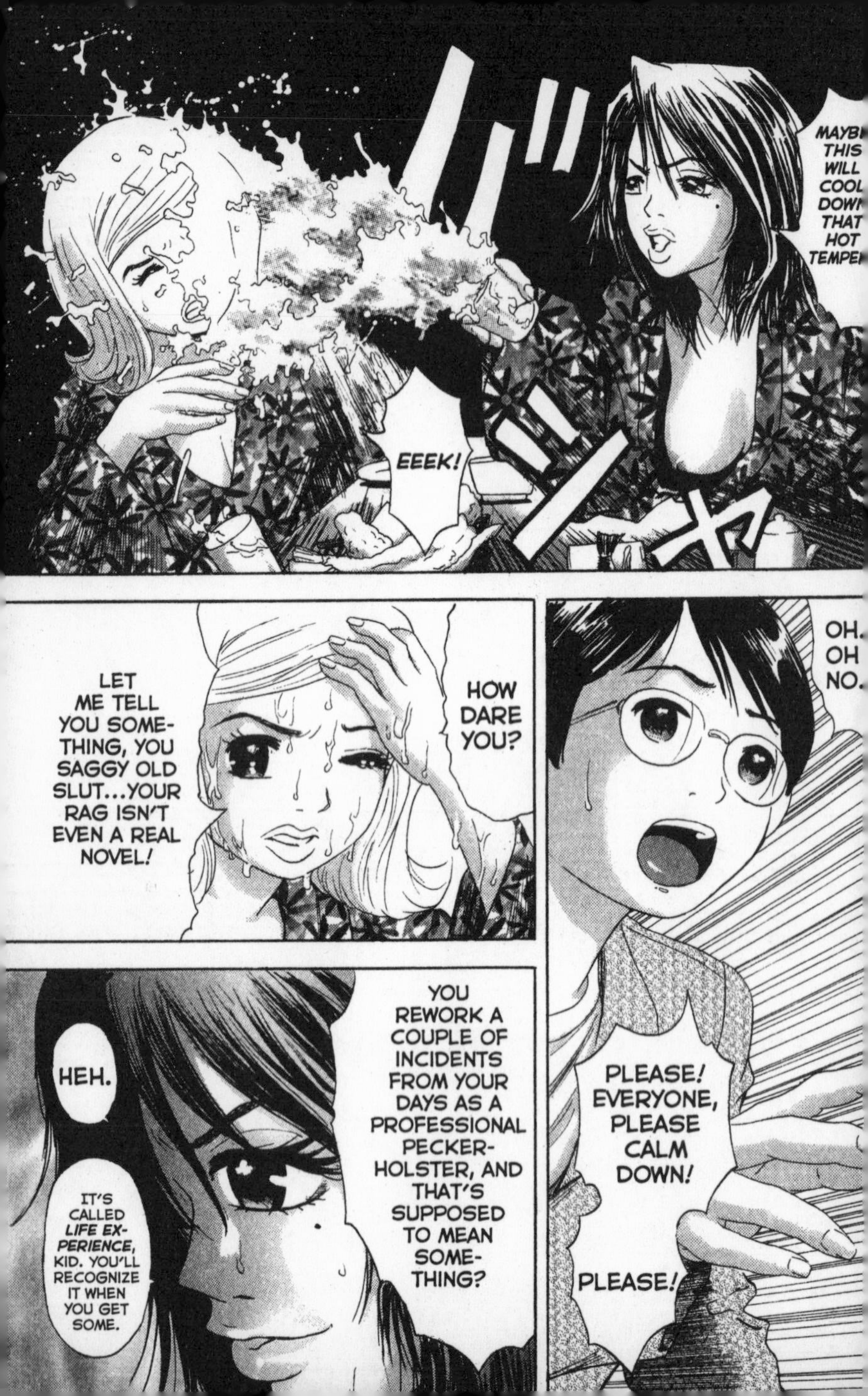
MAYBE THIS WILL COOL DOWN THAT HOT TEMPER
EEEK!
OH... OH NO...
HOW DARE YOU?
LET ME TELL YOU SOMETHING, YOU SAGGY OLD SLUT...YOUR RAG ISN'T EVEN A REAL NOVEL!
PLEASE! EVERYONE, PLEASE CALM DOWN!
PLEASE!
YOU REWORK A COUPLE OF INCIDENTS FROM YOUR DAYS AS A PROFESSIONAL PECKER-HOLSTER, AND THAT'S SUPPOSED TO MEAN SOMETHING?
HEH.
IT'S CALLED LIFE EXPERIENCE, KID. YOU'LL RECOGNIZE IT WHEN YOU GET SOME.

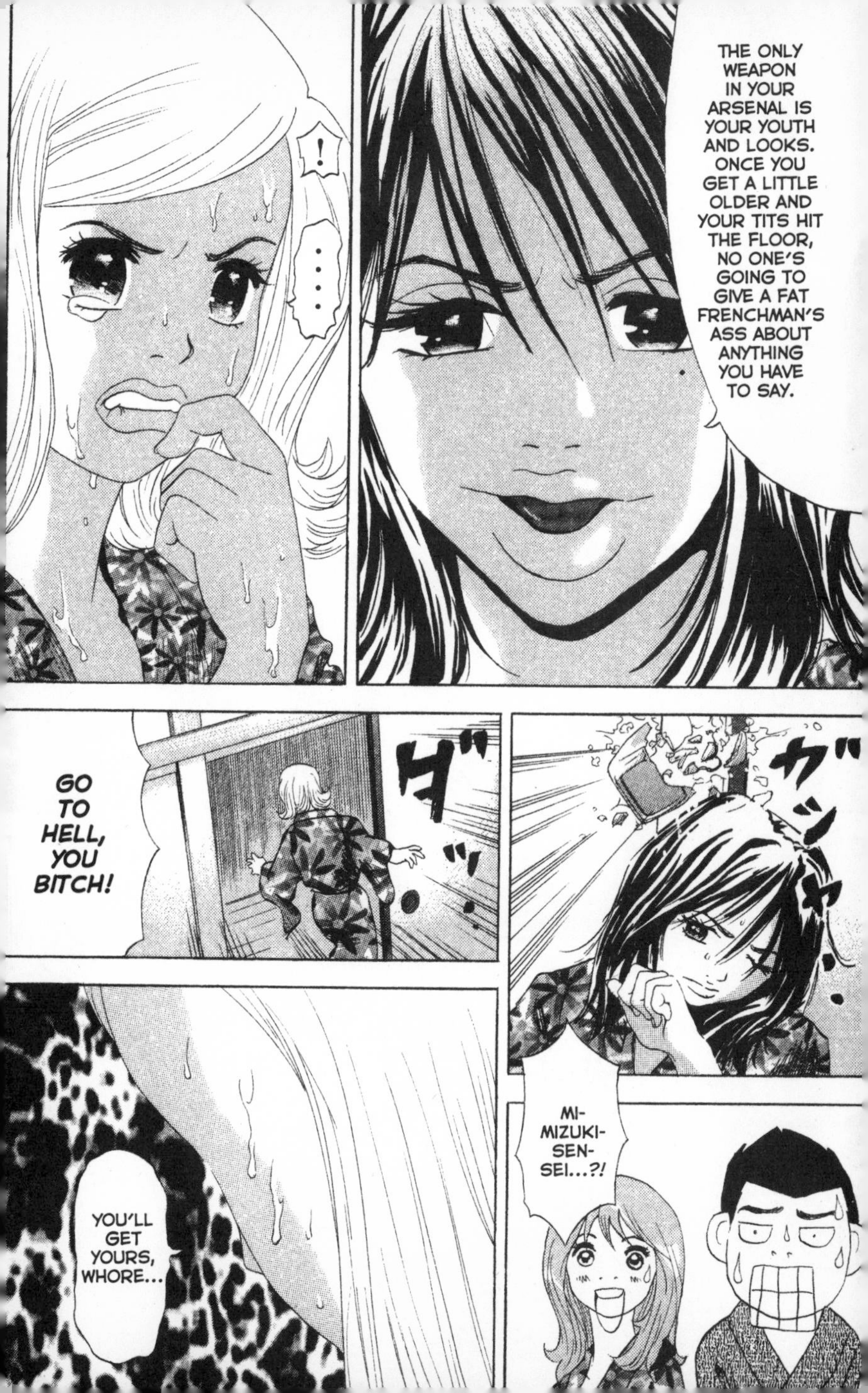
THE ONLY WEAPON IN YOUR ARSENAL IS YOUR YOUTH AND LOOKS. ONCE YOU GET A LITTLE OLDER AND YOUR TITS HIT THE FLOOR, NO ONE'S GOING TO GIVE A FAT FRENCHMAN'S ASS ABOUT ANYTHING YOU HAVE TO SAY.
!
.....
GO TO HELL, YOU BITCH!
MI-MIZUKI-SEN-SEI...?!
YOU'LL GET YOURS, WHORE...

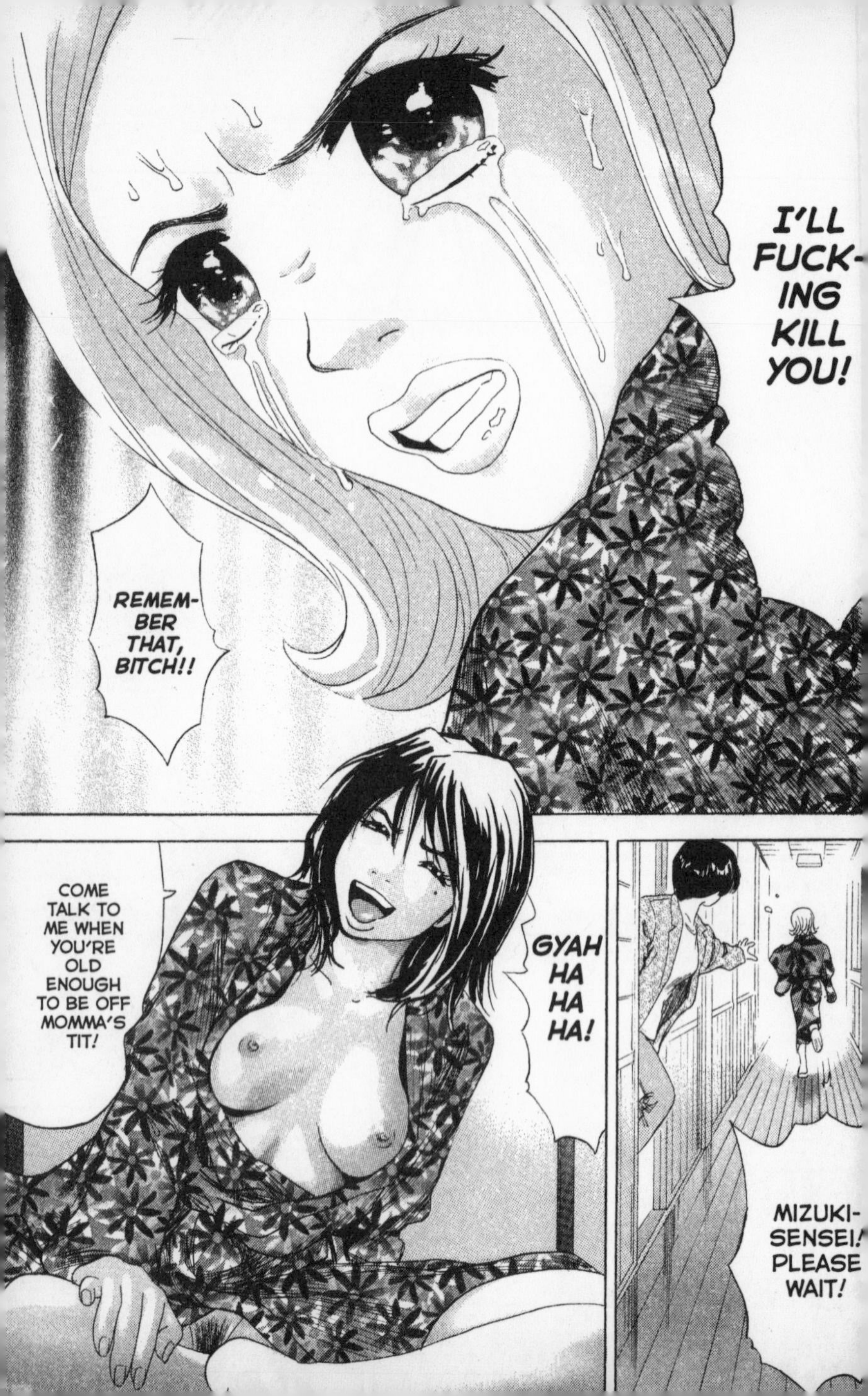
I'LL FUCK-ING KILL YOU!
REMEM-BER THAT, BITCH!!
MIZUKI-SENSEI! PLEASE WAIT!
GYAH HA HA HA HA!
COME TALK TO ME WHEN YOU'RE OLD ENOUGH TO BE OFF MOMMA'S TIT!

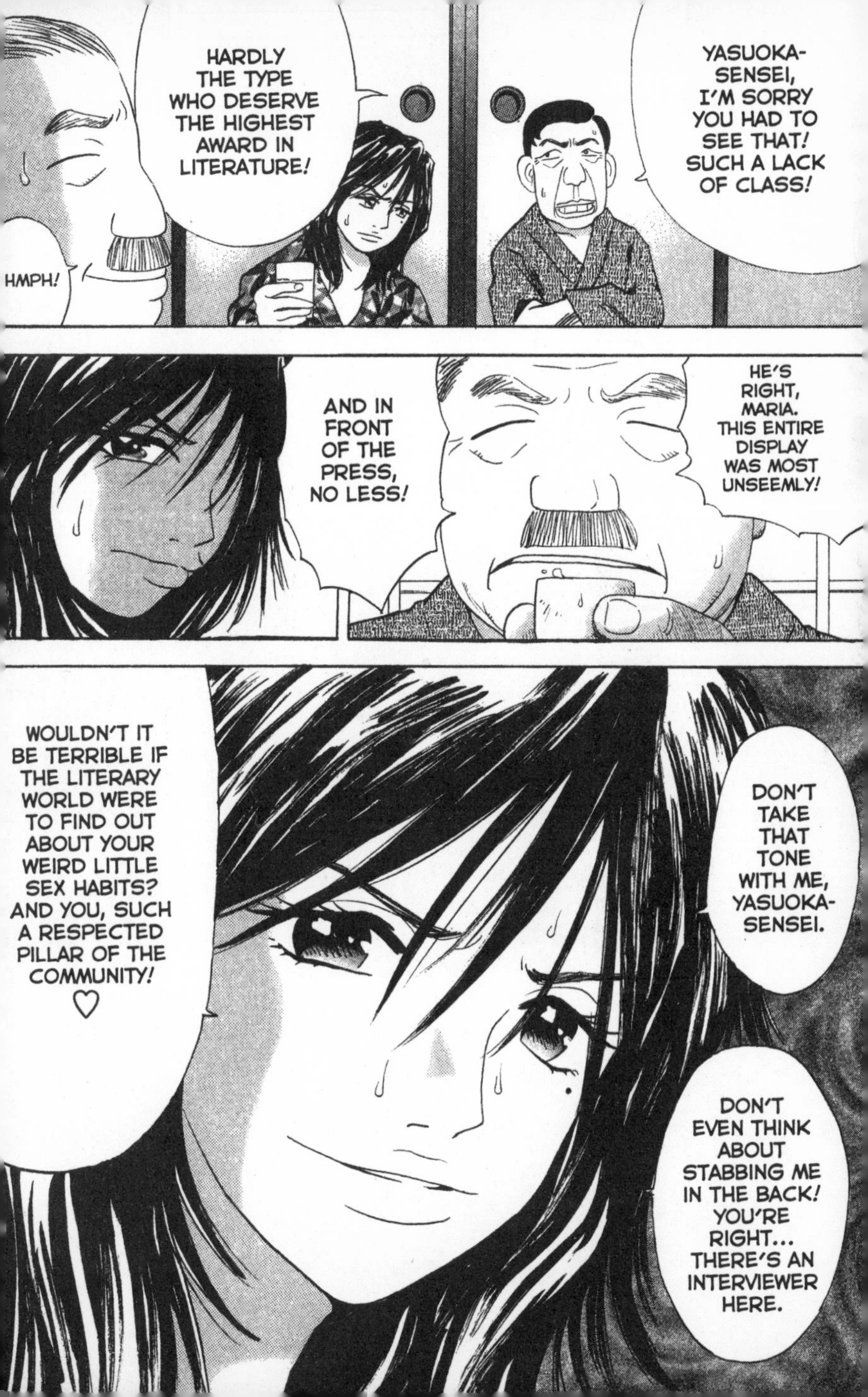
YASUOKA-SENSEI, I'M SORRY YOU HAD TO SEE THAT! SUCH A LACK OF CLASS!
HARDLY THE TYPE WHO DESERVE THE HIGHEST AWARD IN LITERATURE!
HMPH!
HE'S RIGHT, MARIA. THIS ENTIRE DISPLAY WAS MOST UNSEEMLY!
AND IN FRONT OF THE PRESS, NO LESS!
DON'T TAKE THAT TONE WITH ME, YASUOKA-SENSEI.
WOULDN'T IT BE TERRIBLE IF THE LITERARY WORLD WERE TO FIND OUT ABOUT YOUR WEIRD LITTLE SEX HABITS? AND YOU, SUCH A RESPECTED PILLAR OF THE COMMUNITY! ♡
DON'T EVEN THINK ABOUT STABBING ME IN THE BACK! YOU'RE RIGHT... THERE'S AN INTERVIEWER HERE.

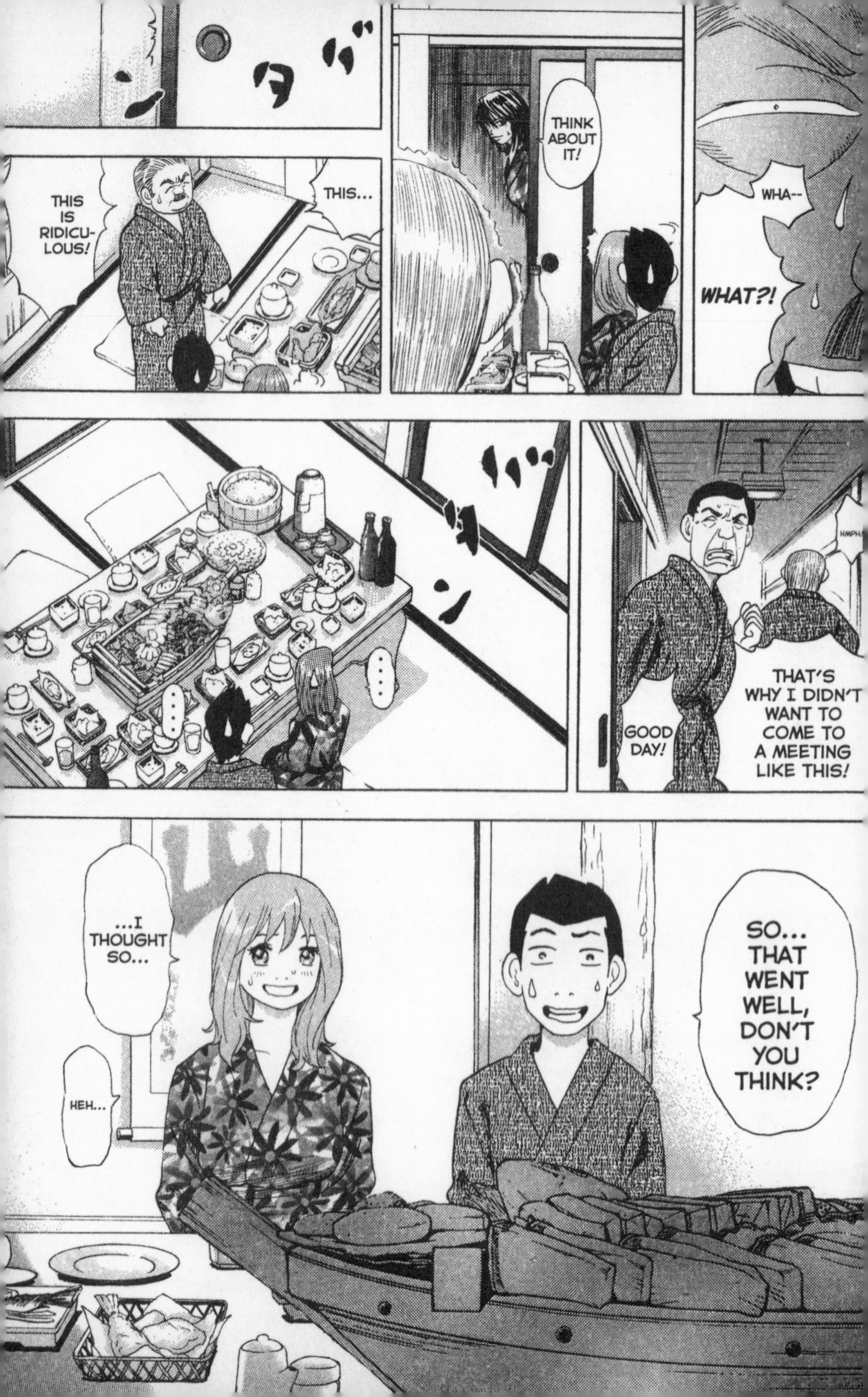
WHA--
WHAT?!
THINK ABOUT IT!
THIS...
THIS IS RIDICU-LOUS!
HMPH!
THAT'S WHY I DIDN'T WANT TO COME TO A MEETING LIKE THIS!
GOOD DAY!
...
...
SO... THAT WENT WELL, DON'T YOU THINK?
...I THOUGHT SO...
HEH...

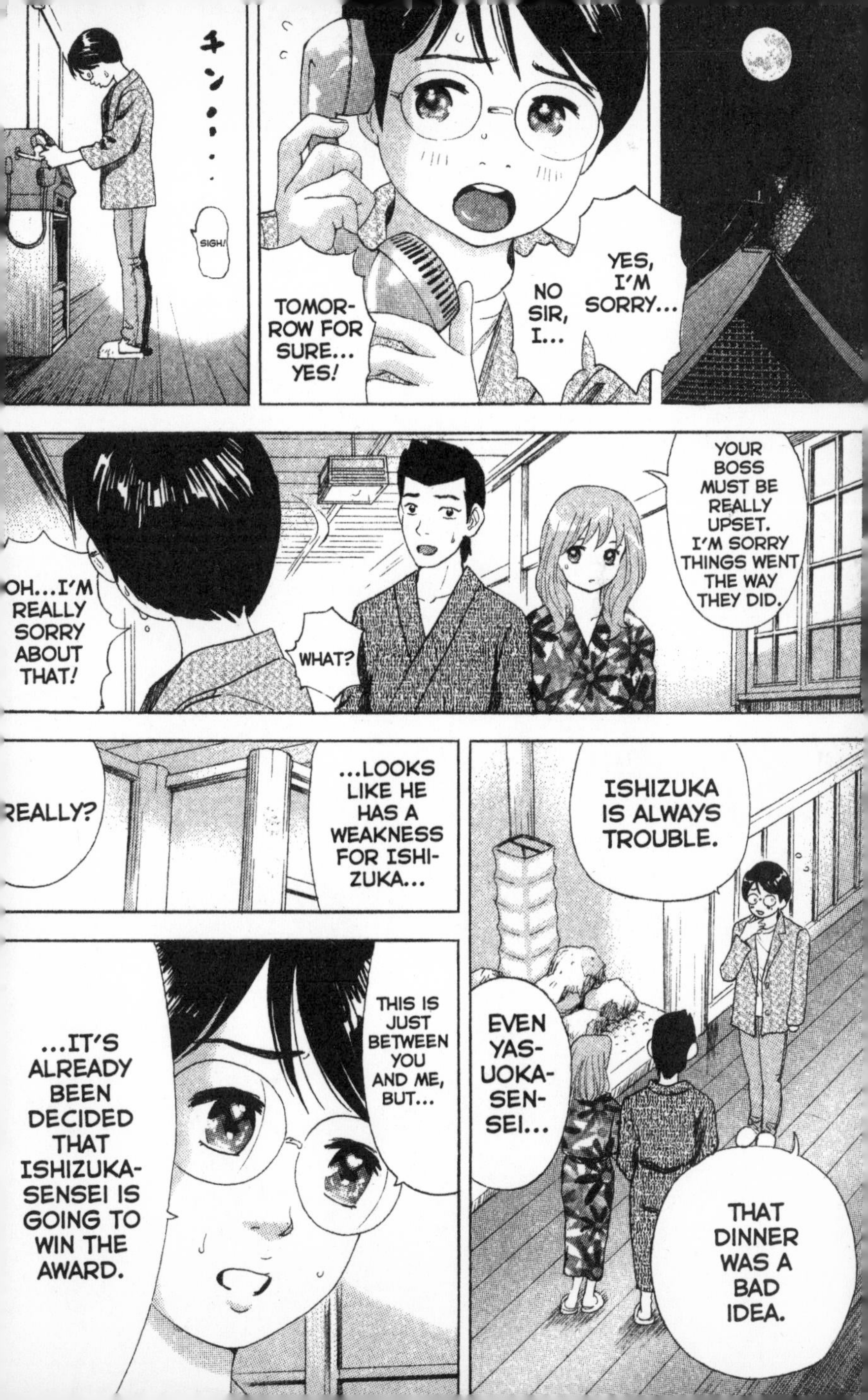
YES, I'M SORRY...
NO SIR, I...
TOMORROW FOR SURE... YES!
チン・・・
SIGH!
YOUR BOSS MUST BE REALLY UPSET. I'M SORRY THINGS WENT THE WAY THEY DID.
WHAT?
OH...I'M REALLY SORRY ABOUT THAT!
ISHIZUKA IS ALWAYS TROUBLE.
THAT DINNER WAS A BAD IDEA.
EVEN YASUOKA-SENSEI...
...LOOKS LIKE HE HAS A WEAKNESS FOR ISHIZUKA...
REALLY?
THIS IS JUST BETWEEN YOU AND ME, BUT...
...IT'S ALREADY BEEN DECIDED THAT ISHIZUKA-SENSEI IS GOING TO WIN THE AWARD.

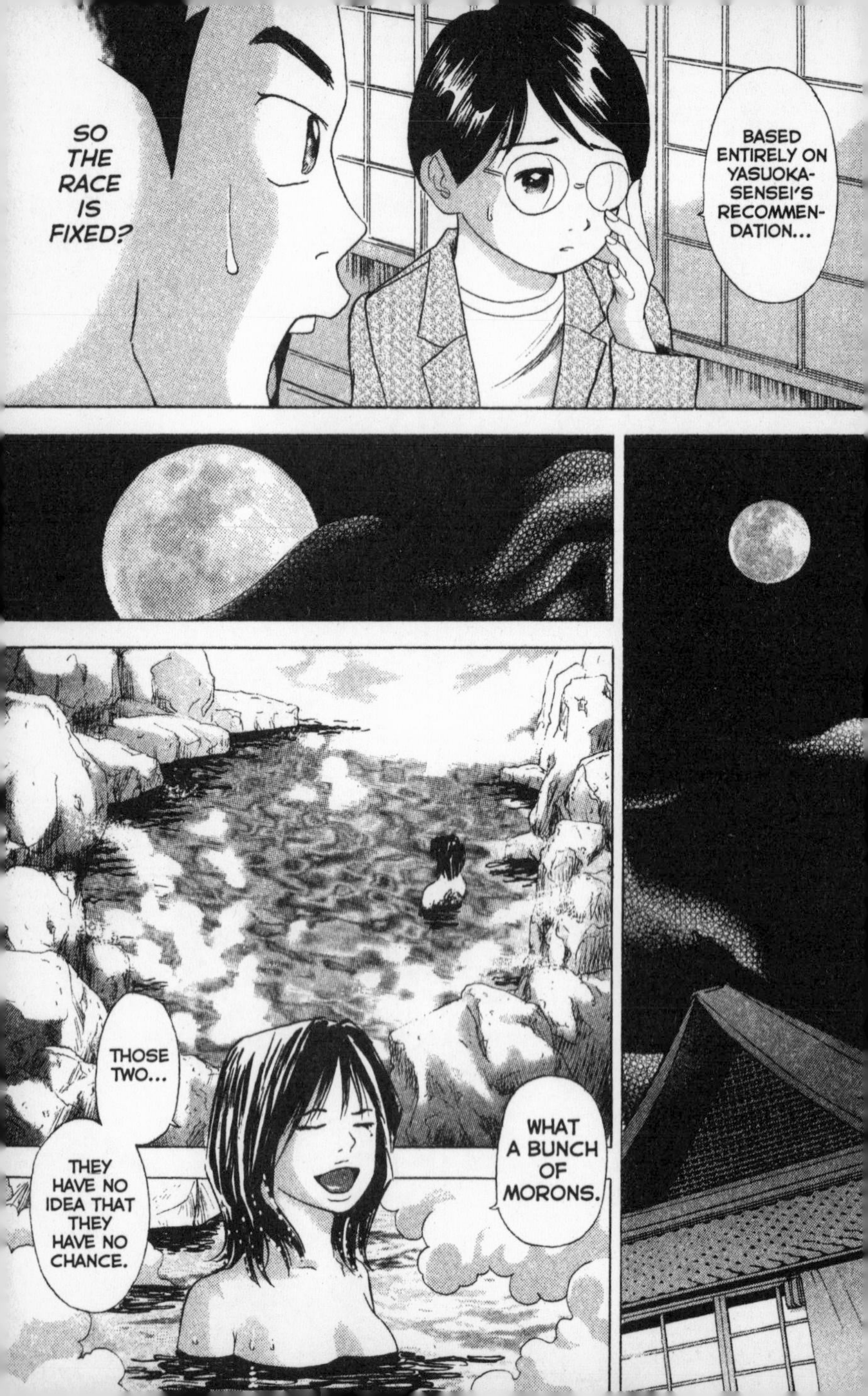
BASED ENTIRELY ON YASUOKA-SENSEI'S RECOMMENDATION...
SO THE RACE IS FIXED?
THOSE TWO...
THEY HAVE NO IDEA THAT THEY HAVE NO CHANCE.
WHAT A BUNCH OF MORONS.

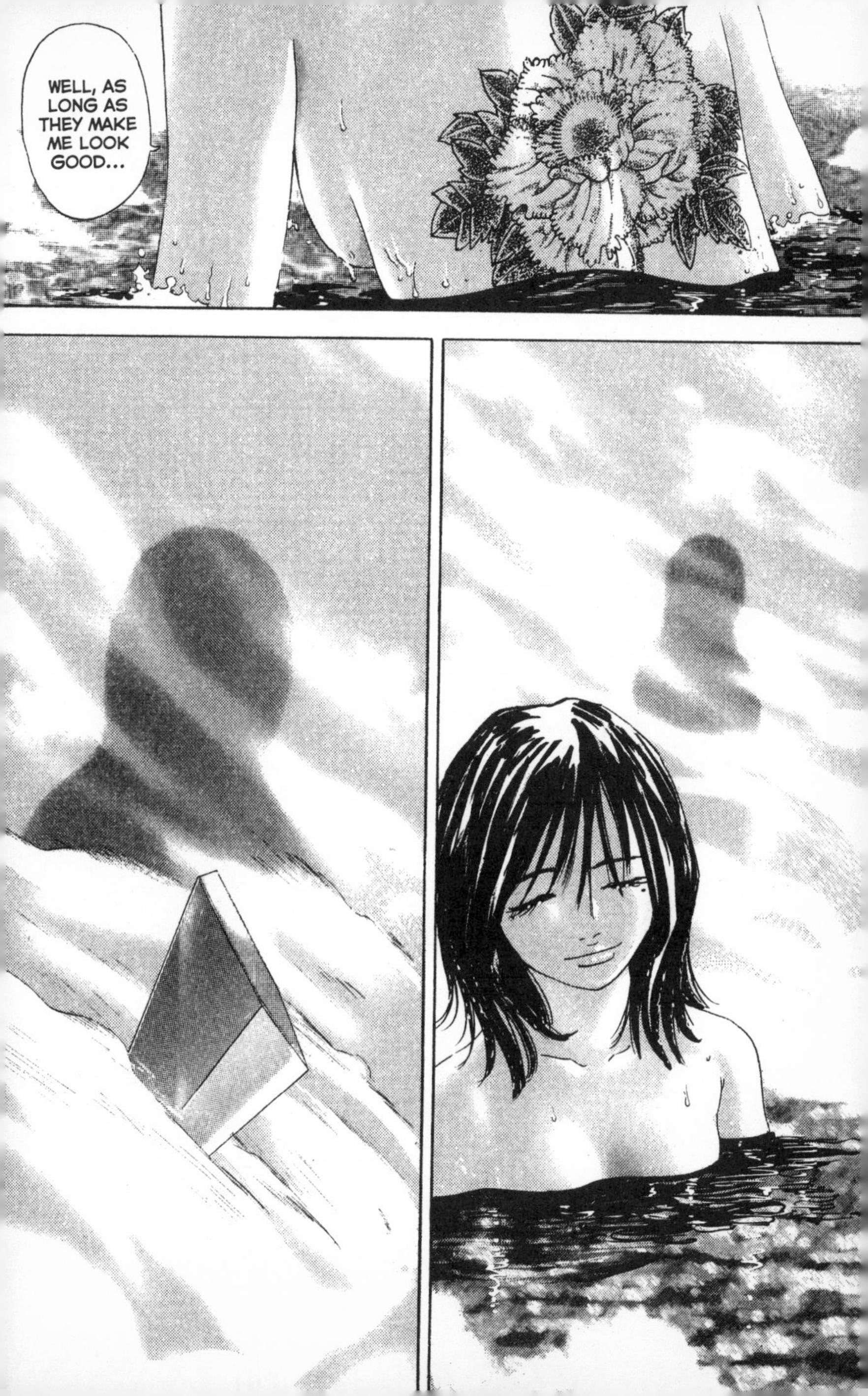
WELL, AS LONG AS THEY MAKE ME LOOK GOOD...

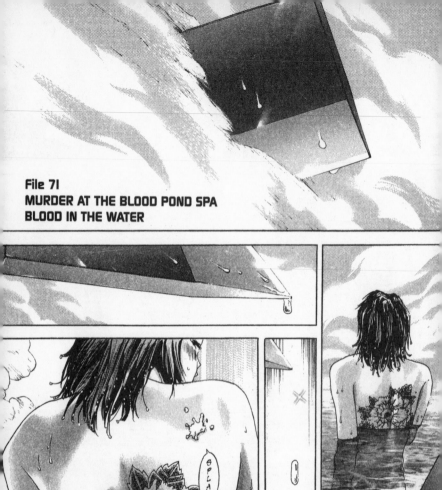

File 71
MURDER AT THE BLOOD POND SPA
BLOOD IN THE WATER

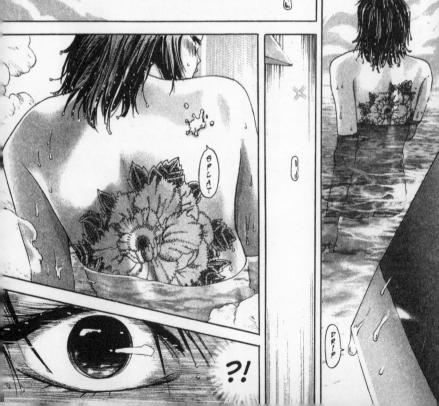

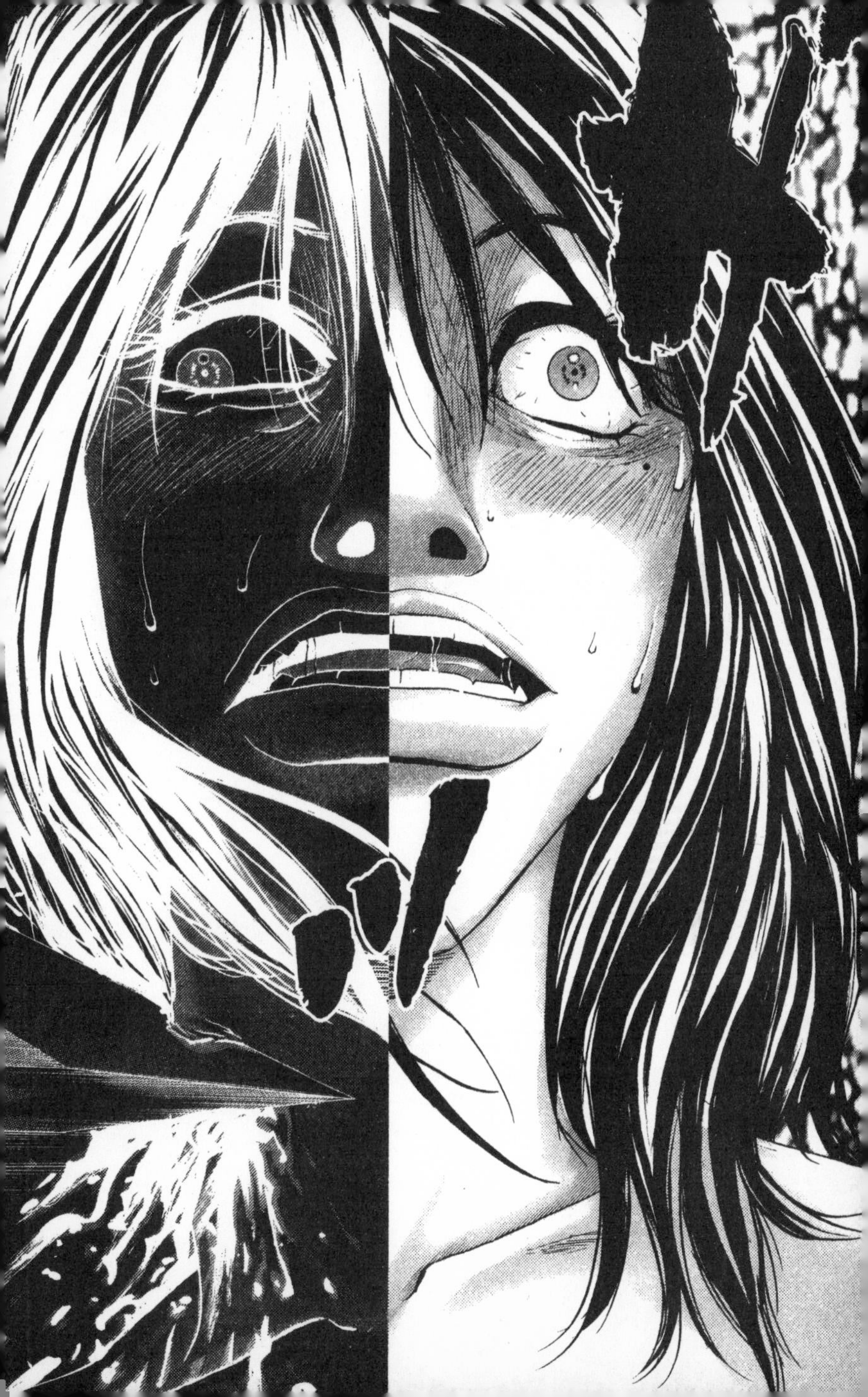

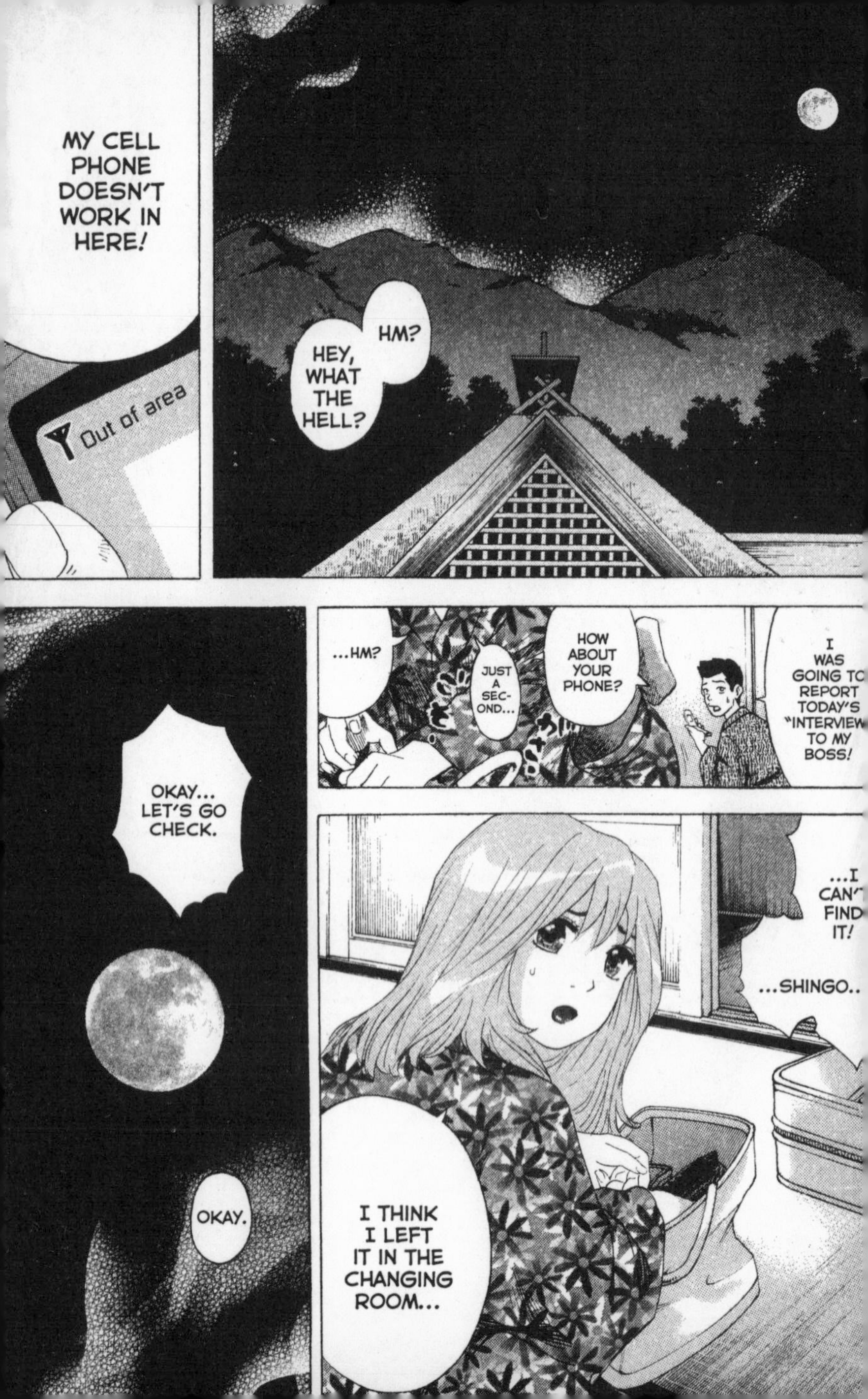
HM?
HEY, WHAT THE HELL?
MY CELL PHONE DOESN'T WORK IN HERE!
Out of area
I WAS GOING TO REPORT TODAY'S "INTERVIEW" TO MY BOSS!
HOW ABOUT YOUR PHONE?
JUST A SEC- OND...
...HM?
...I CAN'T FIND IT!
...SHINGO...
I THINK I LEFT IT IN THE CHANGING ROOM...
OKAY... LET'S GO CHECK.
OKAY.

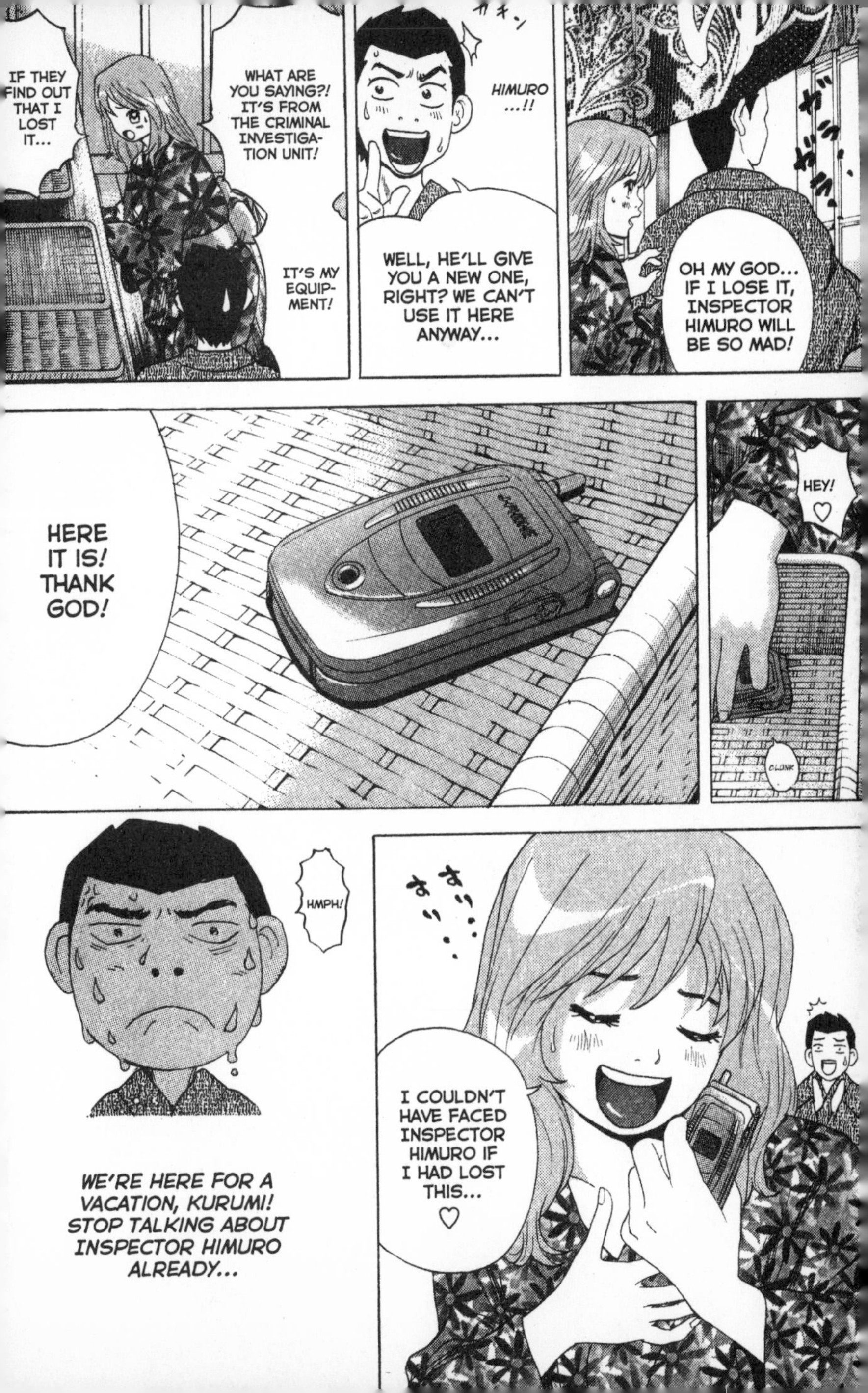
OH MY GOD... IF I LOSE IT, INSPECTOR HIMURO WILL BE SO MAD!
HIMURO ...!!
WELL, HE'LL GIVE YOU A NEW ONE, RIGHT? WE CAN'T USE IT HERE ANYWAY...
WHAT ARE YOU SAYING?! IT'S FROM THE CRIMINAL INVESTIGATION UNIT!
IF THEY FIND OUT THAT I LOST IT...
IT'S MY EQUIPMENT!
HEY! ♡
CLUNK
HERE IT IS! THANK GOD!
I COULDN'T HAVE FACED INSPECTOR HIMURO IF I HAD LOST THIS... ♡
HMPH!
WE'RE HERE FOR A VACATION, KURUMI! STOP TALKING ABOUT INSPECTOR HIMURO ALREADY...

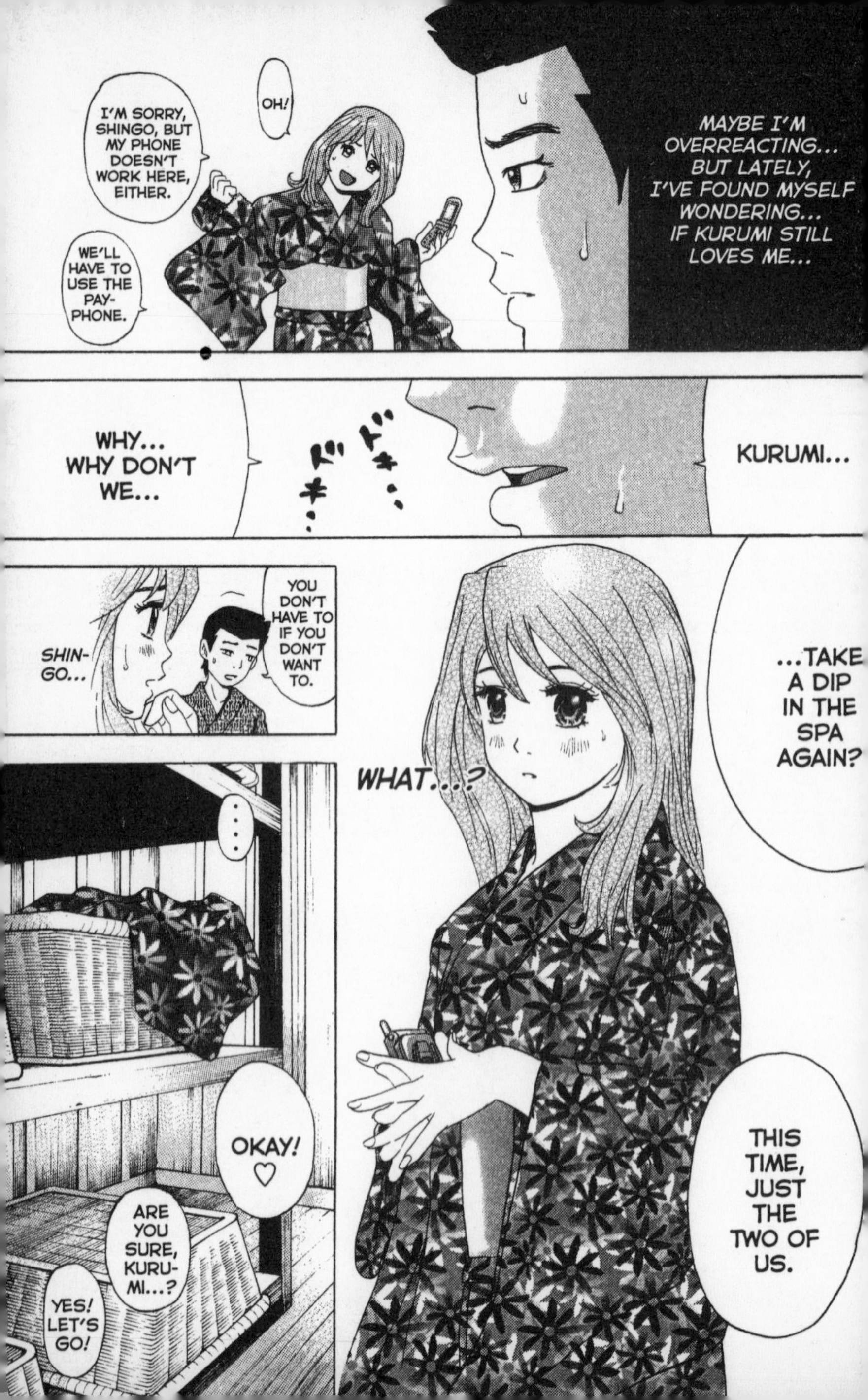
MAYBE I'M OVERREACTING... BUT LATELY, I'VE FOUND MYSELF WONDERING... IF KURUMI STILL LOVES ME...
OH!
I'M SORRY, SHINGO, BUT MY PHONE DOESN'T WORK HERE, EITHER.
WE'LL HAVE TO USE THE PAY-PHONE.
KURUMI...
ドキ、ドキ…
WHY... WHY DON'T WE...
...TAKE A DIP IN THE SPA AGAIN?
WHAT...?
THIS TIME, JUST THE TWO OF US.
YOU DON'T HAVE TO IF YOU DON'T WANT TO.
SHIN-GO...
...
OKAY! ♡
ARE YOU SURE, KURU-MI...?
YES! LET'S GO!

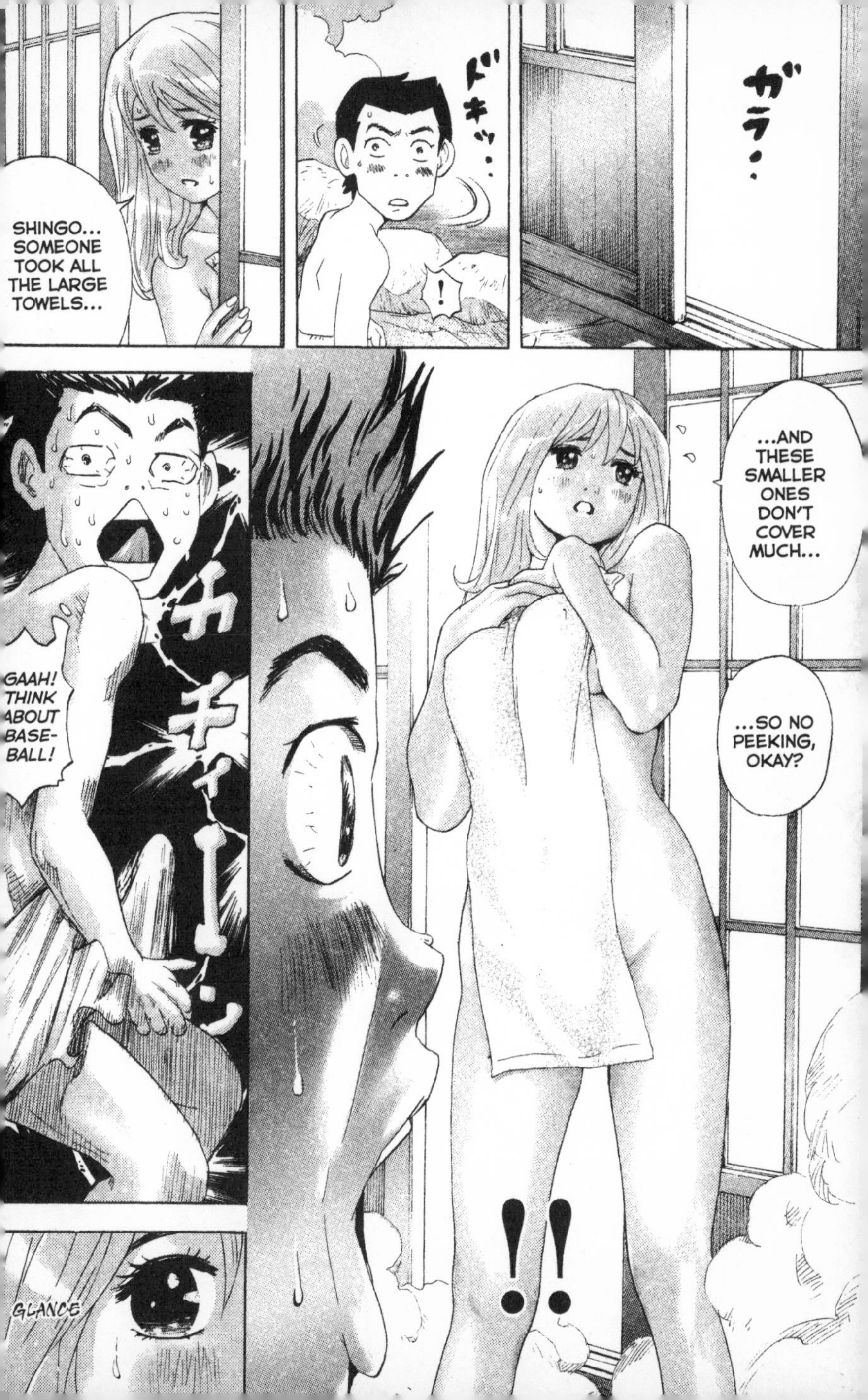

ガラ・・
ドキッ・・
!
SHINGO... SOMEONE TOOK ALL THE LARGE TOWELS...
...AND THESE SMALLER ONES DON'T COVER MUCH...
...SO NO PEEKING, OKAY?
!!
GAAH! THINK ABOUT BASE-BALL!
カキィーン
GLANCE

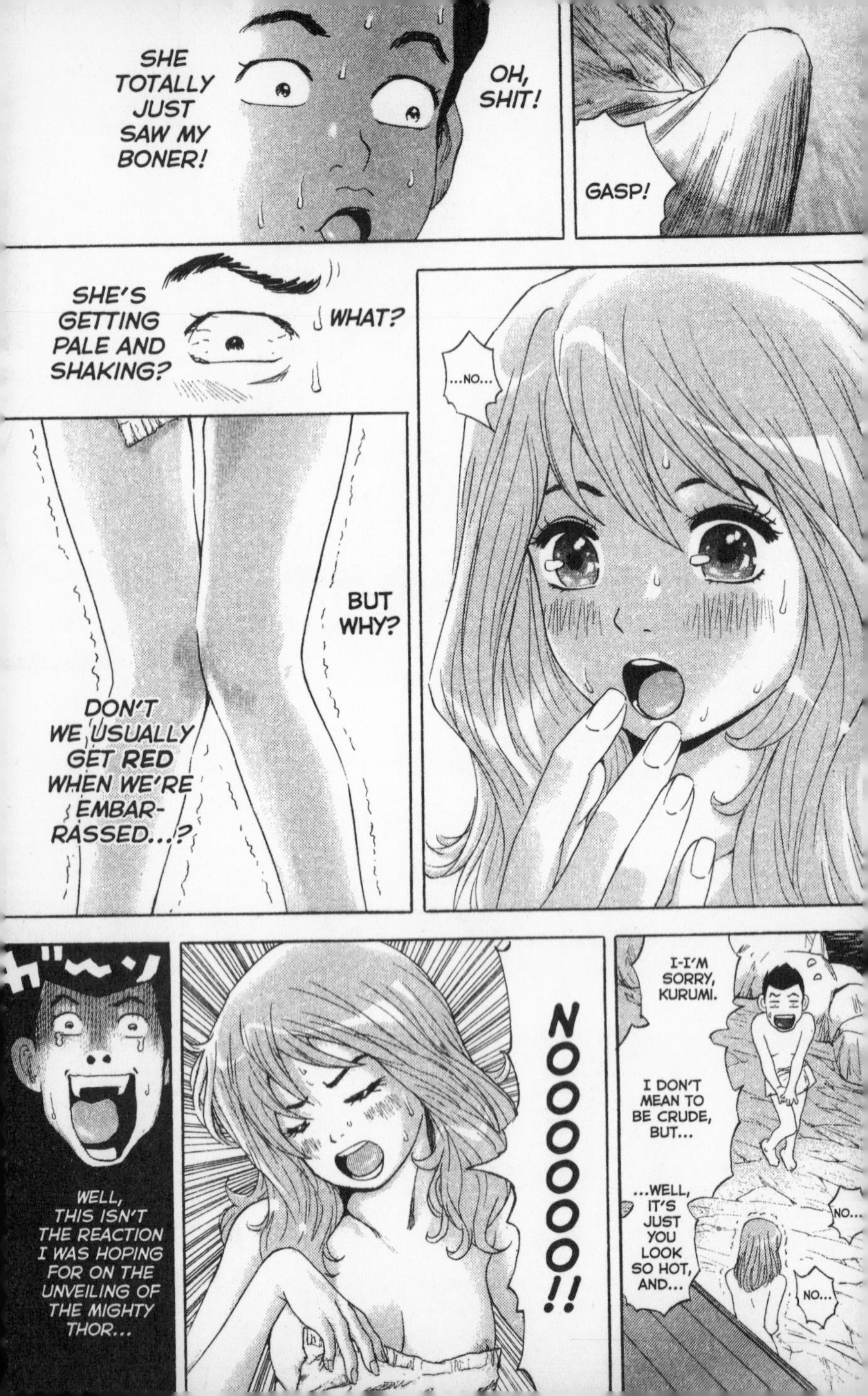
GASP!
OH, SHIT!
SHE TOTALLY JUST SAW MY BONER!
...NO...
WHAT?
SHE'S GETTING PALE AND SHAKING?
BUT WHY?
DON'T WE USUALLY GET RED WHEN WE'RE EMBAR-RASSED...?
I-I'M SORRY, KURUMI.
I DON'T MEAN TO BE CRUDE, BUT...
NO...
...WELL, IT'S JUST YOU LOOK SO HOT, AND...
NO...
NOOOOOOO!!
ガーン
WELL, THIS ISN'T THE REACTION I WAS HOPING FOR ON THE UNVEILING OF THE MIGHTY THOR...

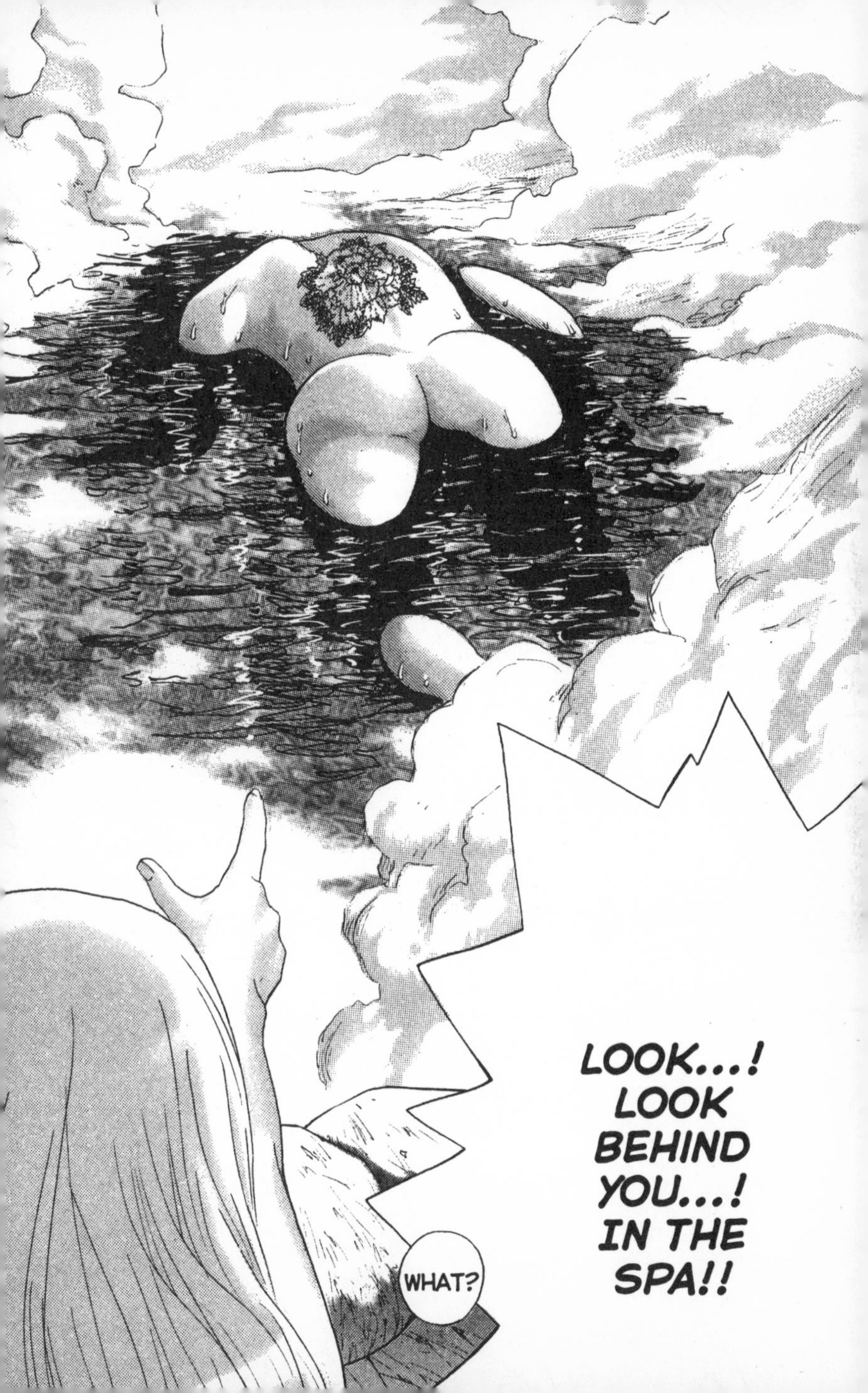
LOOK...! LOOK BEHIND YOU...! IN THE SPA!!
WHAT?

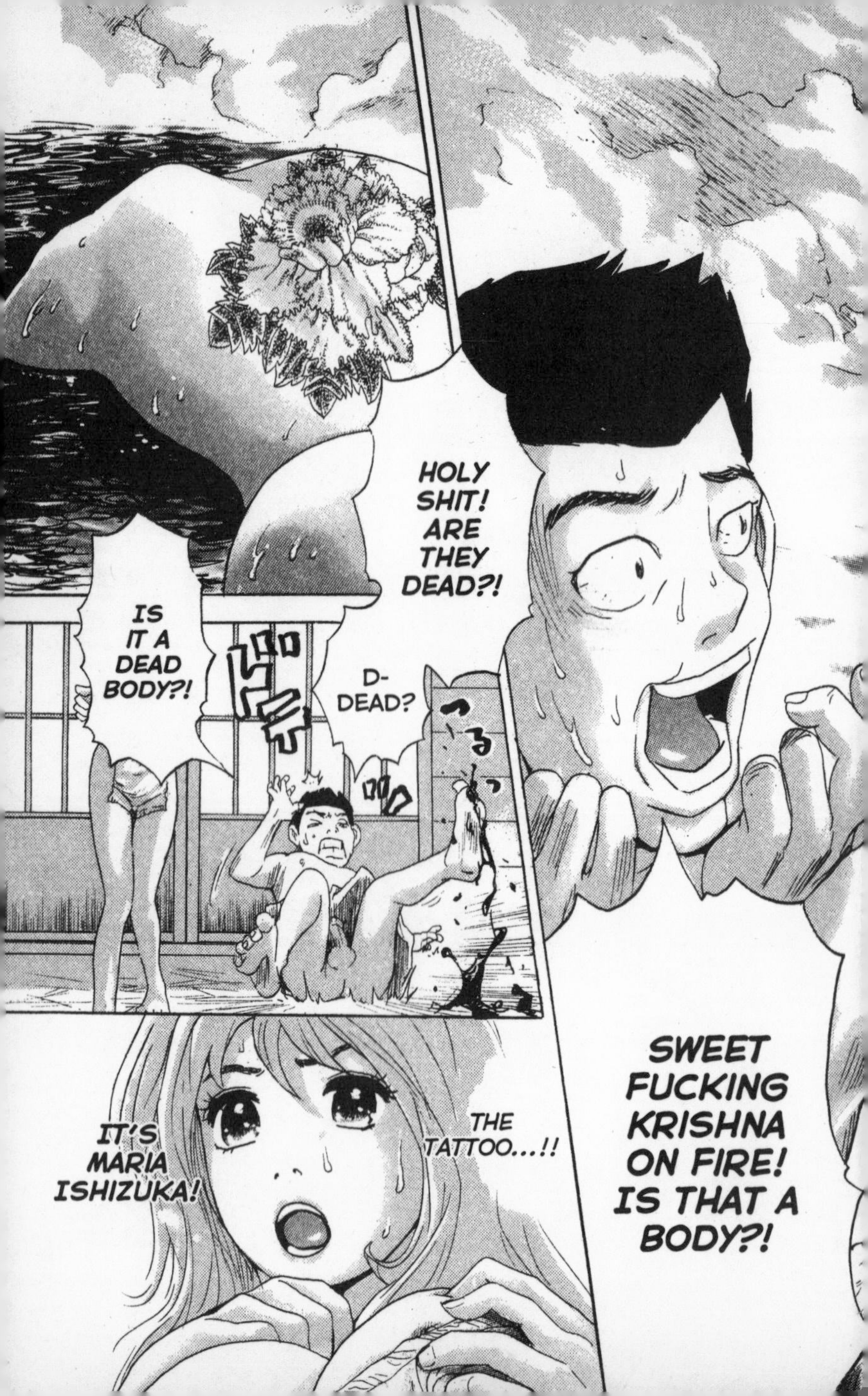
SWEET FUCKING KRISHNA ON FIRE! IS THAT A BODY?!
HOLY SHIT! ARE THEY DEAD?!
IS IT A DEAD BODY?!
D- DEAD?
THE TATTOO...!!
IT'S MARIA ISHIZUKA!

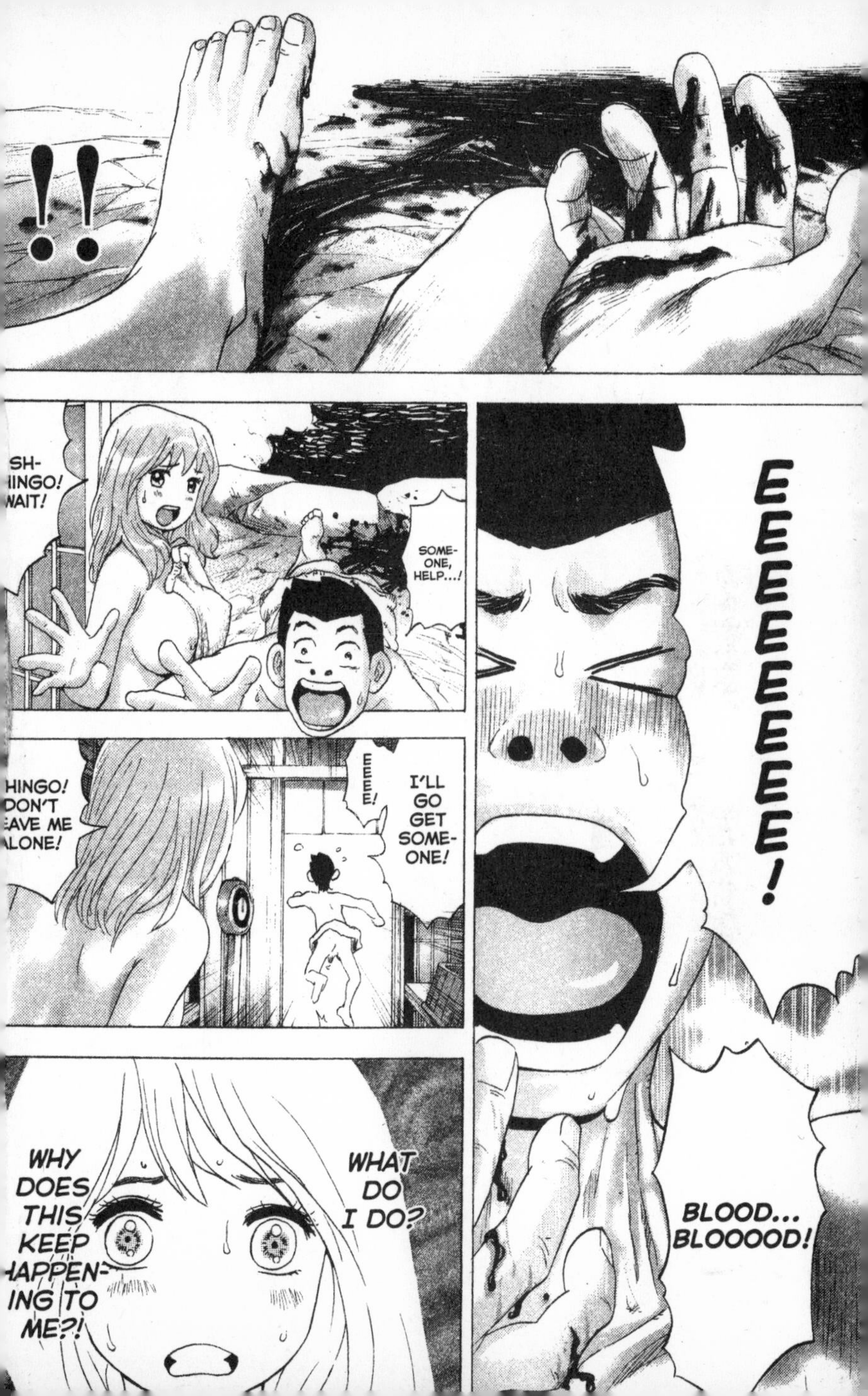
!!
EEEEEEEE!
BLOOD... BLOOOOD!
SH- HINGO! WAIT!
SOME- ONE, HELP...!
I'LL GO GET SOME- ONE!
EEEE!
HINGO! DON'T EAVE ME ALONE!
WHAT DO I DO?
WHY DOES THIS KEEP HAPPEN- ING TO ME?!

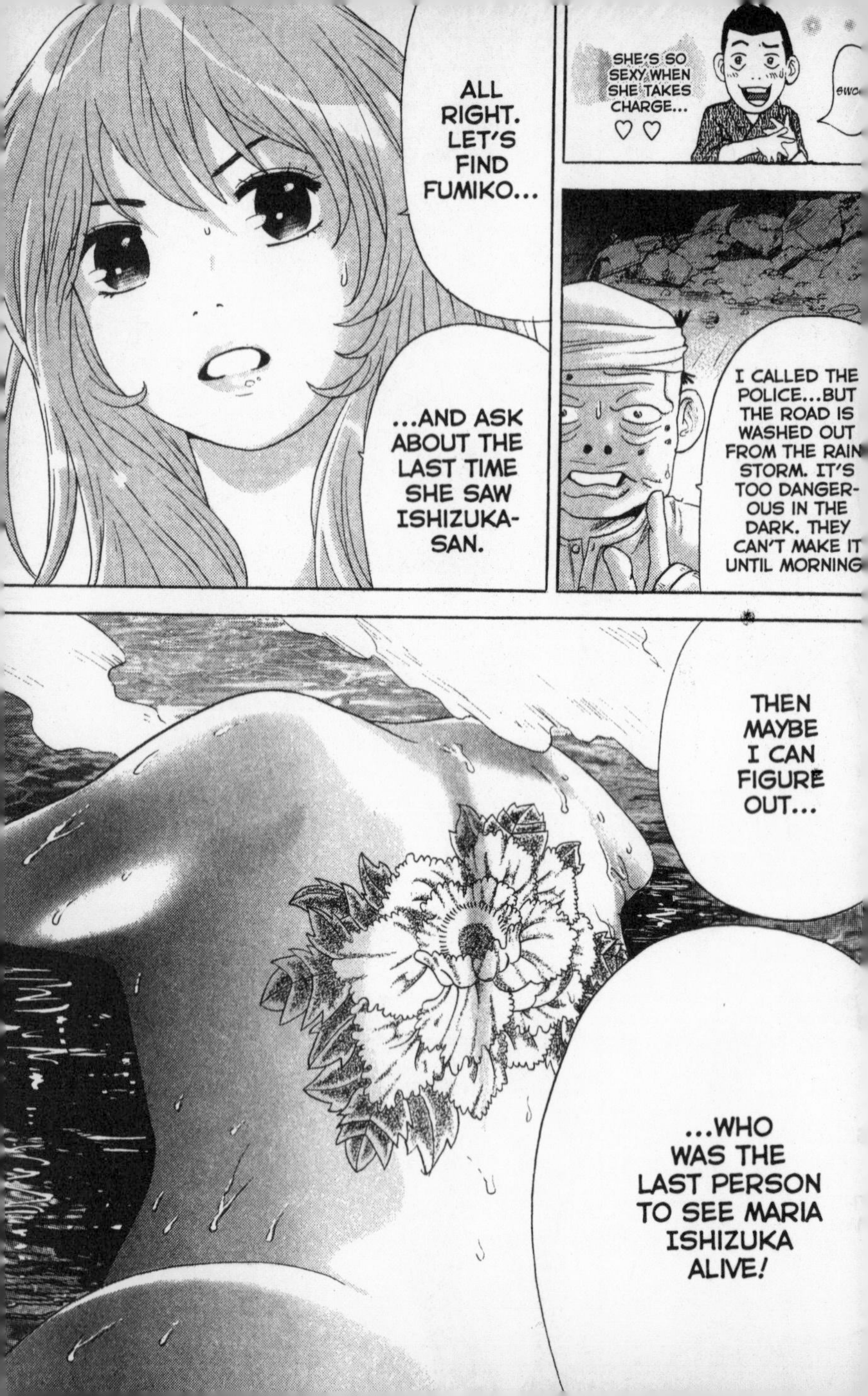

SHE'S SO SEXY WHEN SHE TAKES CHARGE... ♡ ♡
I CALLED THE POLICE...BUT THE ROAD IS WASHED OUT FROM THE RAIN STORM. IT'S TOO DANGER-OUS IN THE DARK. THEY CAN'T MAKE IT UNTIL MORNING
ALL RIGHT. LET'S FIND FUMIKO...
...AND ASK ABOUT THE LAST TIME SHE SAW ISHIZUKA-SAN.
THEN MAYBE I CAN FIGURE OUT...
...WHO WAS THE LAST PERSON TO SEE MARIA ISHIZUKA ALIVE!

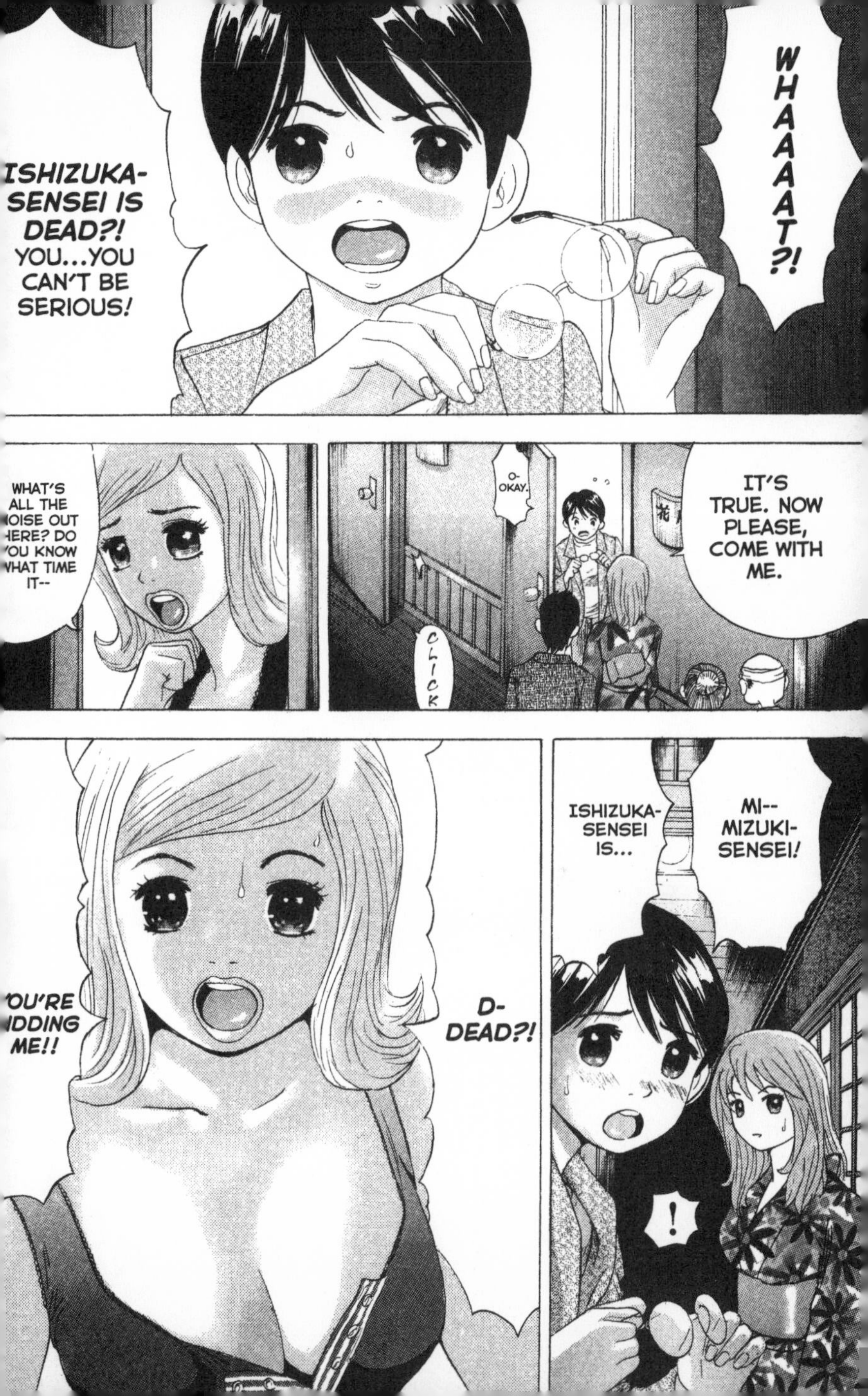
WHAAAAT?!
ISHIZUKA-SENSEI IS DEAD?! YOU...YOU CAN'T BE SERIOUS!
IT'S TRUE. NOW PLEASE, COME WITH ME.
O-OKAY.
CLICK
WHAT'S ALL THE OISE OUT ERE? DO OU KNOW HAT TIME IT--
MI-- MIZUKI-SENSEI!
ISHIZUKA-SENSEI IS...
!
D-DEAD?!
'OU'RE IDDING ME!!

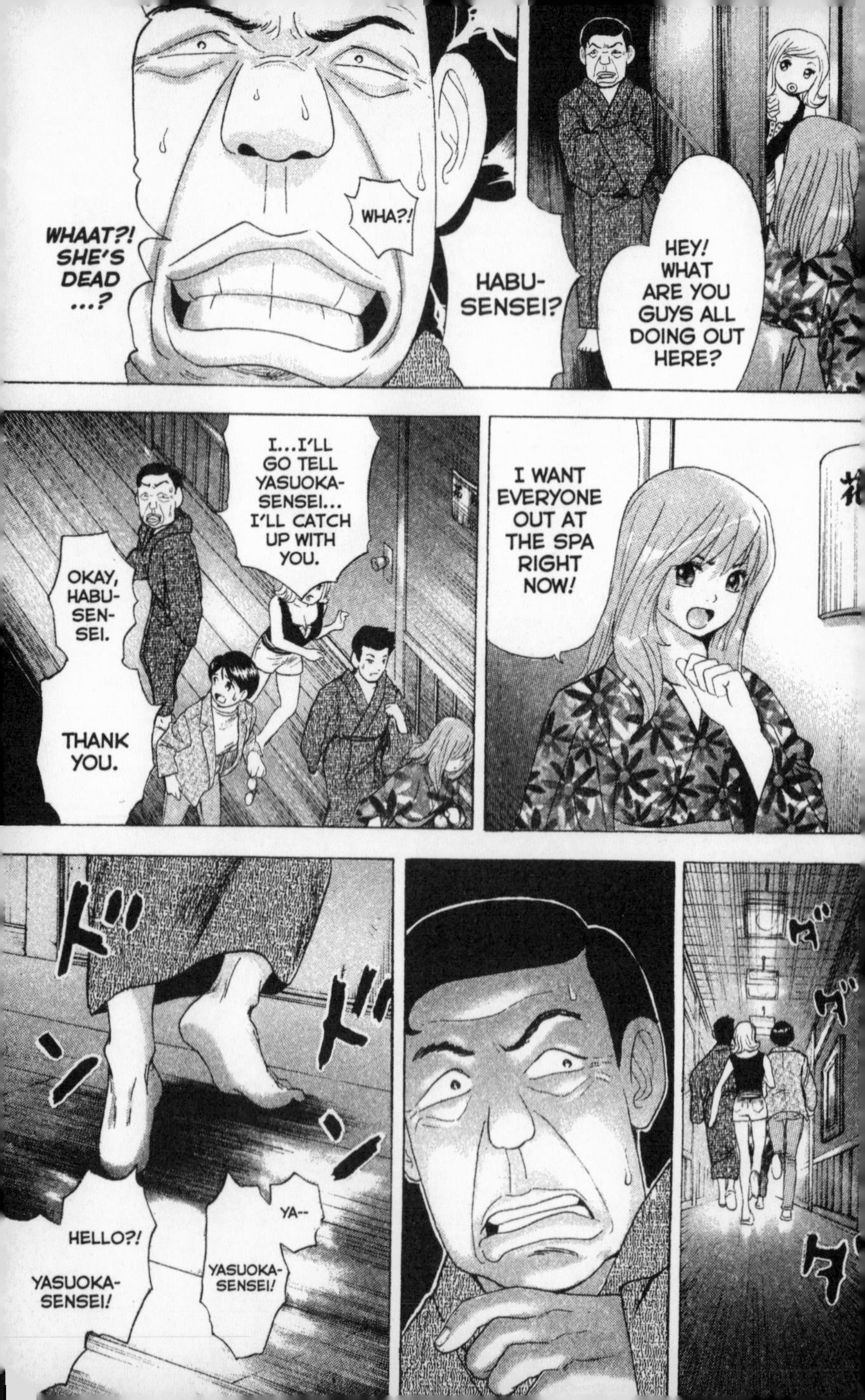
HEY! WHAT ARE YOU GUYS ALL DOING OUT HERE?
HABU-SENSEI?
WHA?!
WHAAT?! SHE'S DEAD ...?
I WANT EVERYONE OUT AT THE SPA RIGHT NOW!
I...I'LL GO TELL YASUOKA-SENSEI... I'LL CATCH UP WITH YOU.
OKAY, HABU-SEN-SEI.
THANK YOU.
YA--
YASUOKA-SENSEI!
HELLO?!
YASUOKA-SENSEI!

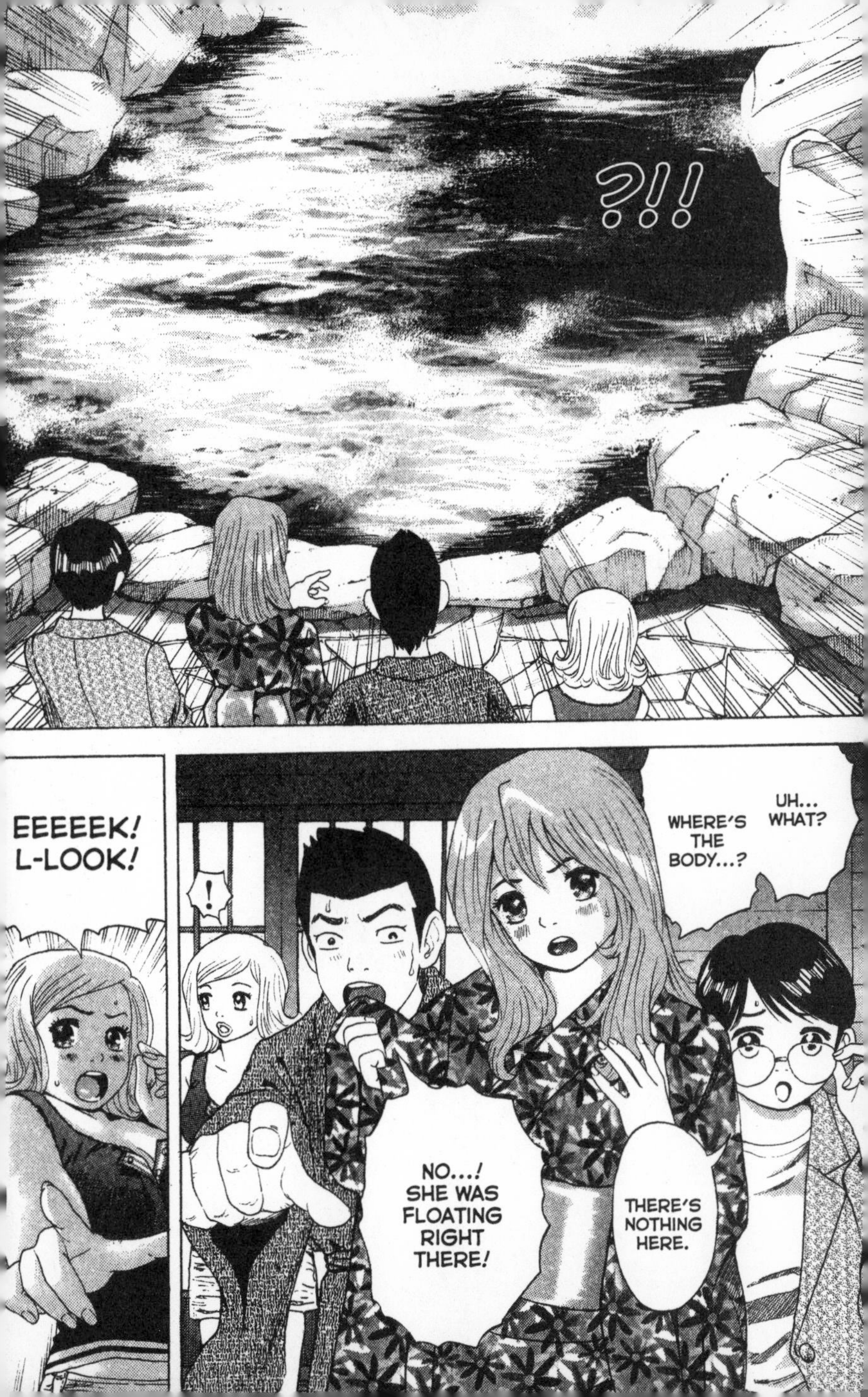
?!!
UH... WHAT?
WHERE'S THE BODY...?
!
THERE'S NOTHING HERE.
NO...! SHE WAS FLOATING RIGHT THERE!
EEEEEK! L-LOOK!

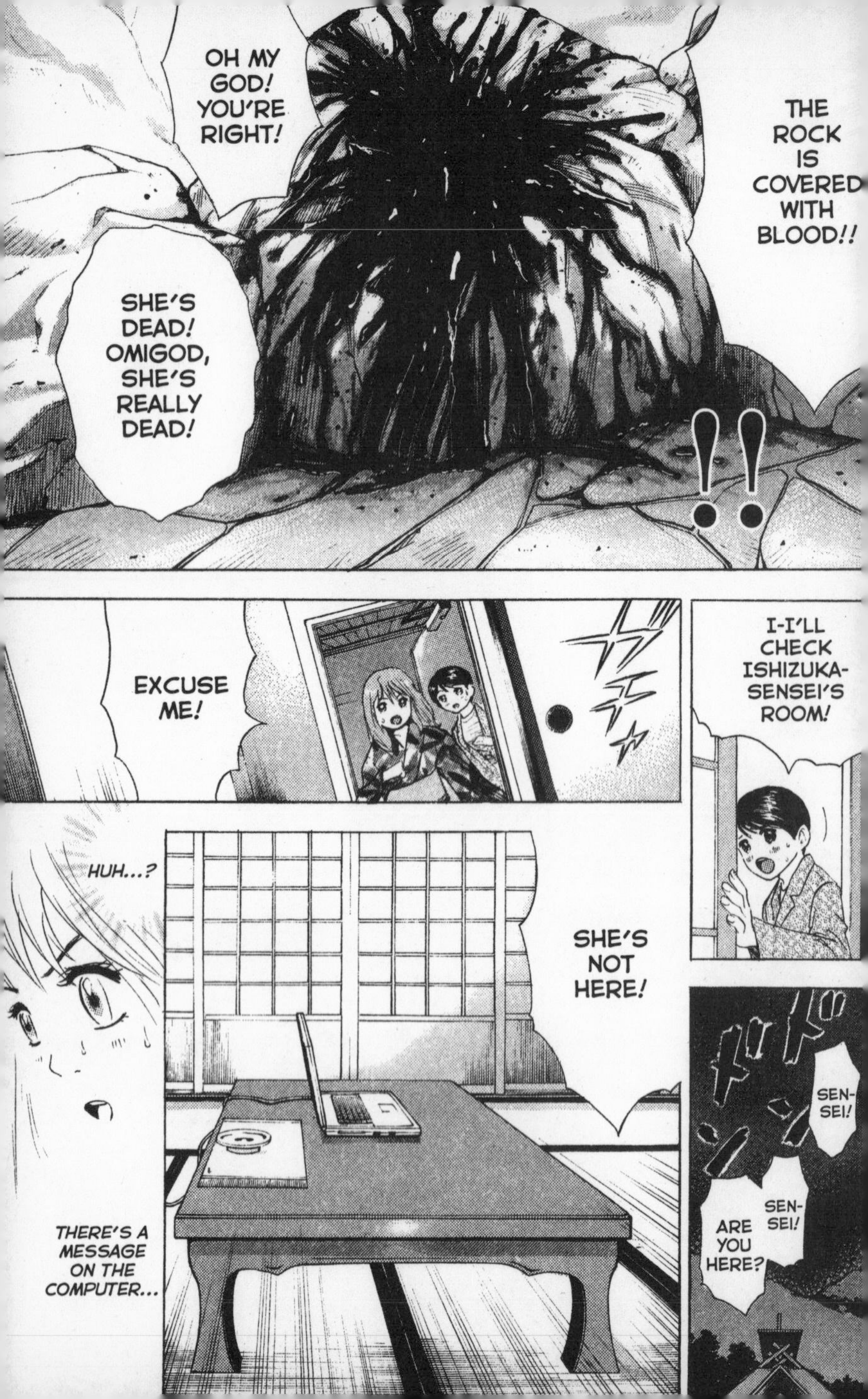
THE ROCK IS COVERED WITH BLOOD!!
OH MY GOD! YOU'RE RIGHT!
SHE'S DEAD! OMIGOD, SHE'S REALLY DEAD!
I-I'LL CHECK ISHIZUKA-SENSEI'S ROOM!
SEN-SEI!
SEN-SEI!
ARE YOU HERE?
EXCUSE ME!
SHE'S NOT HERE!
HUH...?
THERE'S A MESSAGE ON THE COMPUTER...

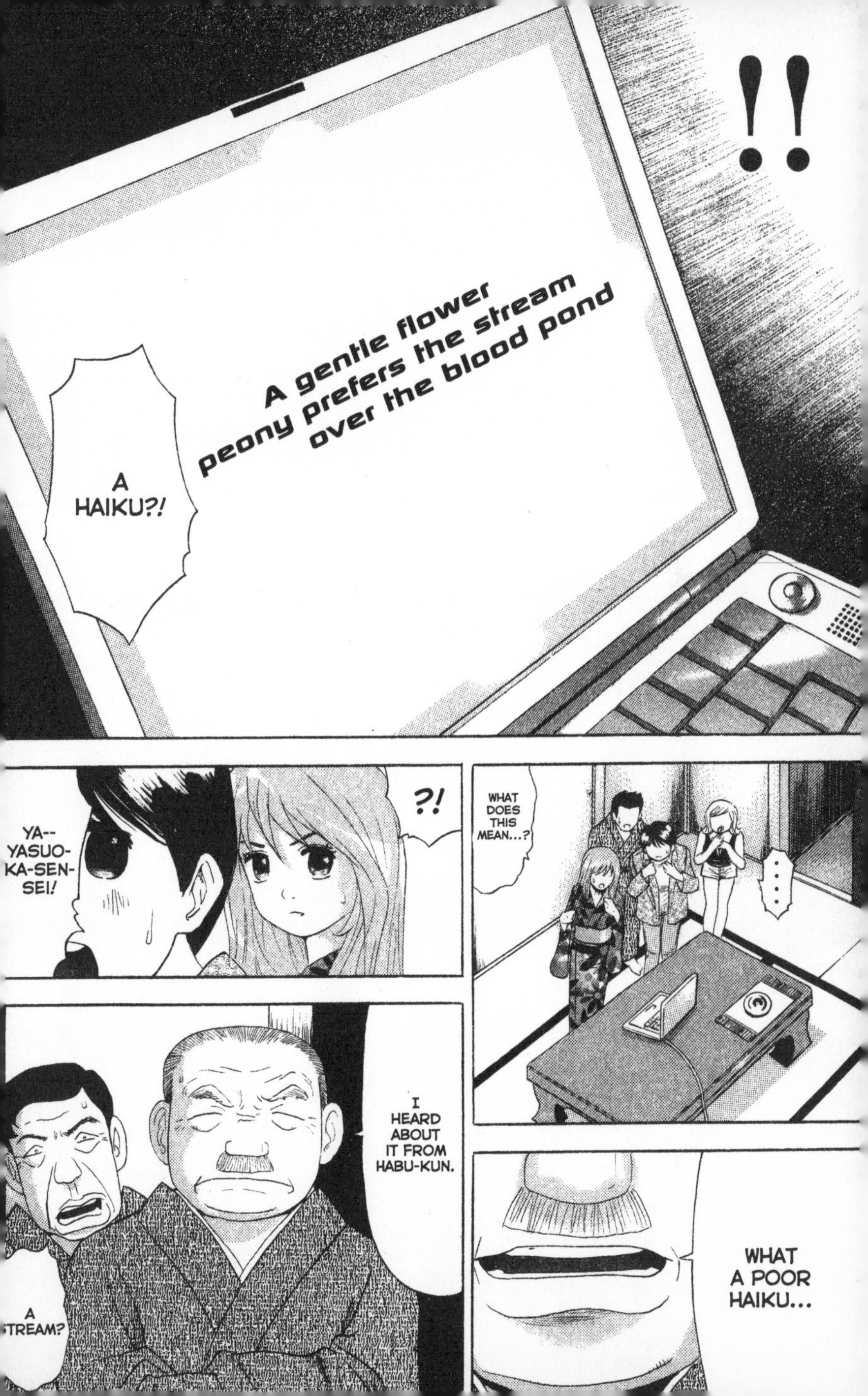
!!
A gentle flower
peony prefers the stream
over the blood pond
A HAIKU?!
WHAT DOES THIS MEAN...?
....
?!
YA-- YASUOKA-SEN-SEI!
WHAT A POOR HAIKU...
I HEARD ABOUT IT FROM HABU-KUN.
A STREAM?

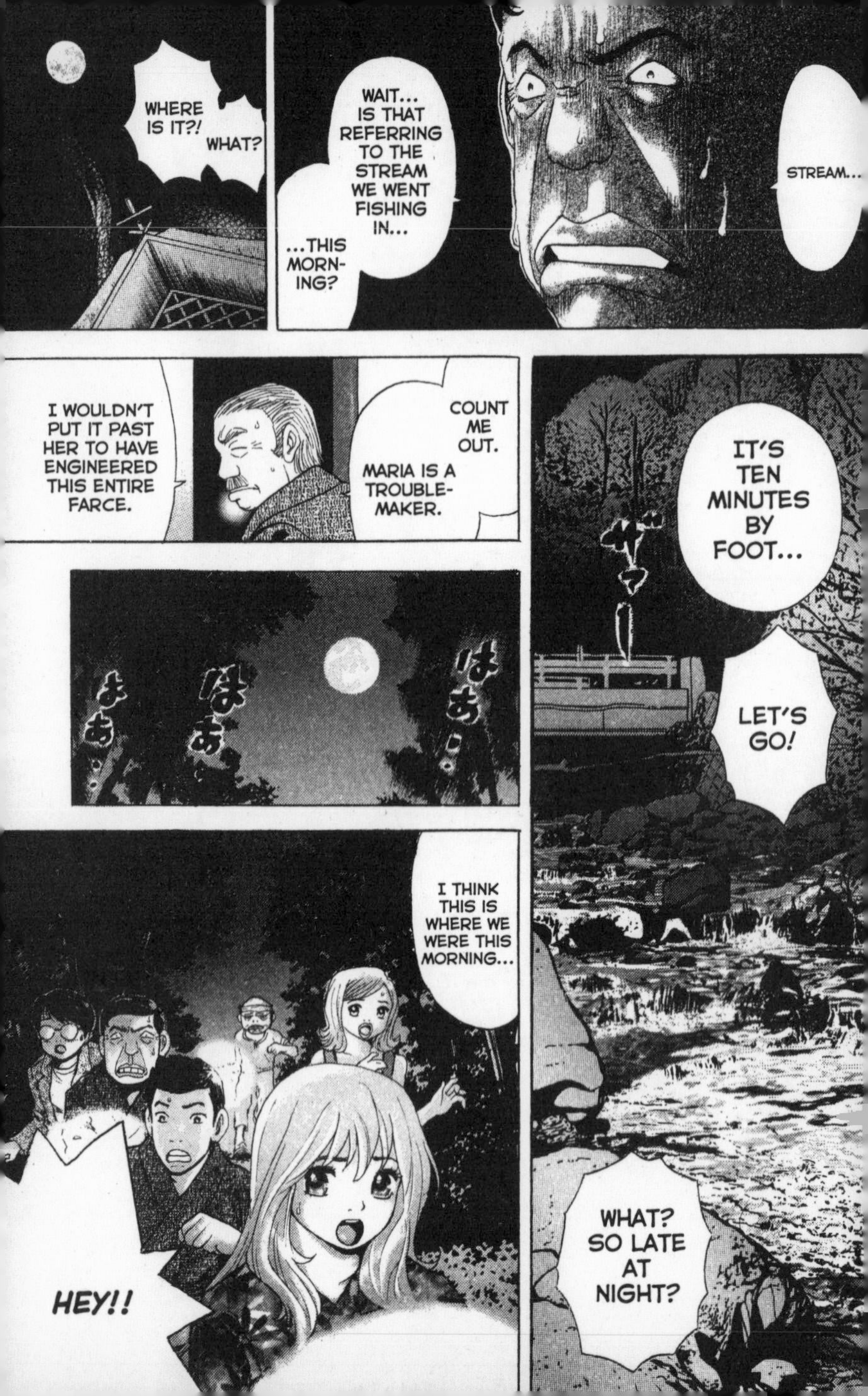
STREAM...
WAIT... IS THAT REFERRING TO THE STREAM WE WENT FISHING IN...
...THIS MORNING?
WHERE IS IT?!
WHAT?
IT'S TEN MINUTES BY FOOT...
LET'S GO!
WHAT? SO LATE AT NIGHT?
COUNT ME OUT.
MARIA IS A TROUBLE-MAKER.
I WOULDN'T PUT IT PAST HER TO HAVE ENGINEERED THIS ENTIRE FARCE.
はあ
はあ
I THINK THIS IS WHERE WE WERE THIS MORNING...
HEY!!

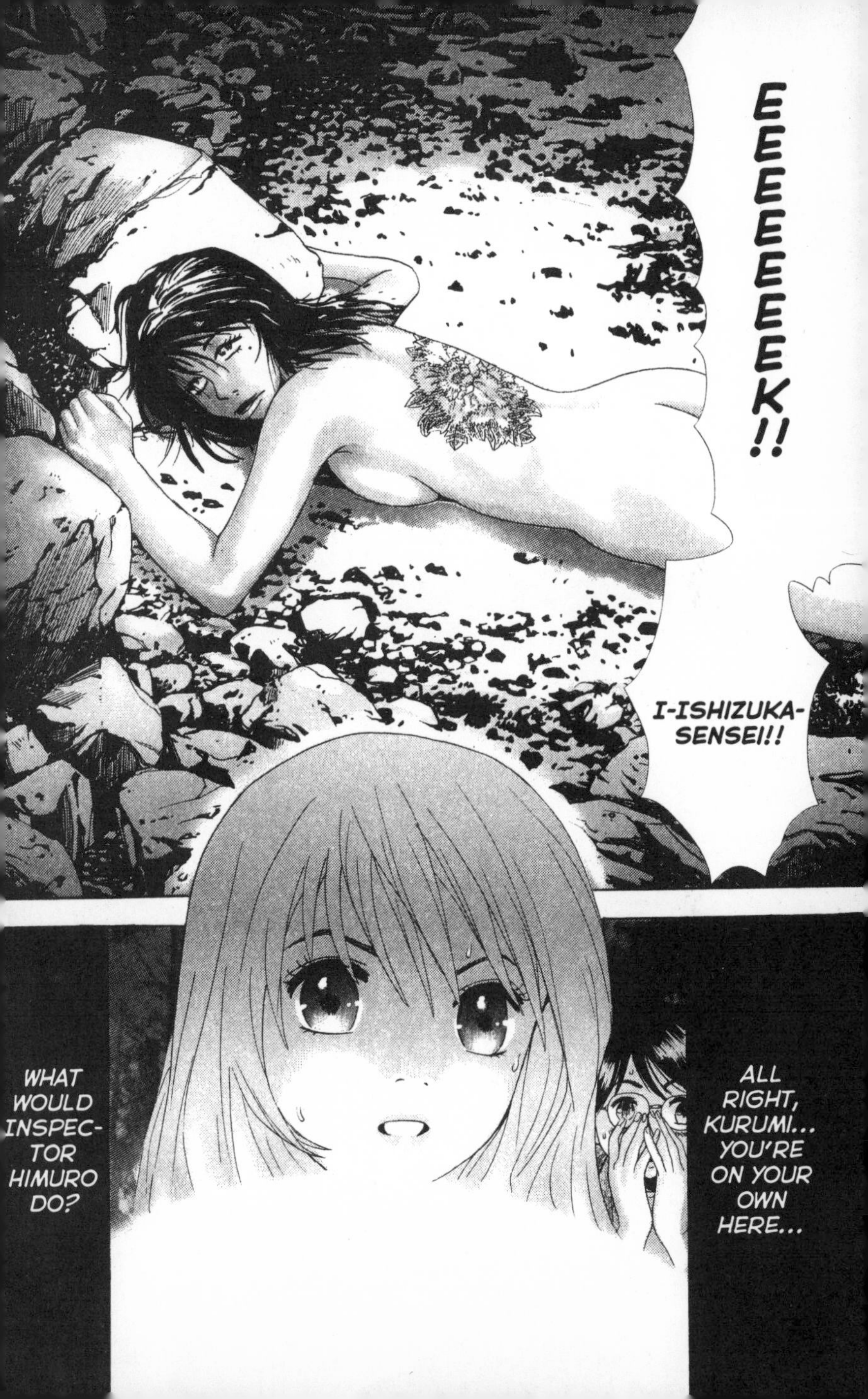

EEEEEEEK!!
I-ISHIZUKA-SENSEI!!
ALL RIGHT, KURUMI... YOU'RE ON YOUR OWN HERE...
WHAT WOULD INSPECTOR HIMURO DO?

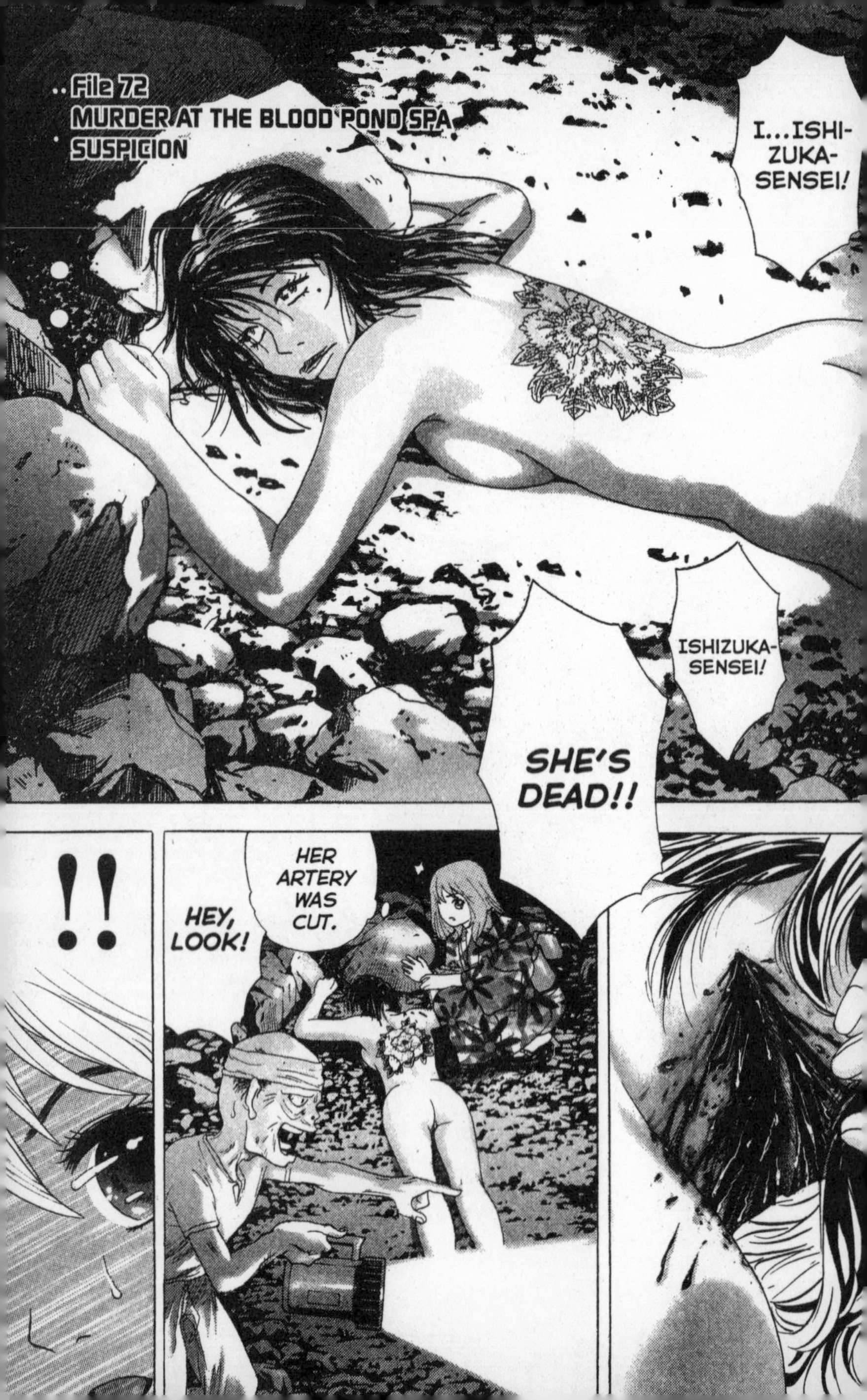
I...ISHI-ZUKA-SENSEI!
File 72
MURDER AT THE BLOOD POND SPA
SUSPICION
ISHIZUKA-SENSEI!
SHE'S DEAD!!
HER ARTERY WAS CUT.
HEY, LOOK!
!!

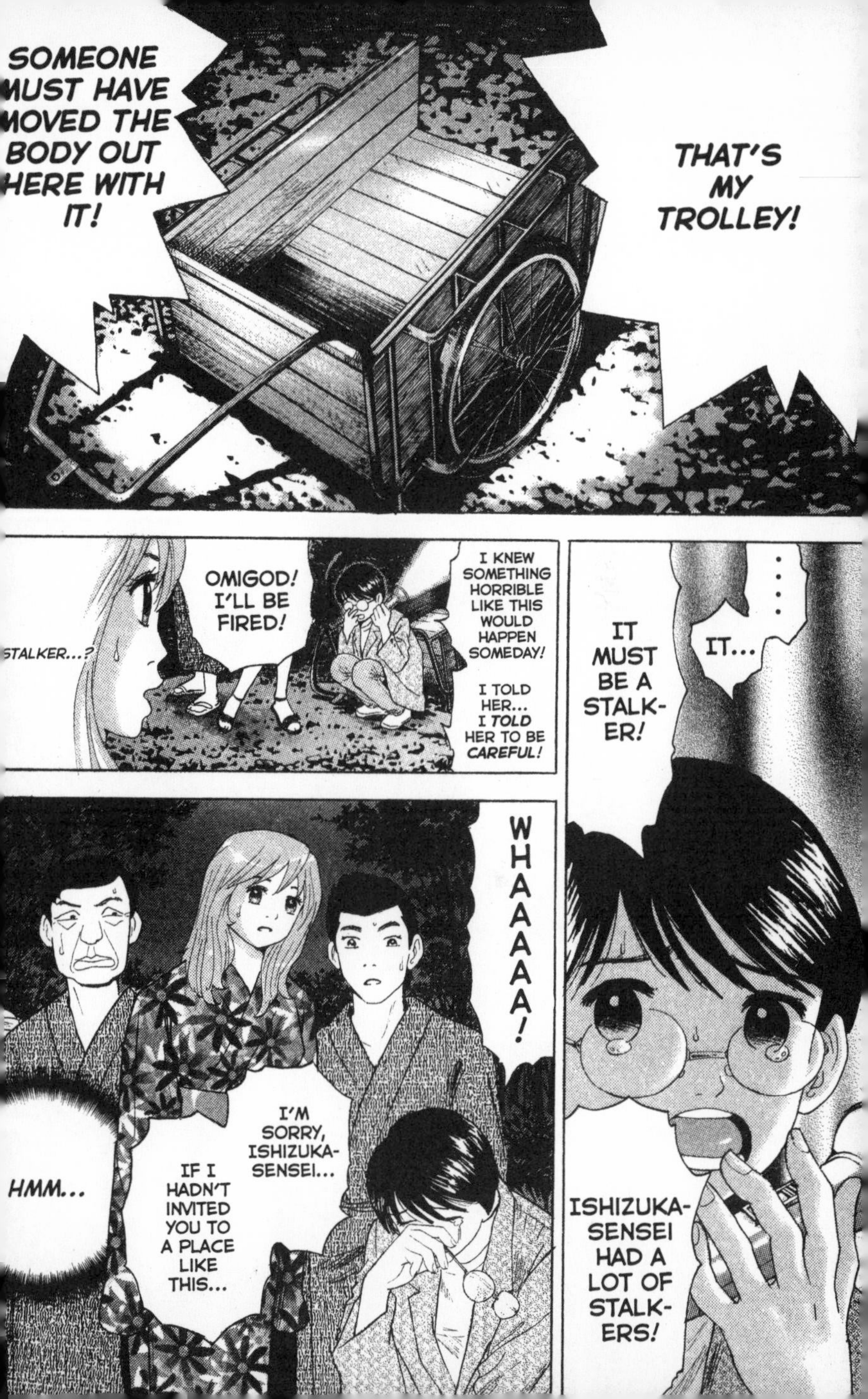
THAT'S MY TROLLEY!
SOMEONE MUST HAVE MOVED THE BODY OUT HERE WITH IT!
....
IT...
IT MUST BE A STALKER!
ISHIZUKA-SENSEI HAD A LOT OF STALKERS!
I KNEW SOMETHING HORRIBLE LIKE THIS WOULD HAPPEN SOMEDAY!
I TOLD HER... I TOLD HER TO BE CAREFUL!
OMIGOD! I'LL BE FIRED!
STALKER...?
WHAAAAAA!
I'M SORRY, ISHIZUKA-SENSEI...
IF I HADN'T INVITED YOU TO A PLACE LIKE THIS...
HMM...

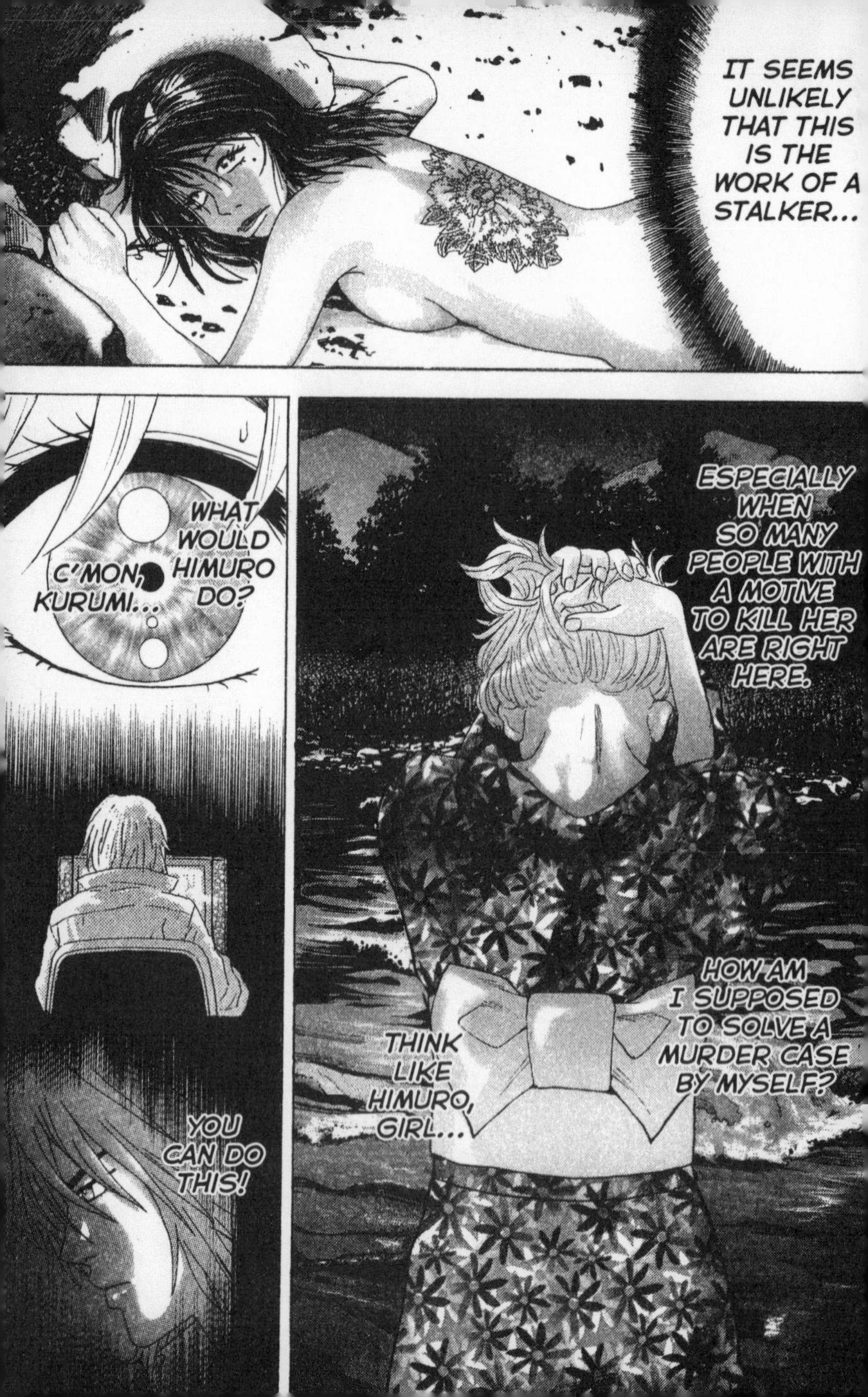
IT SEEMS UNLIKELY THAT THIS IS THE WORK OF A STALKER...
ESPECIALLY WHEN SO MANY PEOPLE WITH A MOTIVE TO KILL HER ARE RIGHT HERE.
HOW AM I SUPPOSED TO SOLVE A MURDER CASE BY MYSELF?
THINK LIKE HIMURO, GIRL...
WHAT WOULD HIMURO DO?
C'MON, KURUMI...
YOU CAN DO THIS!

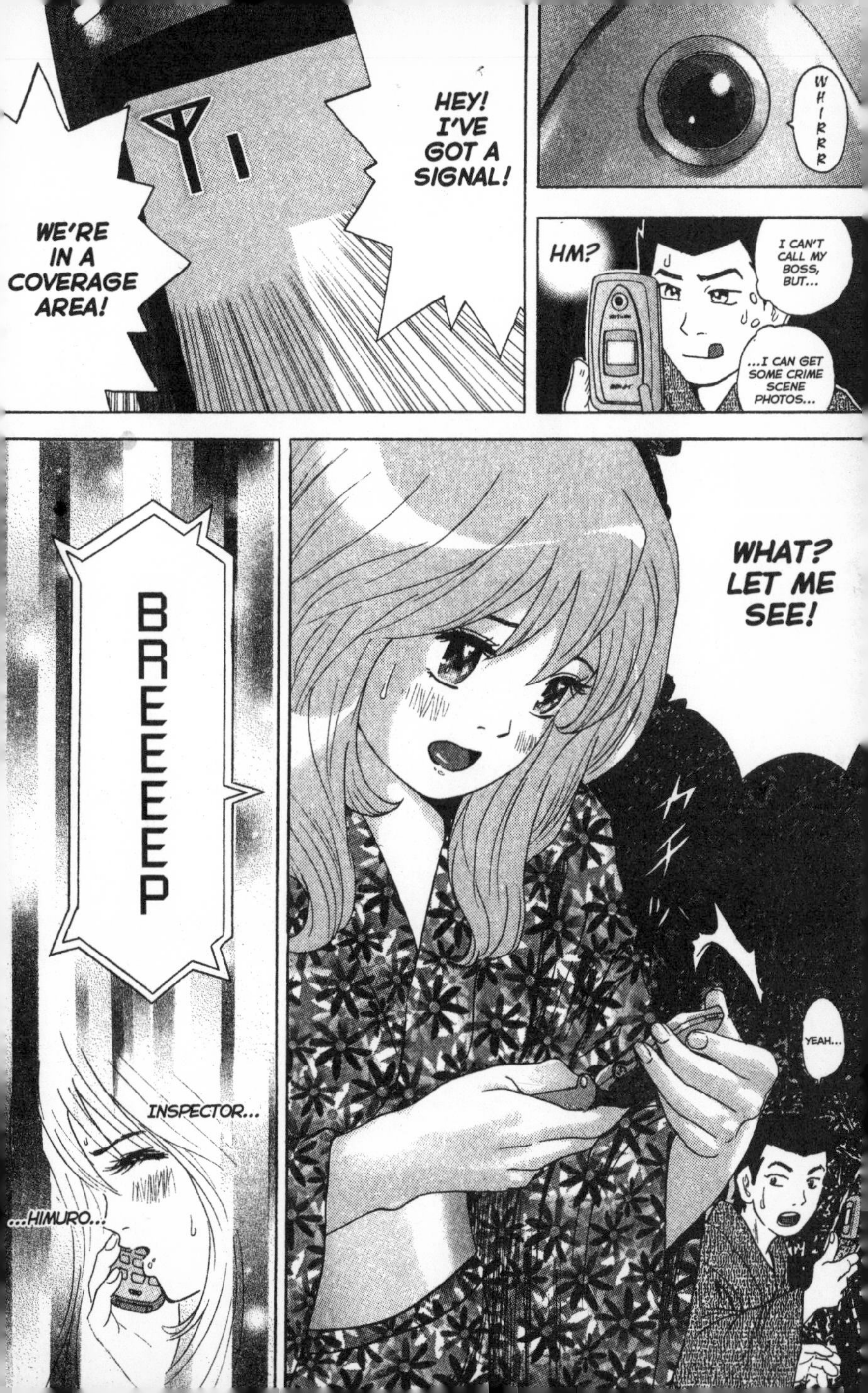
WHIRRR
I CAN'T CALL MY BOSS, BUT...
HM?
...I CAN GET SOME CRIME SCENE PHOTOS...
HEY! I'VE GOT A SIGNAL!
WE'RE IN A COVERAGE AREA!
WHAT? LET ME SEE!
YEAH...
BREEEEP
INSPECTOR...
...HIMURO...

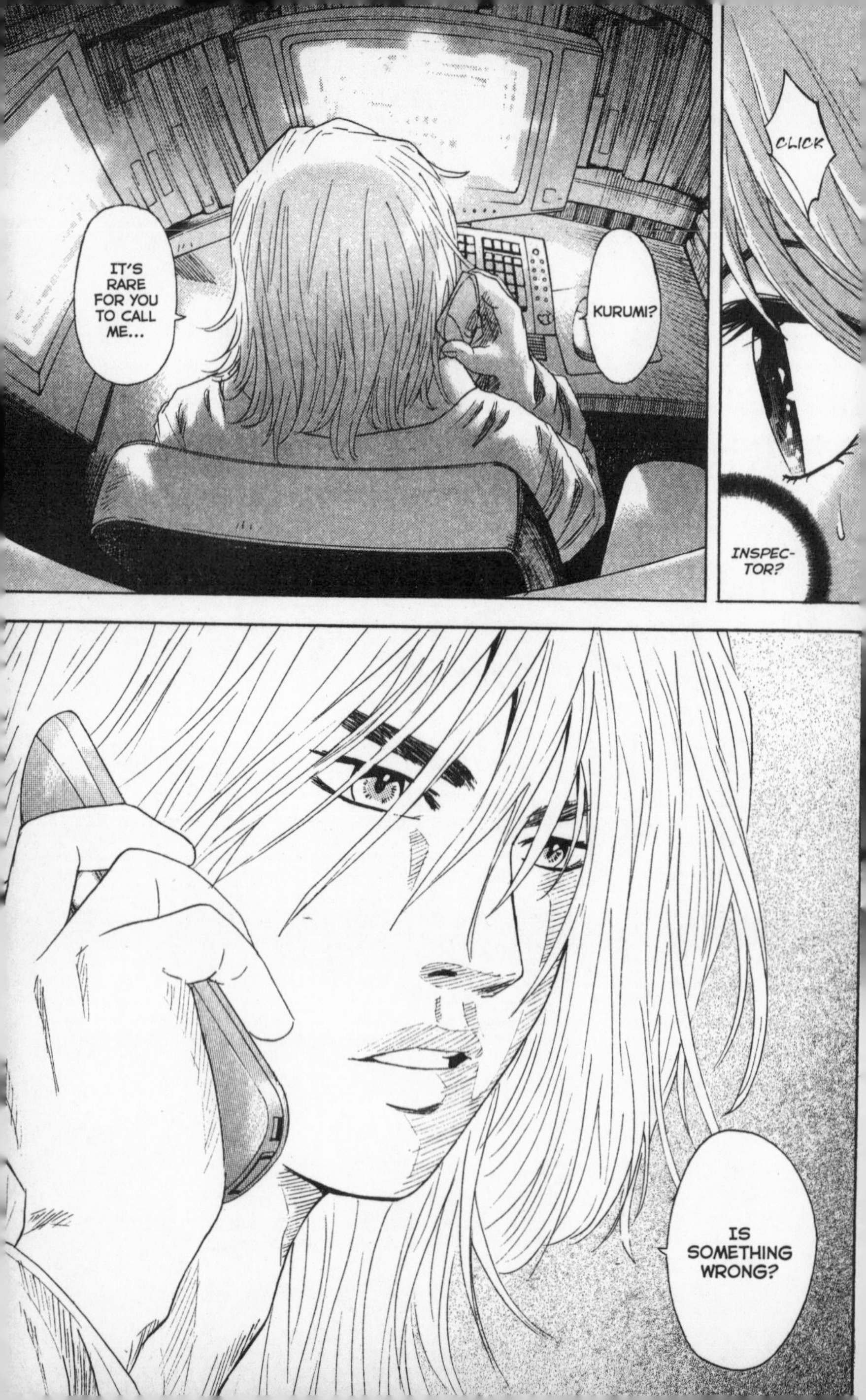
CLICK
INSPECTOR?
KURUMI?
IT'S RARE FOR YOU TO CALL ME...
IS SOMETHING WRONG?

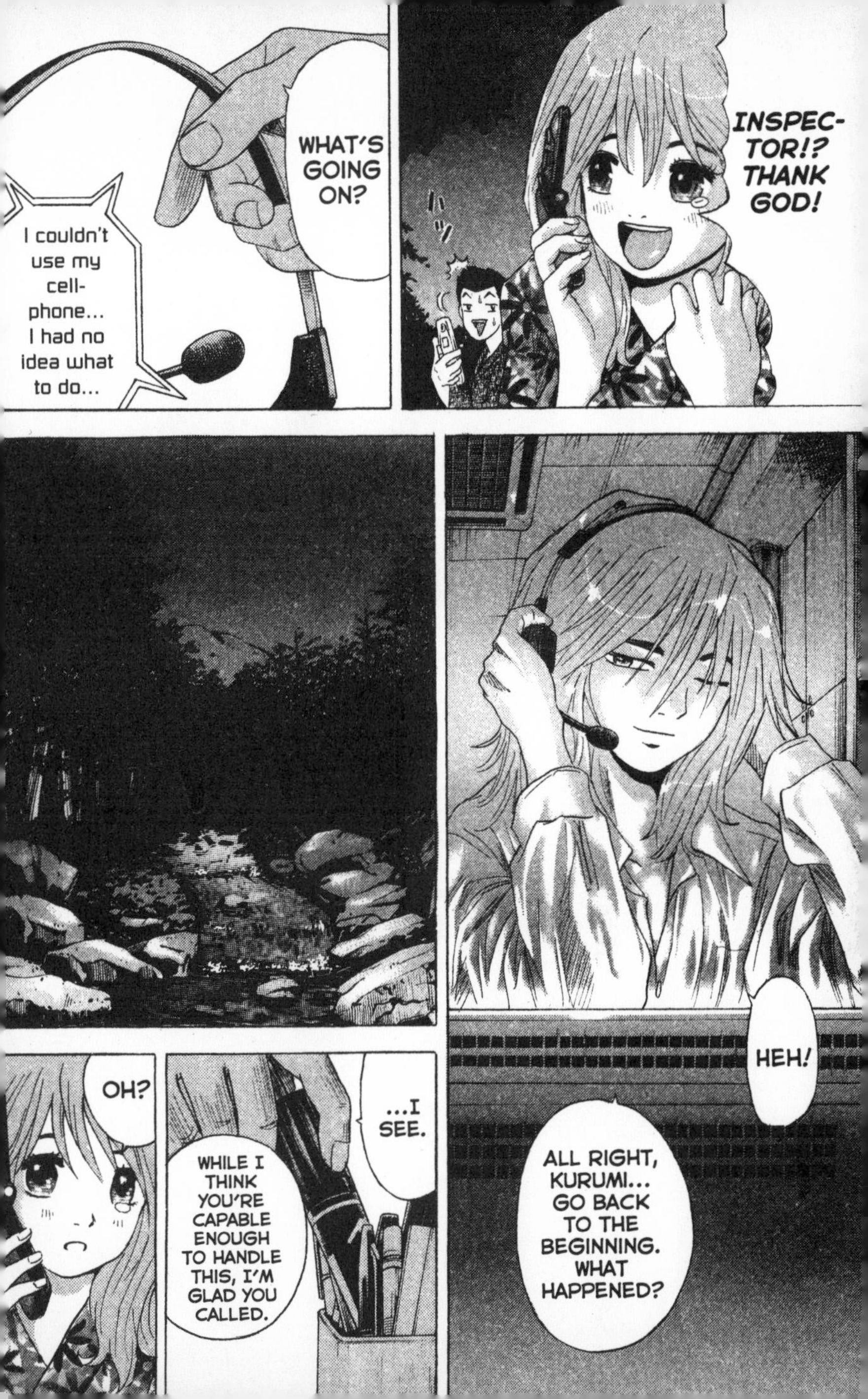
INSPECTOR!? THANK GOD!
WHAT'S GOING ON?
I couldn't use my cell-phone... I had no idea what to do...
HEH!
ALL RIGHT, KURUMI... GO BACK TO THE BEGINNING. WHAT HAPPENED?
...I SEE.
WHILE I THINK YOU'RE CAPABLE ENOUGH TO HANDLE THIS, I'M GLAD YOU CALLED.
OH?

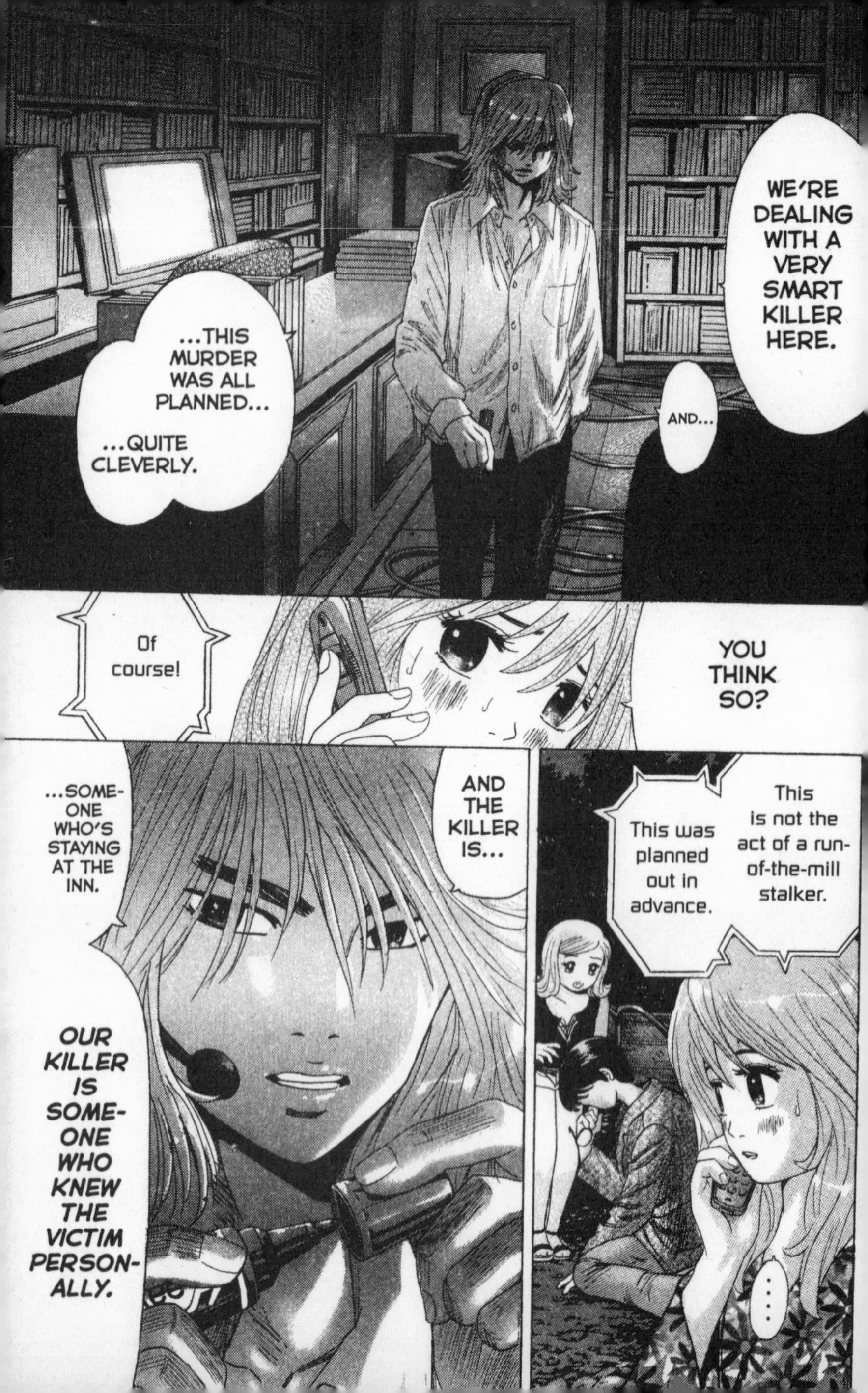
WE'RE DEALING WITH A VERY SMART KILLER HERE.
AND...
...THIS MURDER WAS ALL PLANNED...
...QUITE CLEVERLY.
YOU THINK SO?
Of course!
This is not the act of a run-of-the-mill stalker.
This was planned out in advance.
...
AND THE KILLER IS...
...SOMEONE WHO'S STAYING AT THE INN.
OUR KILLER IS SOMEONE WHO KNEW THE VICTIM PERSONALLY.

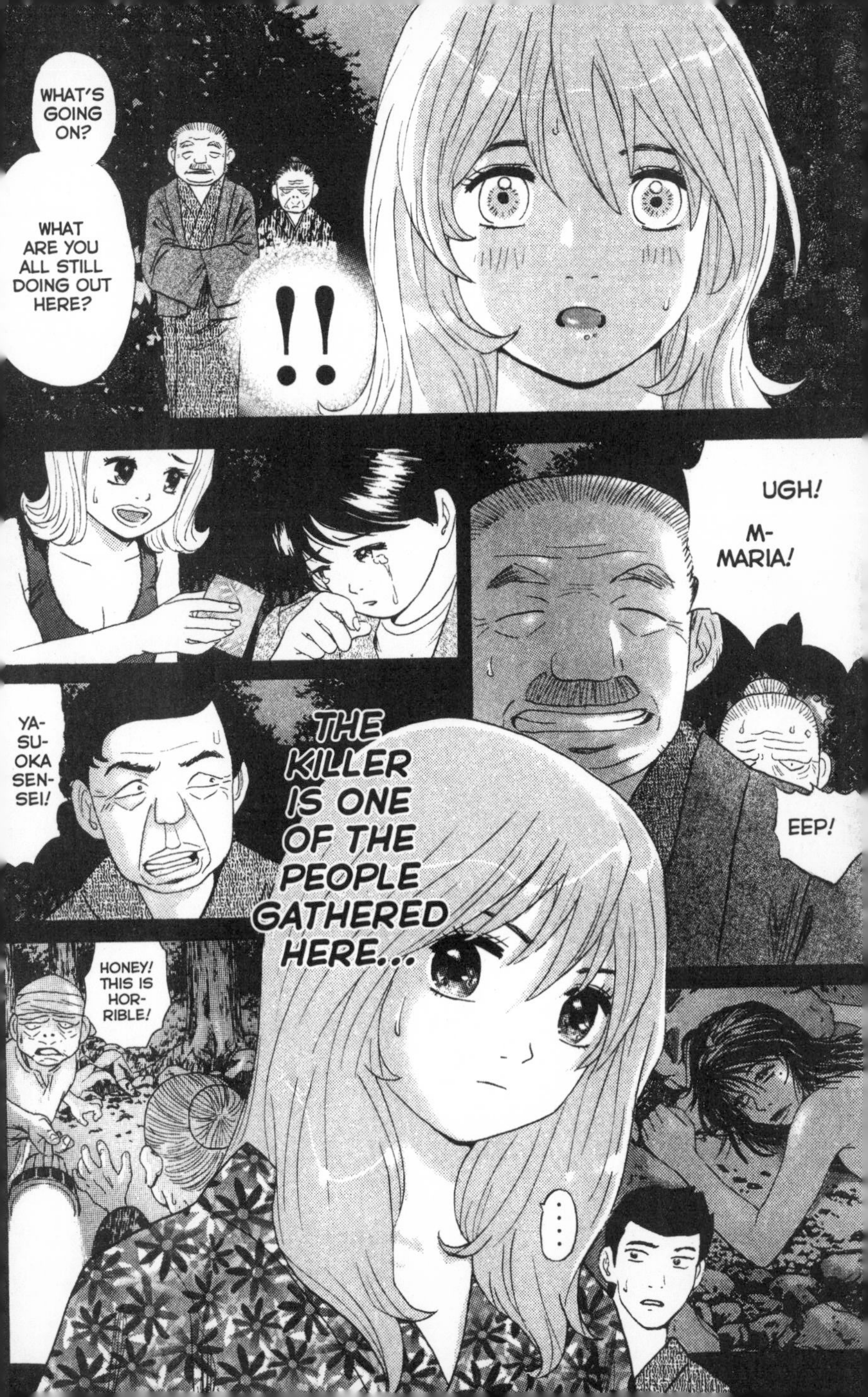
WHAT'S GOING ON?
WHAT ARE YOU ALL STILL DOING OUT HERE?
!!
UGH!
M-MARIA!
EEP!
YA-SU-OKA SEN-SEI!
THE KILLER IS ONE OF THE PEOPLE GATHERED HERE...
HONEY! THIS IS HOR-RIBLE!
....

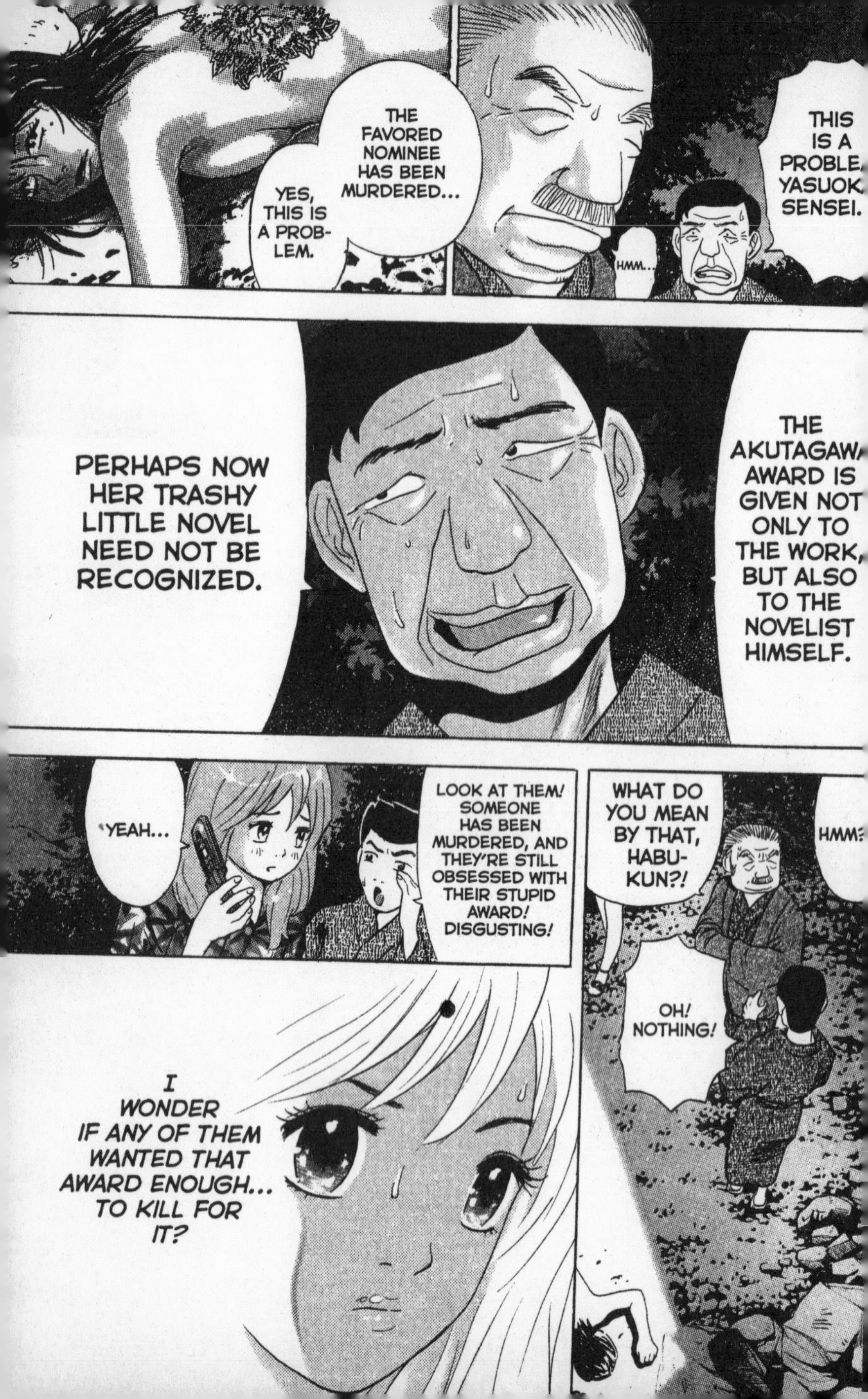
THIS IS A PROBLE YASUOK SENSEI.
HMM...
THE FAVORED NOMINEE HAS BEEN MURDERED...
YES, THIS IS A PROB-LEM.
THE AKUTAGAW AWARD IS GIVEN NOT ONLY TO THE WORK, BUT ALSO TO THE NOVELIST HIMSELF.
PERHAPS NOW HER TRASHY LITTLE NOVEL NEED NOT BE RECOGNIZED.
HMM
WHAT DO YOU MEAN BY THAT, HABU-KUN?!
LOOK AT THEM! SOMEONE HAS BEEN MURDERED, AND THEY'RE STILL OBSESSED WITH THEIR STUPID AWARD! DISGUSTING!
YEAH...
OH! NOTHING!
I WONDER IF ANY OF THEM WANTED THAT AWARD ENOUGH... TO KILL FOR IT?

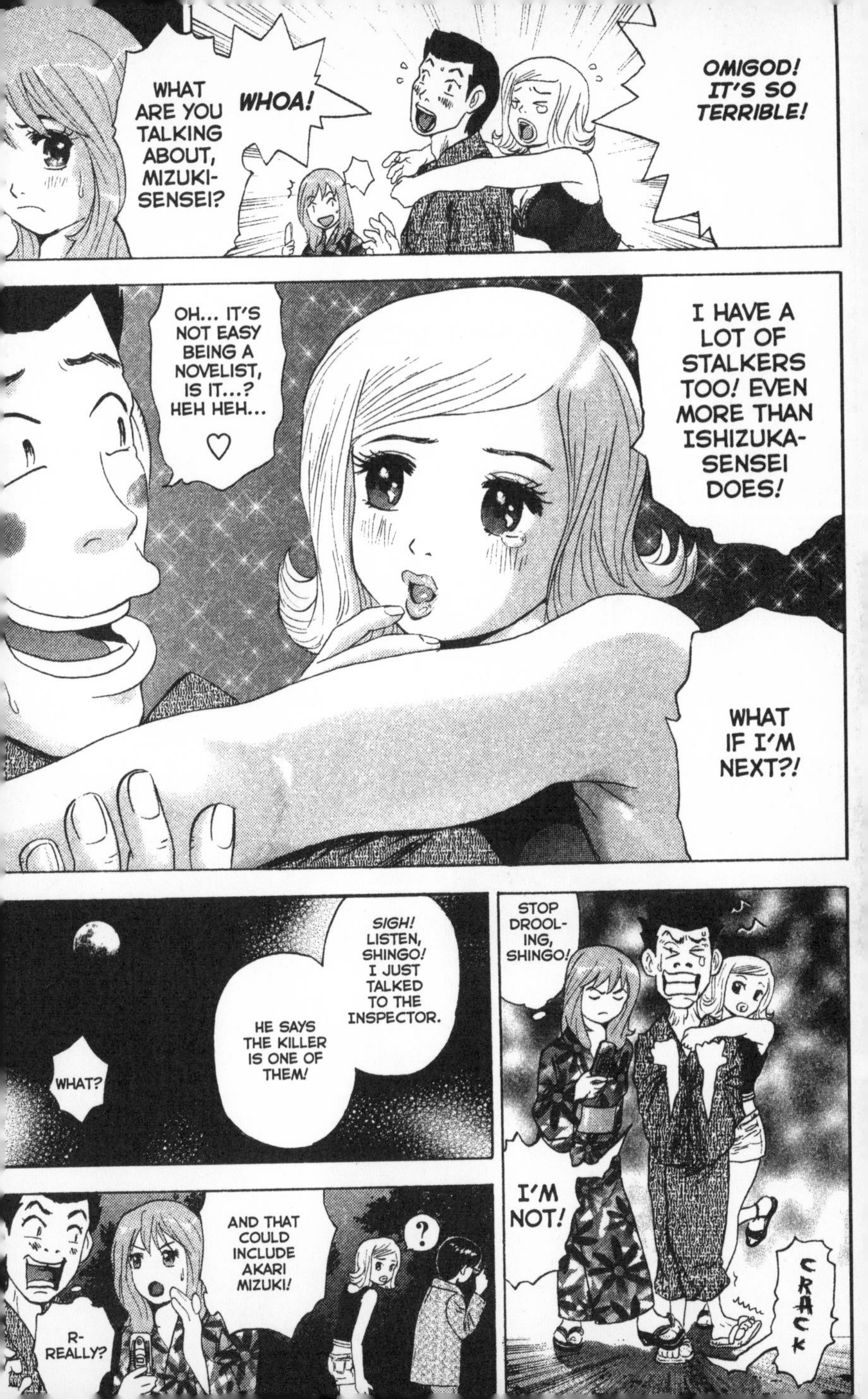
OMIGOD! IT'S SO TERRIBLE!
WHOA!
WHAT ARE YOU TALKING ABOUT, MIZUKI-SENSEI?
I HAVE A LOT OF STALKERS TOO! EVEN MORE THAN ISHIZUKA-SENSEI DOES!
WHAT IF I'M NEXT?!
OH... IT'S NOT EASY BEING A NOVELIST, IS IT...? HEH HEH... ♡
STOP DROOL-ING, SHINGO!
I'M NOT!
CRACK
SIGH! LISTEN, SHINGO! I JUST TALKED TO THE INSPECTOR.
HE SAYS THE KILLER IS ONE OF THEM!
WHAT?
AND THAT COULD INCLUDE AKARI MIZUKI!
?
R-REALLY?

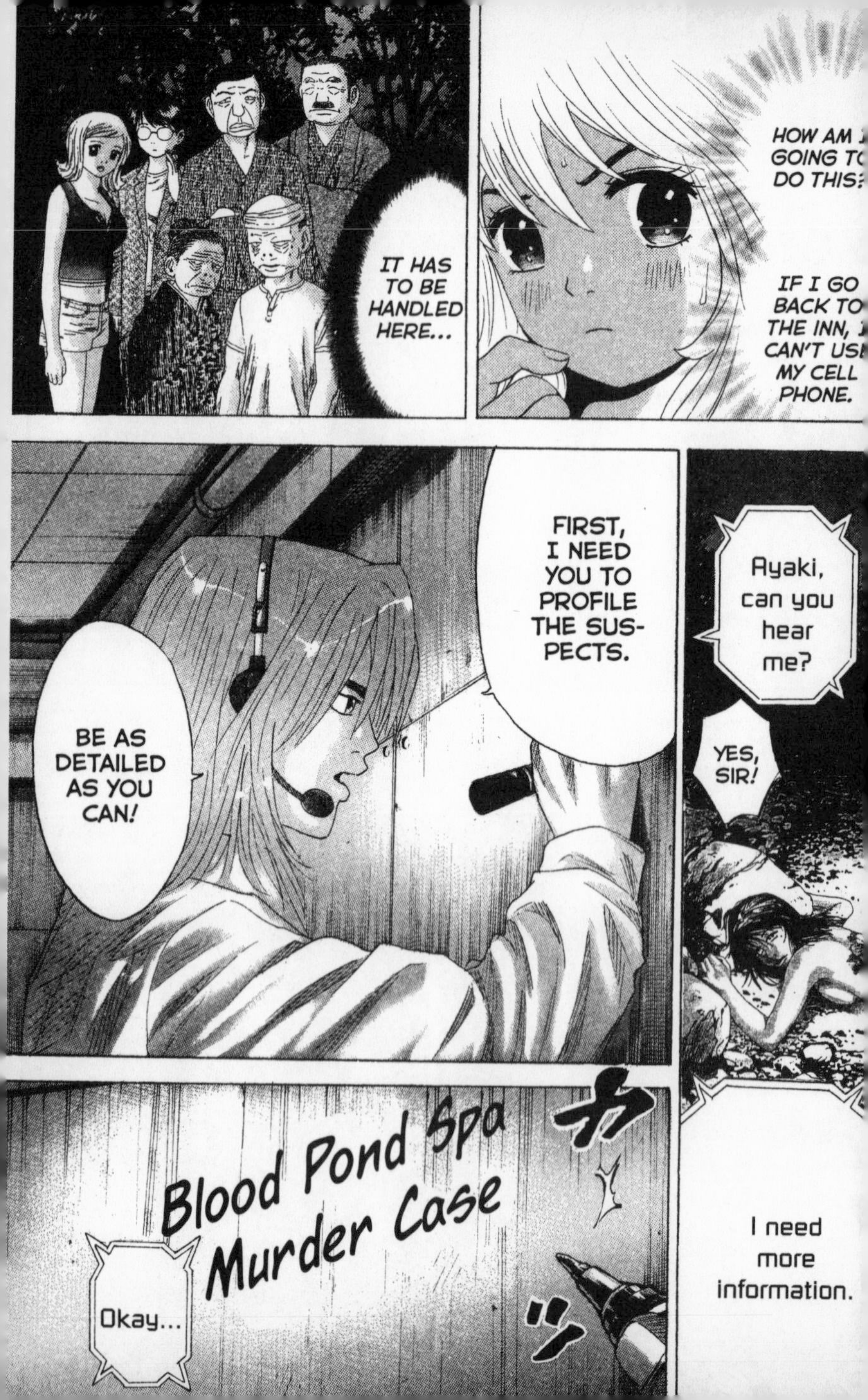
HOW AM I GOING TO DO THIS?
IF I GO BACK TO THE INN, I CAN'T USE MY CELL PHONE.
IT HAS TO BE HANDLED HERE...
Ayaki, can you hear me?
YES, SIR!
I need more information.
FIRST, I NEED YOU TO PROFILE THE SUS-PECTS.
BE AS DETAILED AS YOU CAN!
Blood Pond Spa Murder Case
Okay...

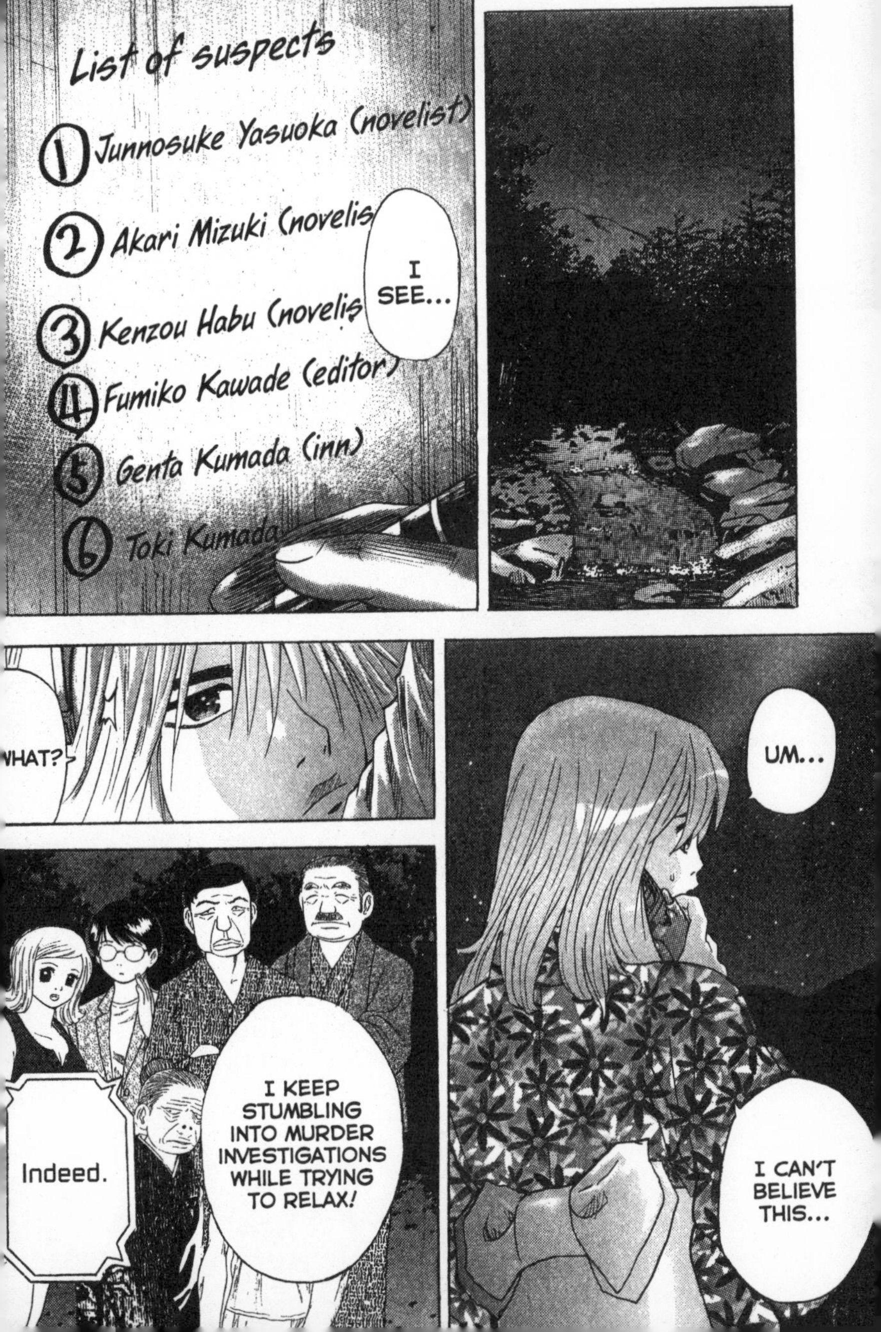

List of suspects
① Junnosuke Yasuoka (novelist)
② Akari Mizuki (novelis
③ Kenzou Habu (novelis
④ Fumiko Kawade (editor)
⑤ Genta Kumada (inn)
⑥ Toki Kumada
I SEE...
UM...
I CAN'T BELIEVE THIS...
WHAT?
I KEEP STUMBLING INTO MURDER INVESTIGATIONS WHILE TRYING TO RELAX!
Indeed.

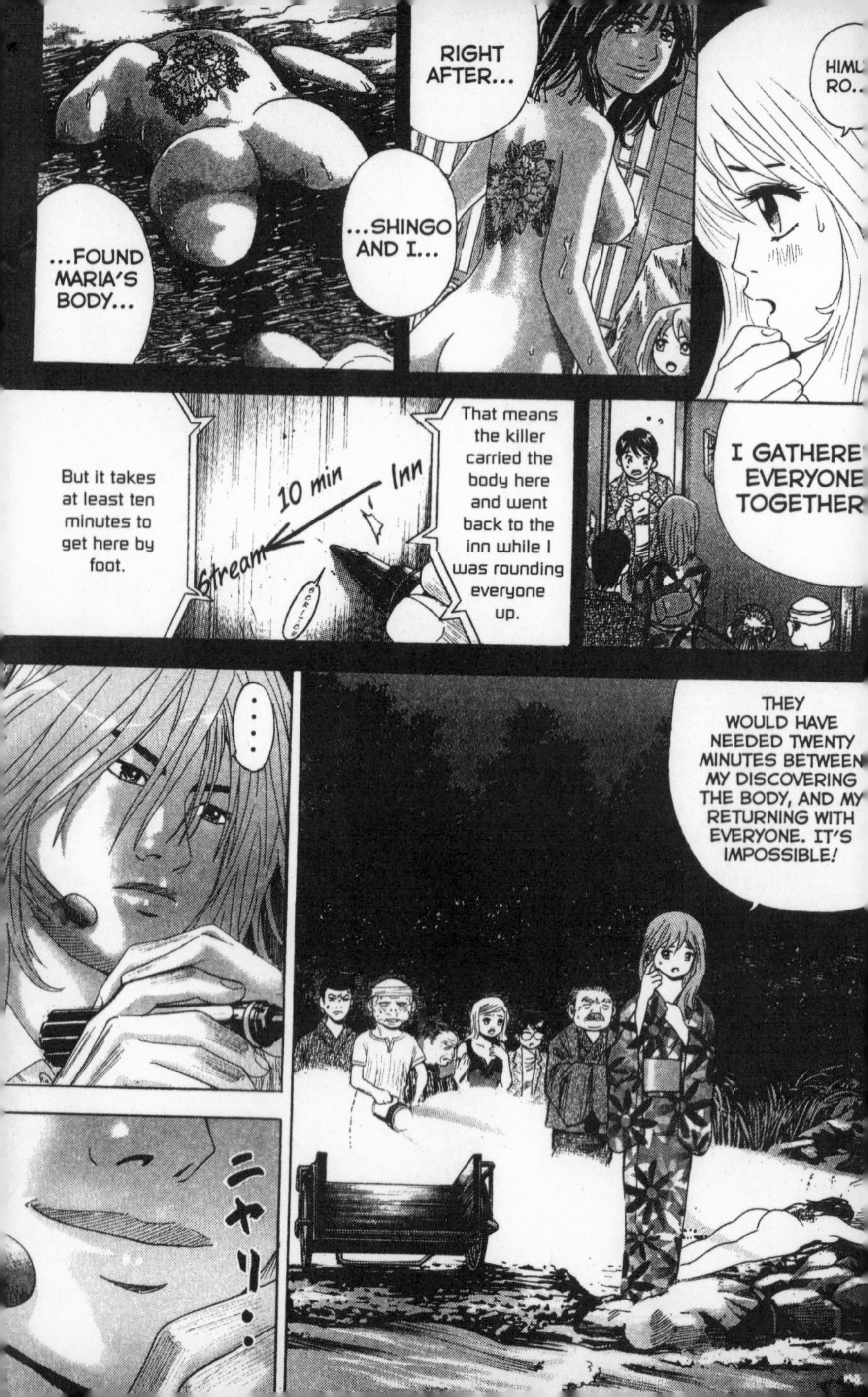
HIMU RO..
RIGHT AFTER...
...SHINGO AND I...
...FOUND MARIA'S BODY...
I GATHERE EVERYONE TOGETHER
That means the killer carried the body here and went back to the inn while I was rounding everyone up.
Inn
10 min
Stream
But it takes at least ten minutes to get here by foot.
THEY WOULD HAVE NEEDED TWENTY MINUTES BETWEEN MY DISCOVERING THE BODY, AND MY RETURNING WITH EVERYONE. IT'S IMPOSSIBLE!
....
ニヤリ…

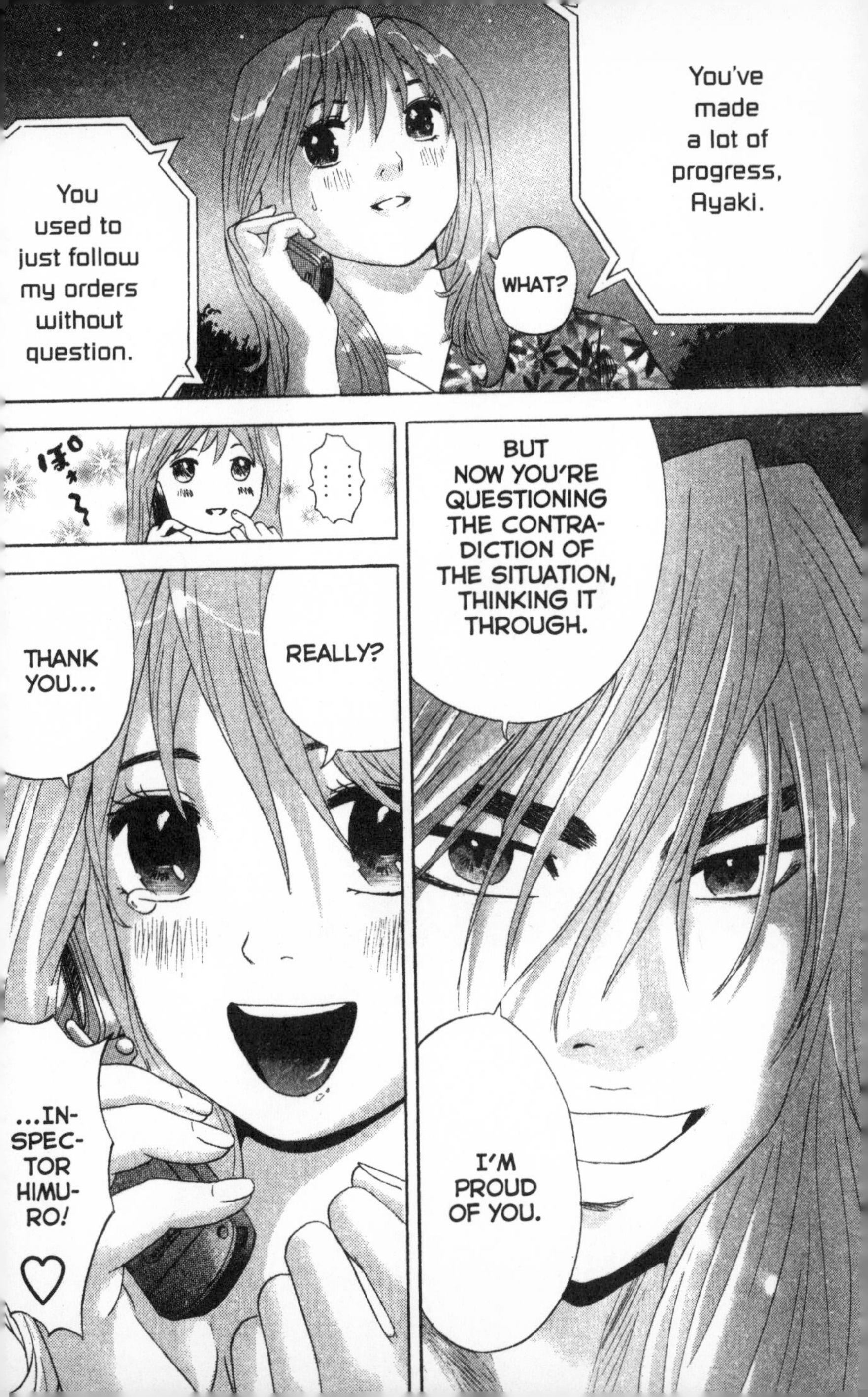
You've made a lot of progress, Ayaki.
WHAT?
You used to just follow my orders without question.
BUT NOW YOU'RE QUESTIONING THE CONTRADICTION OF THE SITUATION, THINKING IT THROUGH.
I'M PROUD OF YOU.
……
REALLY?
THANK YOU...
...INSPECTOR HIMURO! ♡

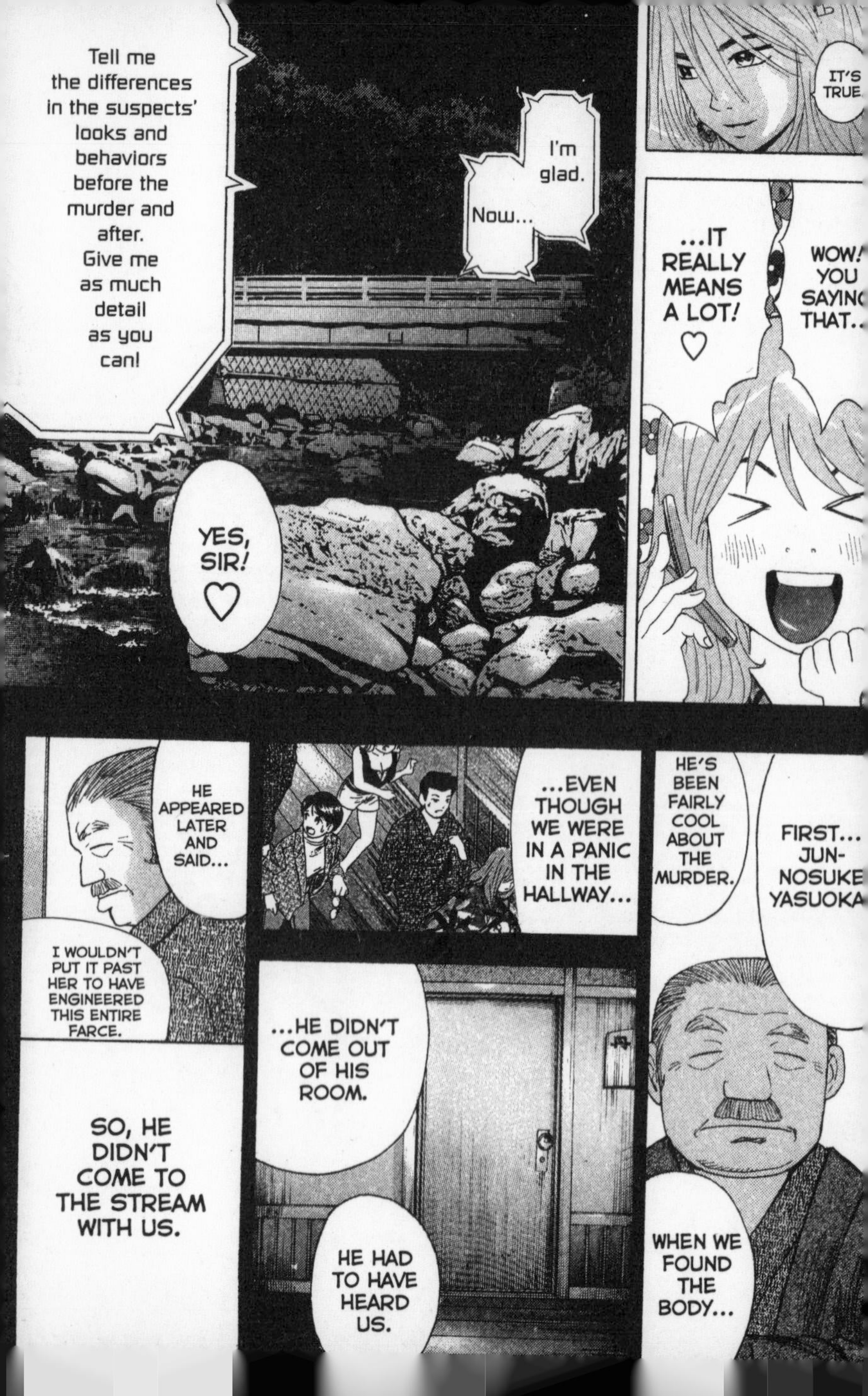

IT'S TRUE.
WOW! YOU SAYING THAT...
...IT REALLY MEANS A LOT! ♡
I'm glad.
Now...
Tell me the differences in the suspects' looks and behaviors before the murder and after. Give me as much detail as you can!
YES, SIR! ♡
FIRST... JUN-NOSUKE YASUOKA
HE'S BEEN FAIRLY COOL ABOUT THE MURDER.
WHEN WE FOUND THE BODY...
...EVEN THOUGH WE WERE IN A PANIC IN THE HALLWAY...
...HE DIDN'T COME OUT OF HIS ROOM.
HE HAD TO HAVE HEARD US.
HE APPEARED LATER AND SAID...
I WOULDN'T PUT IT PAST HER TO HAVE ENGINEERED THIS ENTIRE FARCE.
SO, HE DIDN'T COME TO THE STREAM WITH US.

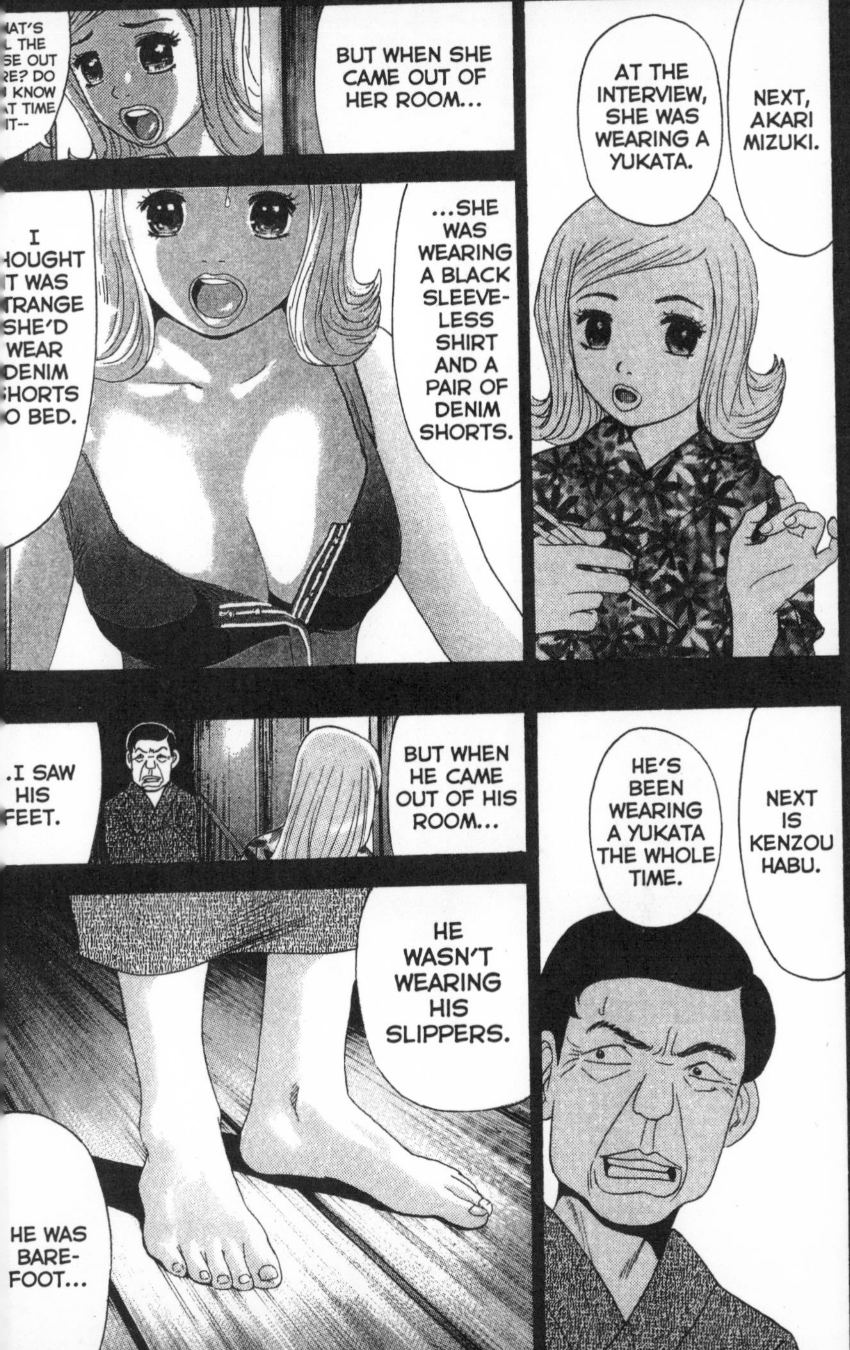
NEXT, AKARI MIZUKI.
AT THE INTERVIEW, SHE WAS WEARING A YUKATA.
BUT WHEN SHE CAME OUT OF HER ROOM...
...SHE WAS WEARING A BLACK SLEEVE-LESS SHIRT AND A PAIR OF DENIM SHORTS.
NEXT IS KENZOU HABU.
HE'S BEEN WEARING A YUKATA THE WHOLE TIME.
BUT WHEN HE CAME OUT OF HIS ROOM...
.I SAW HIS FEET.
HE WASN'T WEARING HIS SLIPPERS.
HE WAS BARE-FOOT...

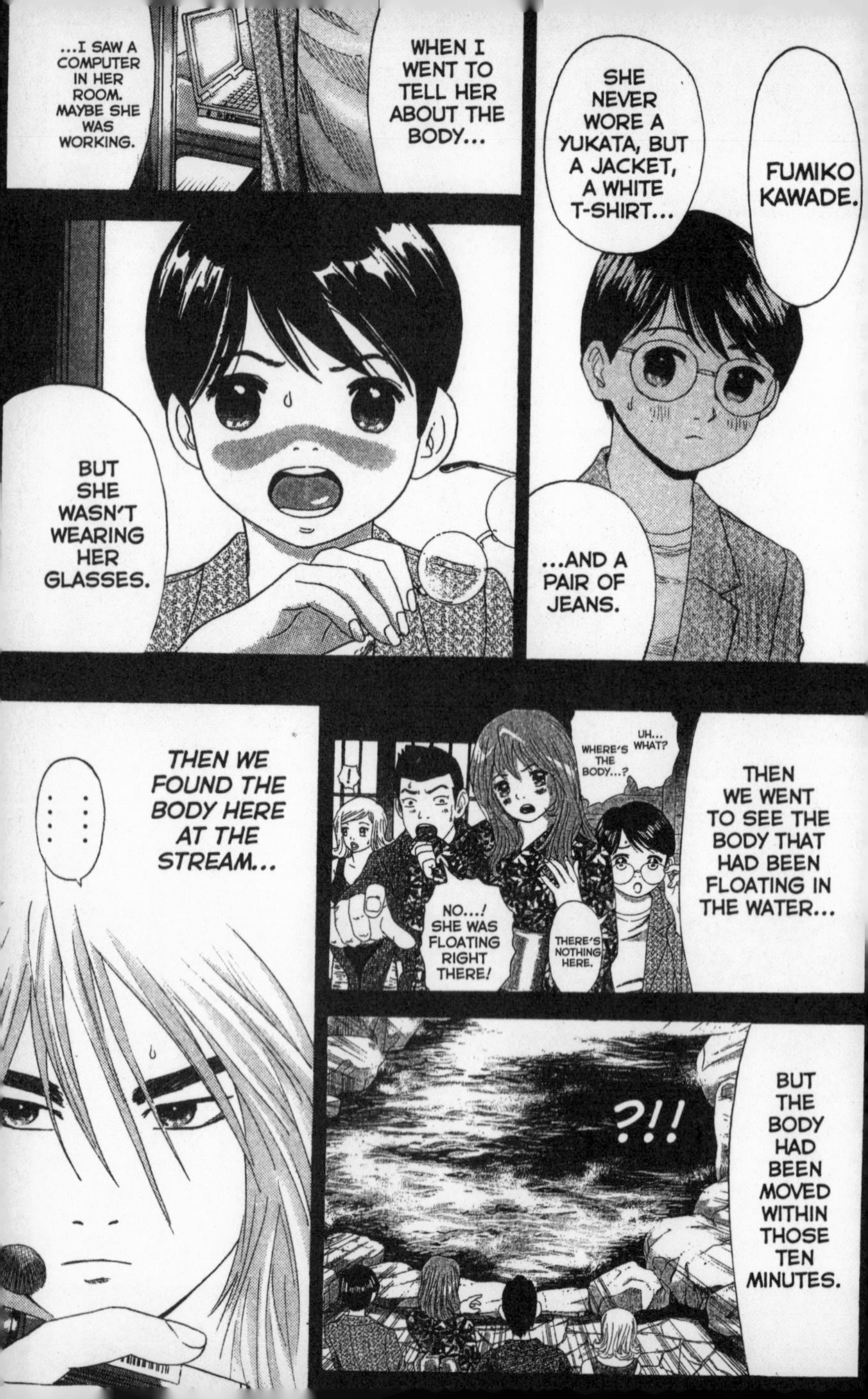
FUMIKO KAWADE.
SHE NEVER WORE A YUKATA, BUT A JACKET, A WHITE T-SHIRT...
...AND A PAIR OF JEANS.
WHEN I WENT TO TELL HER ABOUT THE BODY...
...I SAW A COMPUTER IN HER ROOM. MAYBE SHE WAS WORKING.
BUT SHE WASN'T WEARING HER GLASSES.
THEN WE WENT TO SEE THE BODY THAT HAD BEEN FLOATING IN THE WATER...
UH... WHAT?
WHERE'S THE BODY...?
THERE'S NOTHING HERE.
NO...! SHE WAS FLOATING RIGHT THERE!
BUT THE BODY HAD BEEN MOVED WITHIN THOSE TEN MINUTES.
?!!
THEN WE FOUND THE BODY HERE AT THE STREAM...
....

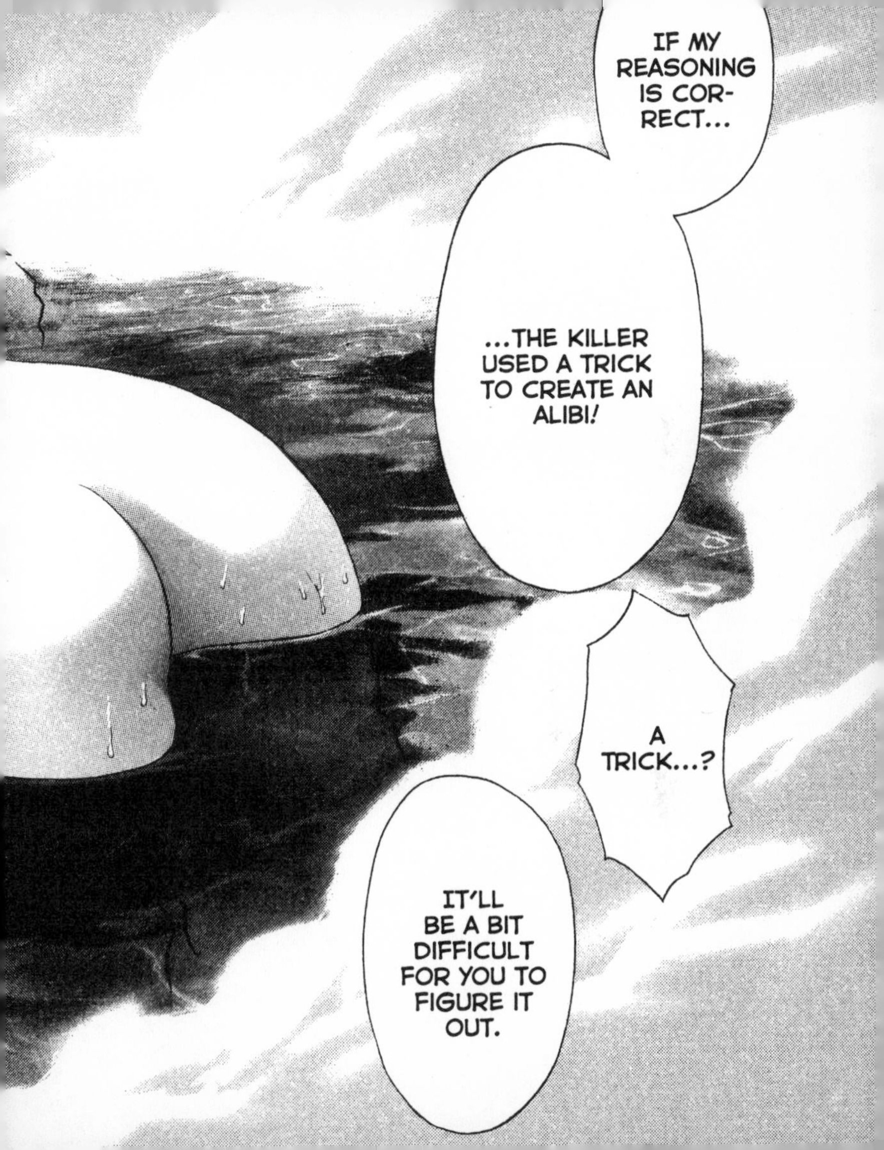
IF MY REASONING IS COR-RECT...
...THE KILLER USED A TRICK TO CREATE AN ALIBI!
A TRICK...?
IT'LL BE A BIT DIFFICULT FOR YOU TO FIGURE IT OUT.

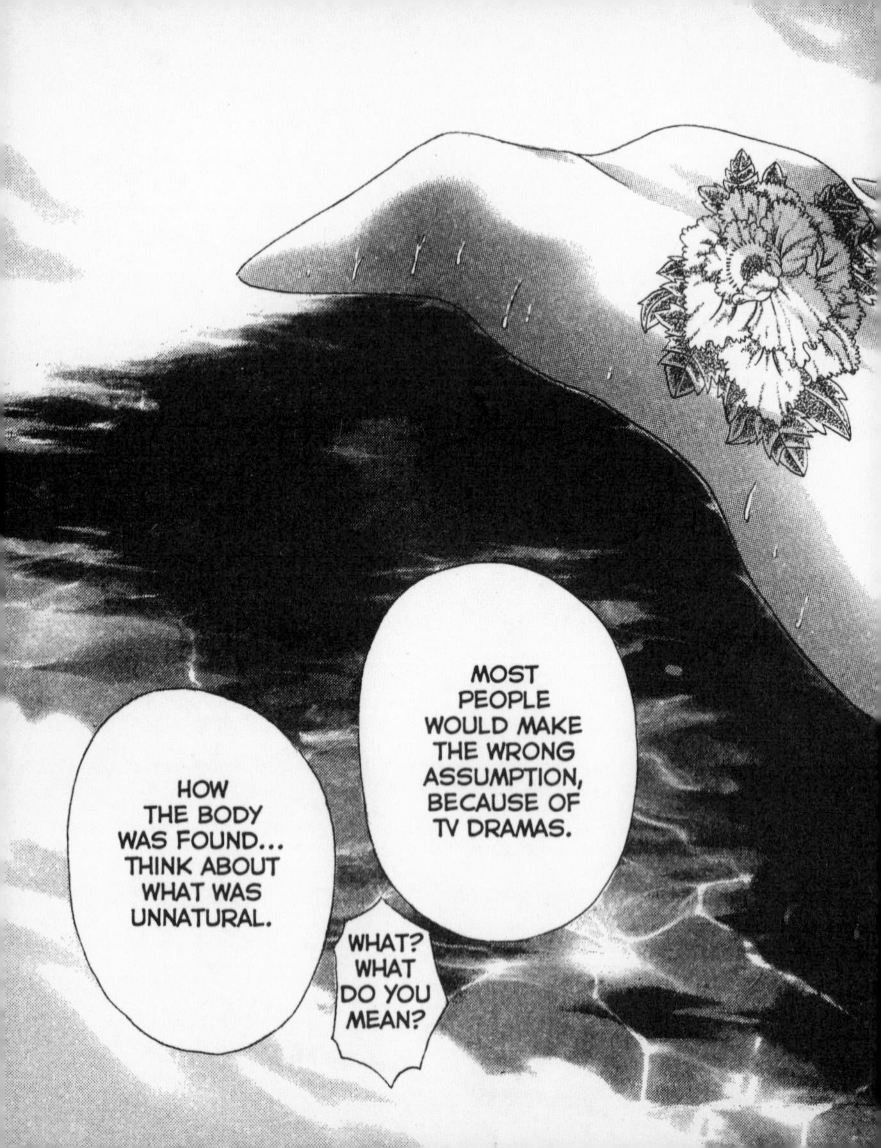
MOST PEOPLE WOULD MAKE THE WRONG ASSUMPTION, BECAUSE OF TV DRAMAS.
HOW THE BODY WAS FOUND... THINK ABOUT WHAT WAS UNNATURAL.
WHAT? WHAT DO YOU MEAN?

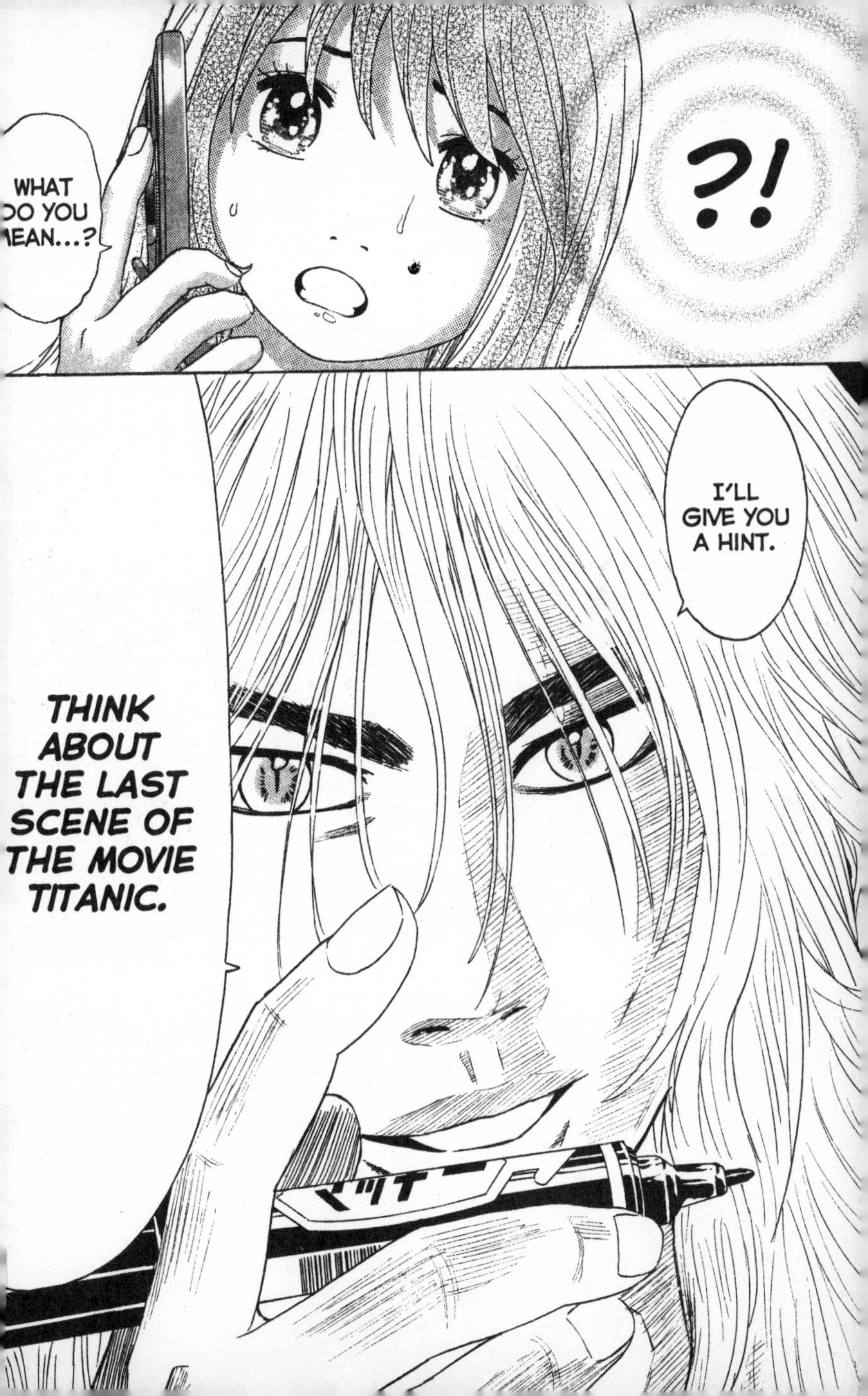
?!
WHAT DO YOU MEAN...?
I'LL GIVE YOU A HINT.
THINK ABOUT THE LAST SCENE OF THE MOVIE TITANIC.

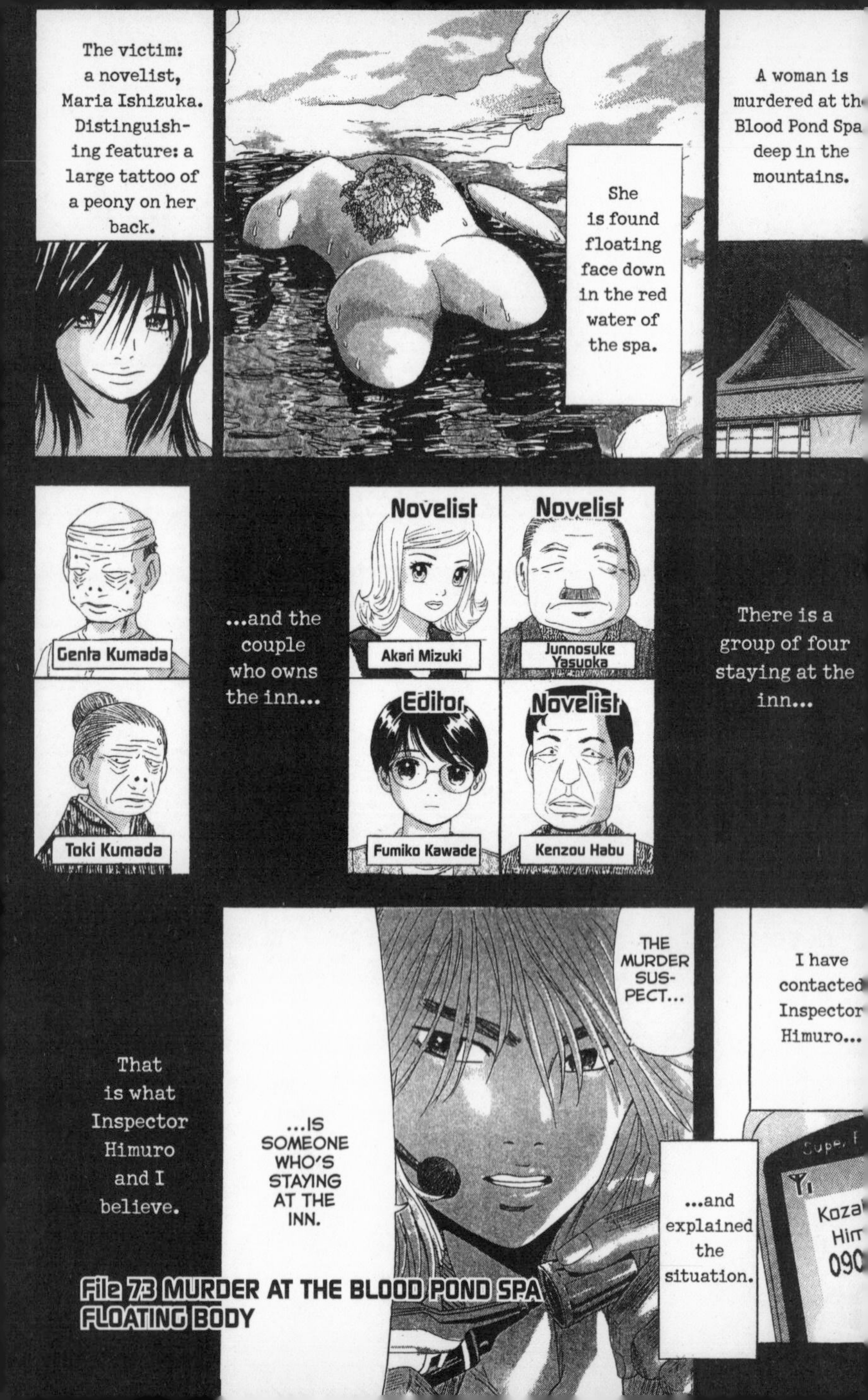
A woman is murdered at th Blood Pond Spa deep in the mountains.
She is found floating face down in the red water of the spa.
The victim: a novelist, Maria Ishizuka. Distinguishing feature: a large tattoo of a peony on her back.
There is a group of four staying at the inn...
Novelist
Junnosuke Yasuoka
Novelist
Akari Mizuki
Novelist
Kenzou Habu
Editor
Fumiko Kawade
...and the couple who owns the inn...
Genta Kumada
Toki Kumada
I have contacted Inspector Himuro...
...and explained the situation.
THE MURDER SUSPECT...
...IS SOMEONE WHO'S STAYING AT THE INN.
That is what Inspector Himuro and I believe.
File 73 MURDER AT THE BLOOD POND SPA
FLOATING BODY

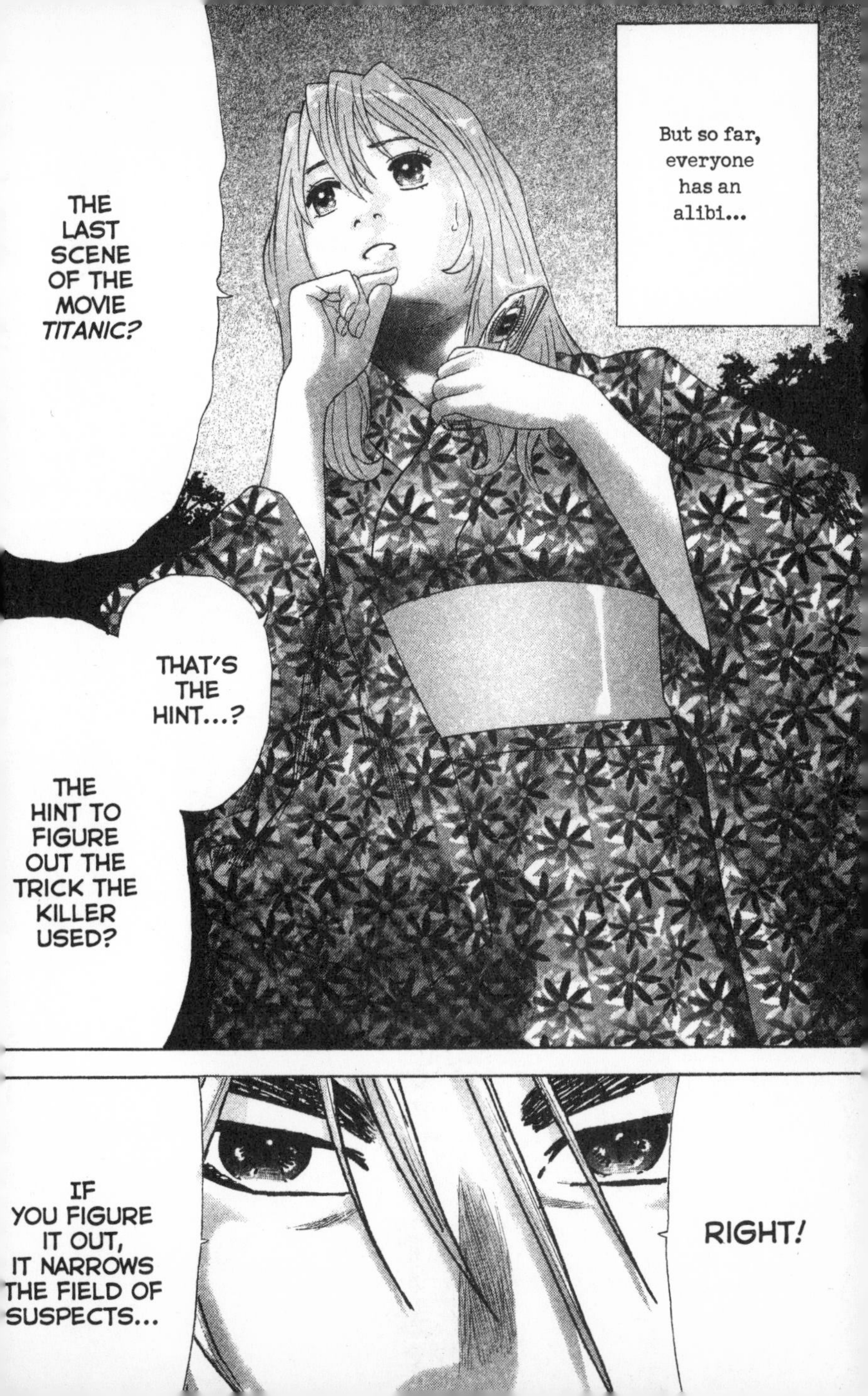
But so far, everyone has an alibi...
THE LAST SCENE OF THE MOVIE *TITANIC?*
THAT'S THE HINT...?
THE HINT TO FIGURE OUT THE TRICK THE KILLER USED?
RIGHT!
IF YOU FIGURE IT OUT, IT NARROWS THE FIELD OF SUSPECTS...

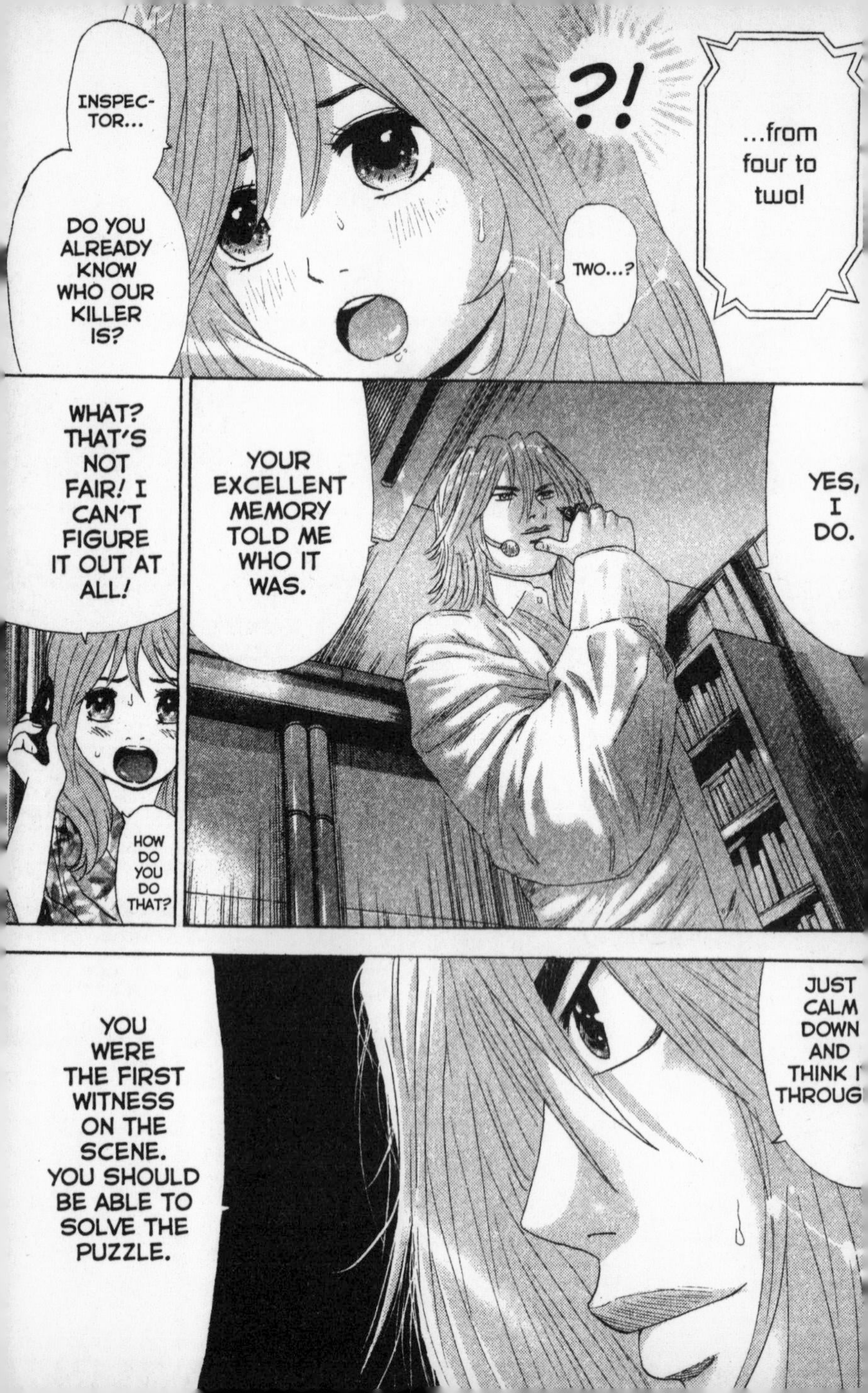
...from four to two!
?!
TWO...?
INSPECTOR...
DO YOU ALREADY KNOW WHO OUR KILLER IS?
YES, I DO.
YOUR EXCELLENT MEMORY TOLD ME WHO IT WAS.
WHAT? THAT'S NOT FAIR! I CAN'T FIGURE IT OUT AT ALL!
HOW DO YOU DO THAT?
JUST CALM DOWN AND THINK I THROUG
YOU WERE THE FIRST WITNESS ON THE SCENE. YOU SHOULD BE ABLE TO SOLVE THE PUZZLE.

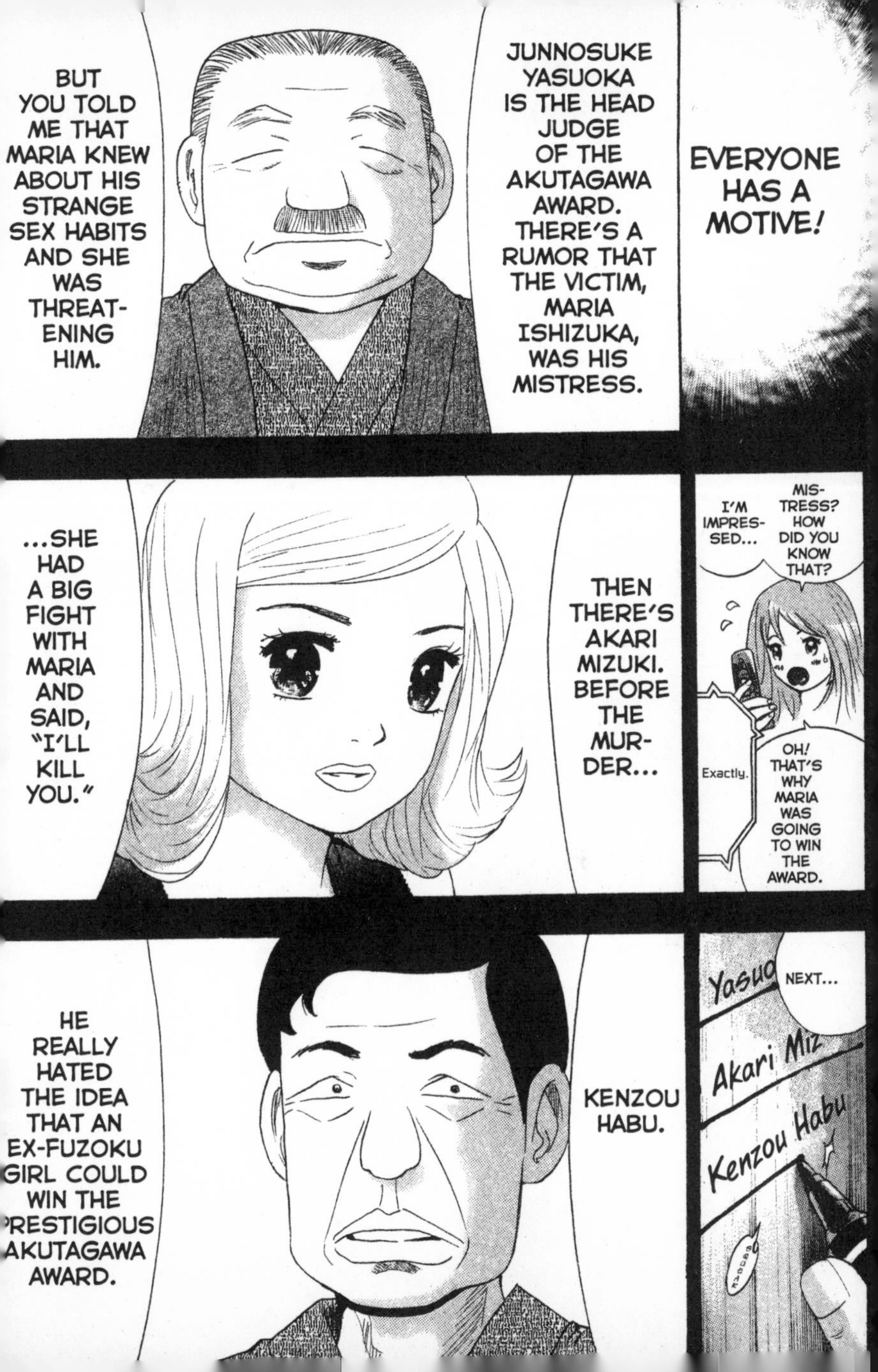
EVERYONE HAS A MOTIVE!
JUNNOSUKE YASUOKA IS THE HEAD JUDGE OF THE AKUTAGAWA AWARD. THERE'S A RUMOR THAT THE VICTIM, MARIA ISHIZUKA, WAS HIS MISTRESS.
BUT YOU TOLD ME THAT MARIA KNEW ABOUT HIS STRANGE SEX HABITS AND SHE WAS THREATENING HIM.
MISTRESS? HOW DID YOU KNOW THAT?
I'M IMPRESSED...
OH! THAT'S WHY MARIA WAS GOING TO WIN THE AWARD.
Exactly.
THEN THERE'S AKARI MIZUKI. BEFORE THE MURDER...
...SHE HAD A BIG FIGHT WITH MARIA AND SAID, "I'LL KILL YOU."
NEXT...
Yasuo
Akari Miz
Kenzou Habu
KENZOU HABU.
HE REALLY HATED THE IDEA THAT AN EX-FUZOKU GIRL COULD WIN THE PRESTIGIOUS AKUTAGAWA AWARD.

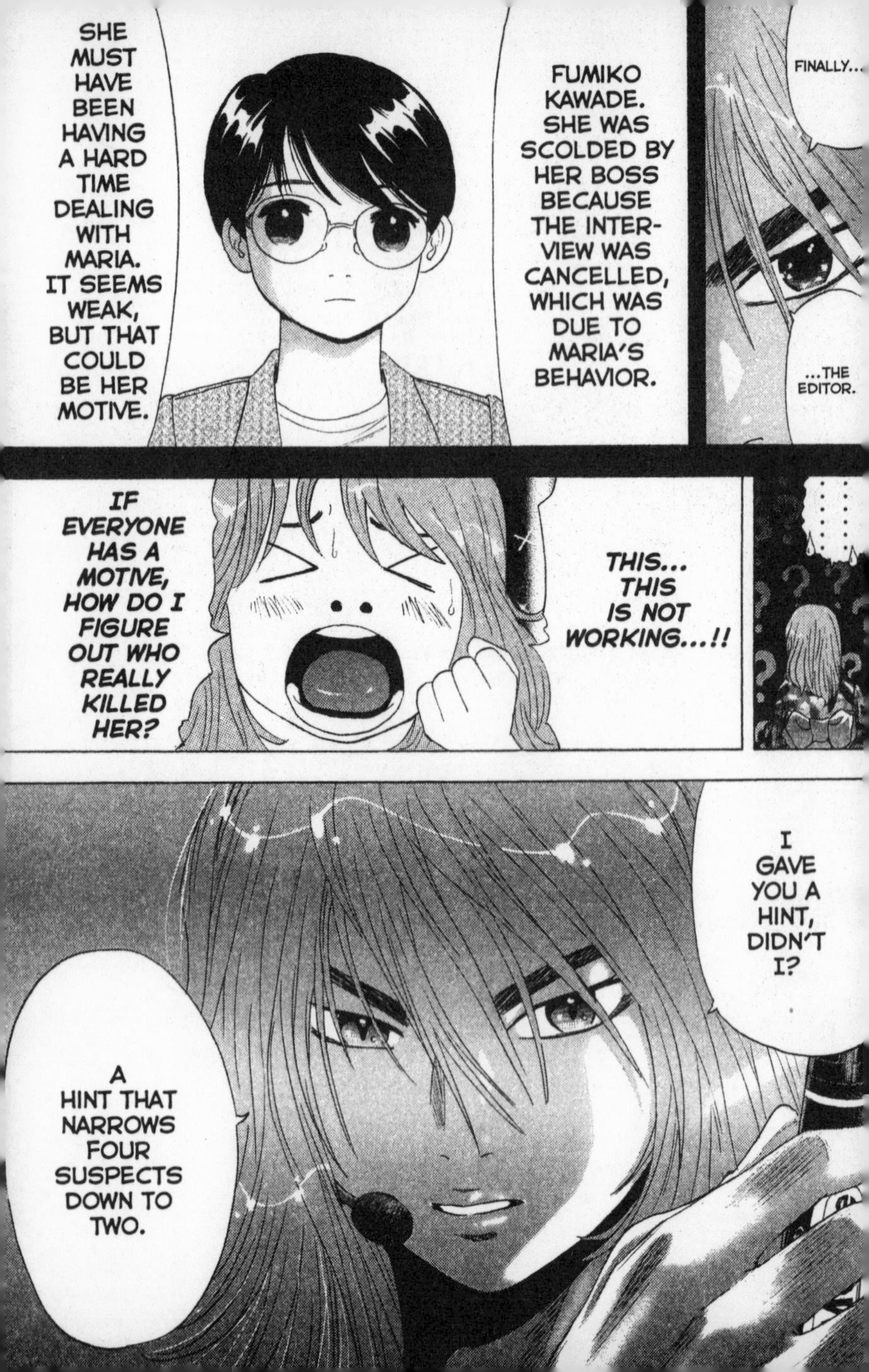
FINALLY...
...THE EDITOR.
FUMIKO KAWADE. SHE WAS SCOLDED BY HER BOSS BECAUSE THE INTER-VIEW WAS CANCELLED, WHICH WAS DUE TO MARIA'S BEHAVIOR.
SHE MUST HAVE BEEN HAVING A HARD TIME DEALING WITH MARIA. IT SEEMS WEAK, BUT THAT COULD BE HER MOTIVE.
THIS... THIS IS NOT WORKING...!!
IF EVERYONE HAS A MOTIVE, HOW DO I FIGURE OUT WHO REALLY KILLED HER?
I GAVE YOU A HINT, DIDN'T I?
A HINT THAT NARROWS FOUR SUSPECTS DOWN TO TWO.

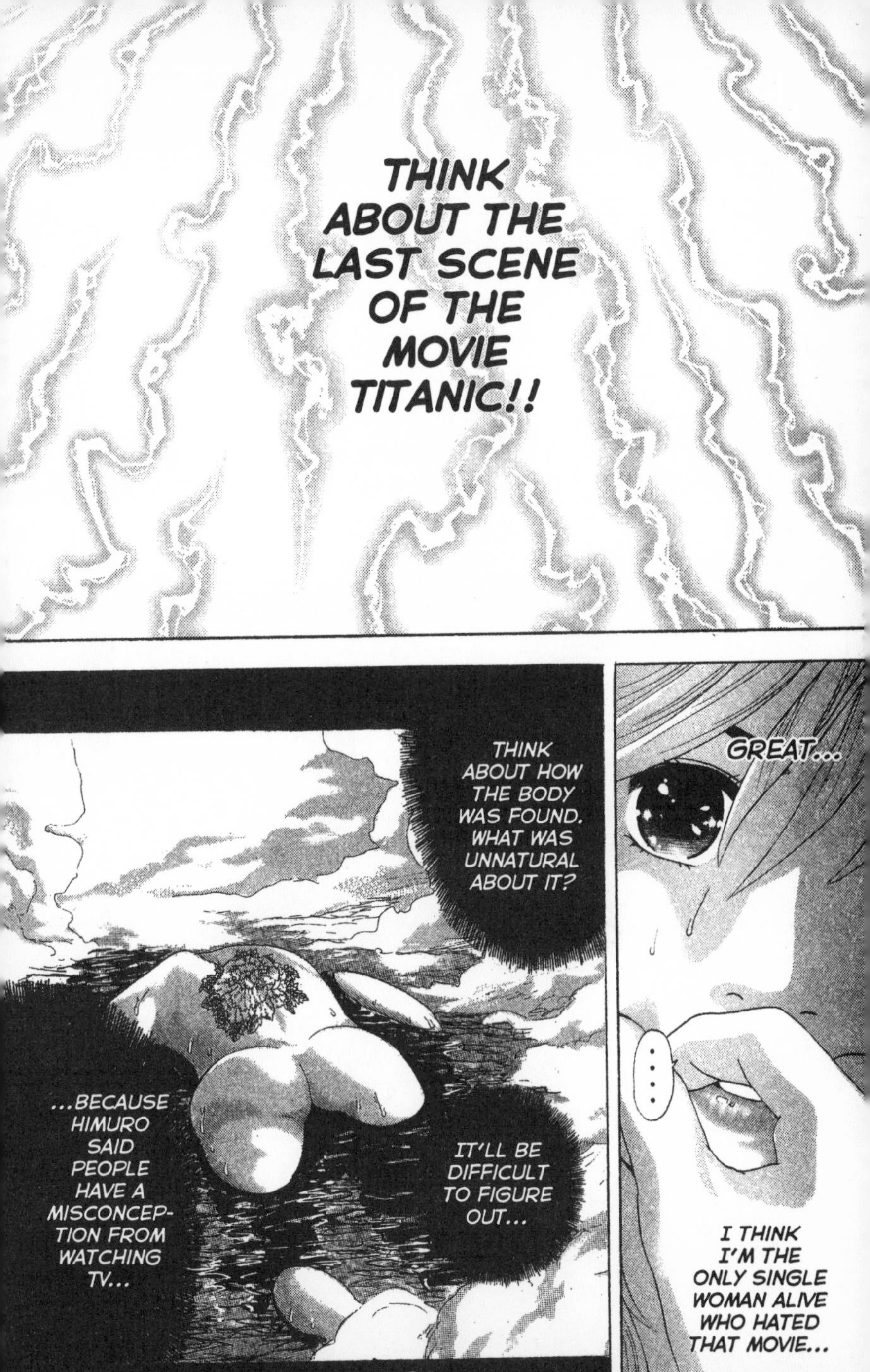
THINK ABOUT THE LAST SCENE OF THE MOVIE TITANIC!!
GREAT...
....
I THINK I'M THE ONLY SINGLE WOMAN ALIVE WHO HATED THAT MOVIE...
THINK ABOUT HOW THE BODY WAS FOUND. WHAT WAS UNNATURAL ABOUT IT?
IT'LL BE DIFFICULT TO FIGURE OUT...
...BECAUSE HIMURO SAID PEOPLE HAVE A MISCONCEP-TION FROM WATCHING TV...

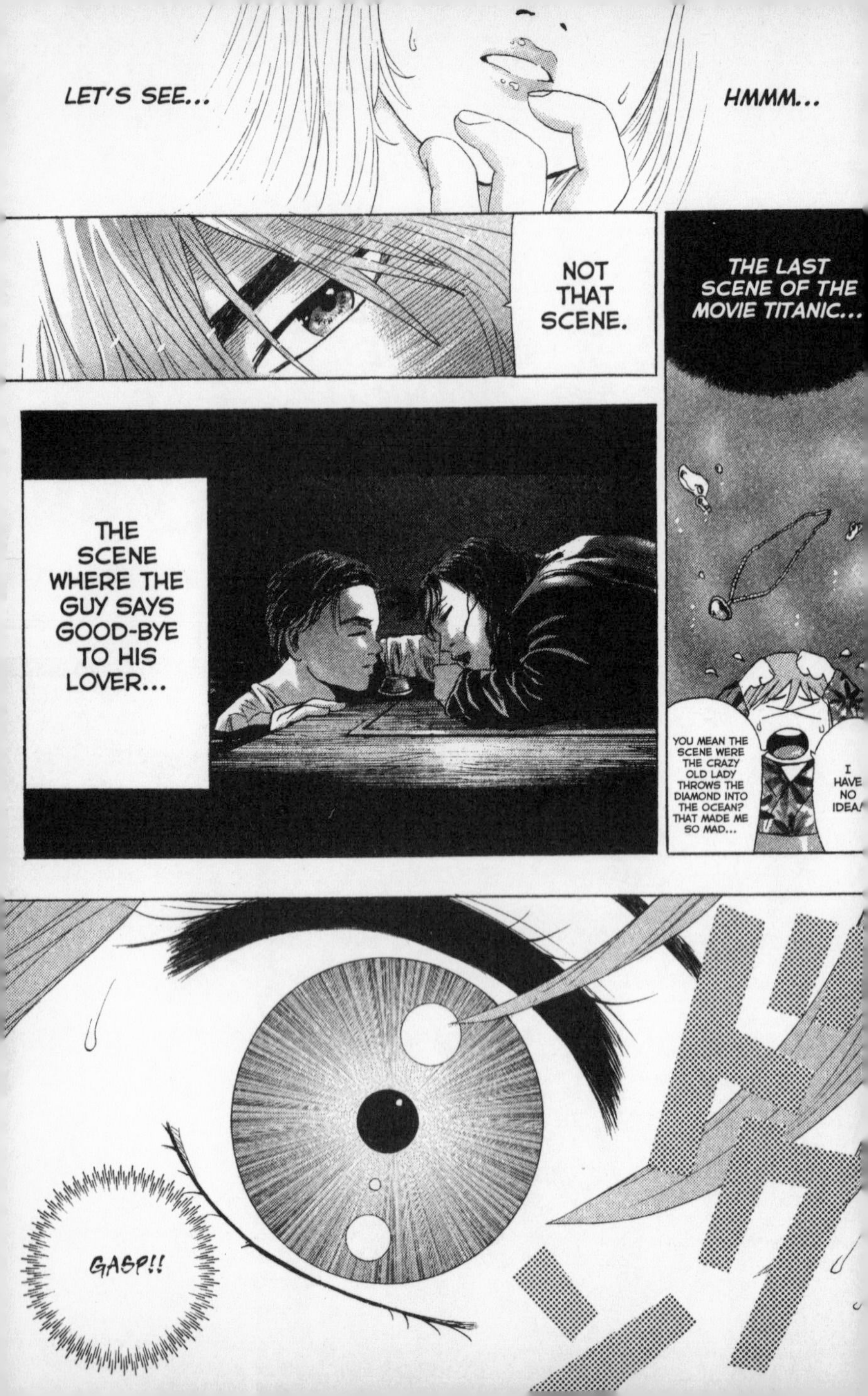
HMMM...
LET'S SEE...
THE LAST SCENE OF THE MOVIE TITANIC...
I HAVE NO IDEA!
YOU MEAN THE SCENE WERE THE CRAZY OLD LADY THROWS THE DIAMOND INTO THE OCEAN? THAT MADE ME SO MAD...
NOT THAT SCENE.
THE SCENE WHERE THE GUY SAYS GOOD-BYE TO HIS LOVER...
GASP!!

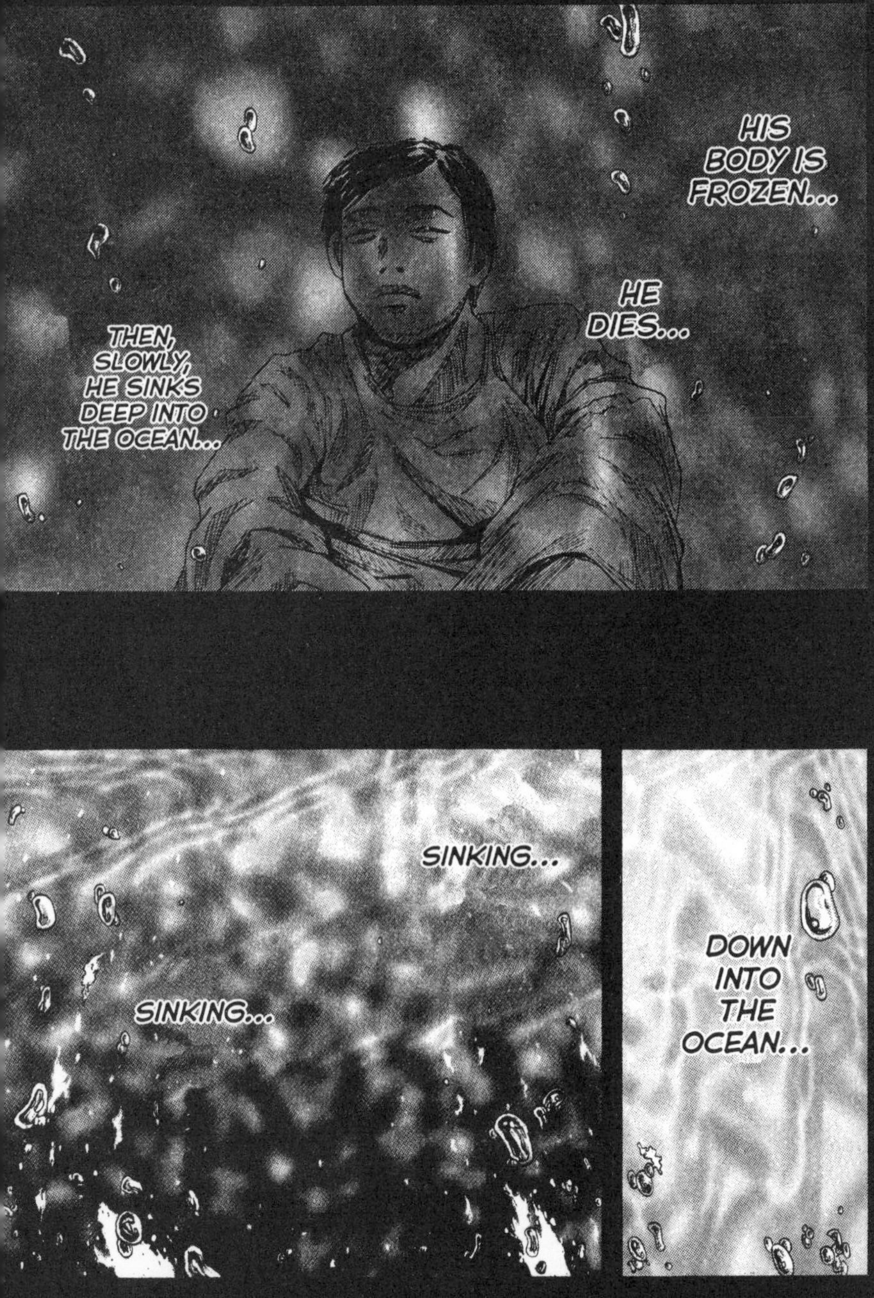
HIS BODY IS FROZEN...
HE DIES...
THEN, SLOWLY, HE SINKS DEEP INTO THE OCEAN...
DOWN INTO THE OCEAN...
SINKING...
SINKING...

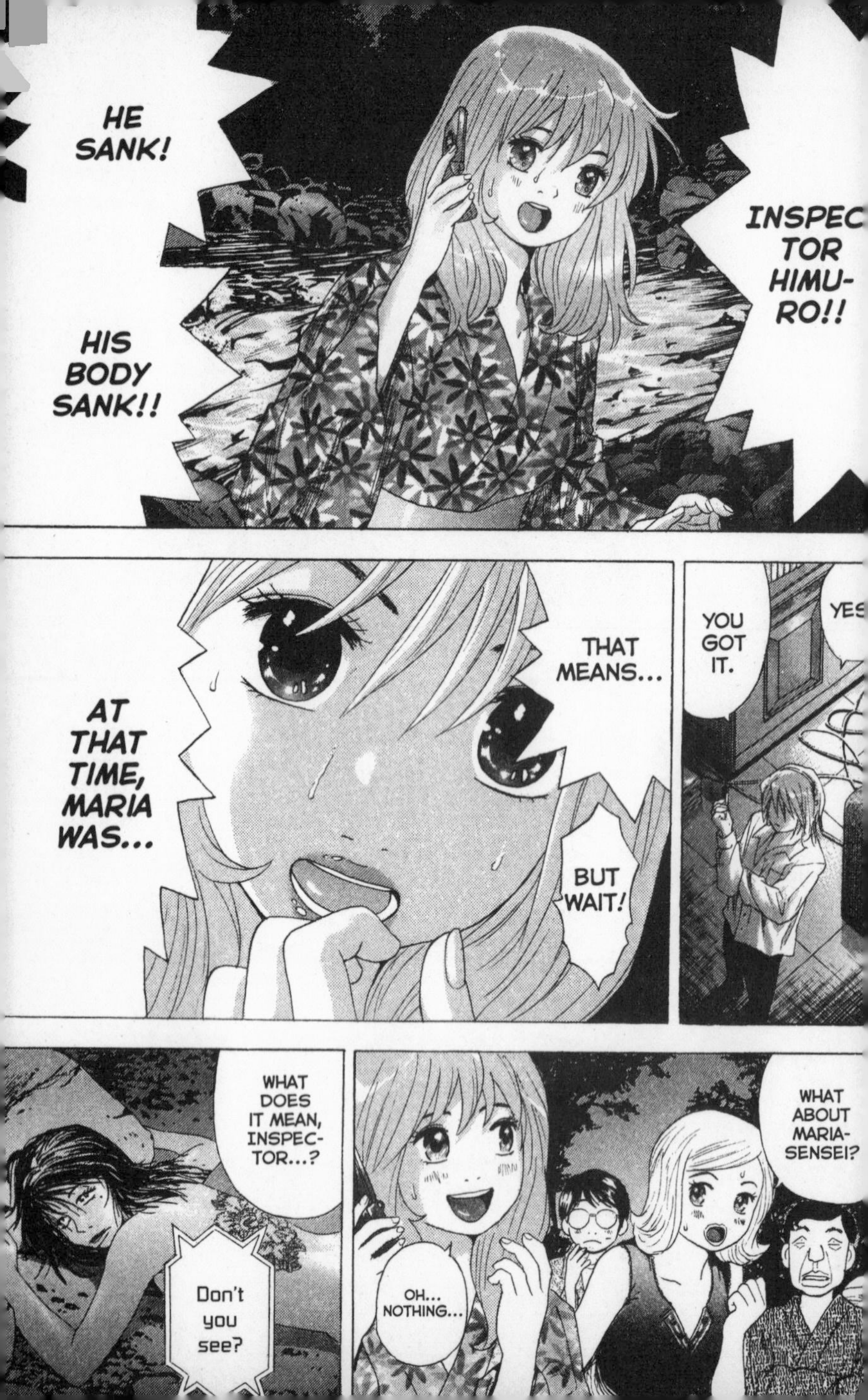
INSPECTOR HIMURO!!
HE SANK!
HIS BODY SANK!!
YES
YOU GOT IT.
THAT MEANS...
AT THAT TIME, MARIA WAS...
BUT WAIT!
WHAT ABOUT MARIA-SENSEI?
OH... NOTHING...
WHAT DOES IT MEAN, INSPECTOR...?
Don't you see?

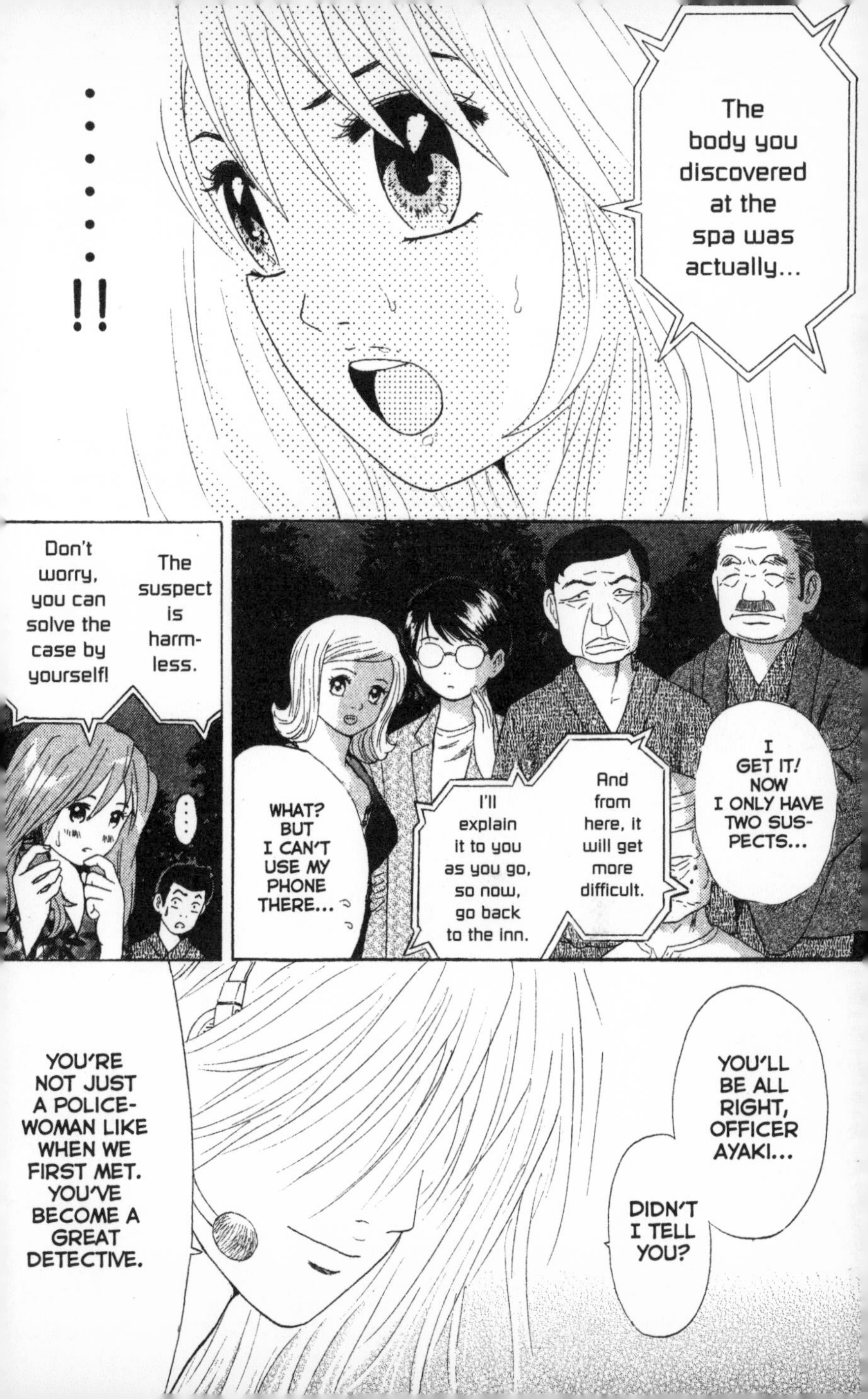
The body you discovered at the spa was actually...
......!!
I GET IT! NOW I ONLY HAVE TWO SUSPECTS...
And from here, it will get more difficult.
I'll explain it to you as you go, so now, go back to the inn.
WHAT? BUT I CAN'T USE MY PHONE THERE...
The suspect is harmless.
Don't worry, you can solve the case by yourself!
...
YOU'LL BE ALL RIGHT, OFFICER AYAKI...
DIDN'T I TELL YOU?
YOU'RE NOT JUST A POLICEWOMAN LIKE WHEN WE FIRST MET. YOU'VE BECOME A GREAT DETECTIVE.

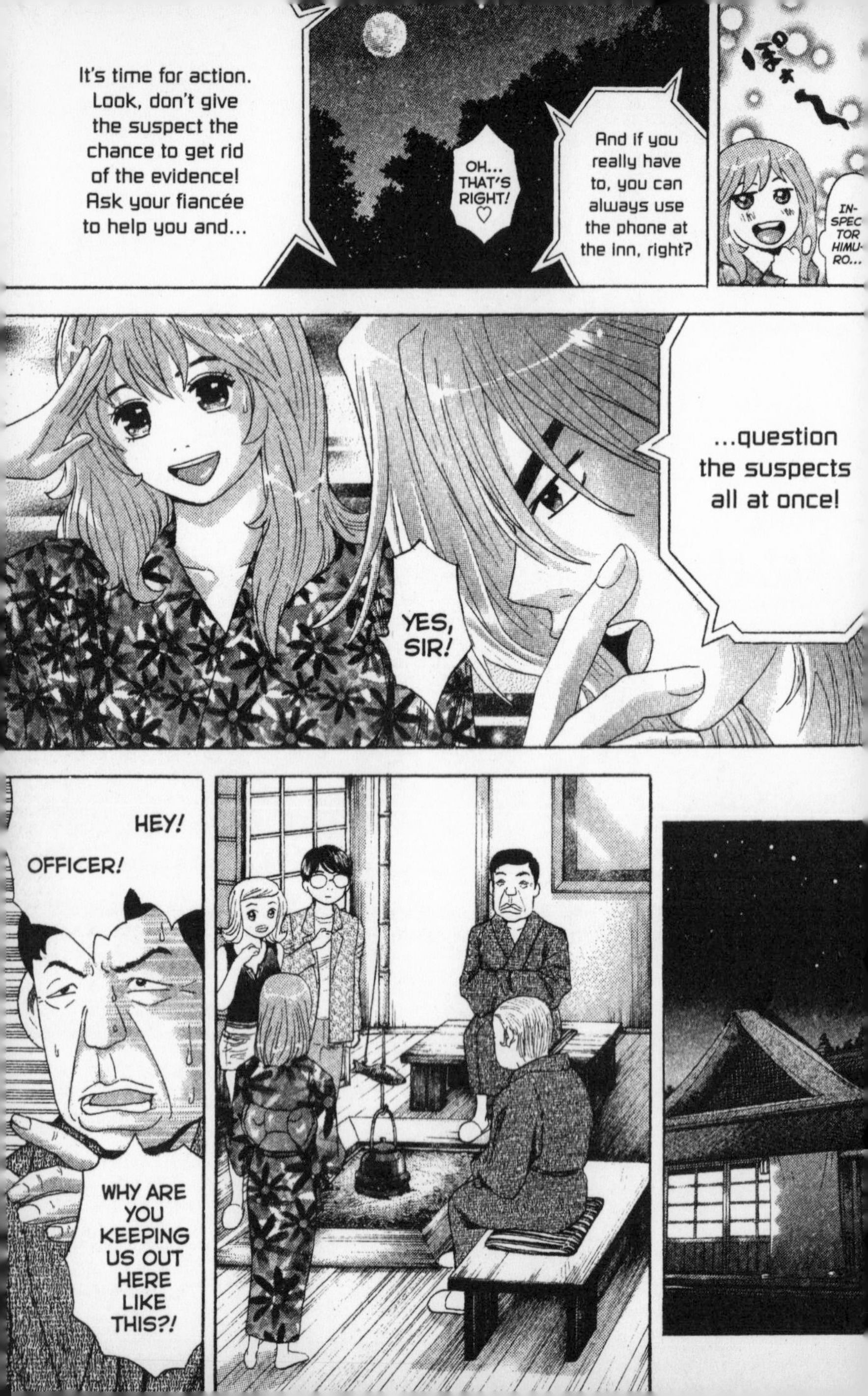
INSPECTOR HIMURO...
And if you really have to, you can always use the phone at the inn, right?
OH... THAT'S RIGHT! ♡
It's time for action. Look, don't give the suspect the chance to get rid of the evidence! Ask your fiancée to help you and...
...question the suspects all at once!
YES, SIR!
HEY!
OFFICER!
WHY ARE YOU KEEPING US OUT HERE LIKE THIS?!

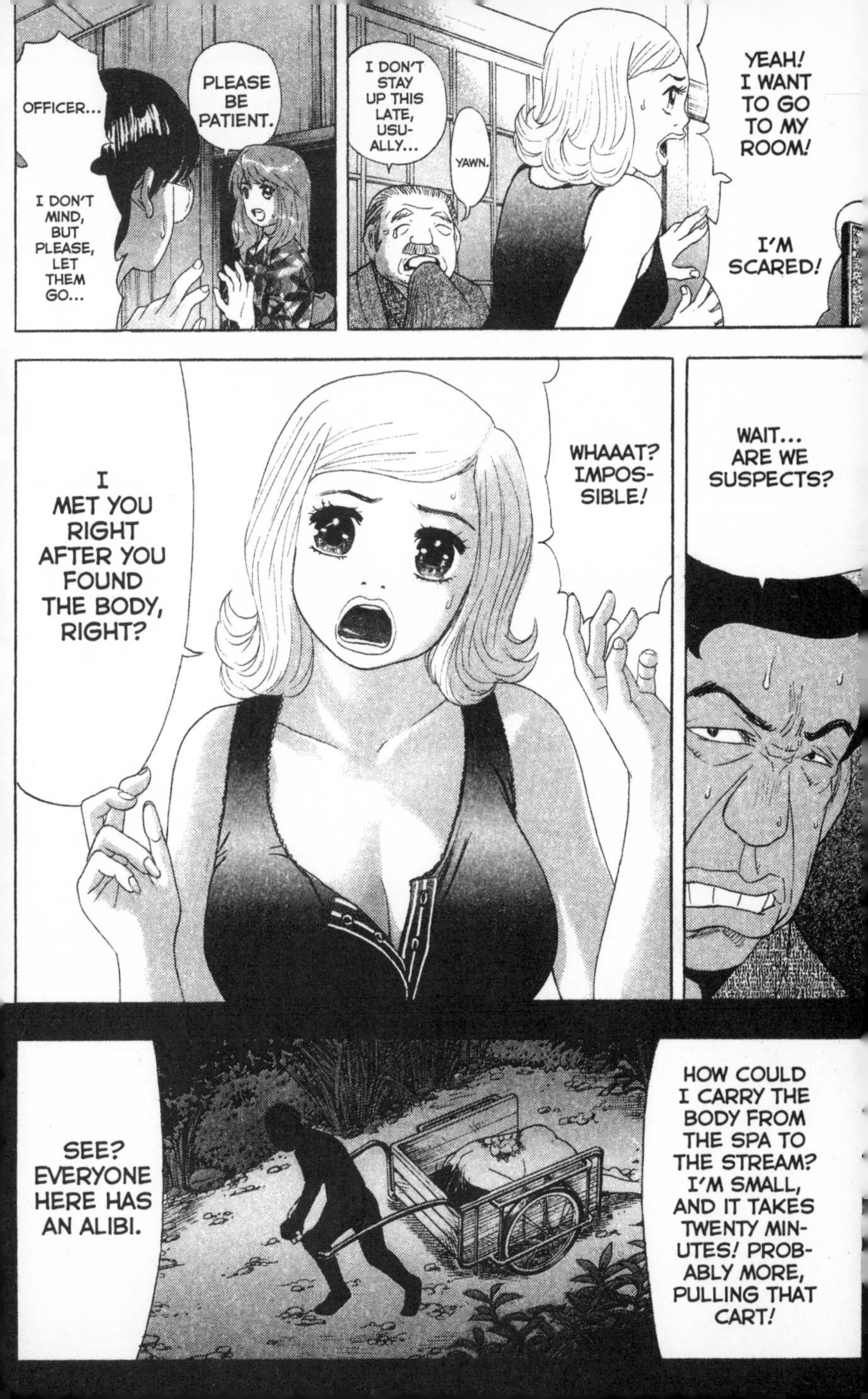

YEAH! I WANT TO GO TO MY ROOM!
I'M SCARED!
I DON'T STAY UP THIS LATE, USUALLY...
YAWN.
PLEASE BE PATIENT.
OFFICER...
I DON'T MIND, BUT PLEASE, LET THEM GO...
WAIT... ARE WE SUSPECTS?
WHAAAT? IMPOSSIBLE!
I MET YOU RIGHT AFTER YOU FOUND THE BODY, RIGHT?
HOW COULD I CARRY THE BODY FROM THE SPA TO THE STREAM? I'M SMALL, AND IT TAKES TWENTY MINUTES! PROBABLY MORE, PULLING THAT CART!
SEE? EVERYONE HERE HAS AN ALIBI.

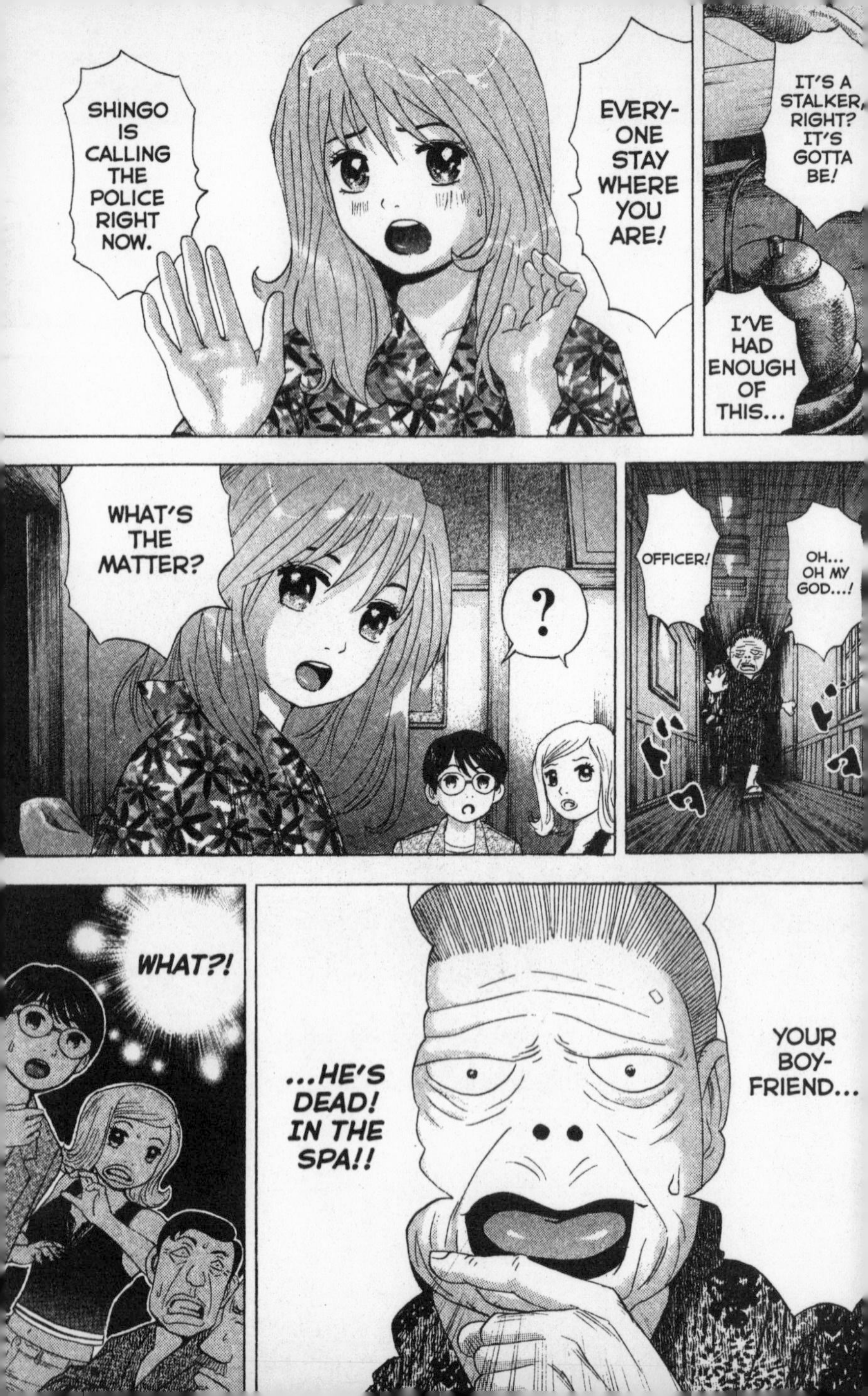
IT'S A STALKER, RIGHT? IT'S GOTTA BE!
I'VE HAD ENOUGH OF THIS...
EVERY-ONE STAY WHERE YOU ARE!
SHINGO IS CALLING THE POLICE RIGHT NOW.
OH... OH MY GOD...!
OFFICER!
WHAT'S THE MATTER?
?
YOUR BOY-FRIEND...
...HE'S DEAD! IN THE SPA!!
WHAT?!

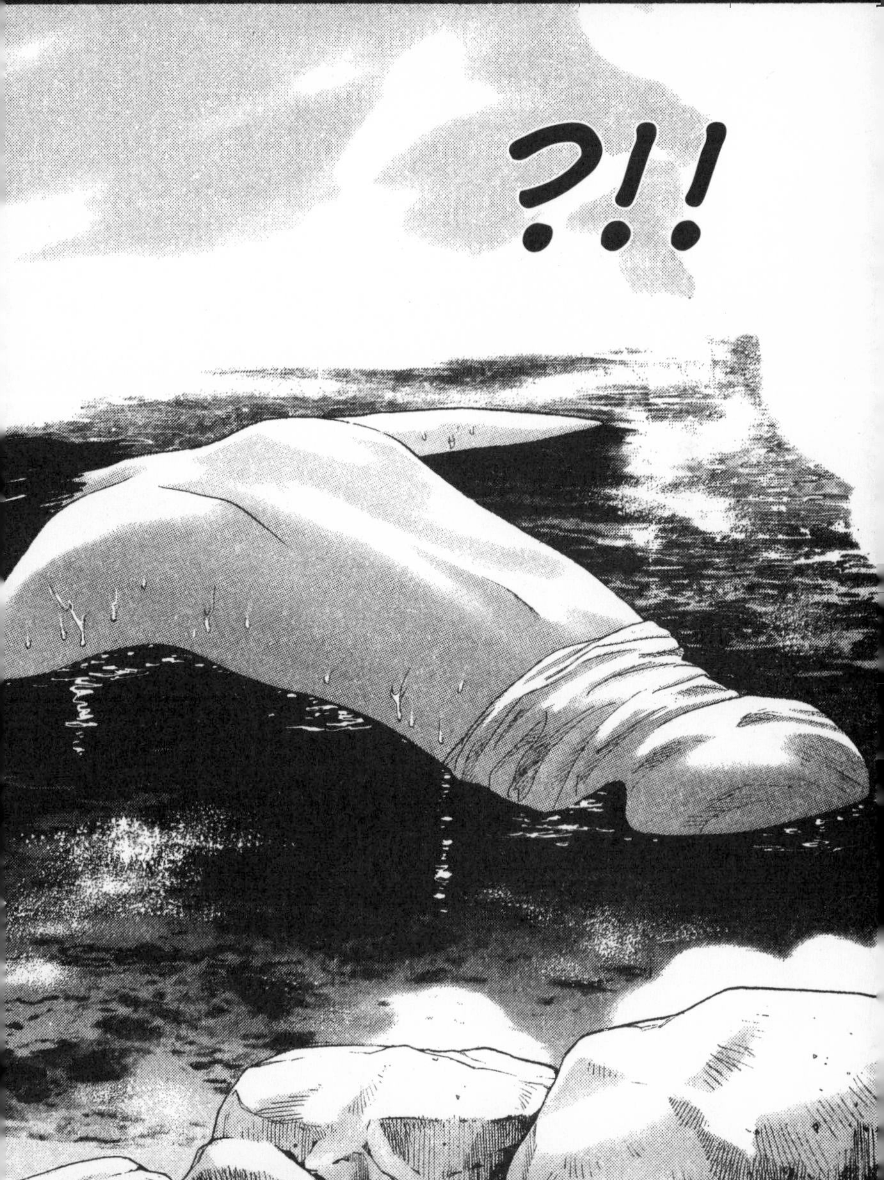
?!!

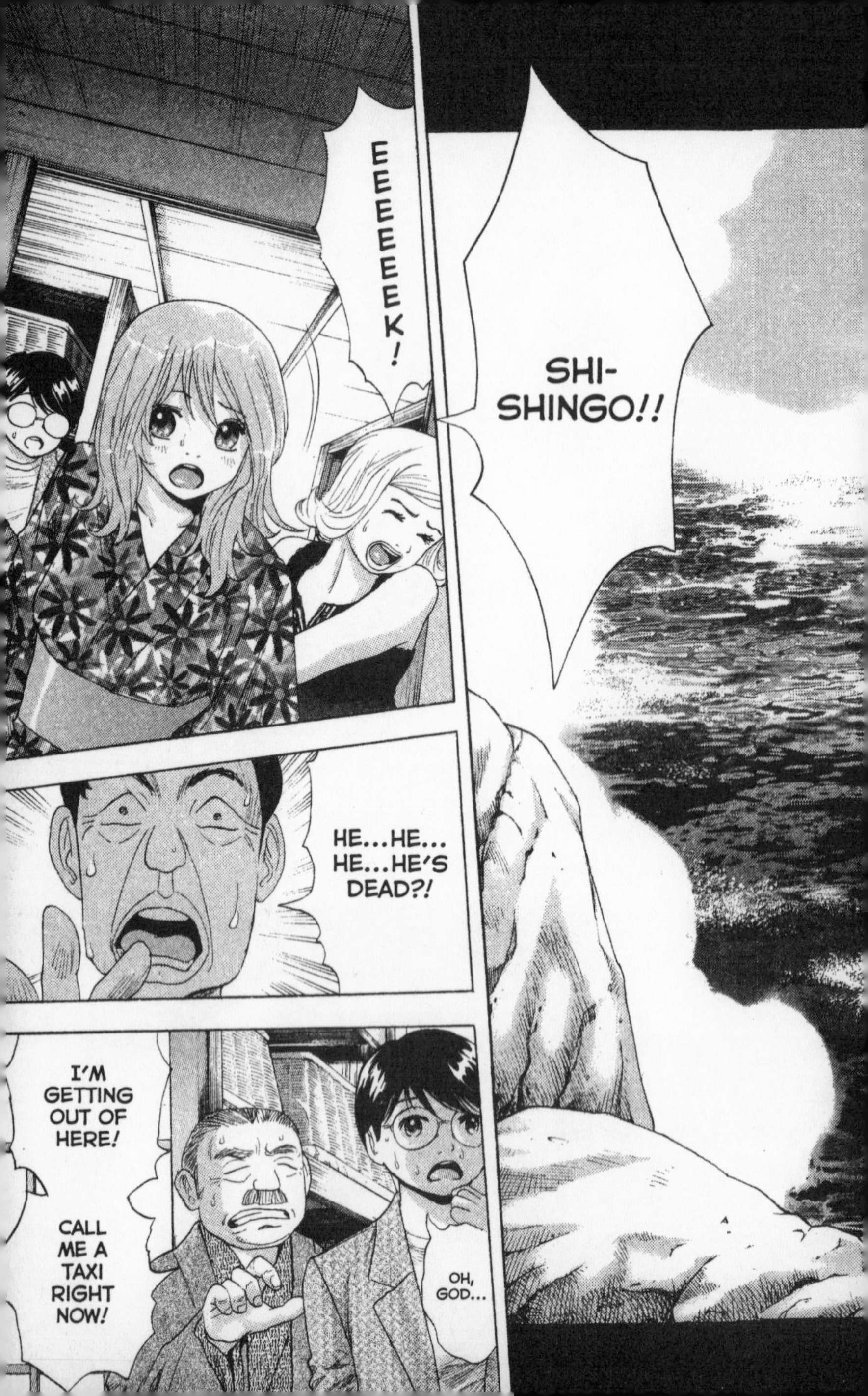
SHI-SHINGO!!
EEEEEEEK!
HE...HE... HE...HE'S DEAD?!
I'M GETTING OUT OF HERE!
CALL ME A TAXI RIGHT NOW!
OH, GOD...

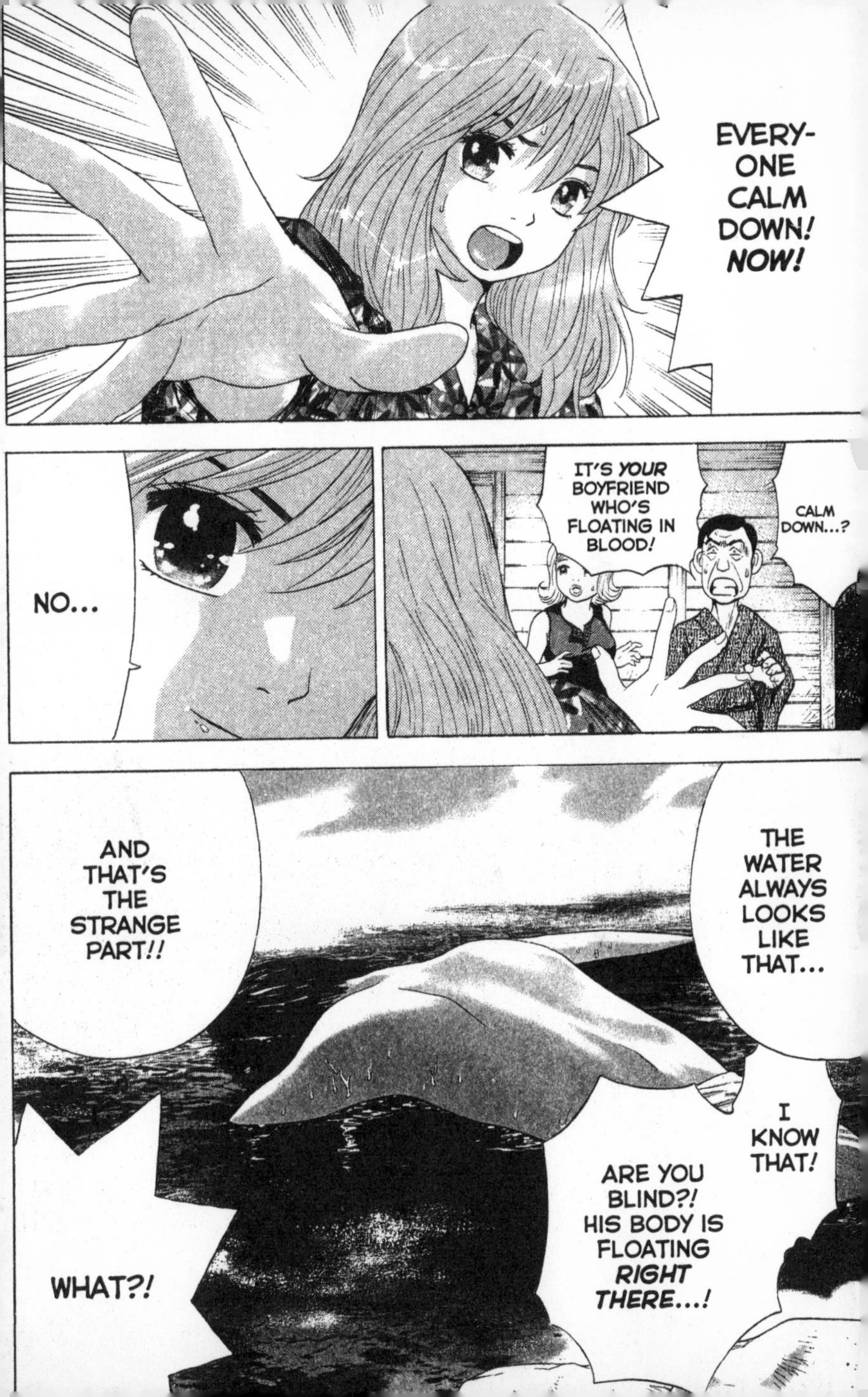
EVERY-ONE CALM DOWN! NOW!
CALM DOWN...?
IT'S YOUR BOYFRIEND WHO'S FLOATING IN BLOOD!
NO...
THE WATER ALWAYS LOOKS LIKE THAT...
AND THAT'S THE STRANGE PART!!
I KNOW THAT!
ARE YOU BLIND?! HIS BODY IS FLOATING RIGHT THERE...!
WHAT?!

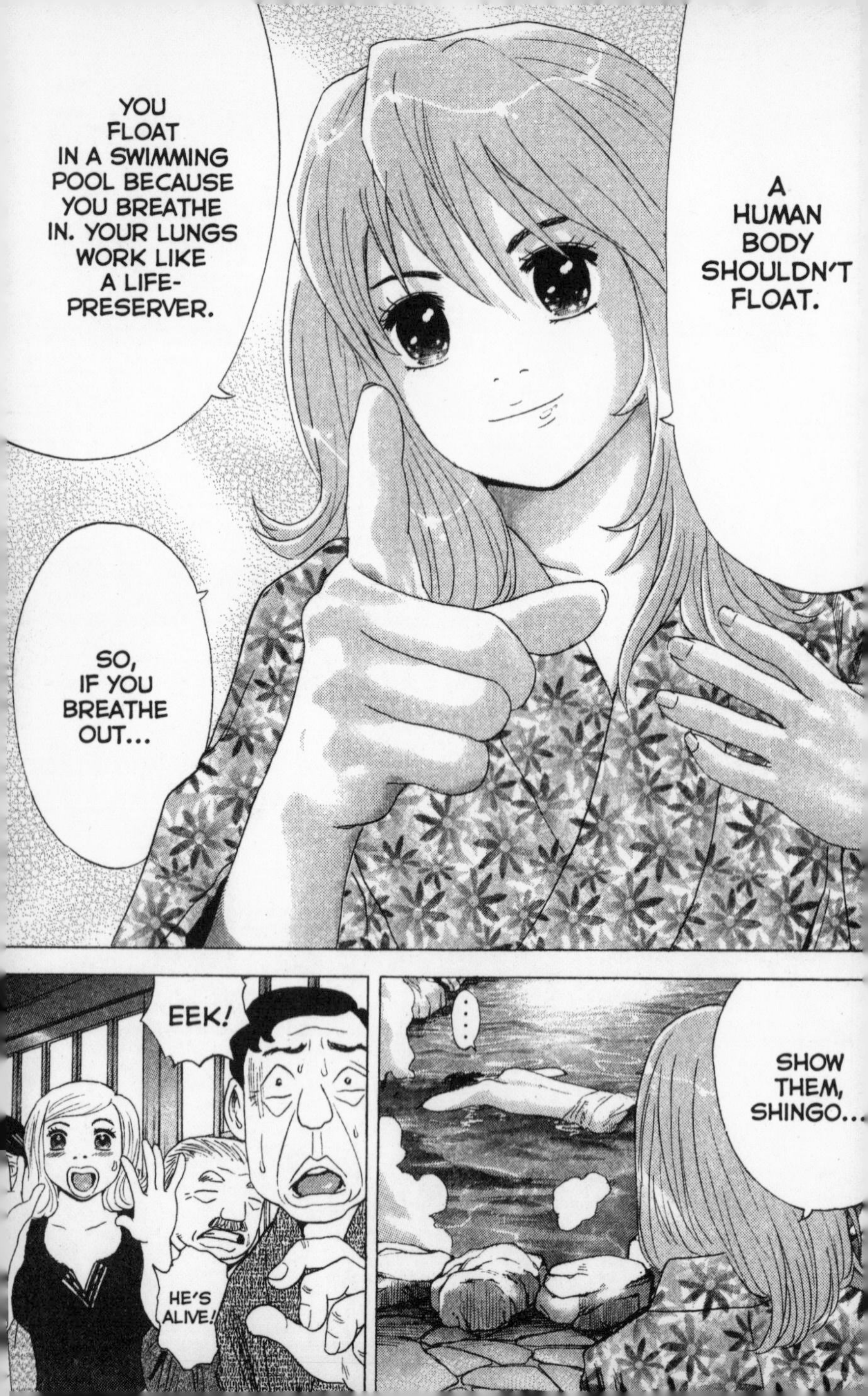
A HUMAN BODY SHOULDN'T FLOAT.
YOU FLOAT IN A SWIMMING POOL BECAUSE YOU BREATHE IN. YOUR LUNGS WORK LIKE A LIFE-PRESERVER.
SO, IF YOU BREATHE OUT...
SHOW THEM, SHINGO...
...
EEK!
HE'S ALIVE!

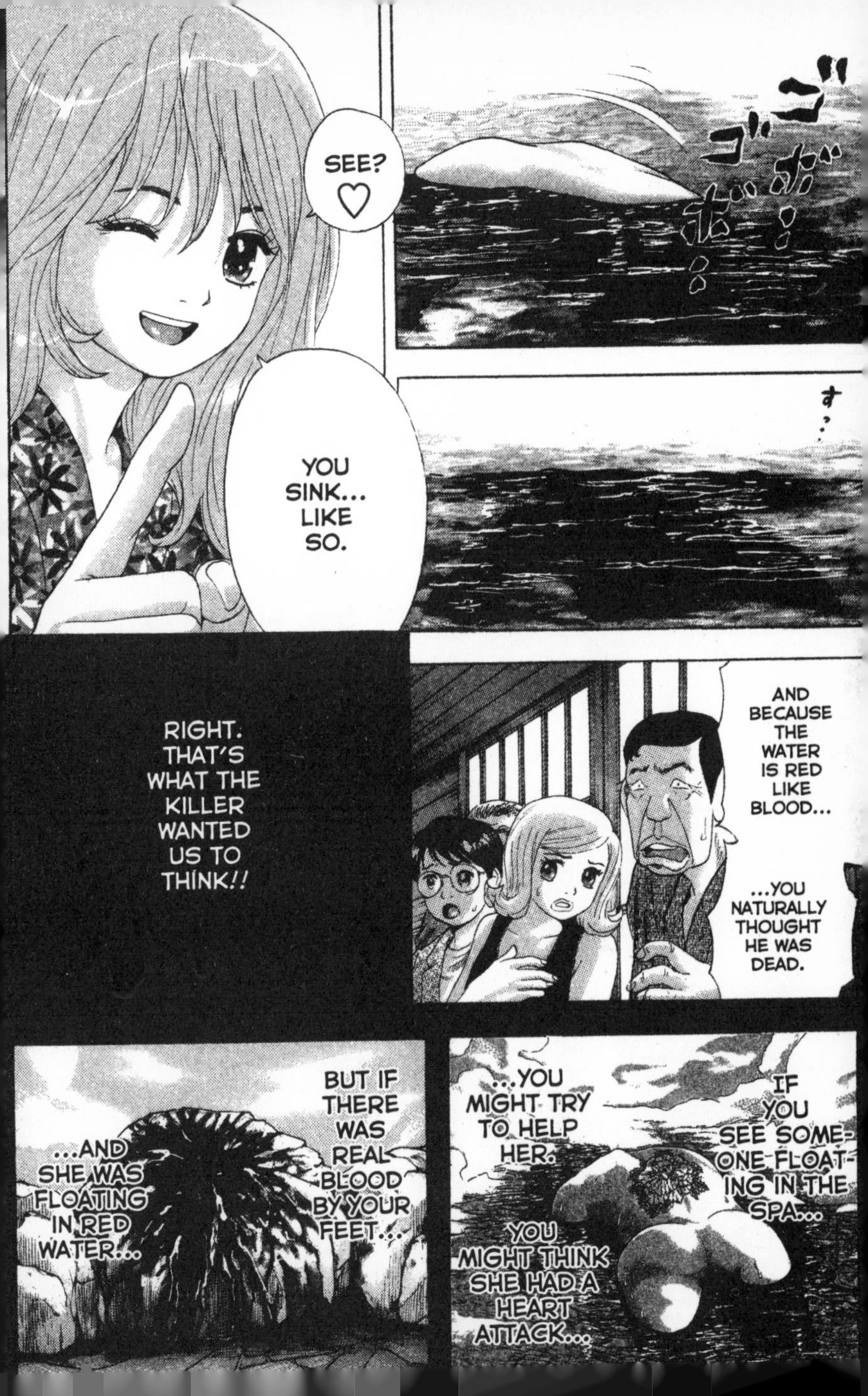
ゴボゴボ…
す…
SEE? ♡
YOU SINK... LIKE SO.
AND BECAUSE THE WATER IS RED LIKE BLOOD...
...YOU NATURALLY THOUGHT HE WAS DEAD.
RIGHT. THAT'S WHAT THE KILLER WANTED US TO THINK!!
IF YOU SEE SOME-ONE FLOAT-ING IN THE SPA...
...YOU MIGHT TRY TO HELP HER.
YOU MIGHT THINK SHE HAD A HEART ATTACK...
BUT IF THERE WAS REAL BLOOD BY YOUR FEET...
...AND SHE WAS FLOATING IN RED WATER...

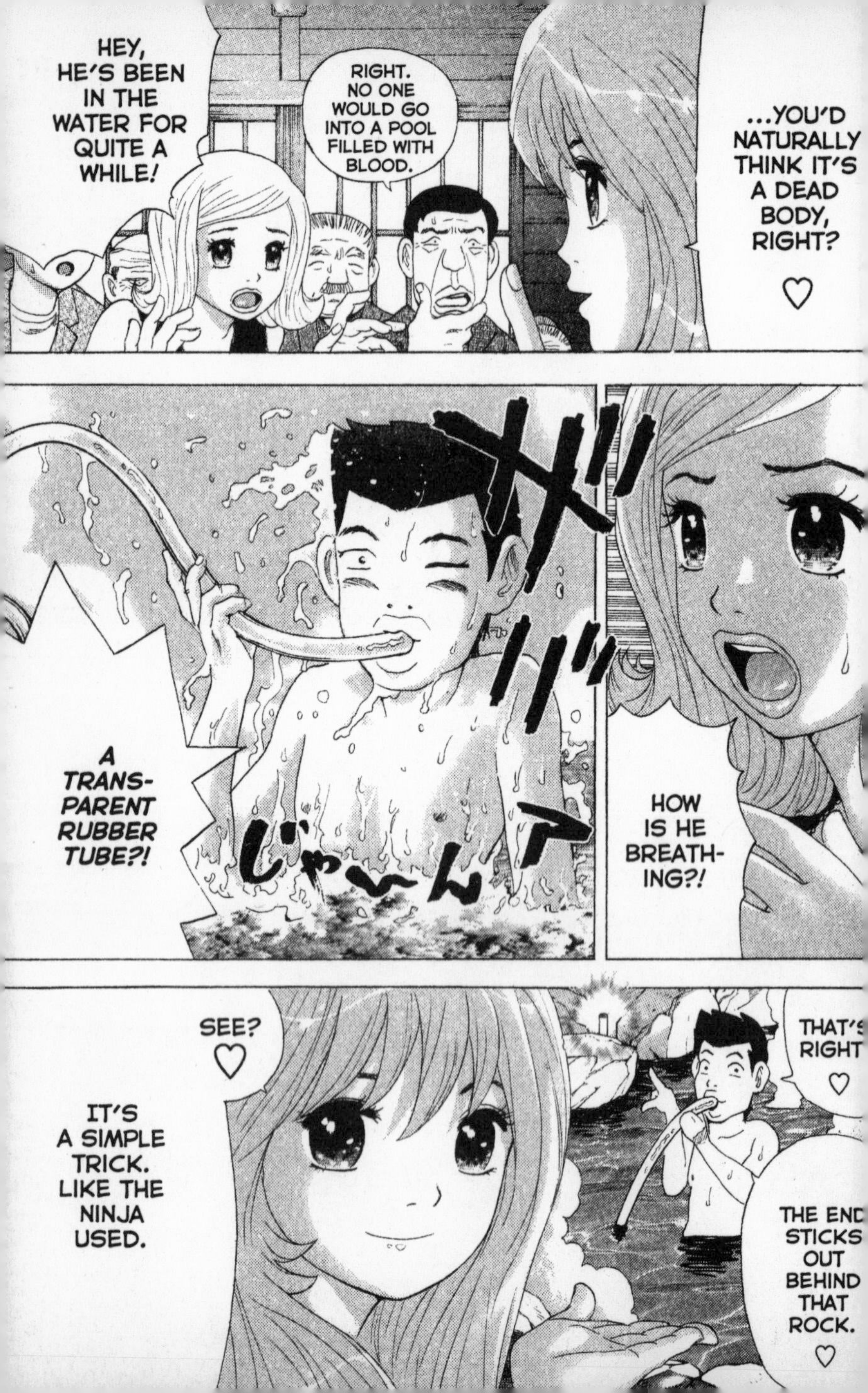

...YOU'D NATURALLY THINK IT'S A DEAD BODY, RIGHT? ♡
RIGHT. NO ONE WOULD GO INTO A POOL FILLED WITH BLOOD.
HEY, HE'S BEEN IN THE WATER FOR QUITE A WHILE!
HOW IS HE BREATHING?!
じゃ～ん
A TRANS-PARENT RUBBER TUBE?!
THAT'S RIGHT ♡
THE END STICKS OUT BEHIND THAT ROCK. ♡
SEE? ♡
IT'S A SIMPLE TRICK. LIKE THE NINJA USED.

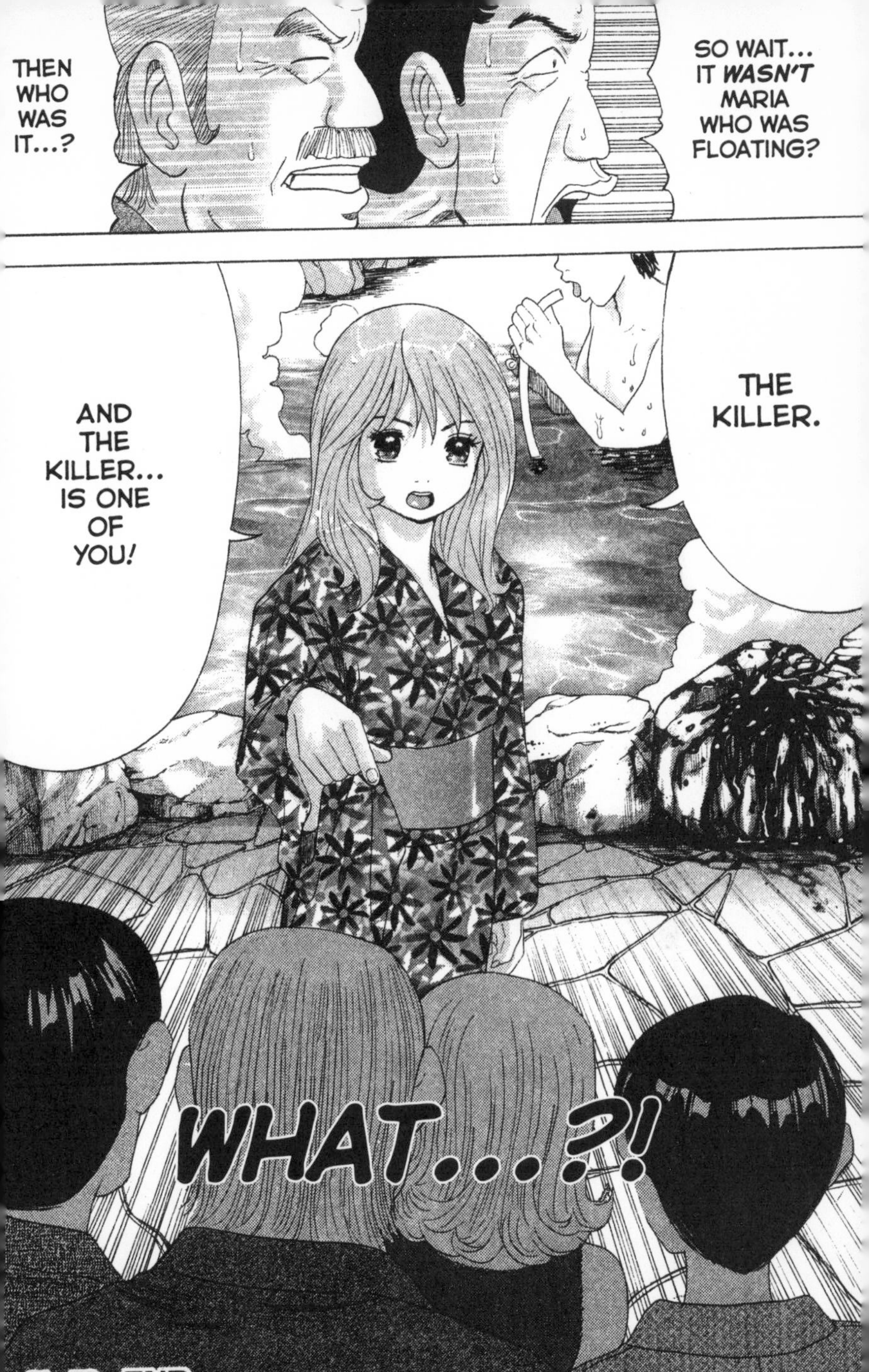
SO WAIT... IT *WASN'T* MARIA WHO WAS FLOATING?
THEN WHO WAS IT...?
THE KILLER.
AND THE KILLER... IS ONE OF YOU!
WHAT...?!

file 73 END

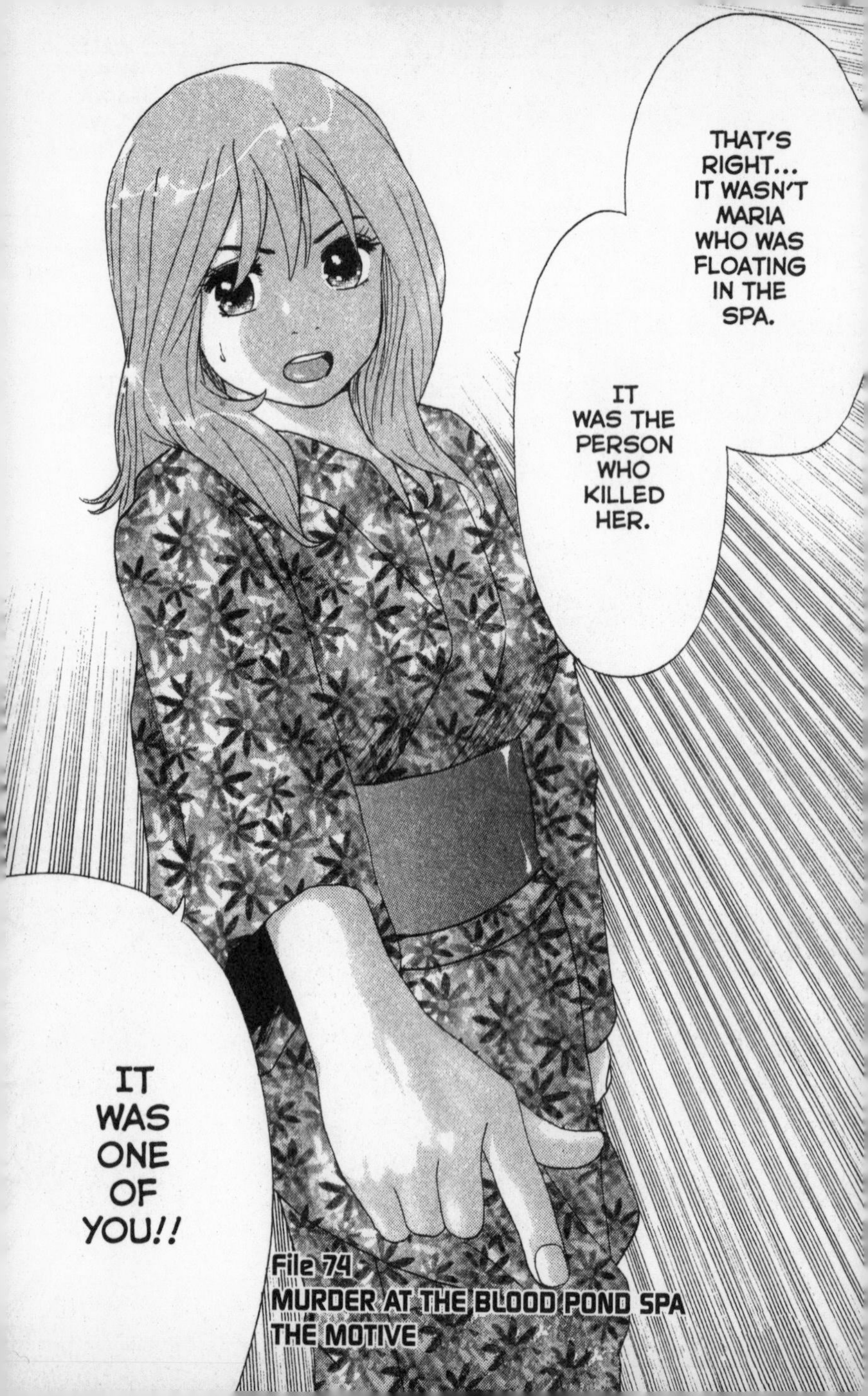
THAT'S RIGHT... IT WASN'T MARIA WHO WAS FLOATING IN THE SPA.
IT WAS THE PERSON WHO KILLED HER.
IT WAS ONE OF YOU!!

File 74
MURDER AT THE BLOOD POND SPA
THE MOTIVE

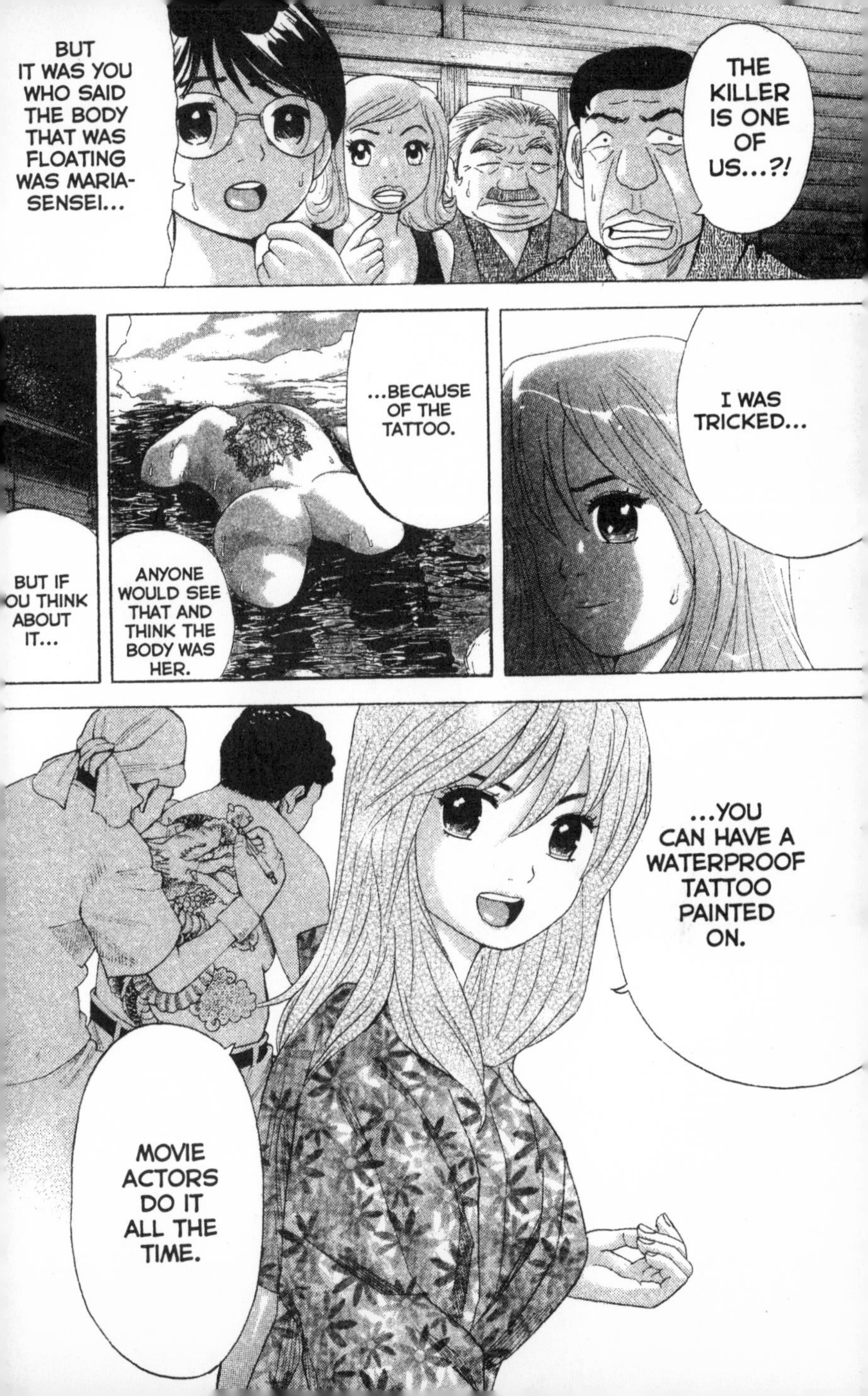
THE KILLER IS ONE OF US...?!
BUT IT WAS YOU WHO SAID THE BODY THAT WAS FLOATING WAS MARIA-SENSEI...
I WAS TRICKED...
...BECAUSE OF THE TATTOO.
ANYONE WOULD SEE THAT AND THINK THE BODY WAS HER.
BUT IF OU THINK ABOUT IT...
...YOU CAN HAVE A WATERPROOF TATTOO PAINTED ON.
MOVIE ACTORS DO IT ALL THE TIME.

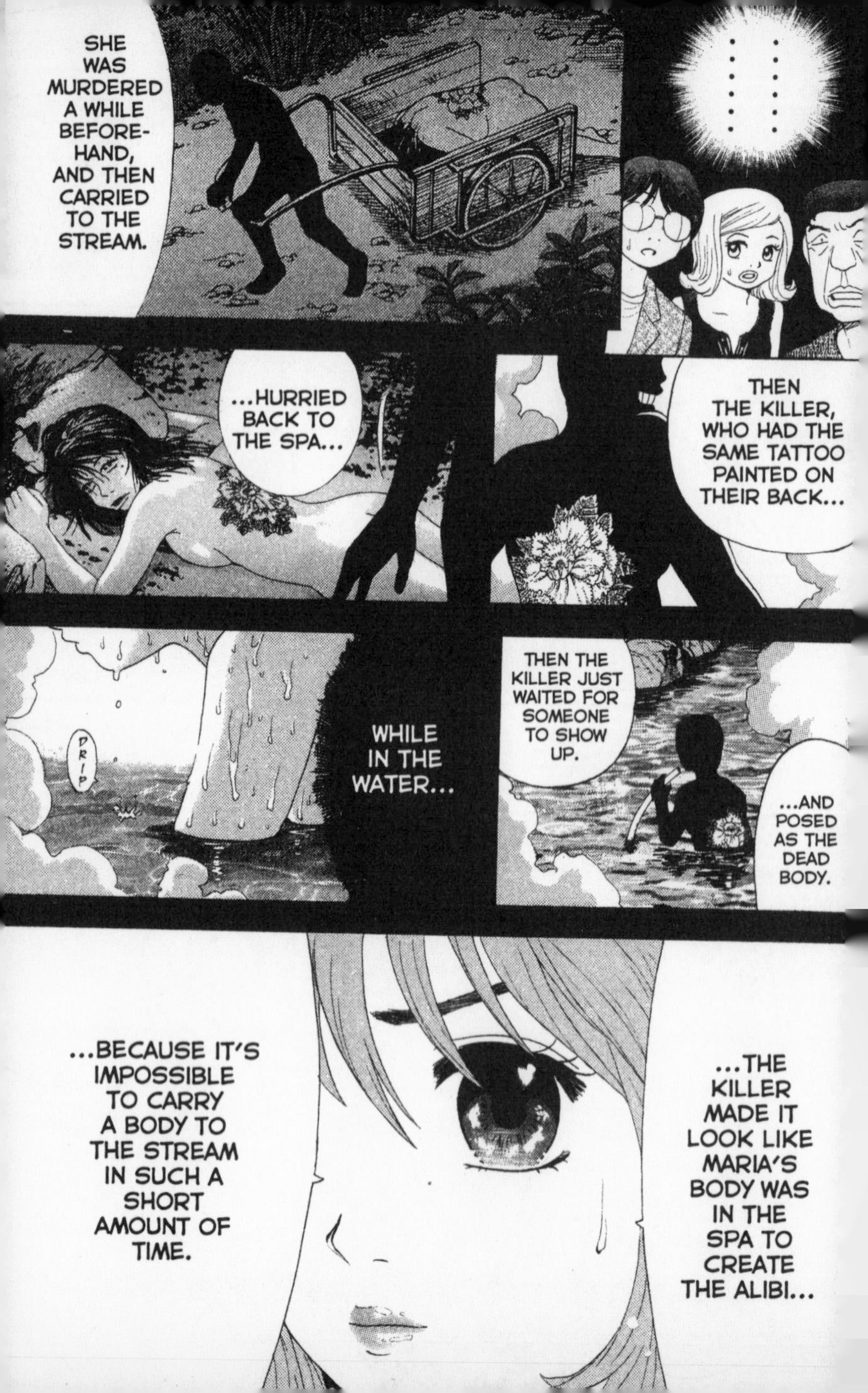
......
SHE WAS MURDERED A WHILE BEFORE-HAND, AND THEN CARRIED TO THE STREAM.
THEN THE KILLER, WHO HAD THE SAME TATTOO PAINTED ON THEIR BACK...
...HURRIED BACK TO THE SPA...
WHILE IN THE WATER...
...AND POSED AS THE DEAD BODY.
THEN THE KILLER JUST WAITED FOR SOMEONE TO SHOW UP.
DRIP
...THE KILLER MADE IT LOOK LIKE MARIA'S BODY WAS IN THE SPA TO CREATE THE ALIBI...
...BECAUSE IT'S IMPOSSIBLE TO CARRY A BODY TO THE STREAM IN SUCH A SHORT AMOUNT OF TIME.

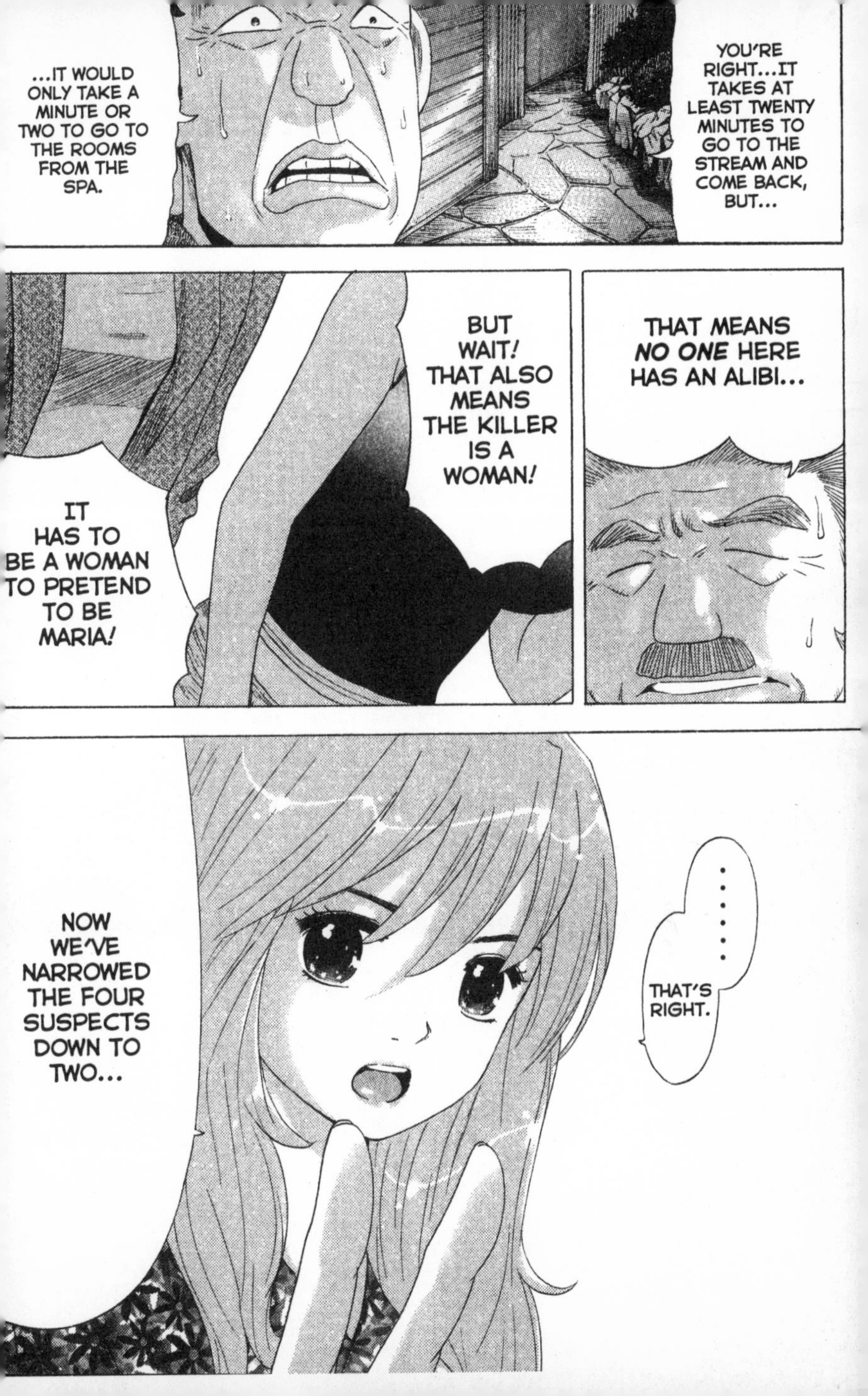
YOU'RE RIGHT...IT TAKES AT LEAST TWENTY MINUTES TO GO TO THE STREAM AND COME BACK, BUT...
...IT WOULD ONLY TAKE A MINUTE OR TWO TO GO TO THE ROOMS FROM THE SPA.
THAT MEANS *NO ONE* HERE HAS AN ALIBI...
BUT WAIT! THAT ALSO MEANS THE KILLER IS A WOMAN!
IT HAS TO BE A WOMAN TO PRETEND TO BE MARIA!
...... THAT'S RIGHT.
NOW WE'VE NARROWED THE FOUR SUSPECTS DOWN TO TWO...

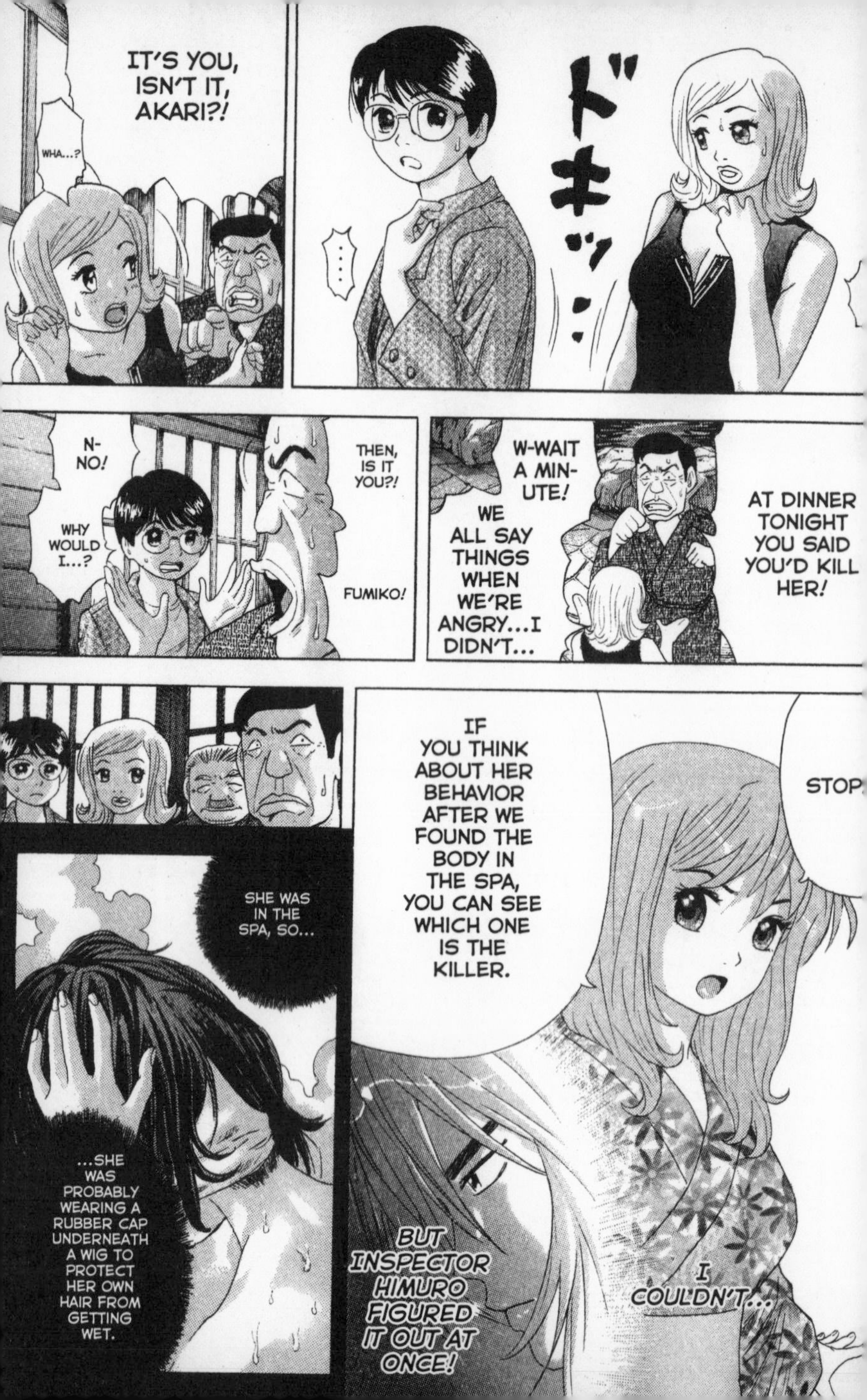
ドキッ
....
IT'S YOU, ISN'T IT, AKARI?!
WHA...?
AT DINNER TONIGHT YOU SAID YOU'D KILL HER!
W-WAIT A MIN-UTE!
WE ALL SAY THINGS WHEN WE'RE ANGRY...I DIDN'T...
THEN, IS IT YOU?!
FUMIKO!
N-NO!
WHY WOULD I...?
STOP
IF YOU THINK ABOUT HER BEHAVIOR AFTER WE FOUND THE BODY IN THE SPA, YOU CAN SEE WHICH ONE IS THE KILLER.
I COULDN'T...
BUT INSPECTOR HIMURO FIGURED IT OUT AT ONCE!
SHE WAS IN THE SPA, SO...
...SHE WAS PROBABLY WEARING A RUBBER CAP UNDERNEATH A WIG TO PROTECT HER OWN HAIR FROM GETTING WET.

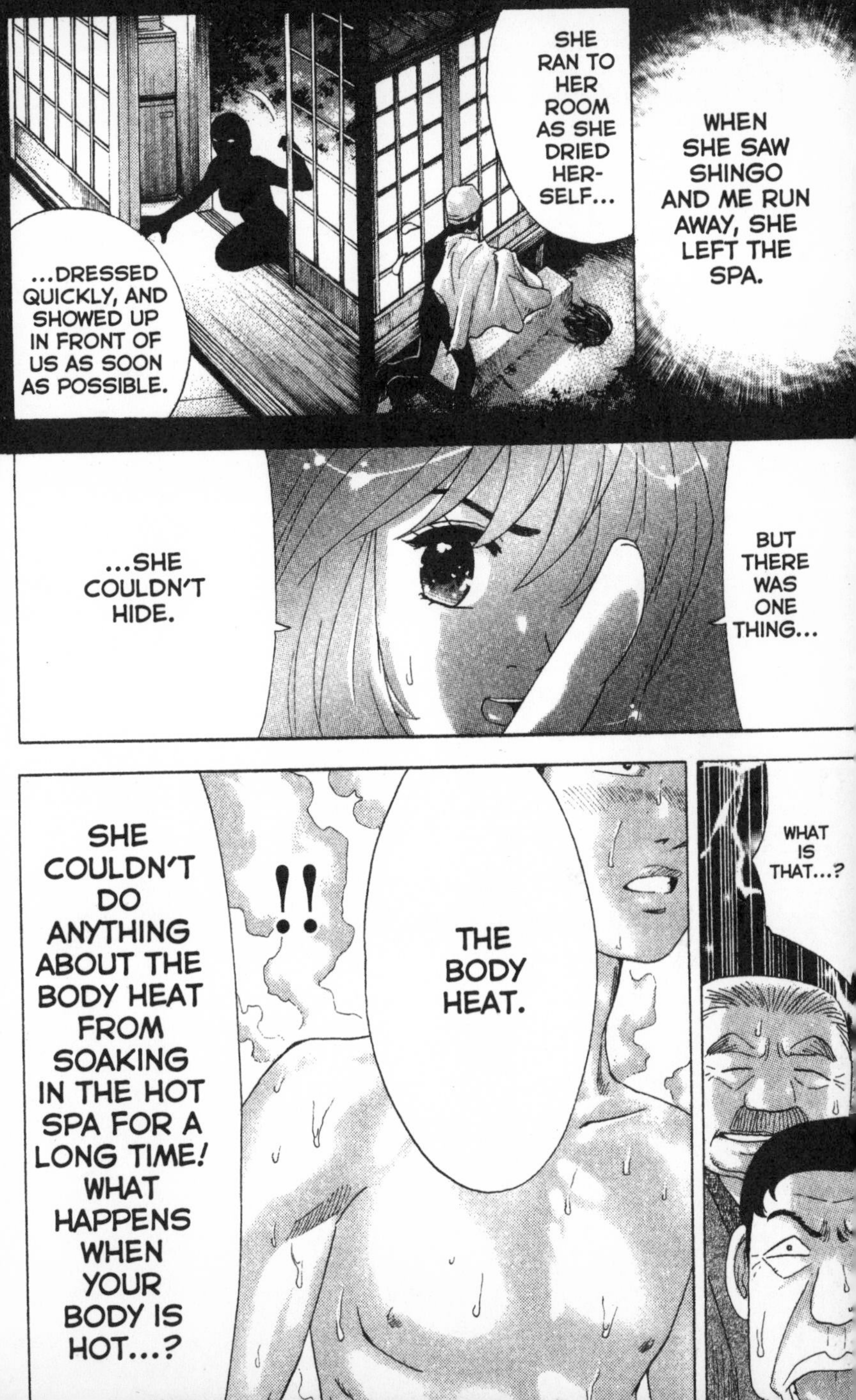
WHEN SHE SAW SHINGO AND ME RUN AWAY, SHE LEFT THE SPA.
SHE RAN TO HER ROOM AS SHE DRIED HER-SELF...
...DRESSED QUICKLY, AND SHOWED UP IN FRONT OF US AS SOON AS POSSIBLE.
BUT THERE WAS ONE THING...
...SHE COULDN'T HIDE.
WHAT IS THAT...?
THE BODY HEAT.
!!
SHE COULDN'T DO ANYTHING ABOUT THE BODY HEAT FROM SOAKING IN THE HOT SPA FOR A LONG TIME! WHAT HAPPENS WHEN YOUR BODY IS HOT...?

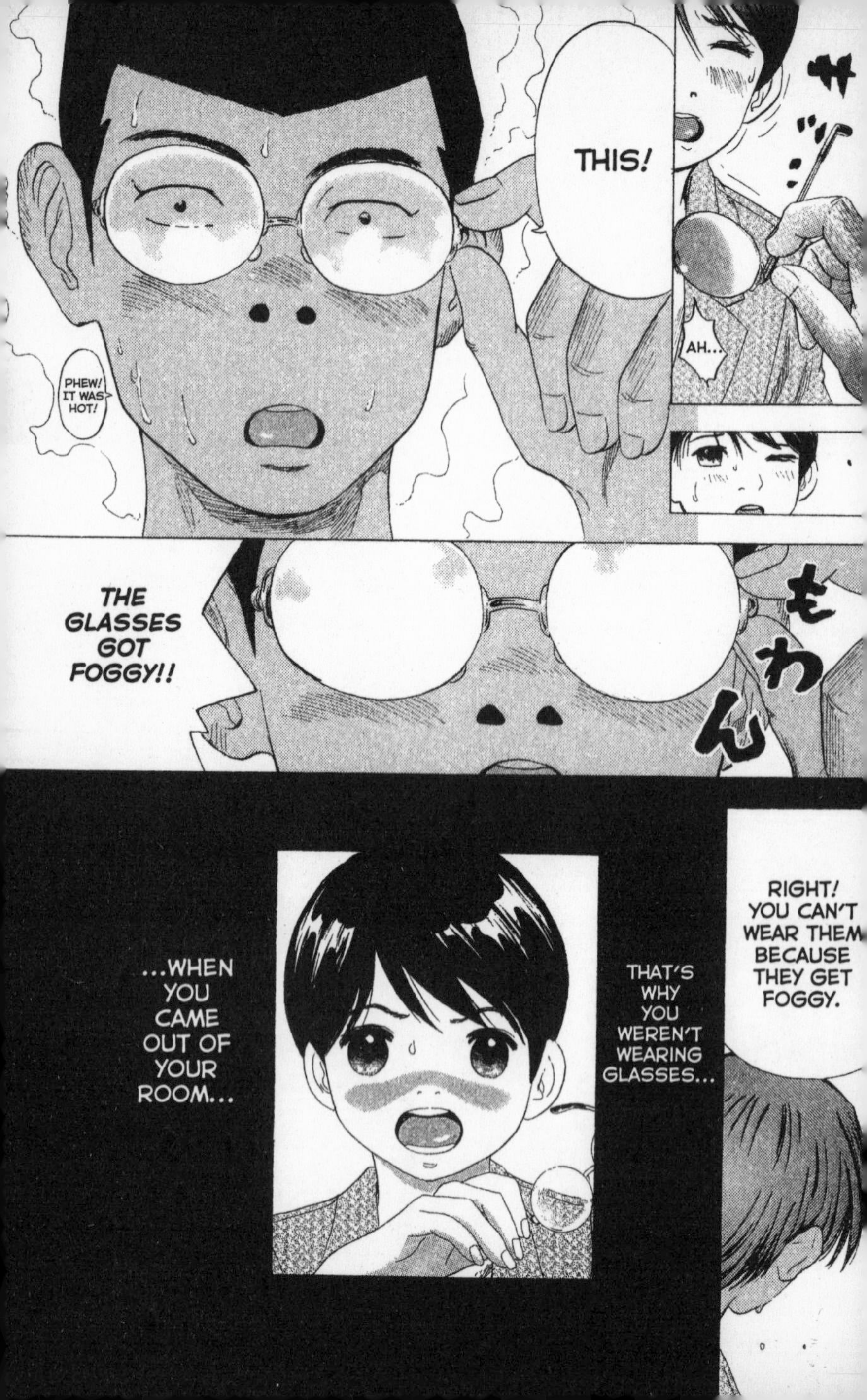
AH...
THIS!
PHEW! IT WAS HOT!
もわん
THE GLASSES GOT FOGGY!!
RIGHT! YOU CAN'T WEAR THEM BECAUSE THEY GET FOGGY.
THAT'S WHY YOU WEREN'T WEARING GLASSES...
...WHEN YOU CAME OUT OF YOUR ROOM...

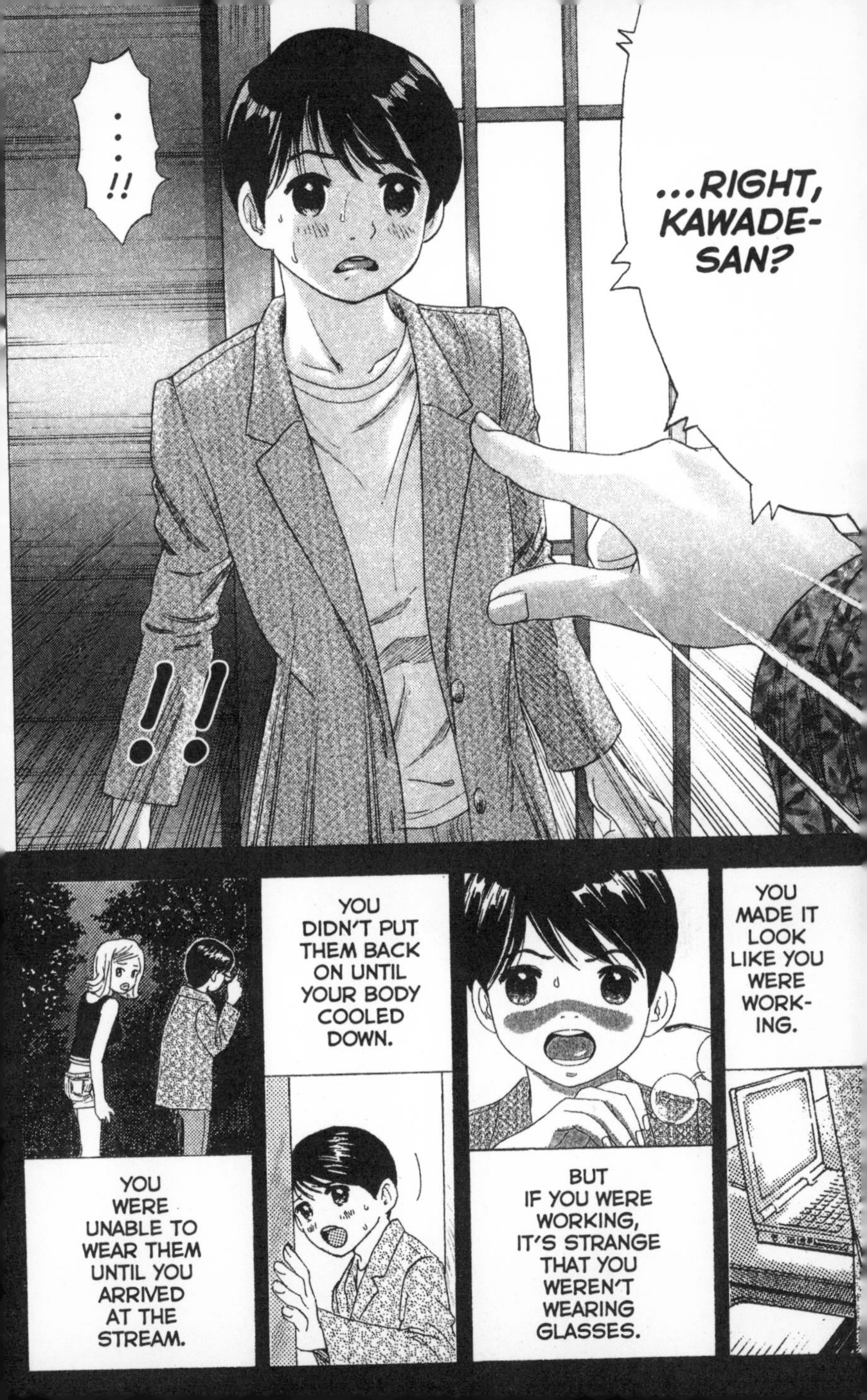
...RIGHT, KAWADE-SAN?
....!!
!!
YOU MADE IT LOOK LIKE YOU WERE WORK-ING.
BUT IF YOU WERE WORKING, IT'S STRANGE THAT YOU WEREN'T WEARING GLASSES.
YOU DIDN'T PUT THEM BACK ON UNTIL YOUR BODY COOLED DOWN.
YOU WERE UNABLE TO WEAR THEM UNTIL YOU ARRIVED AT THE STREAM.

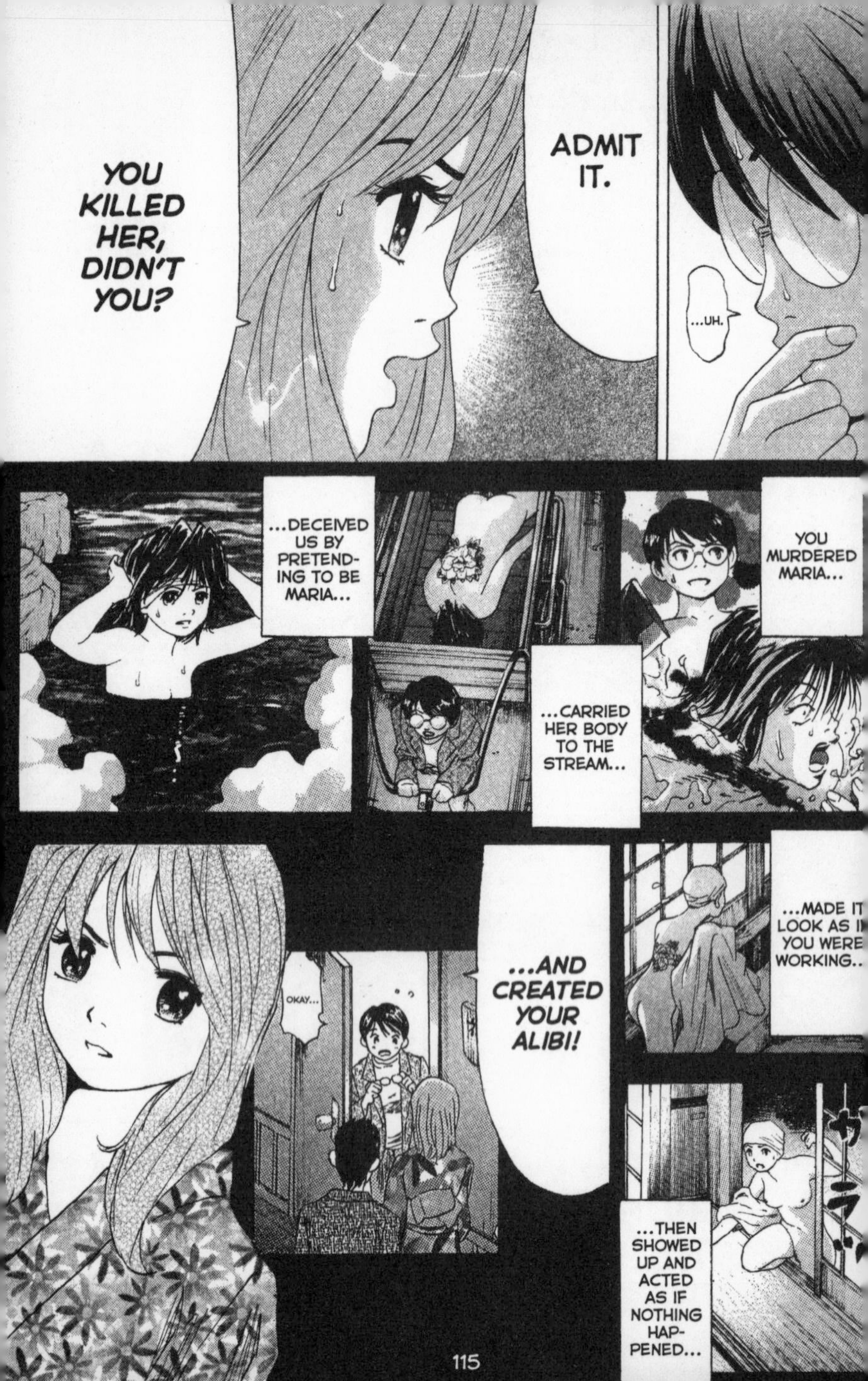
...UH.
ADMIT IT.
YOU KILLED HER, DIDN'T YOU?
YOU MURDERED MARIA...
...CARRIED HER BODY TO THE STREAM...
...DECEIVED US BY PRETENDING TO BE MARIA...
...MADE IT LOOK AS I YOU WERE WORKING..
...THEN SHOWED UP AND ACTED AS IF NOTHING HAPPENED...
...AND CREATED YOUR ALIBI!
OKAY...

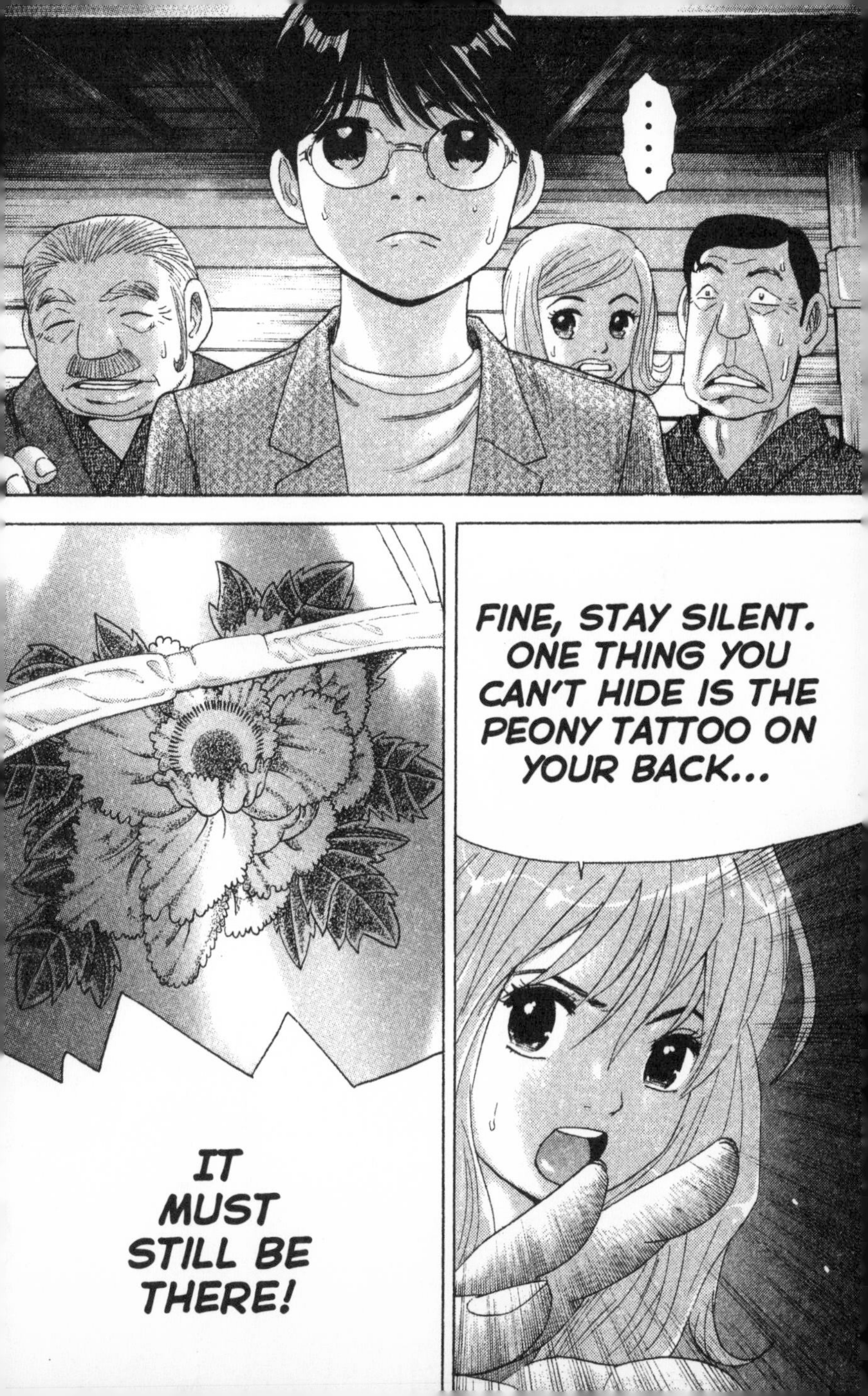
....!
FINE, STAY SILENT. ONE THING YOU CAN'T HIDE IS THE PEONY TATTOO ON YOUR BACK...
IT MUST STILL BE THERE!

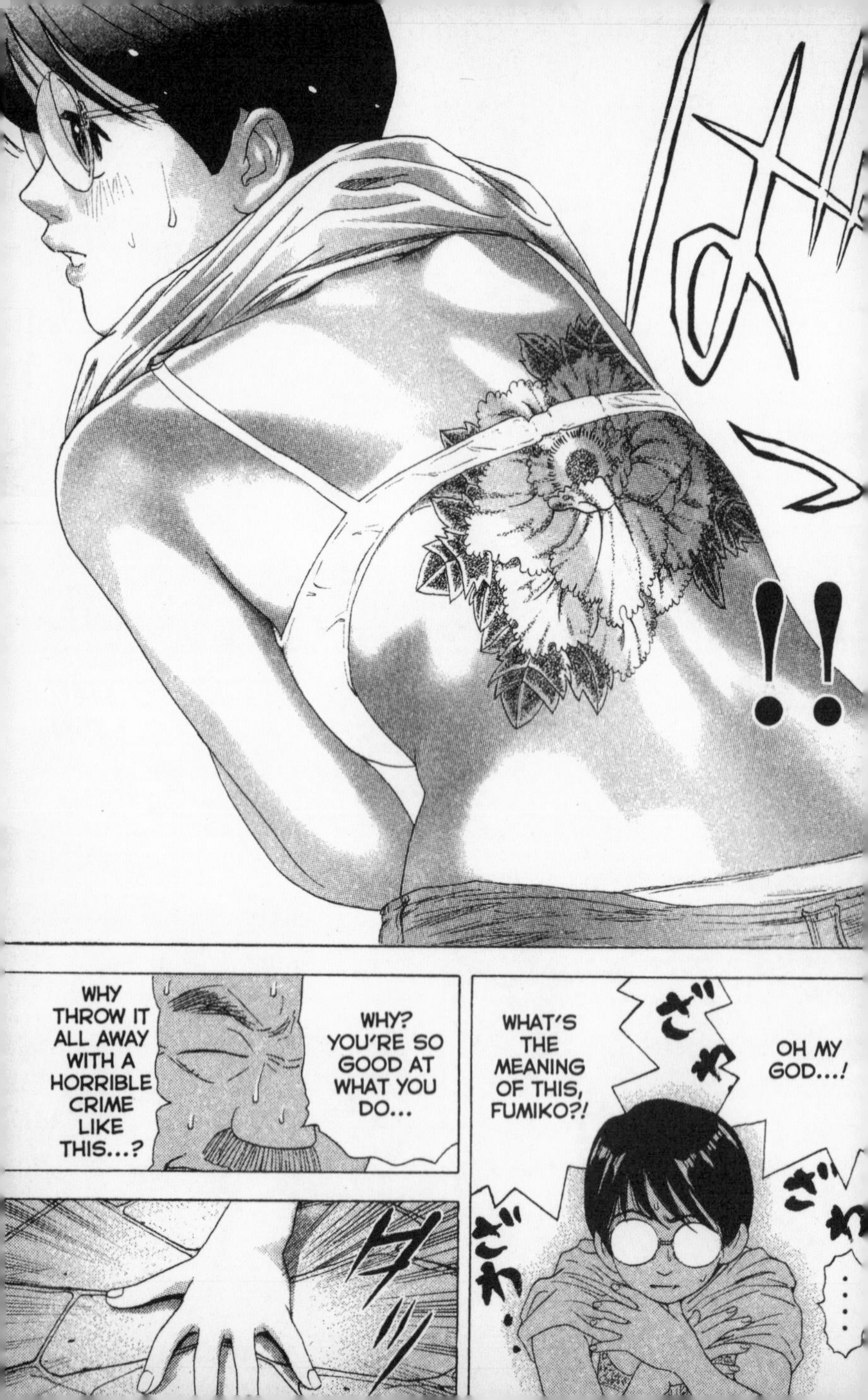

!!
OH MY GOD...!
WHAT'S THE MEANING OF THIS, FUMIKO?!
ざわ
ざわ
ざわ…
……
WHY? YOU'RE SO GOOD AT WHAT YOU DO...
WHY THROW IT ALL AWAY WITH A HORRIBLE CRIME LIKE THIS...?

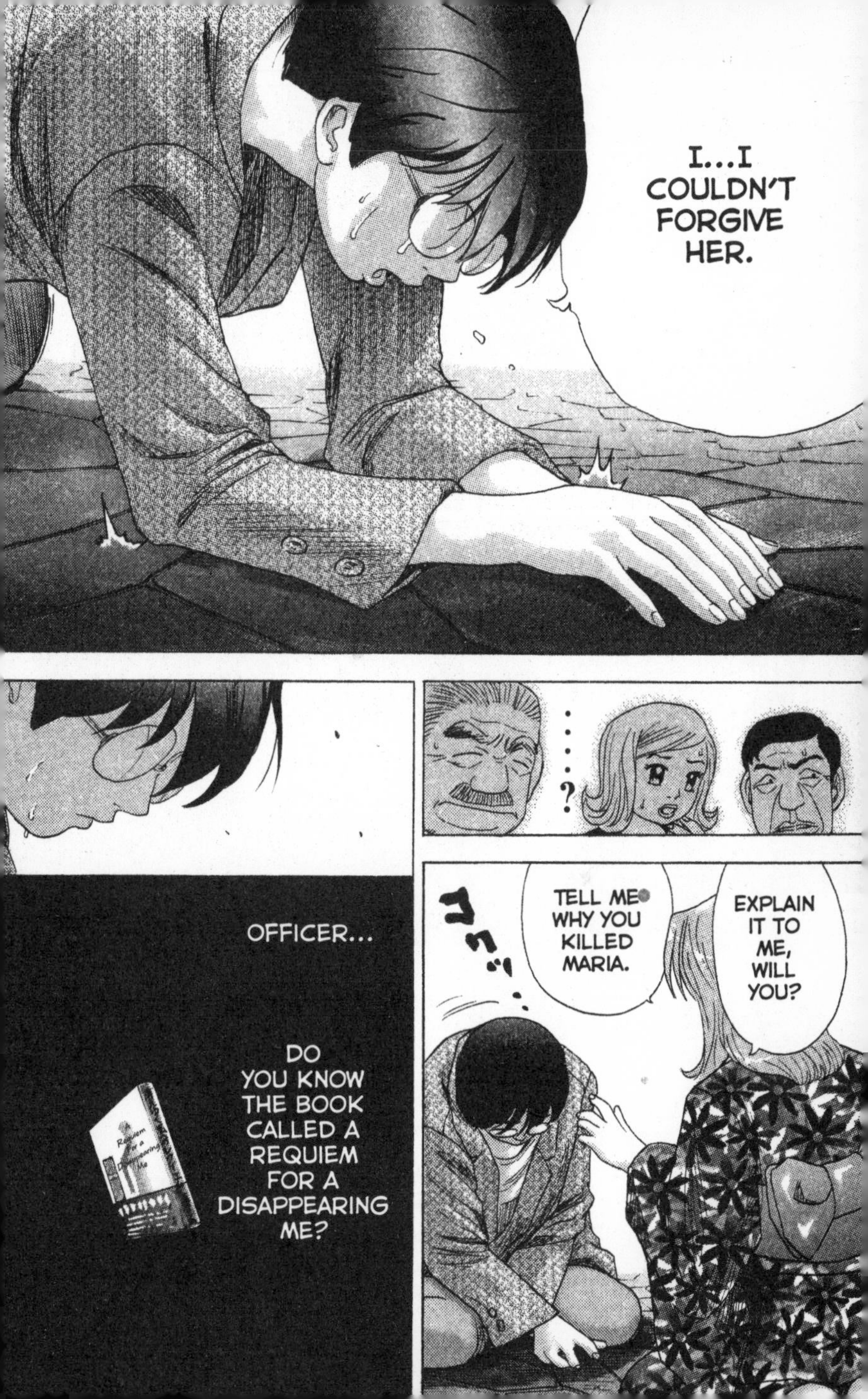
I...I COULDN'T FORGIVE HER.
....?
EXPLAIN IT TO ME, WILL YOU?
TELL ME WHY YOU KILLED MARIA.
OFFICER...
DO YOU KNOW THE BOOK CALLED A REQUIEM FOR A DISAPPEARING ME?

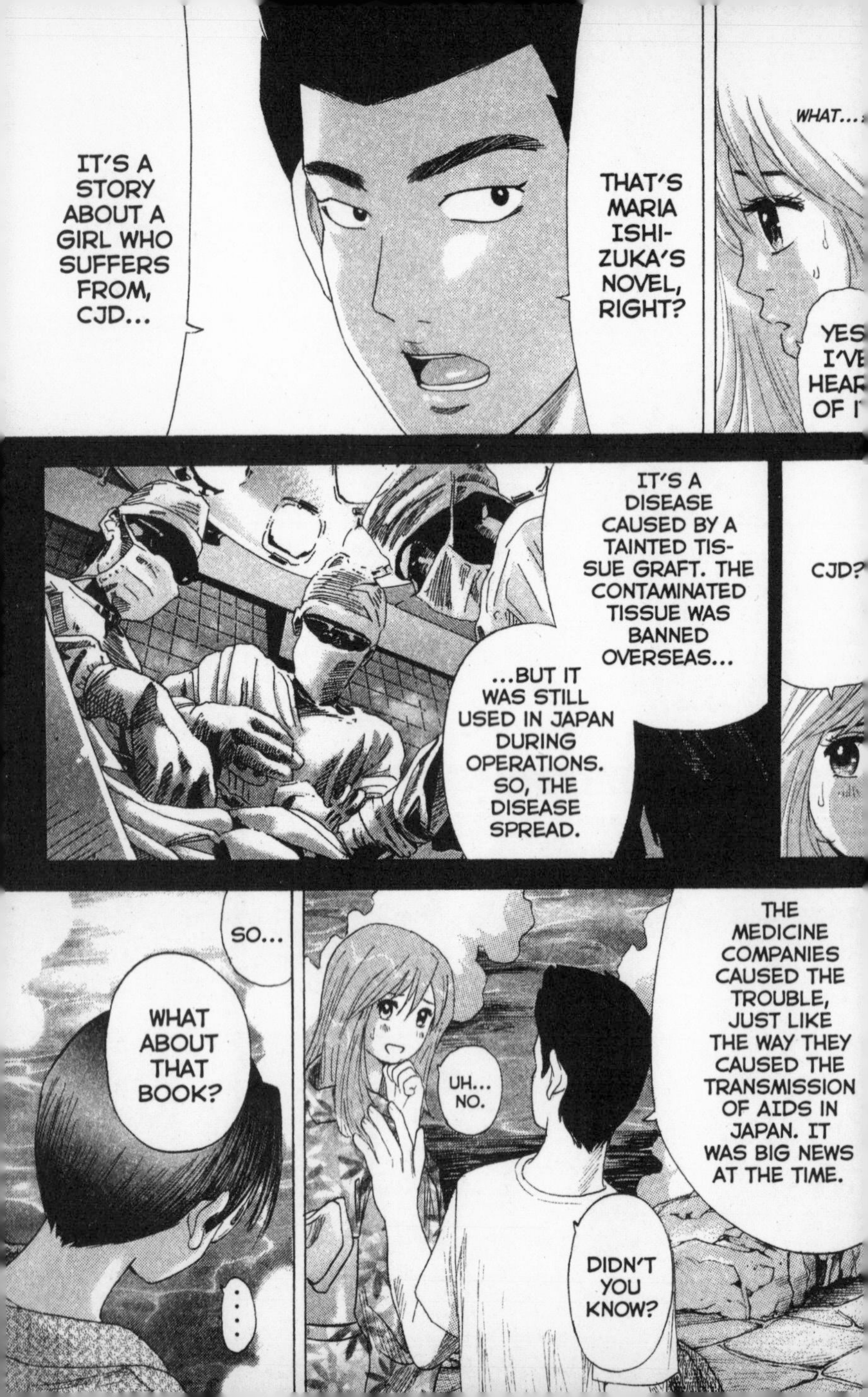
WHAT...
YES I'VE HEAR OF I
THAT'S MARIA ISHI-ZUKA'S NOVEL, RIGHT?
IT'S A STORY ABOUT A GIRL WHO SUFFERS FROM, CJD...
CJD?
IT'S A DISEASE CAUSED BY A TAINTED TIS-SUE GRAFT. THE CONTAMINATED TISSUE WAS BANNED OVERSEAS...
...BUT IT WAS STILL USED IN JAPAN DURING OPERATIONS. SO, THE DISEASE SPREAD.
THE MEDICINE COMPANIES CAUSED THE TROUBLE, JUST LIKE THE WAY THEY CAUSED THE TRANSMISSION OF AIDS IN JAPAN. IT WAS BIG NEWS AT THE TIME.
DIDN'T YOU KNOW?
UH... NO.
SO...
WHAT ABOUT THAT BOOK?
...

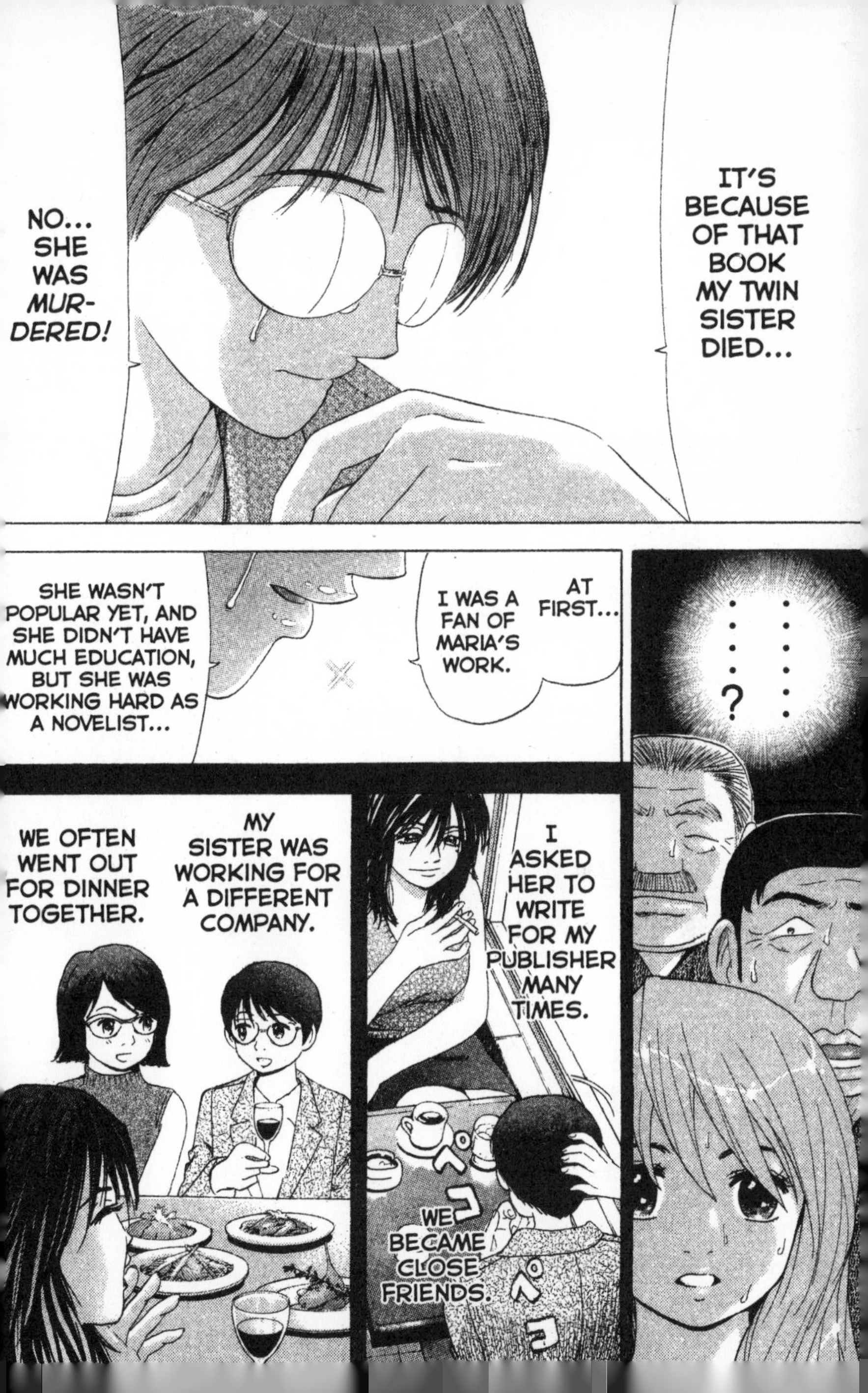
IT'S BECAUSE OF THAT BOOK MY TWIN SISTER DIED...
NO... SHE WAS *MURDERED!*
......
......?
AT FIRST...
I WAS A FAN OF MARIA'S WORK.
SHE WASN'T POPULAR YET, AND SHE DIDN'T HAVE MUCH EDUCATION, BUT SHE WAS WORKING HARD AS A NOVELIST...
I ASKED HER TO WRITE FOR MY PUBLISHER MANY TIMES.
ペコ
WE BECAME CLOSE FRIENDS.
ペコ
MY SISTER WAS WORKING FOR A DIFFERENT COMPANY.
WE OFTEN WENT OUT FOR DINNER TOGETHER.

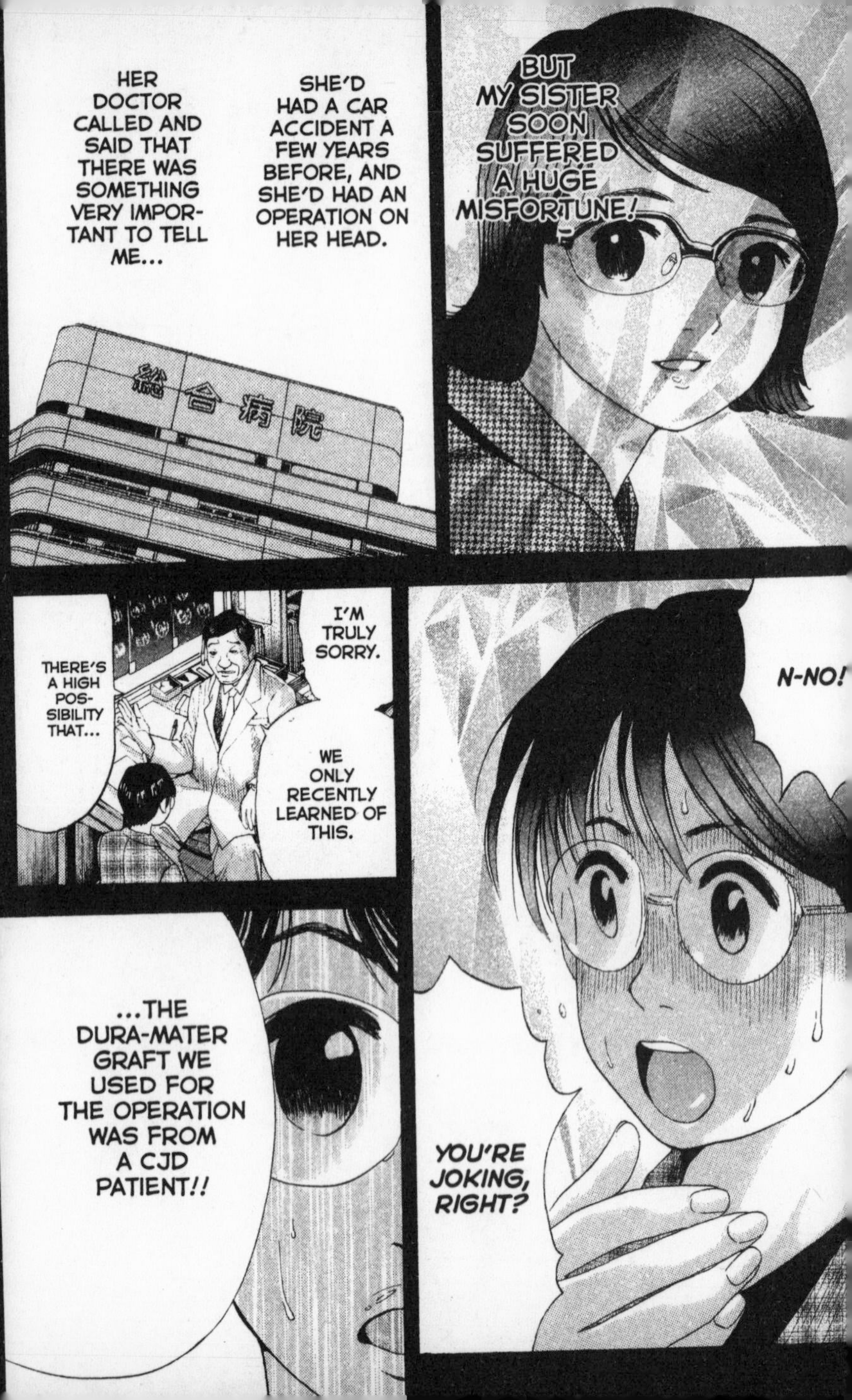
BUT MY SISTER SOON SUFFERED A HUGE MISFORTUNE!
SHE'D HAD A CAR ACCIDENT A FEW YEARS BEFORE, AND SHE'D HAD AN OPERATION ON HER HEAD.
HER DOCTOR CALLED AND SAID THAT THERE WAS SOMETHING VERY IMPOR-TANT TO TELL ME...
総合病院
N-NO!
YOU'RE JOKING, RIGHT?
I'M TRULY SORRY.
WE ONLY RECENTLY LEARNED OF THIS.
THERE'S A HIGH POS-SIBILITY THAT...
...THE DURA-MATER GRAFT WE USED FOR THE OPERATION WAS FROM A CJD PATIENT!!

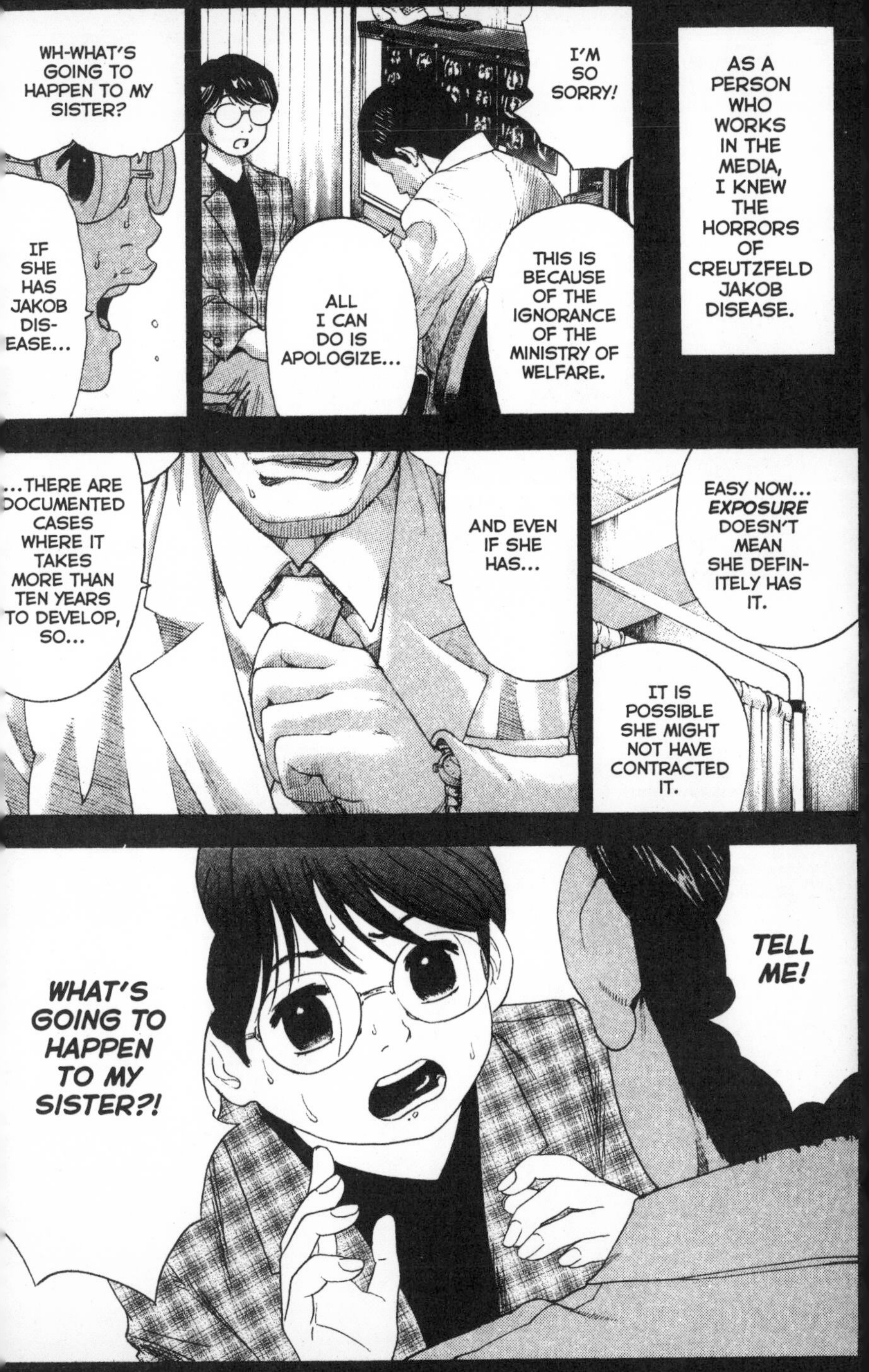
AS A PERSON WHO WORKS IN THE MEDIA, I KNEW THE HORRORS OF CREUTZFELD JAKOB DISEASE.
I'M SO SORRY!
THIS IS BECAUSE OF THE IGNORANCE OF THE MINISTRY OF WELFARE.
ALL I CAN DO IS APOLOGIZE...
WH-WHAT'S GOING TO HAPPEN TO MY SISTER?
IF SHE HAS JAKOB DISEASE...
EASY NOW... *EXPOSURE* DOESN'T MEAN SHE DEFINITELY HAS IT.
IT IS POSSIBLE SHE MIGHT NOT HAVE CONTRACTED IT.
AND EVEN IF SHE HAS...
...THERE ARE DOCUMENTED CASES WHERE IT TAKES MORE THAN TEN YEARS TO DEVELOP, SO...
TELL ME!
WHAT'S GOING TO HAPPEN TO MY SISTER?!

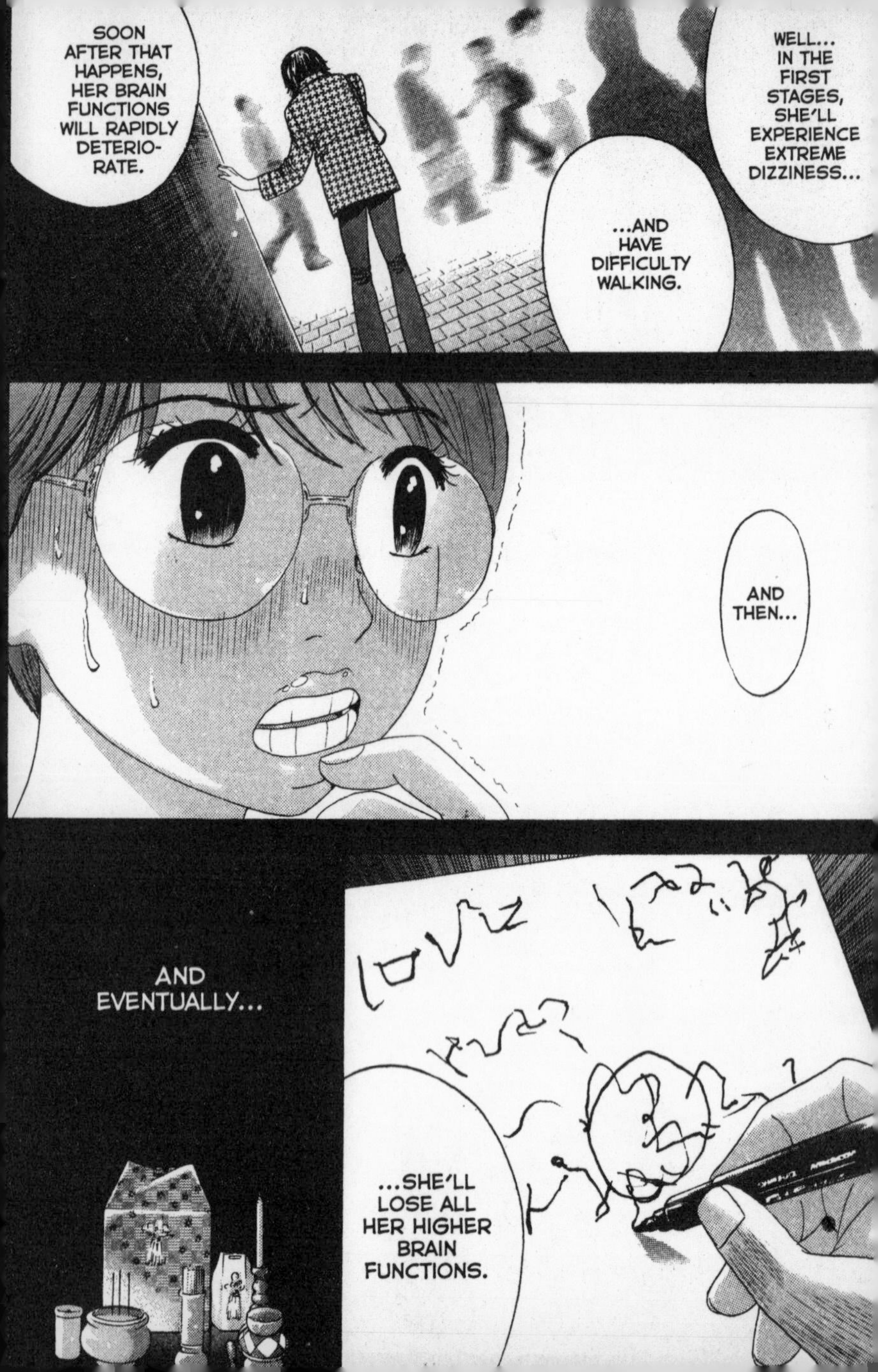
WELL... IN THE FIRST STAGES, SHE'LL EXPERIENCE EXTREME DIZZINESS...
...AND HAVE DIFFICULTY WALKING.
SOON AFTER THAT HAPPENS, HER BRAIN FUNCTIONS WILL RAPIDLY DETERIO-RATE.
AND THEN...
AND EVENTUALLY...
...SHE'LL LOSE ALL HER HIGHER BRAIN FUNCTIONS.

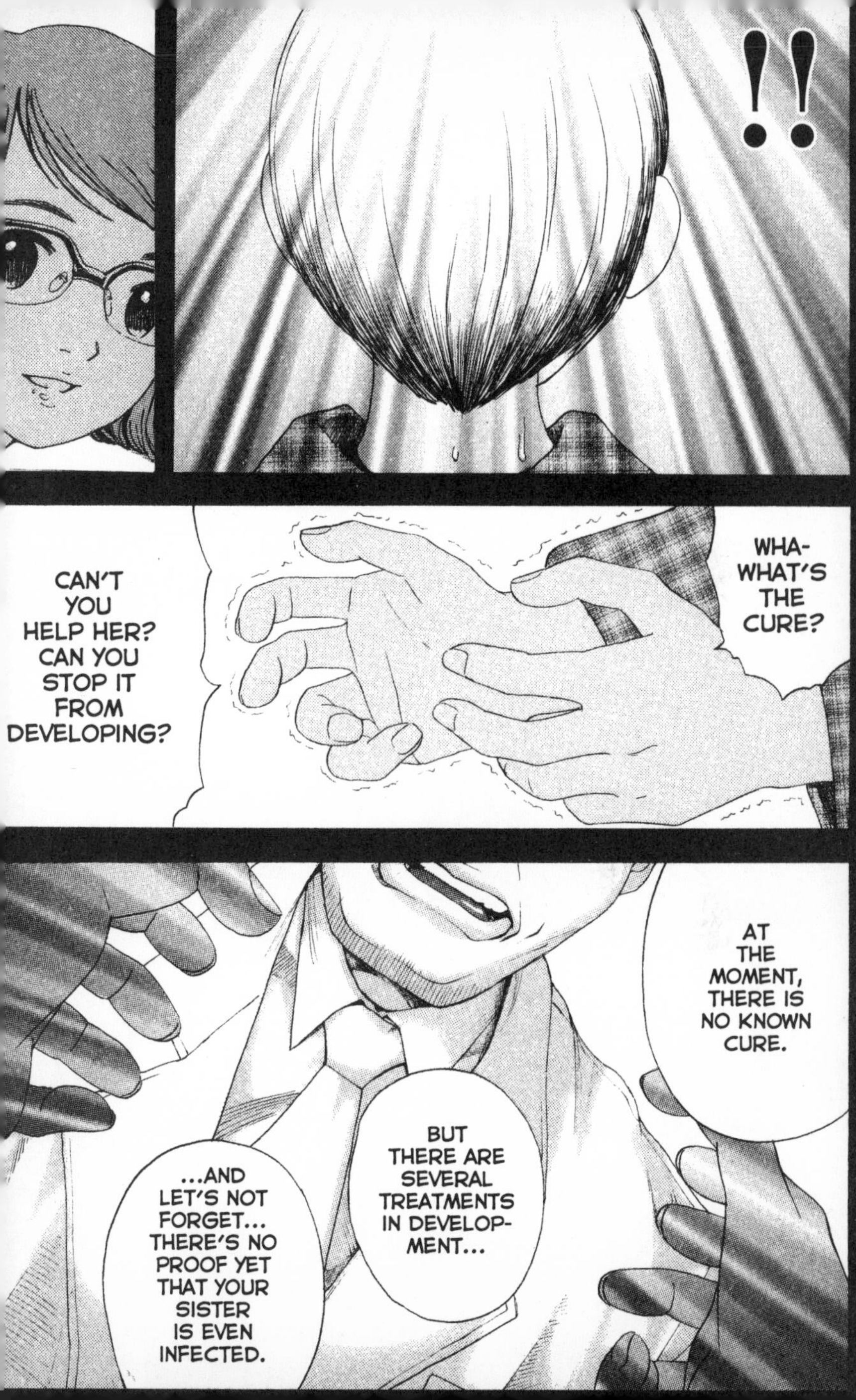
!!
WHA-WHAT'S THE CURE?
CAN'T YOU HELP HER? CAN YOU STOP IT FROM DEVELOPING?
AT THE MOMENT, THERE IS NO KNOWN CURE.
BUT THERE ARE SEVERAL TREATMENTS IN DEVELOP-MENT...
...AND LET'S NOT FORGET... THERE'S NO PROOF YET THAT YOUR SISTER IS EVEN INFECTED.

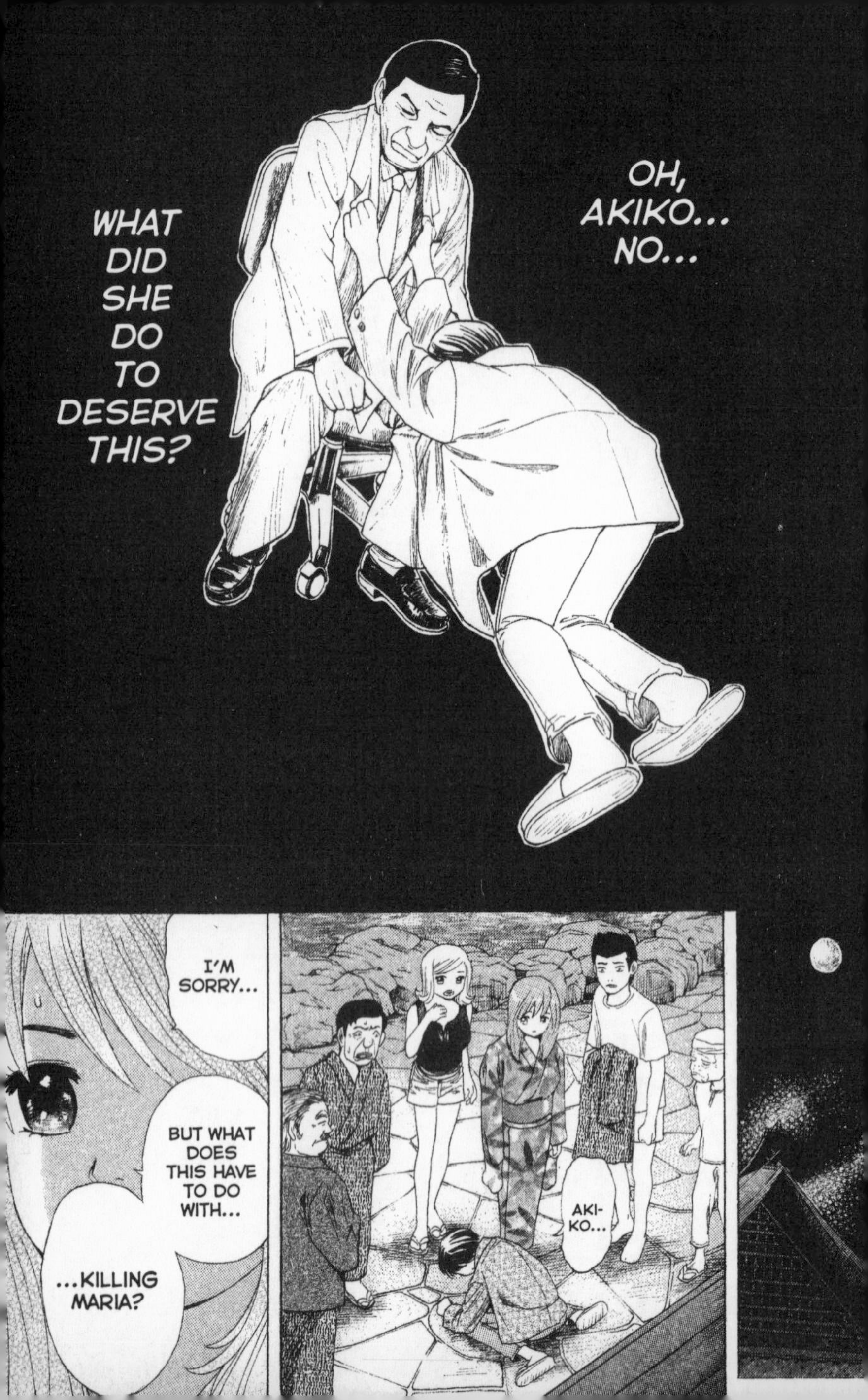
OH, AKIKO... NO...
WHAT DID SHE DO TO DESERVE THIS?
AKI-KO...
I'M SORRY...
BUT WHAT DOES THIS HAVE TO DO WITH...
...KILLING MARIA?

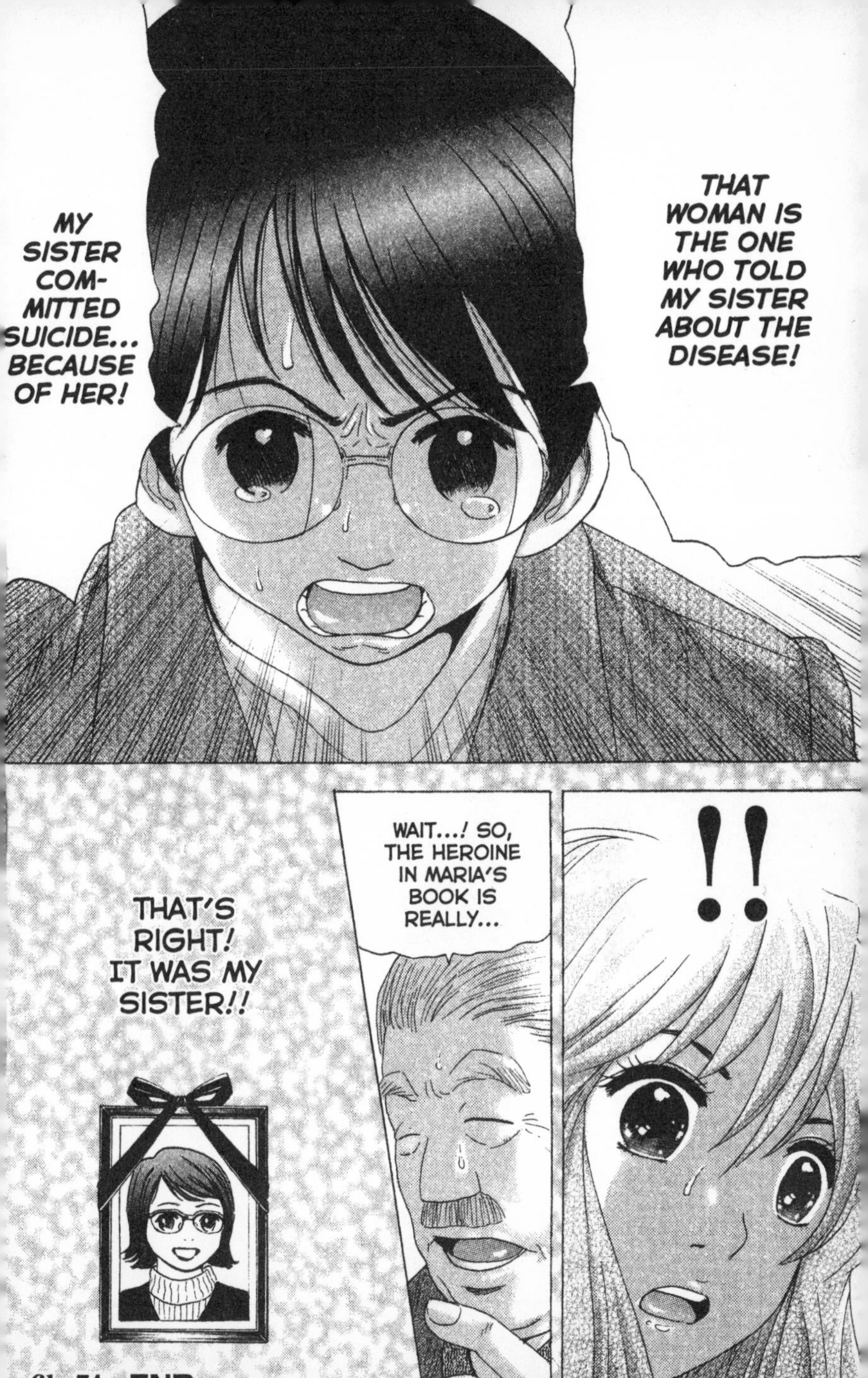
THAT WOMAN IS THE ONE WHO TOLD MY SISTER ABOUT THE DISEASE!
MY SISTER COM-MITTED SUICIDE... BECAUSE OF HER!
!!
WAIT...! SO, THE HEROINE IN MARIA'S BOOK IS REALLY...
THAT'S RIGHT! IT WAS MY SISTER!!

file.74 END

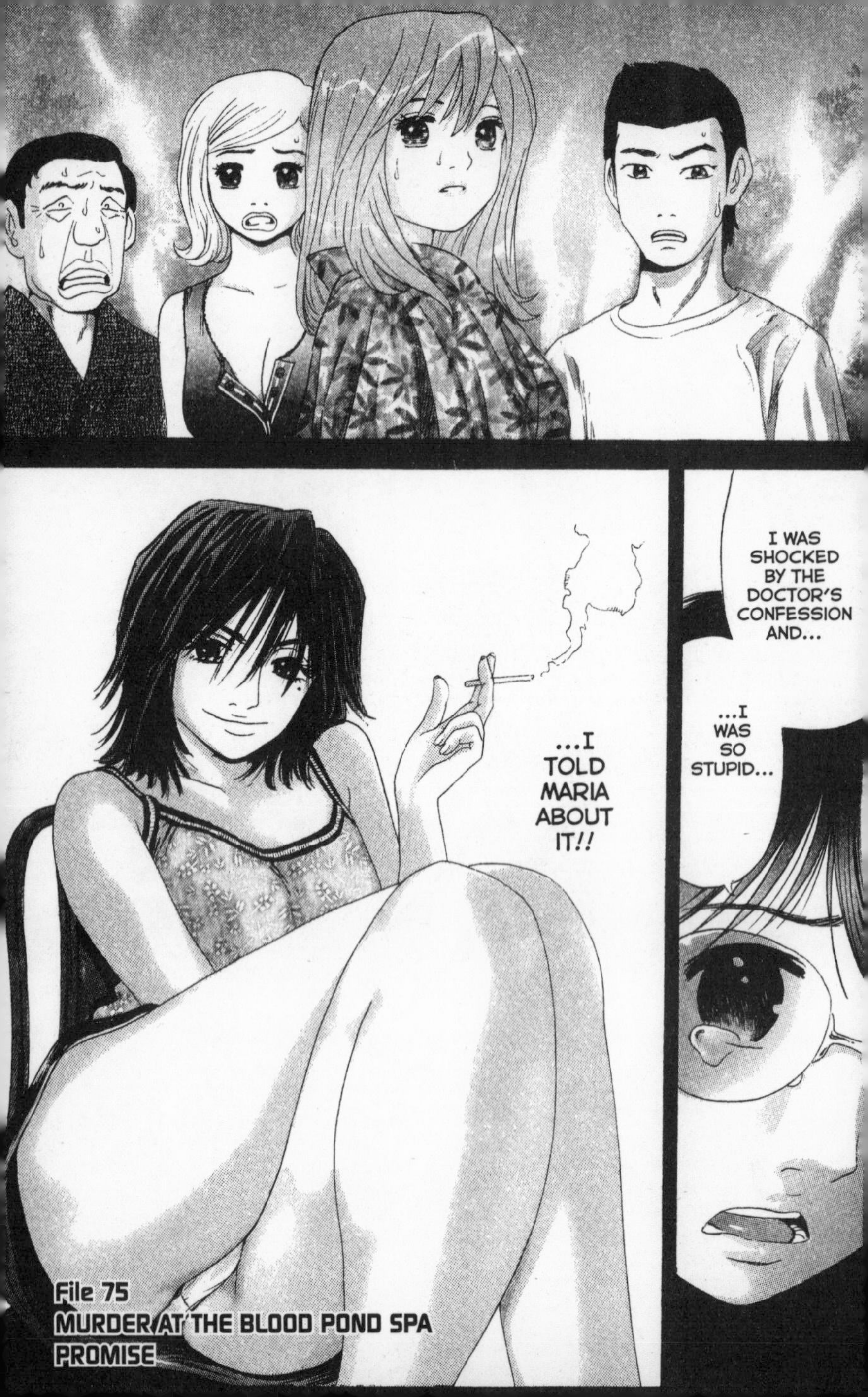
I WAS SHOCKED BY THE DOCTOR'S CONFESSION AND...
...I WAS SO STUPID...
...I TOLD MARIA ABOUT IT!!
File 75
MURDER AT THE BLOOD POND SPA
PROMISE

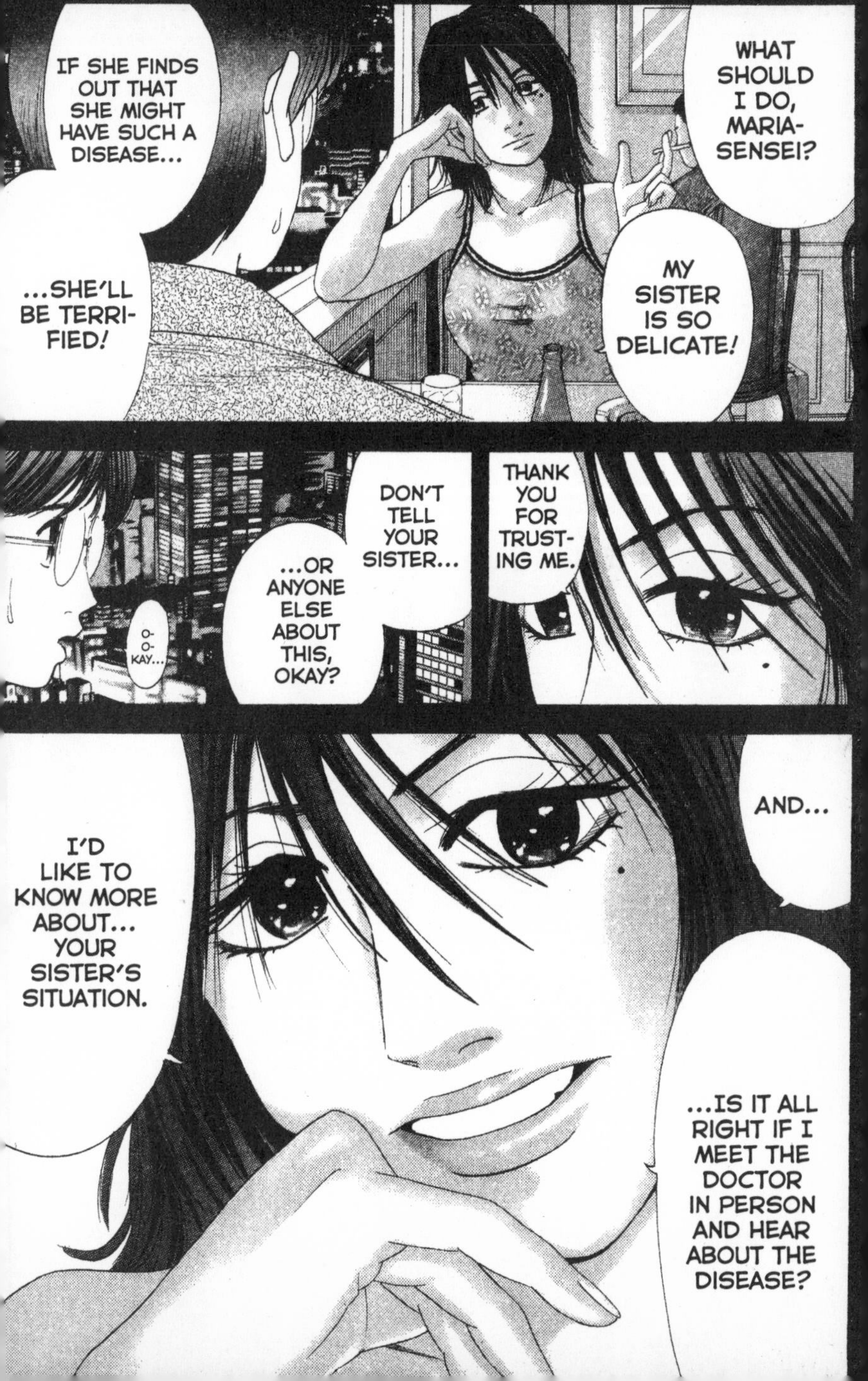
WHAT SHOULD I DO, MARIA-SENSEI?
MY SISTER IS SO DELICATE!
IF SHE FINDS OUT THAT SHE MIGHT HAVE SUCH A DISEASE...
...SHE'LL BE TERRI-FIED!
THANK YOU FOR TRUST-ING ME.
DON'T TELL YOUR SISTER...
...OR ANYONE ELSE ABOUT THIS, OKAY?
O-O-KAY...
AND...
I'D LIKE TO KNOW MORE ABOUT... YOUR SISTER'S SITUATION.
...IS IT ALL RIGHT IF I MEET THE DOCTOR IN PERSON AND HEAR ABOUT THE DISEASE?

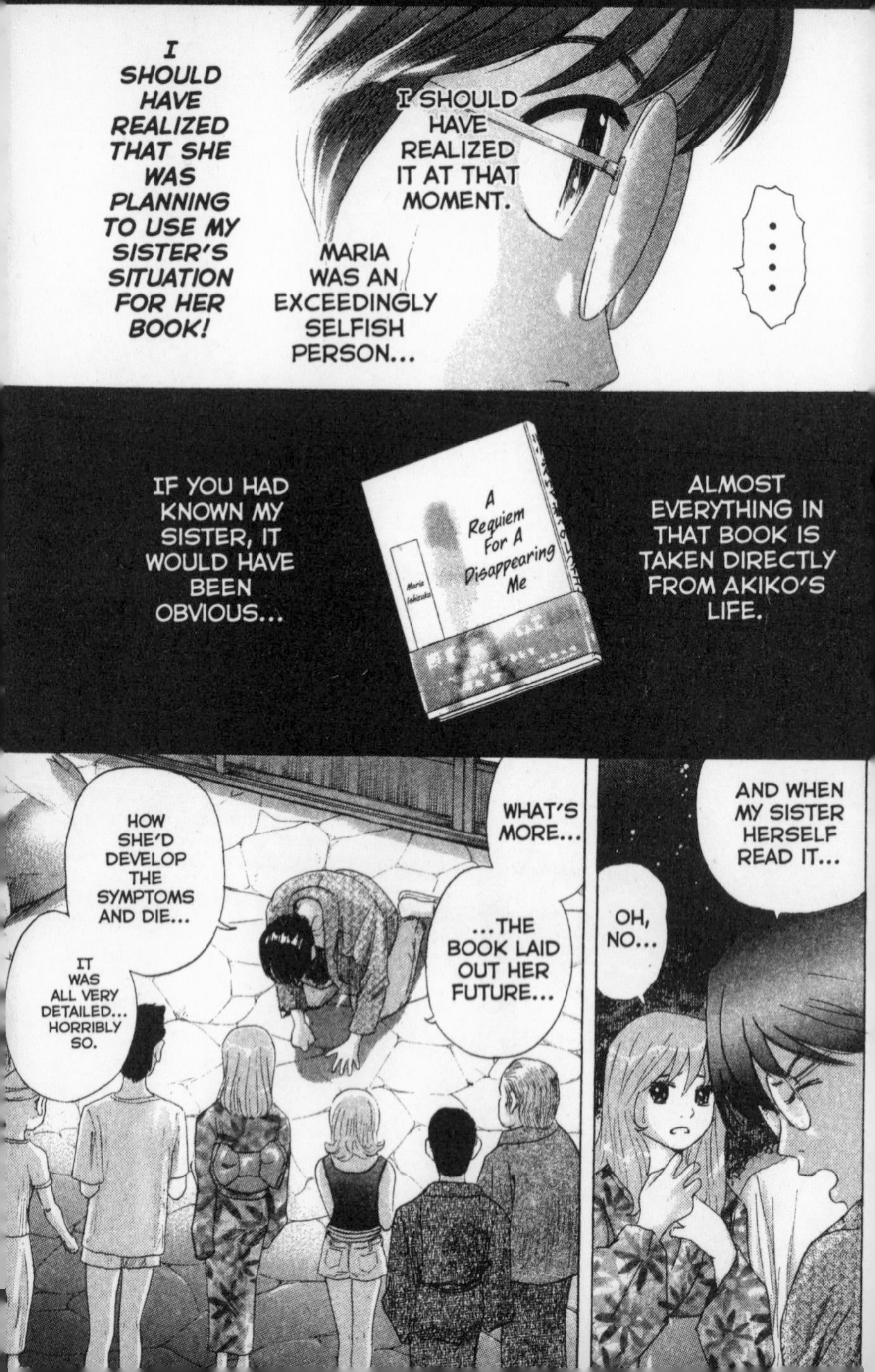
....
I SHOULD HAVE REALIZED IT AT THAT MOMENT.
MARIA WAS AN EXCEEDINGLY SELFISH PERSON...
I SHOULD HAVE REALIZED THAT SHE WAS PLANNING TO USE MY SISTER'S SITUATION FOR HER BOOK!
ALMOST EVERYTHING IN THAT BOOK IS TAKEN DIRECTLY FROM AKIKO'S LIFE.
A Requiem For A Disappearing Me
IF YOU HAD KNOWN MY SISTER, IT WOULD HAVE BEEN OBVIOUS...
AND WHEN MY SISTER HERSELF READ IT...
OH, NO...
WHAT'S MORE...
...THE BOOK LAID OUT HER FUTURE...
HOW SHE'D DEVELOP THE SYMPTOMS AND DIE...
IT WAS ALL VERY DETAILED... HORRIBLY SO.

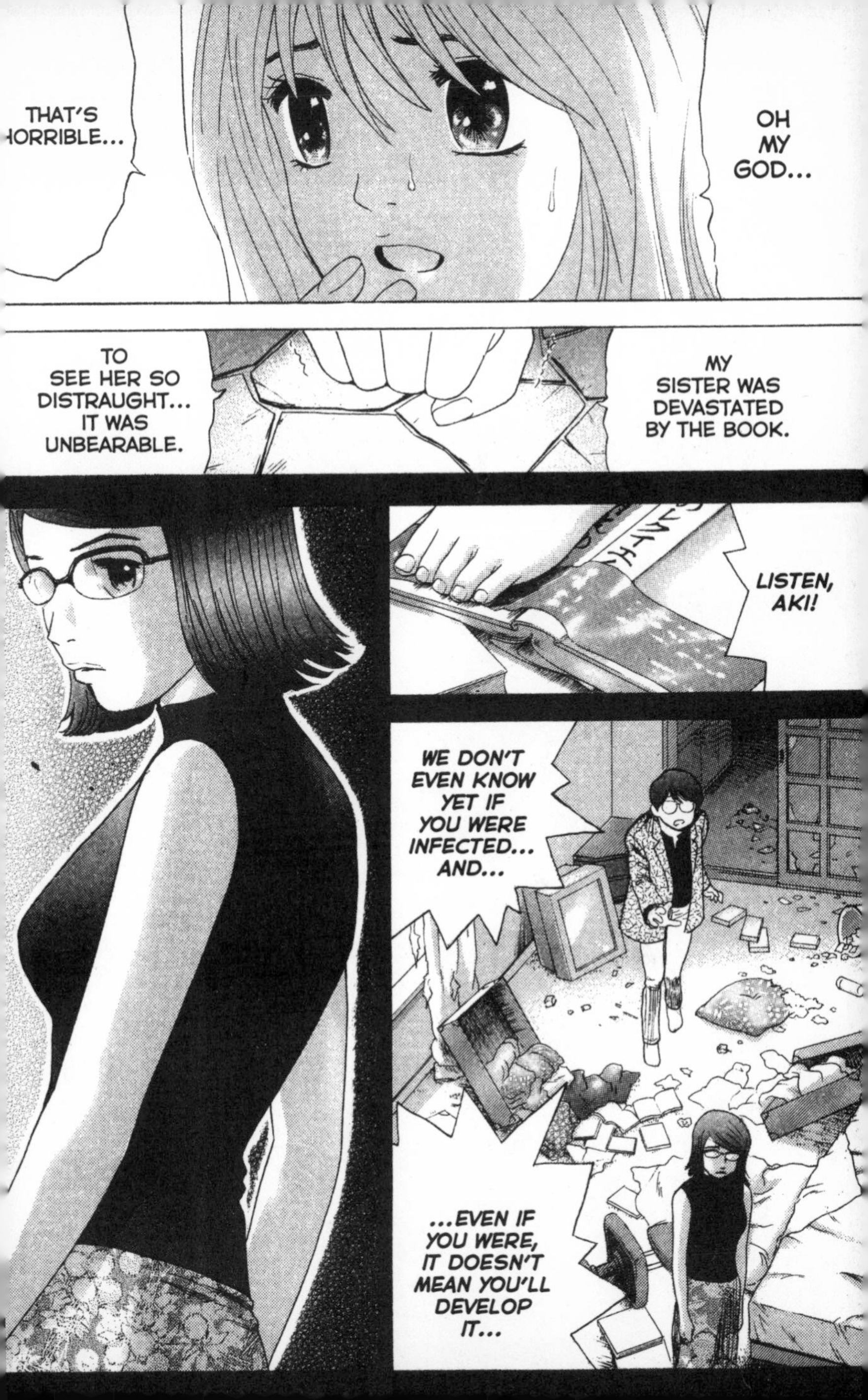
OH MY GOD...
THAT'S HORRIBLE...
MY SISTER WAS DEVASTATED BY THE BOOK.
TO SEE HER SO DISTRAUGHT... IT WAS UNBEARABLE.
LISTEN, AKI!
WE DON'T EVEN KNOW YET IF YOU WERE INFECTED... AND...
...EVEN IF YOU WERE, IT DOESN'T MEAN YOU'LL DEVELOP IT...

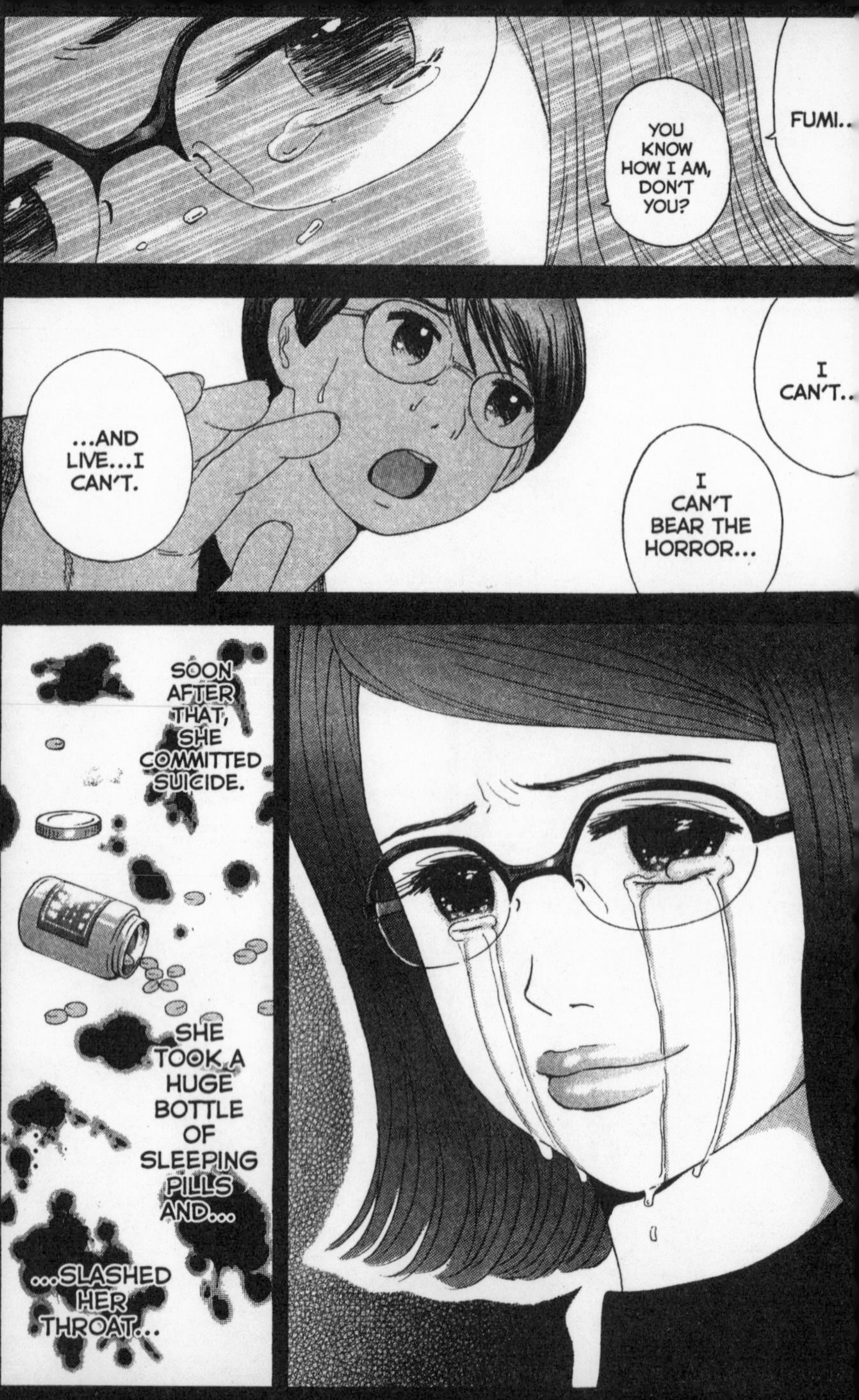
FUMI...
YOU KNOW HOW I AM, DON'T YOU?
I CAN'T...
I CAN'T BEAR THE HORROR...
...AND LIVE...I CAN'T.
SOON AFTER THAT, SHE COMMITTED SUICIDE.
SHE TOOK A HUGE BOTTLE OF SLEEPING PILLS AND...
...SLASHED HER THROAT...

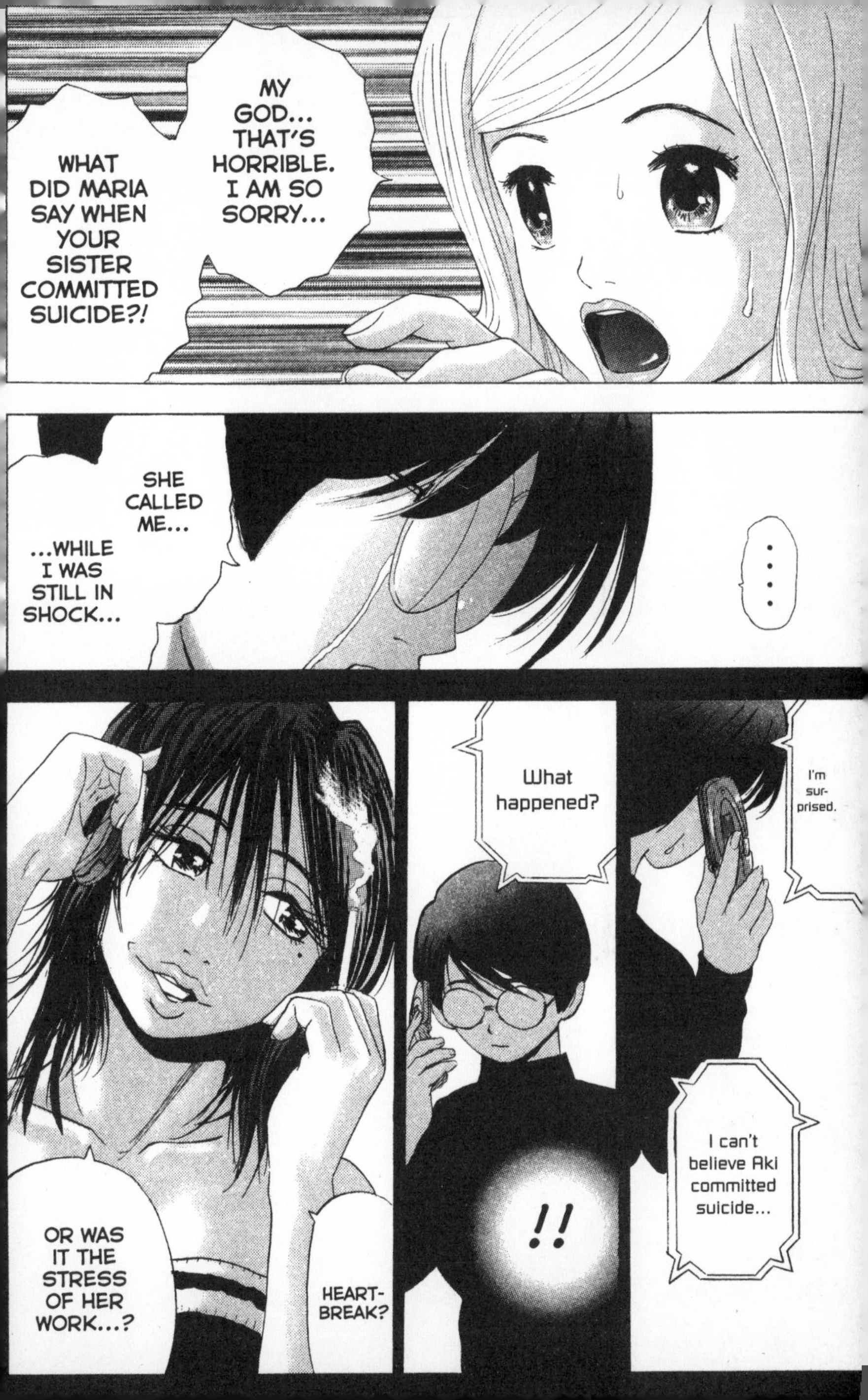
MY GOD... THAT'S HORRIBLE. I AM SO SORRY...
WHAT DID MARIA SAY WHEN YOUR SISTER COMMITTED SUICIDE?!
....
SHE CALLED ME...
...WHILE I WAS STILL IN SHOCK...
I'm sur-prised.
What happened?
I can't believe Aki committed suicide...
!!
HEART-BREAK?
OR WAS IT THE STRESS OF HER WORK...?

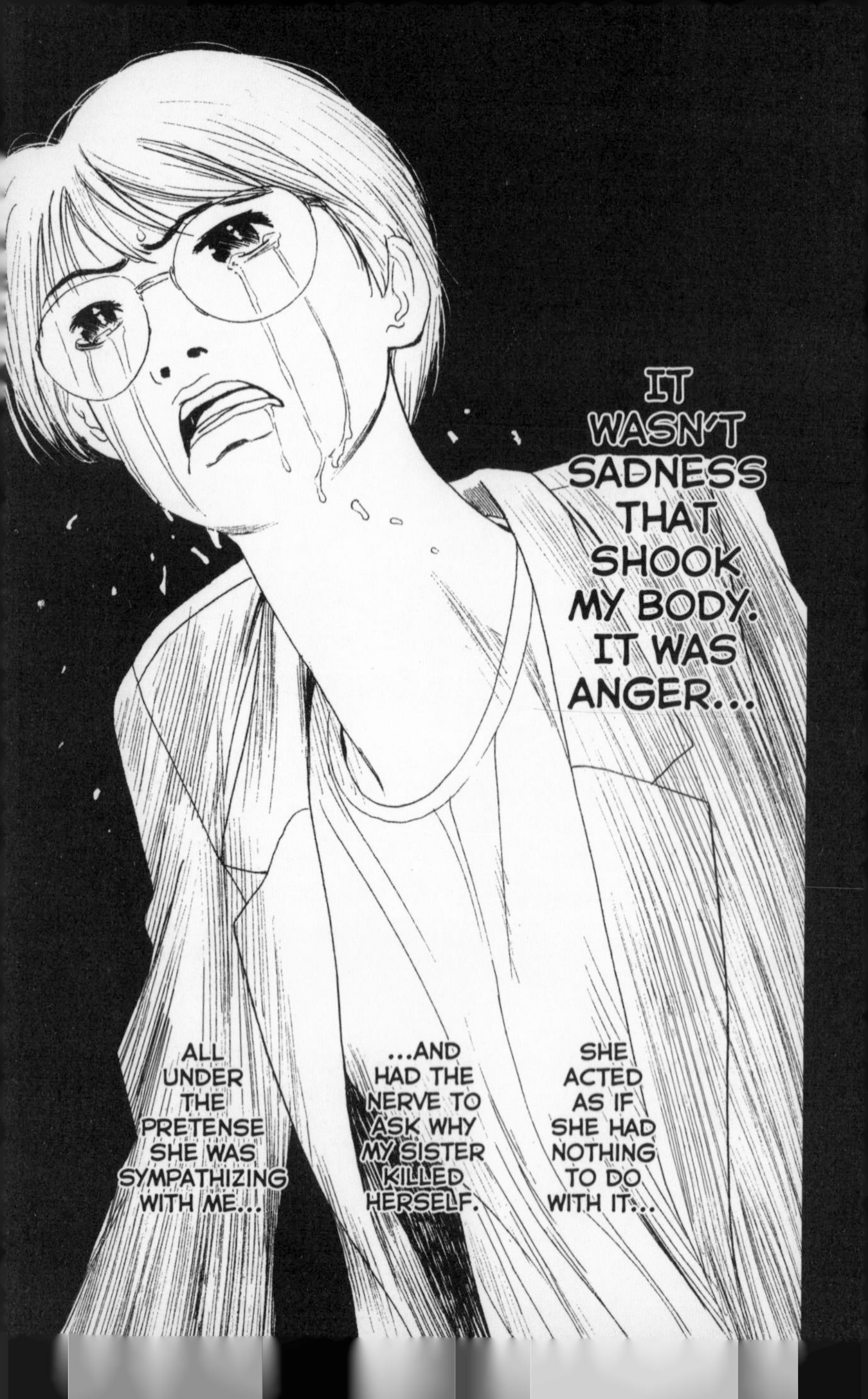
IT WASN'T SADNESS THAT SHOOK MY BODY. IT WAS ANGER...
SHE ACTED AS IF SHE HAD NOTHING TO DO WITH IT...
...AND HAD THE NERVE TO ASK WHY MY SISTER KILLED HERSELF.
ALL UNDER THE PRETENSE SHE WAS SYMPATHIZING WITH ME...

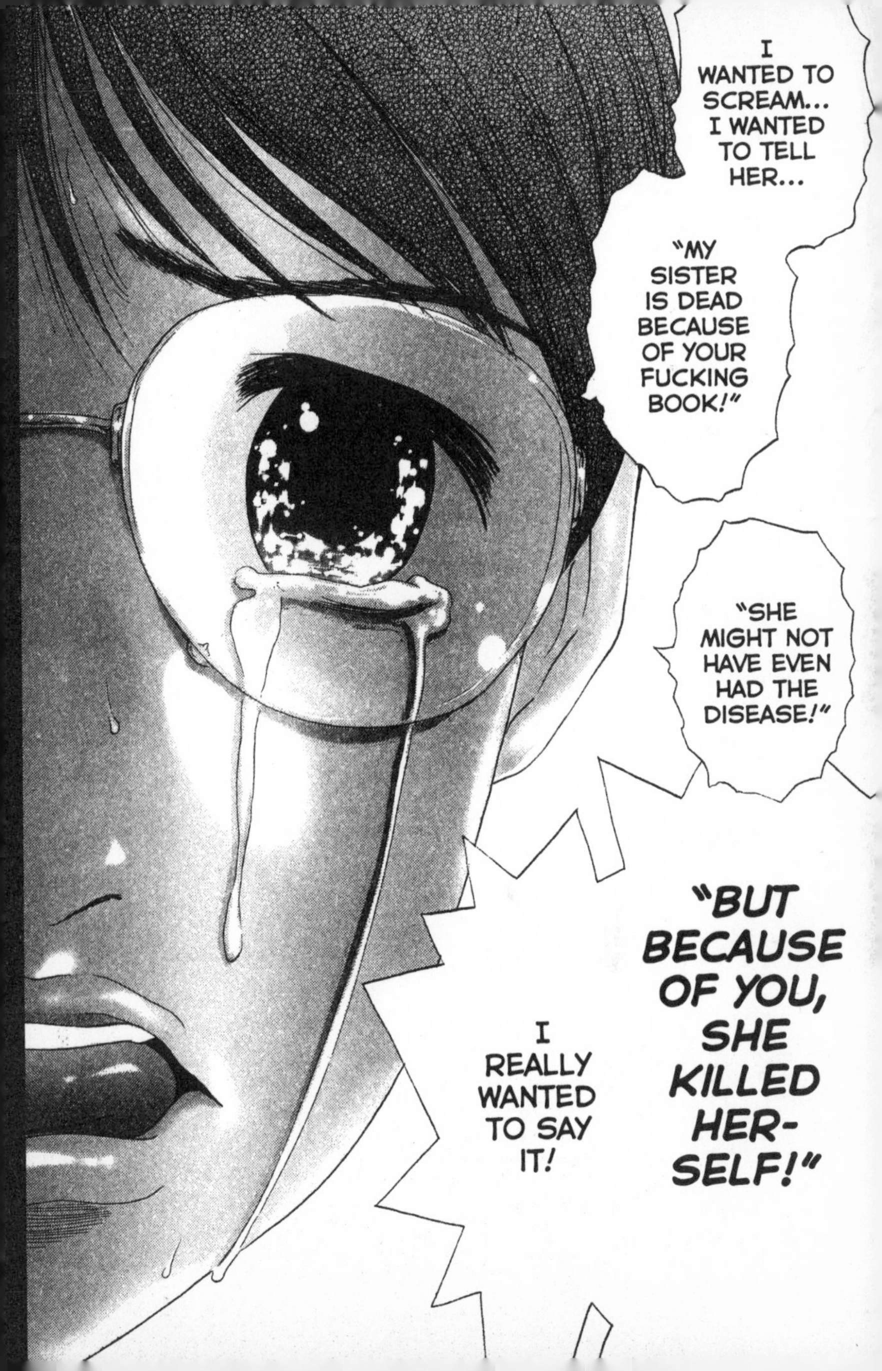
I WANTED TO SCREAM... I WANTED TO TELL HER...
"MY SISTER IS DEAD BECAUSE OF YOUR FUCKING BOOK!"
"SHE MIGHT NOT HAVE EVEN HAD THE DISEASE!"
"BUT BECAUSE OF YOU, SHE KILLED HER-SELF!"
I REALLY WANTED TO SAY IT!

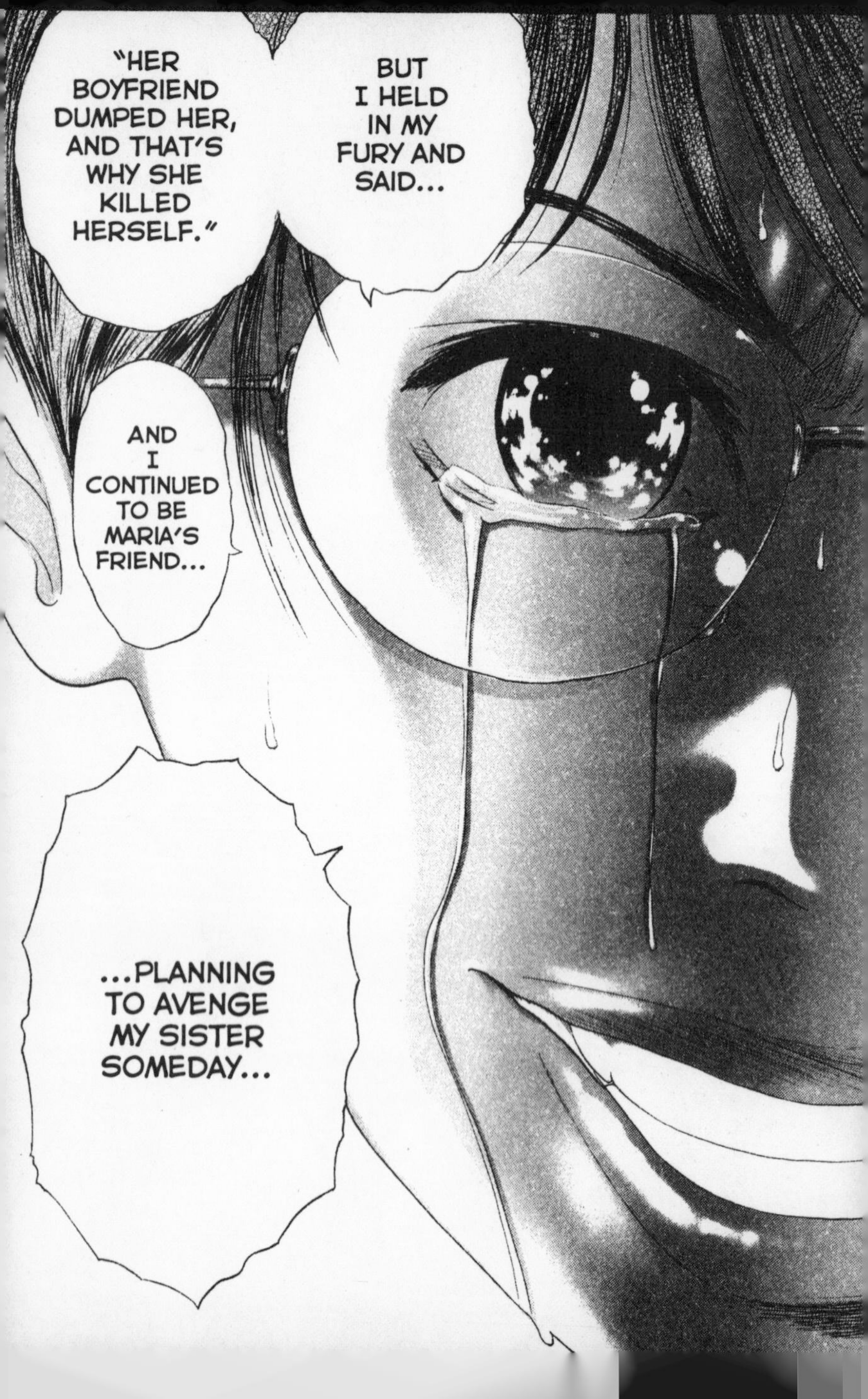
BUT I HELD IN MY FURY AND SAID...
"HER BOYFRIEND DUMPED HER, AND THAT'S WHY SHE KILLED HERSELF."
AND I CONTINUED TO BE MARIA'S FRIEND...
...PLANNING TO AVENGE MY SISTER SOMEDAY...

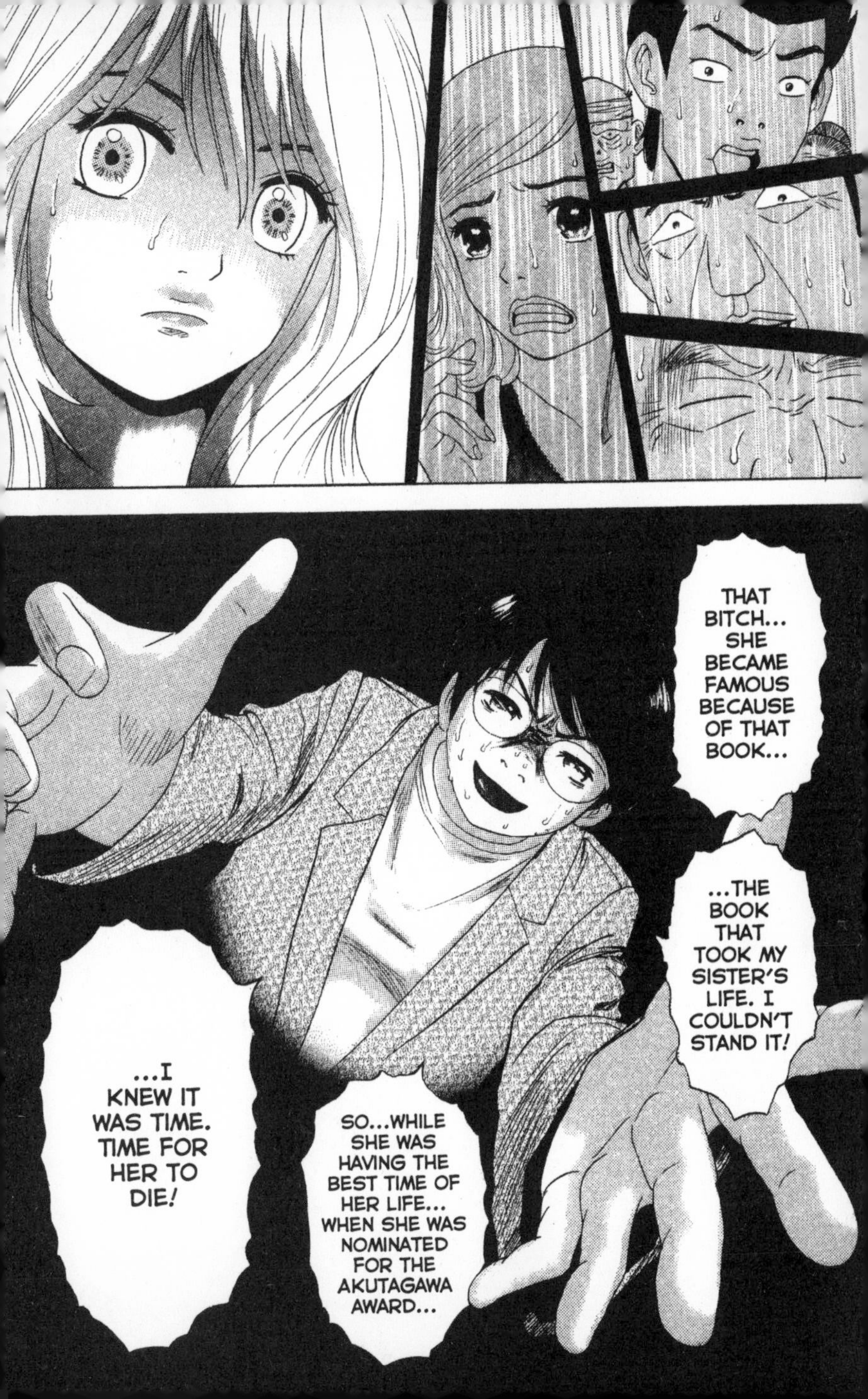
THAT BITCH... SHE BECAME FAMOUS BECAUSE OF THAT BOOK...
...THE BOOK THAT TOOK MY SISTER'S LIFE. I COULDN'T STAND IT!
SO...WHILE SHE WAS HAVING THE BEST TIME OF HER LIFE... WHEN SHE WAS NOMINATED FOR THE AKUTAGAWA AWARD...
...I KNEW IT WAS TIME. TIME FOR HER TO DIE!

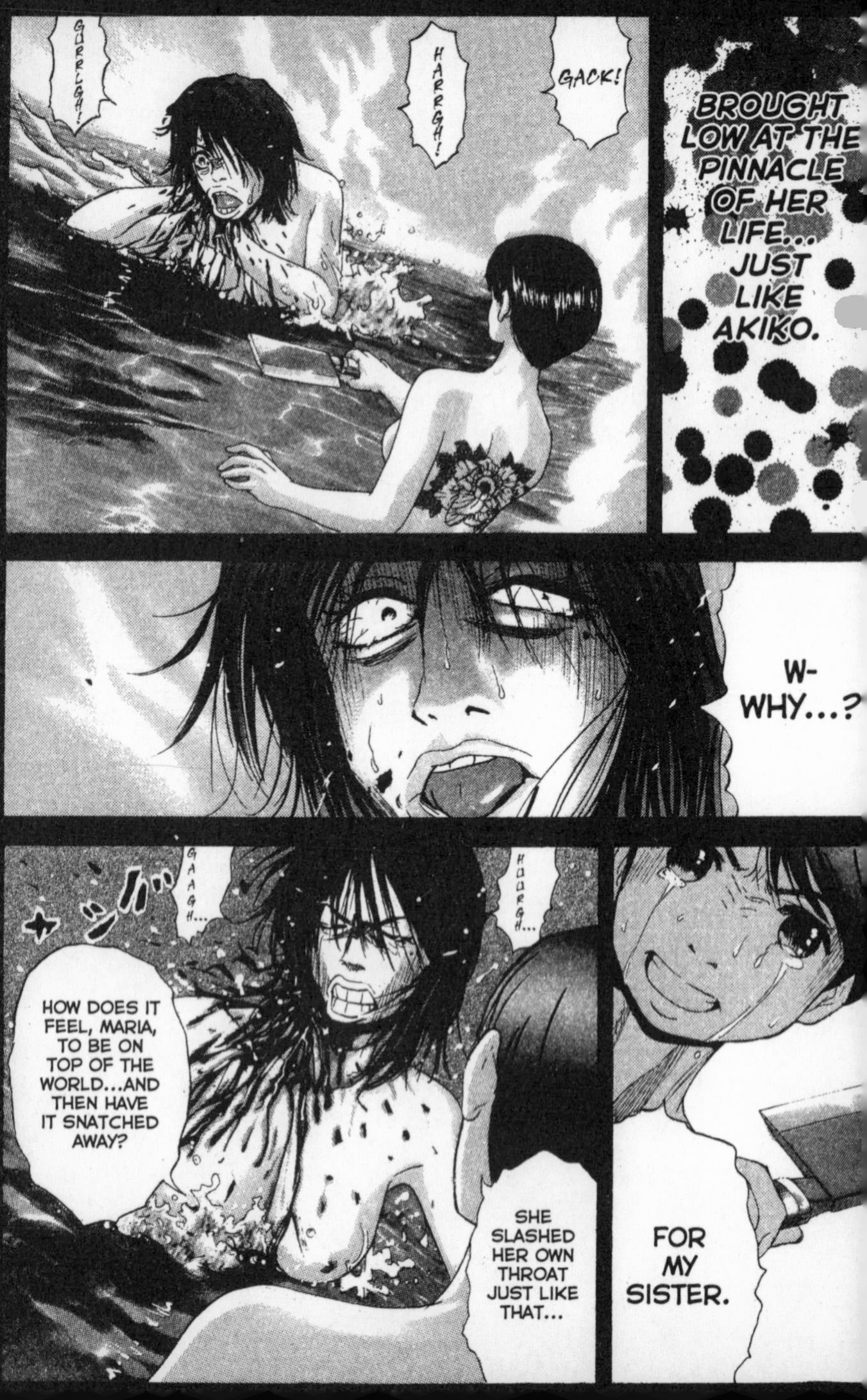
BROUGHT LOW AT THE PINNACLE OF HER LIFE... JUST LIKE AKIKO.
GACK!
HARRGH!
GURRLGH!
W-WHY...?
FOR MY SISTER.
HUURGH...
GAAAGH...
HOW DOES IT FEEL, MARIA, TO BE ON TOP OF THE WORLD...AND THEN HAVE IT SNATCHED AWAY?
SHE SLASHED HER OWN THROAT JUST LIKE THAT...

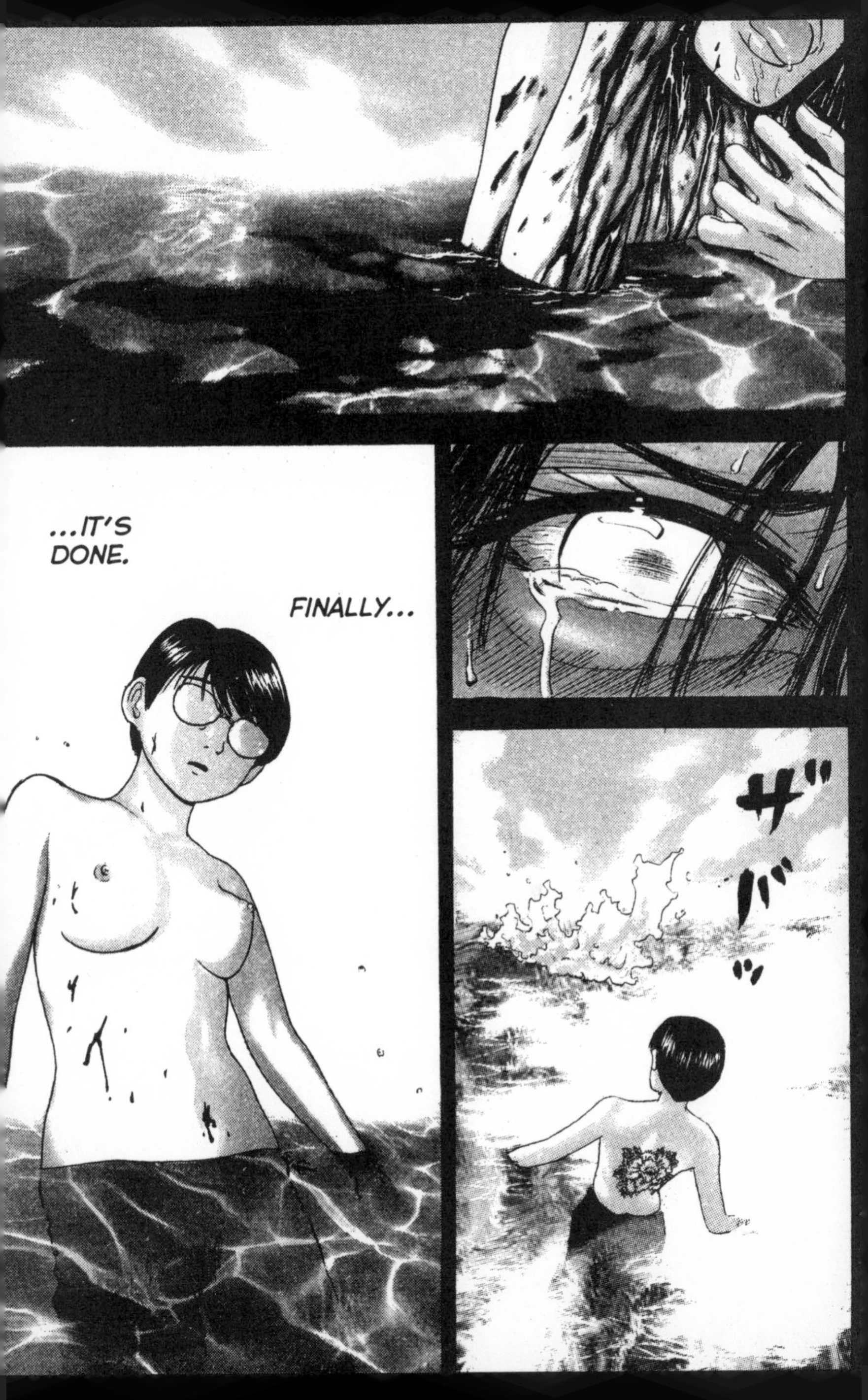
ザバッ
...IT'S DONE.
FINALLY...

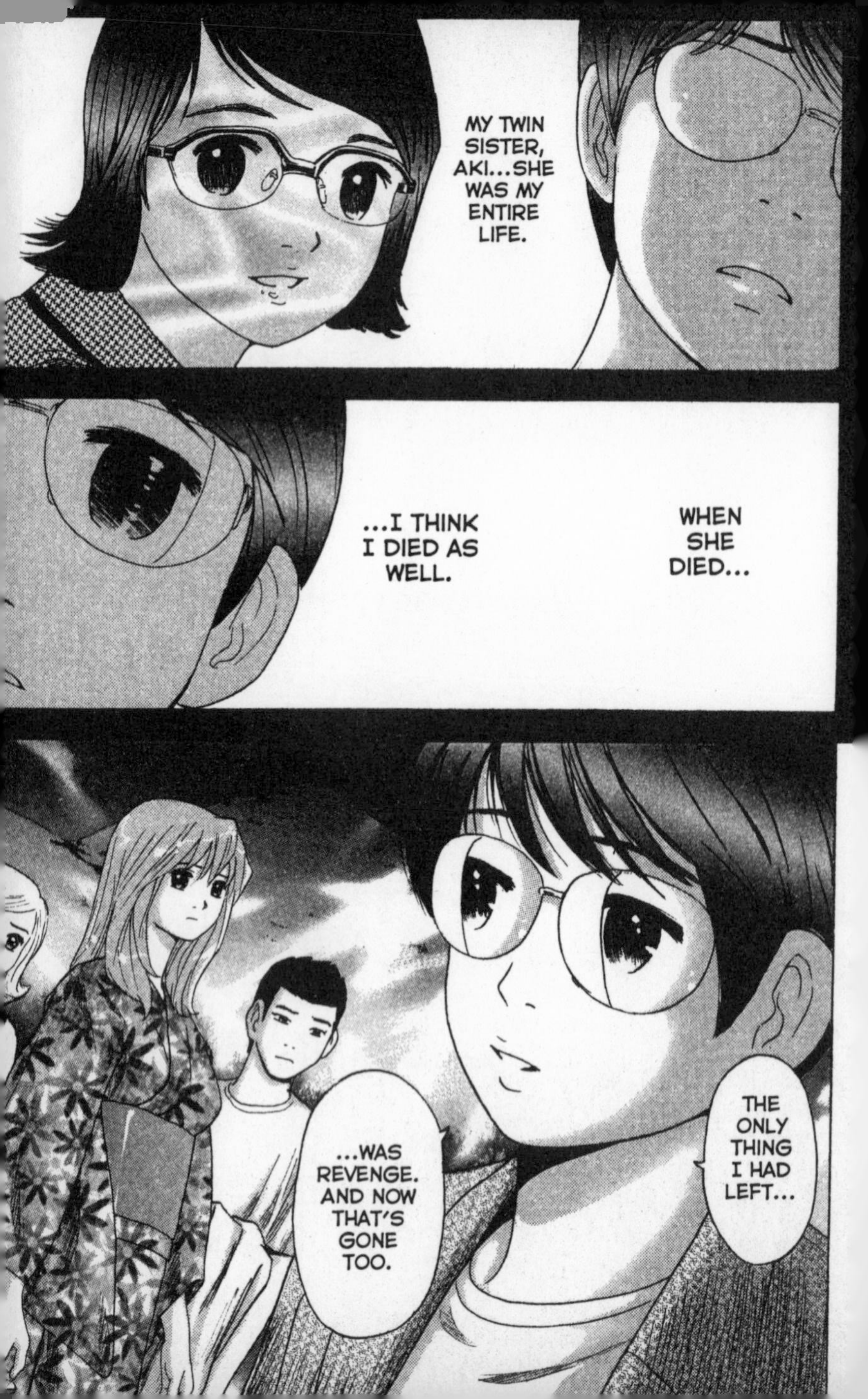
MY TWIN SISTER, AKI...SHE WAS MY ENTIRE LIFE.
WHEN SHE DIED...
...I THINK I DIED AS WELL.
THE ONLY THING I HAD LEFT...
...WAS REVENGE. AND NOW THAT'S GONE TOO.

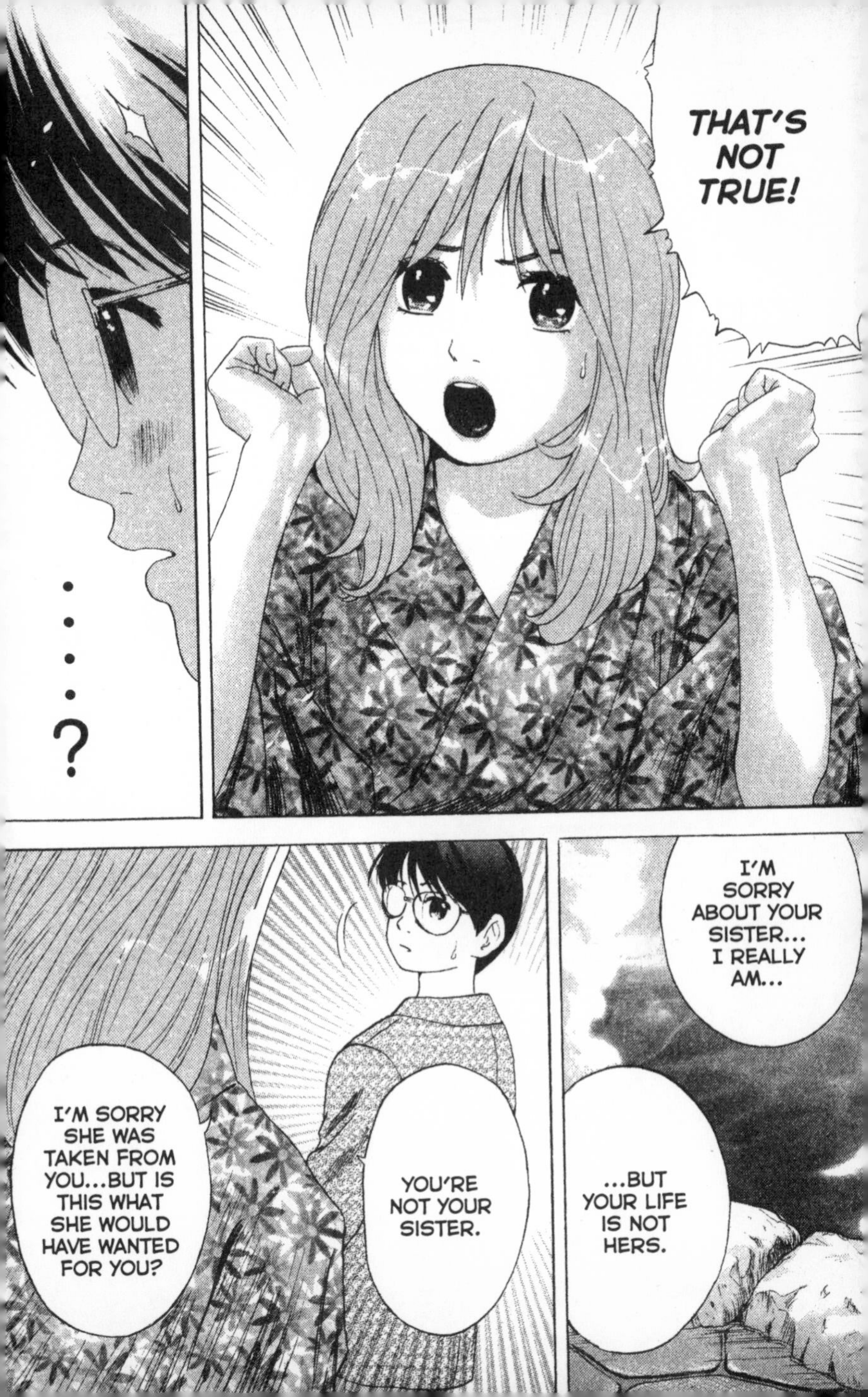
THAT'S NOT TRUE!
....?
I'M SORRY ABOUT YOUR SISTER... I REALLY AM...
...BUT YOUR LIFE IS NOT HERS.
YOU'RE NOT YOUR SISTER.
I'M SORRY SHE WAS TAKEN FROM YOU...BUT IS THIS WHAT SHE WOULD HAVE WANTED FOR YOU?

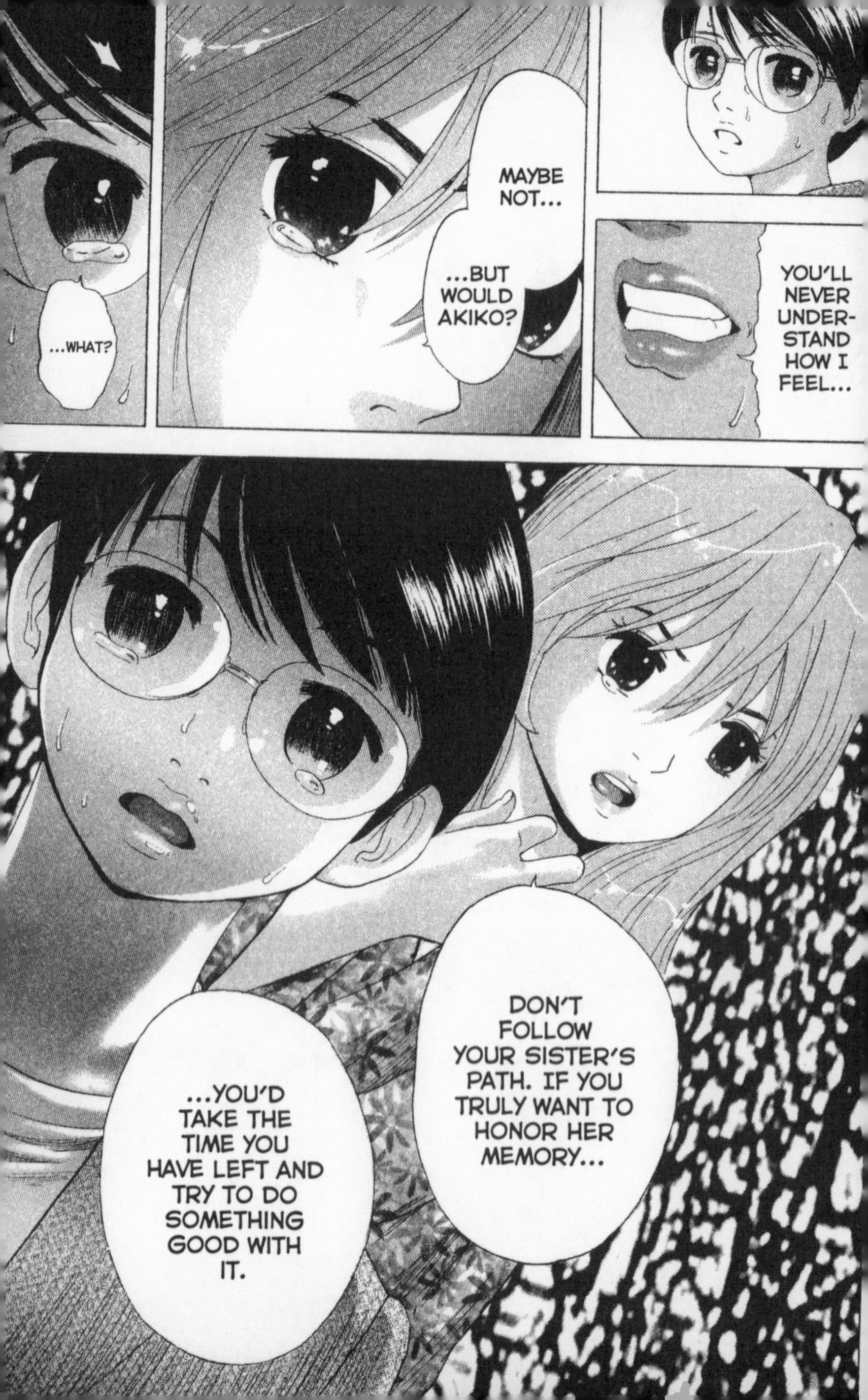
YOU'LL NEVER UNDER-STAND HOW I FEEL...
MAYBE NOT...
...BUT WOULD AKIKO?
...WHAT?
DON'T FOLLOW YOUR SISTER'S PATH. IF YOU TRULY WANT TO HONOR HER MEMORY...
...YOU'D TAKE THE TIME YOU HAVE LEFT AND TRY TO DO SOMETHING GOOD WITH IT.

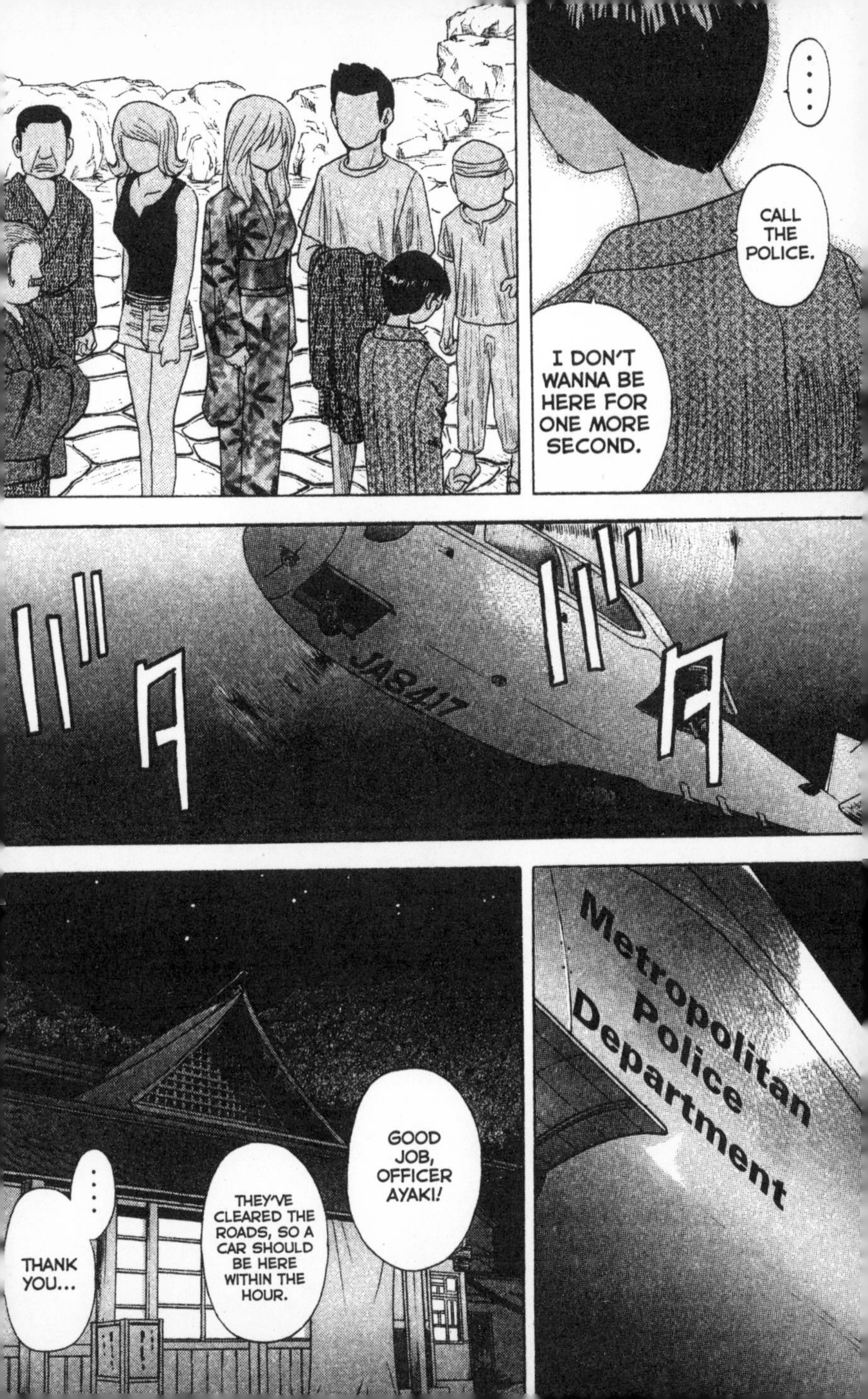
...
CALL THE POLICE.
I DON'T WANNA BE HERE FOR ONE MORE SECOND.
バタ
JA8417
バタ
Metropolitan Police Department
GOOD JOB, OFFICER AYAKI!
THEY'VE CLEARED THE ROADS, SO A CAR SHOULD BE HERE WITHIN THE HOUR.
...
THANK YOU...

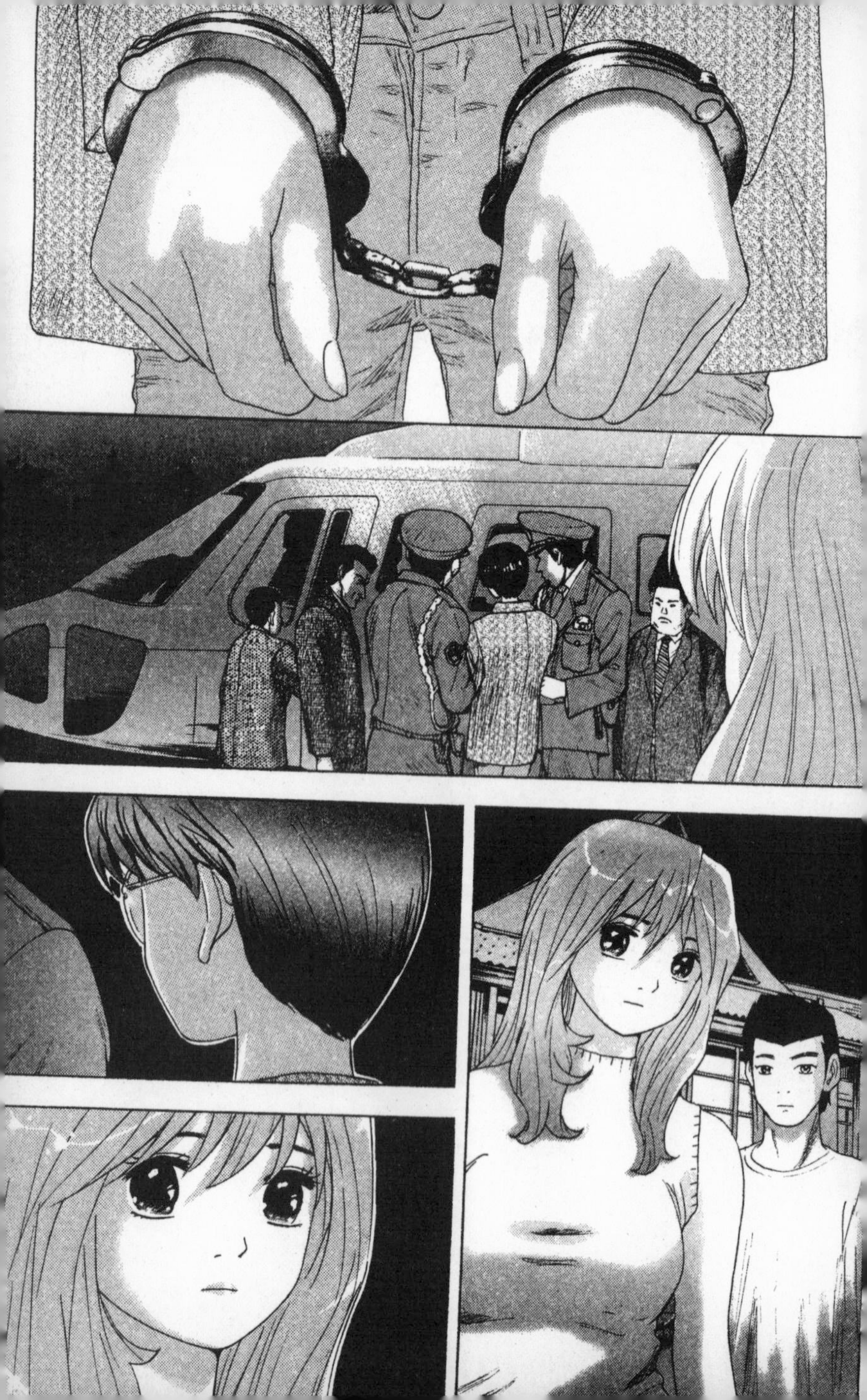

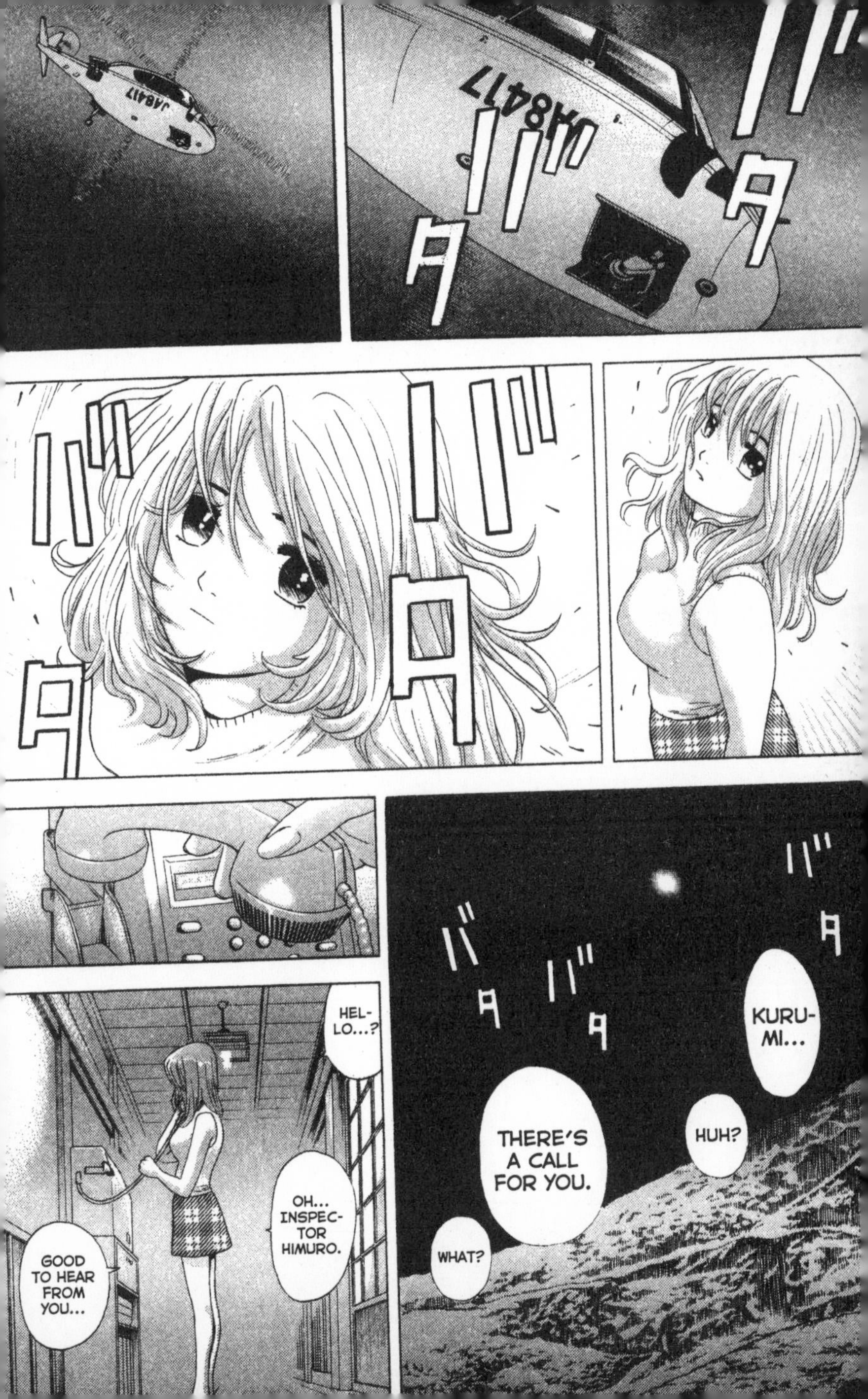
バタ
バタ
JA8417
JA8417
バタ
バタ
バタ
バタ
バタ
バタ
KURU-MI...
HUH?
THERE'S A CALL FOR YOU.
WHAT?
HEL-LO...?
OH... INSPECTOR HIMURO.
GOOD TO HEAR FROM YOU...

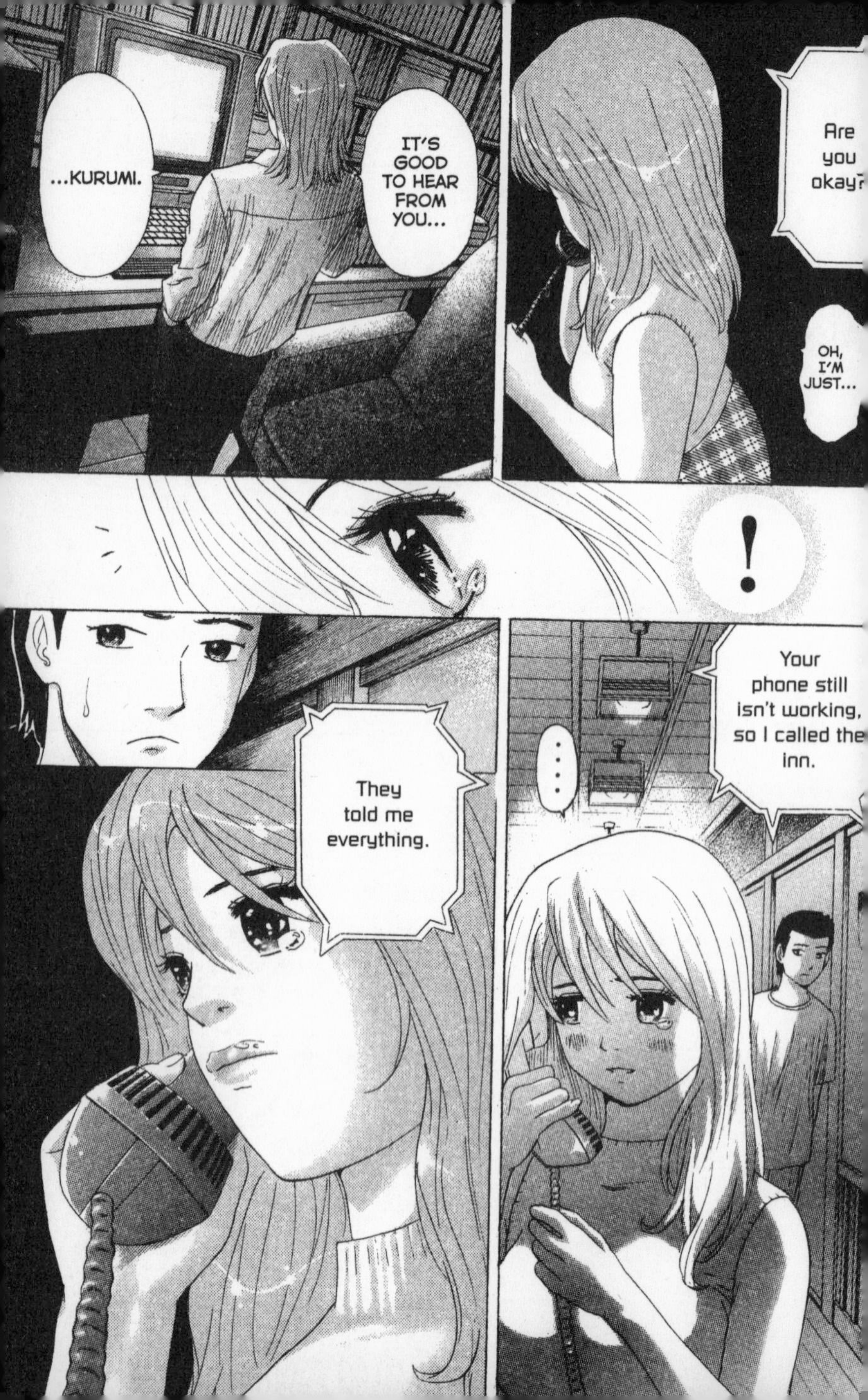
Are you okay?
OH, I'M JUST...
IT'S GOOD TO HEAR FROM YOU...
...KURUMI.
!
Your phone still isn't working, so I called the inn.
....
They told me everything.

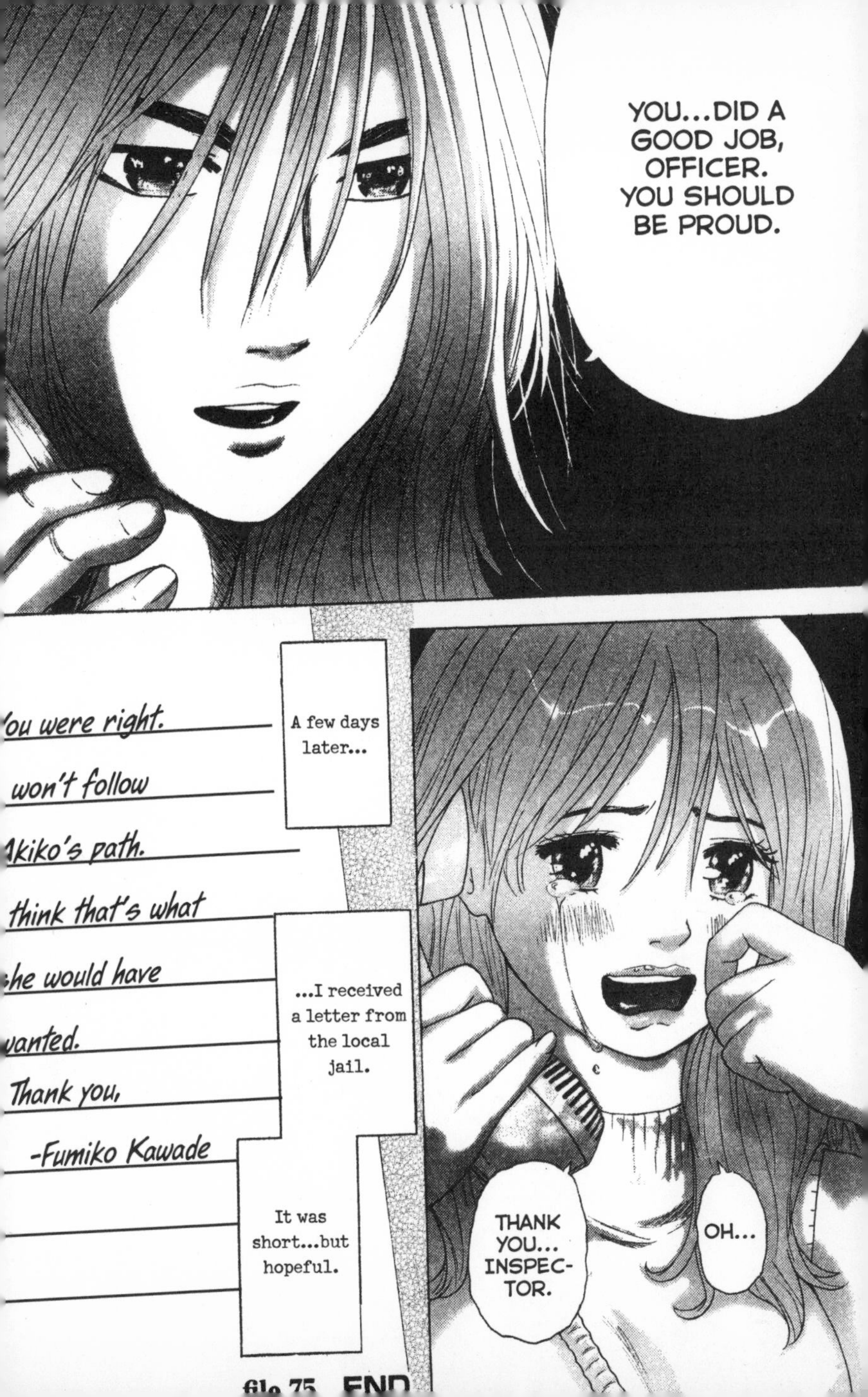
YOU...DID A GOOD JOB, OFFICER. YOU SHOULD BE PROUD.
OH...
THANK YOU... INSPEC- TOR.
A few days later...
...I received a letter from the local jail.
ou were right.
won't follow
kiko's path.
think that's what
he would have
vanted.
Thank you,
-Fumiko Kawade
It was short...but hopeful.
file 75 END

CHAPTER 9
Murder in the Ghost Building

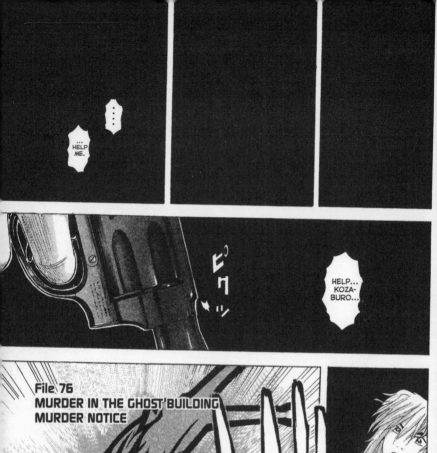

... HELP ME.

HELP... KOZA- BURO...

File 76
MURDER IN THE GHOST BUILDING
MURDER NOTICE

YUKA?!

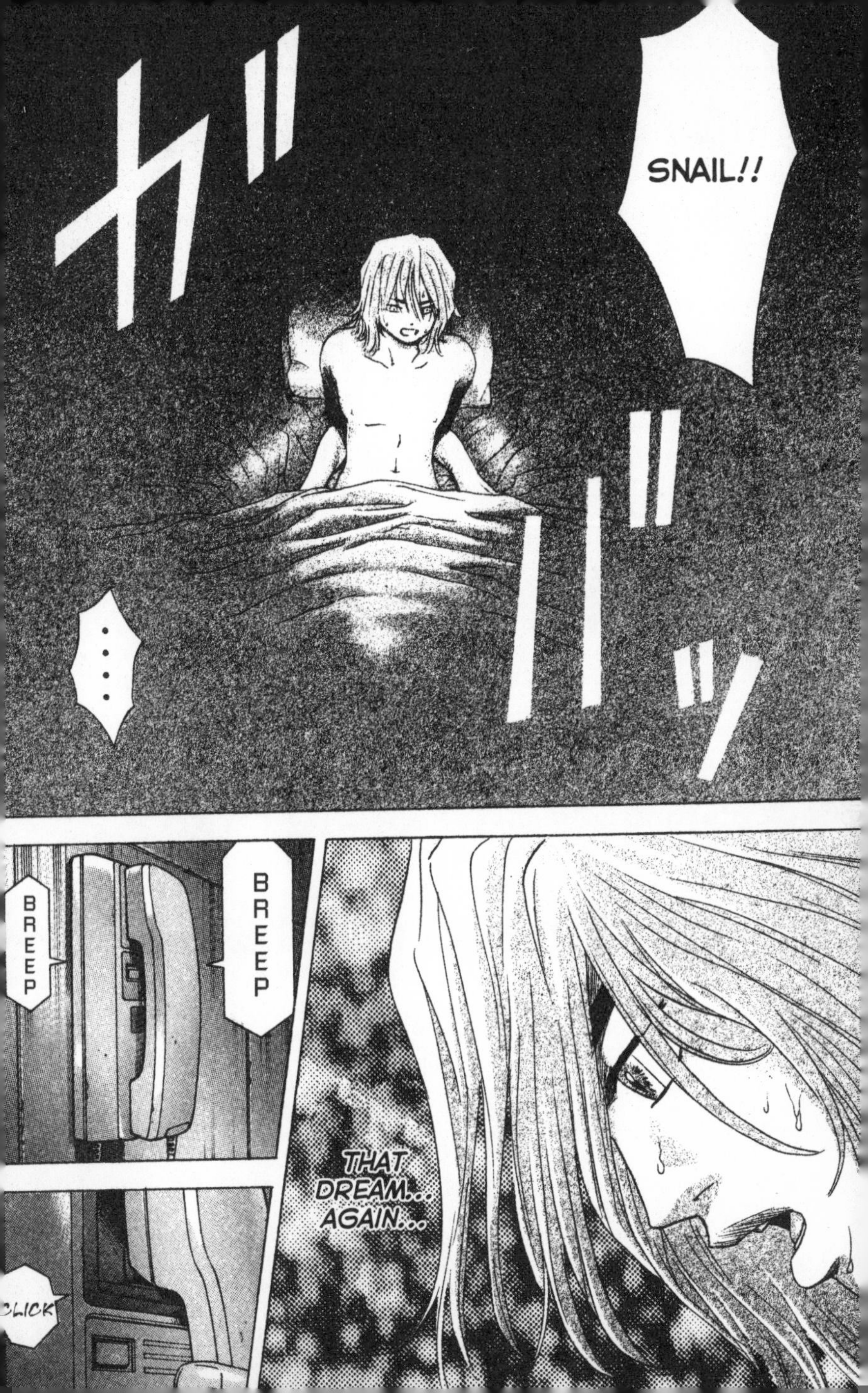

SNAIL!!
....
THAT DREAM... AGAIN...
BREEP
BREEP
CLICK

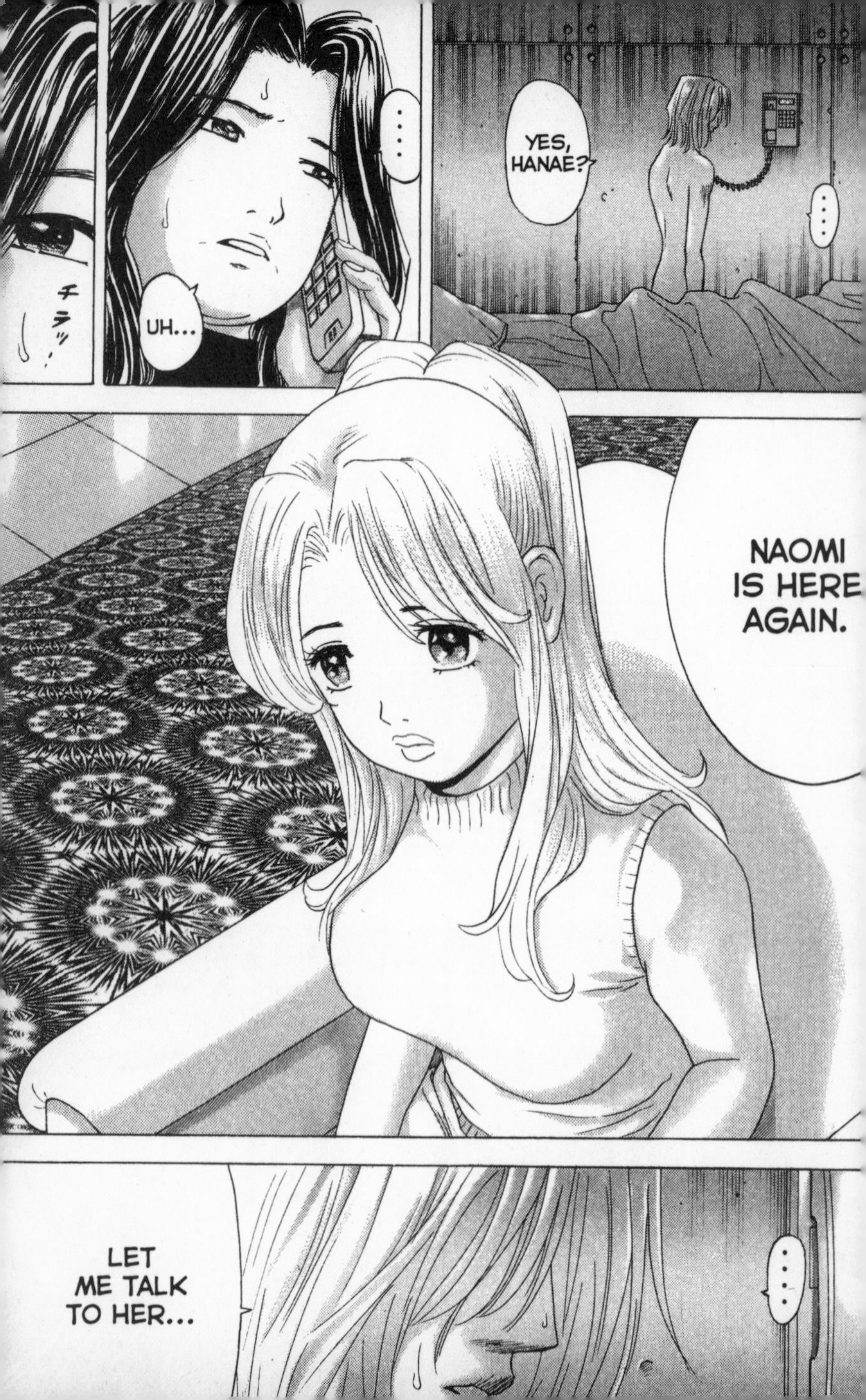
YES, HANAE?
....
....
UH...
チラッ
NAOMI IS HERE AGAIN.
....
LET ME TALK TO HER...

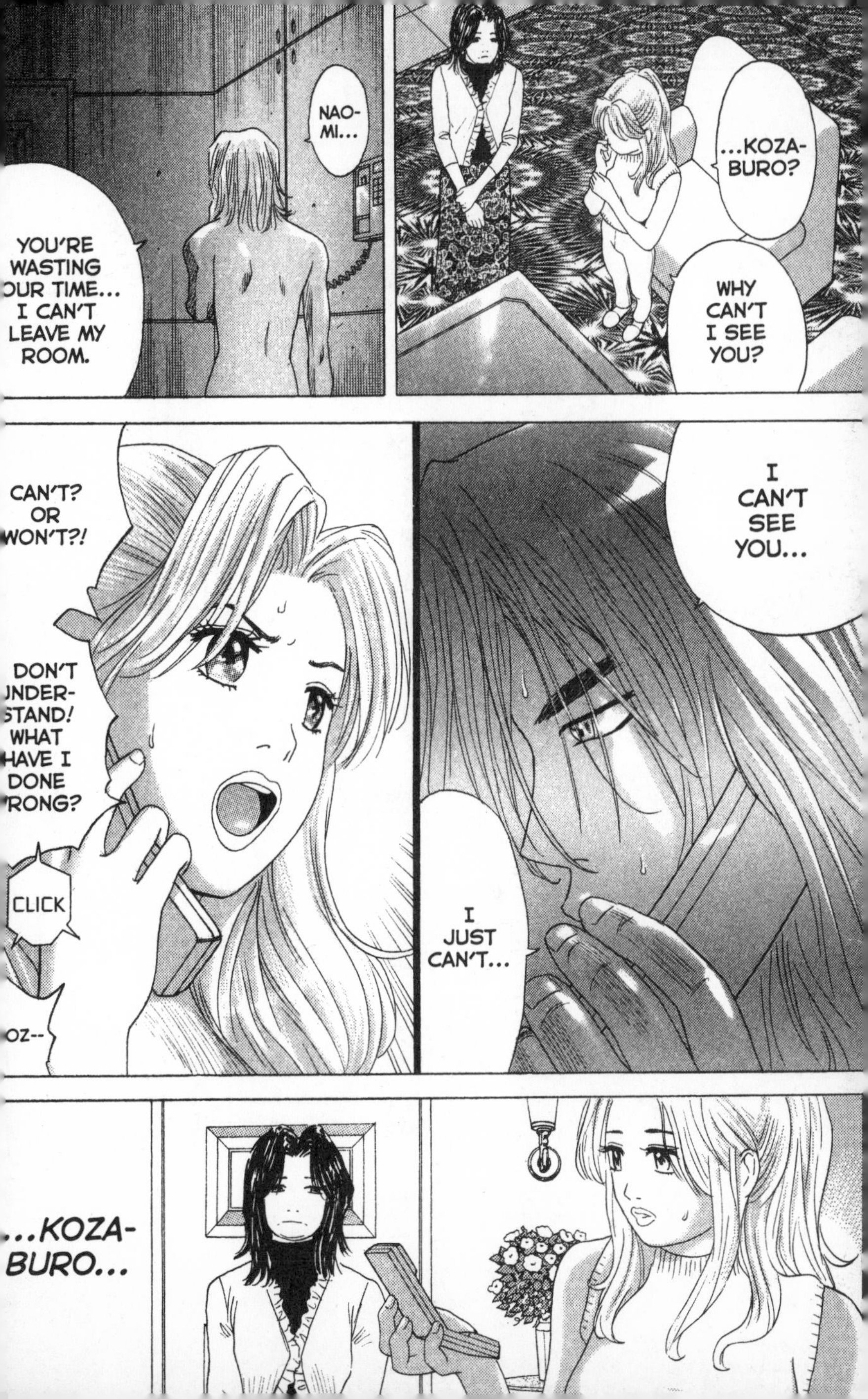

...KOZABURO?
WHY CAN'T I SEE YOU?
NAOMI...
YOU'RE WASTING OUR TIME... I CAN'T LEAVE MY ROOM.
I CAN'T SEE YOU...
I JUST CAN'T...
CAN'T? OR WON'T?!
DON'T UNDERSTAND! WHAT HAVE I DONE WRONG?
CLICK
OZ--
...KOZABURO...

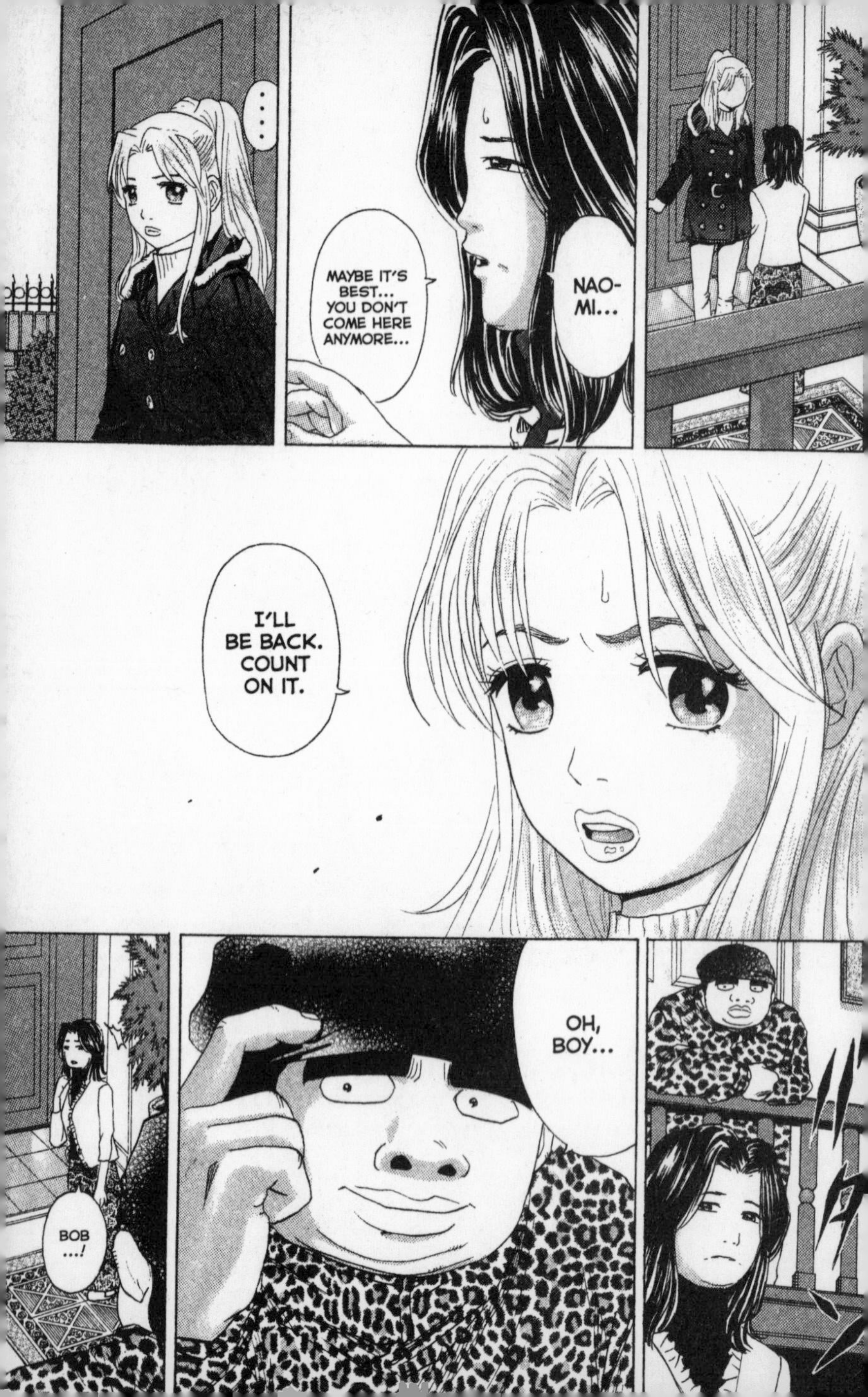
NAO-MI...
MAYBE IT'S BEST... YOU DON'T COME HERE ANYMORE...
....
I'LL BE BACK. COUNT ON IT.
OH, BOY...
BOB ...!

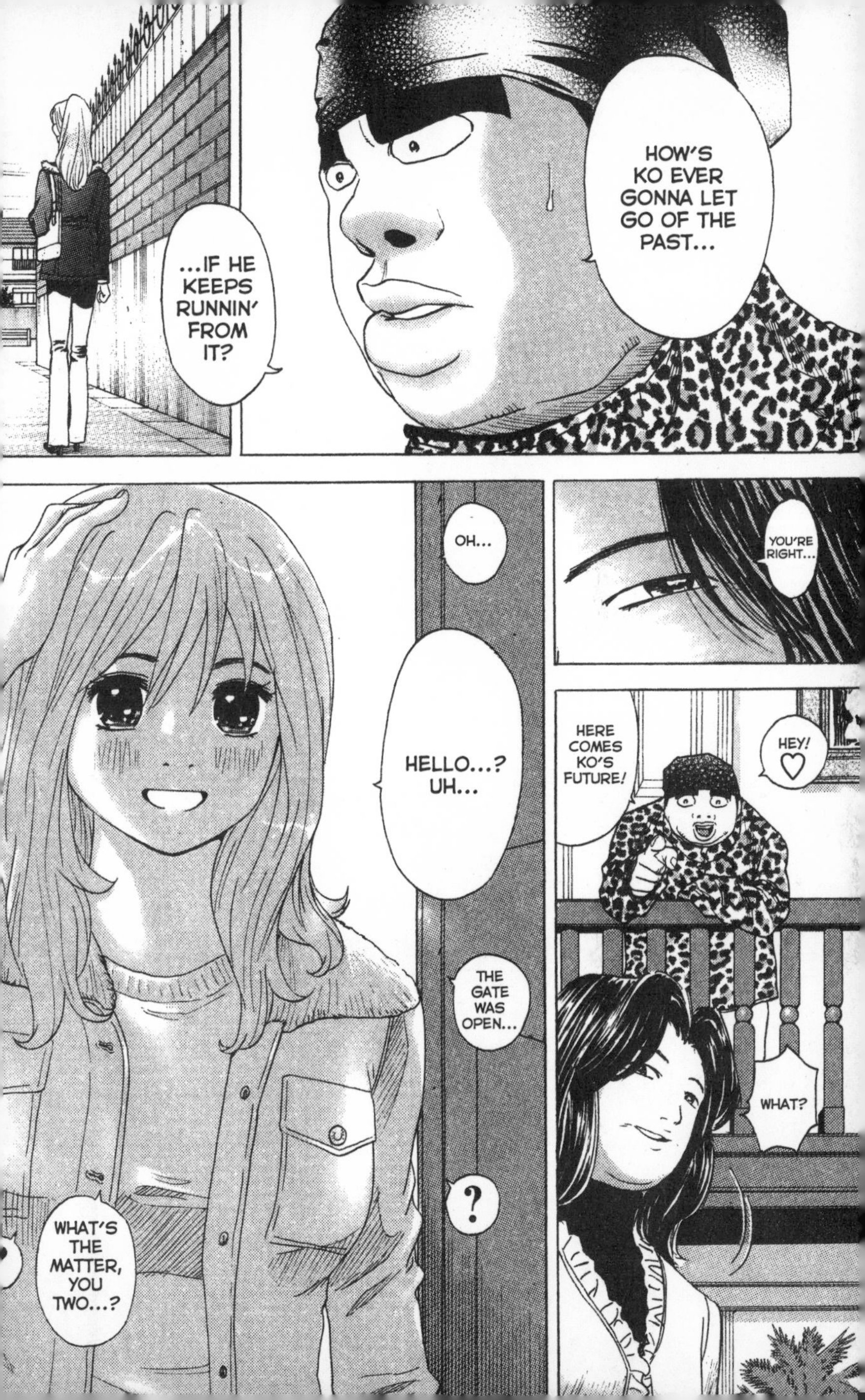
HOW'S KO EVER GONNA LET GO OF THE PAST...
...IF HE KEEPS RUNNIN' FROM IT?
YOU'RE RIGHT...
HEY! ♡
HERE COMES KO'S FUTURE!
WHAT?
OH...
HELLO...? UH...
THE GATE WAS OPEN...
?
WHAT'S THE MATTER, YOU TWO...?

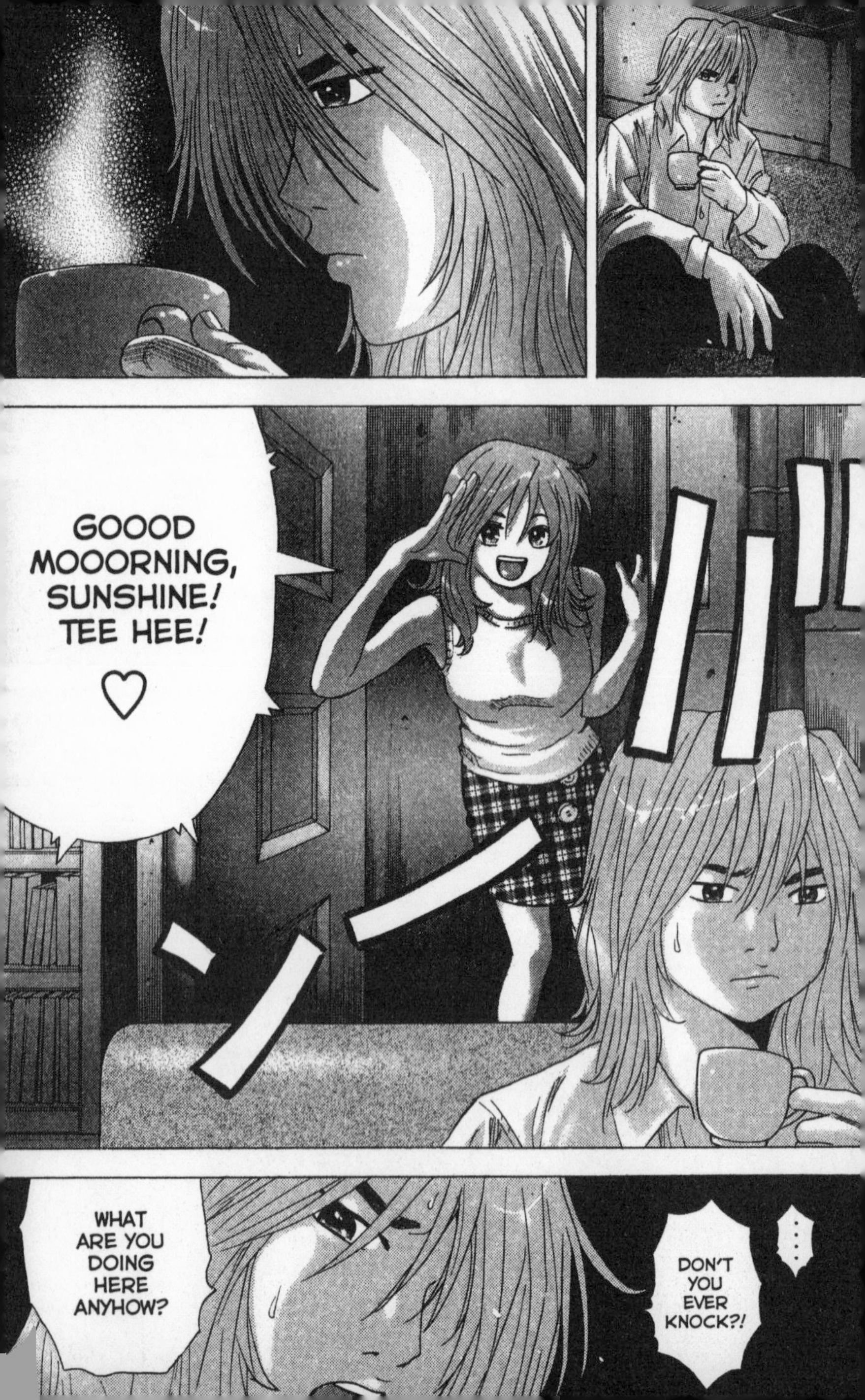
GOOOD MOOORNING, SUNSHINE! TEE HEE! ♡
...
DON'T YOU EVER KNOCK?!
WHAT ARE YOU DOING HERE ANYHOW?

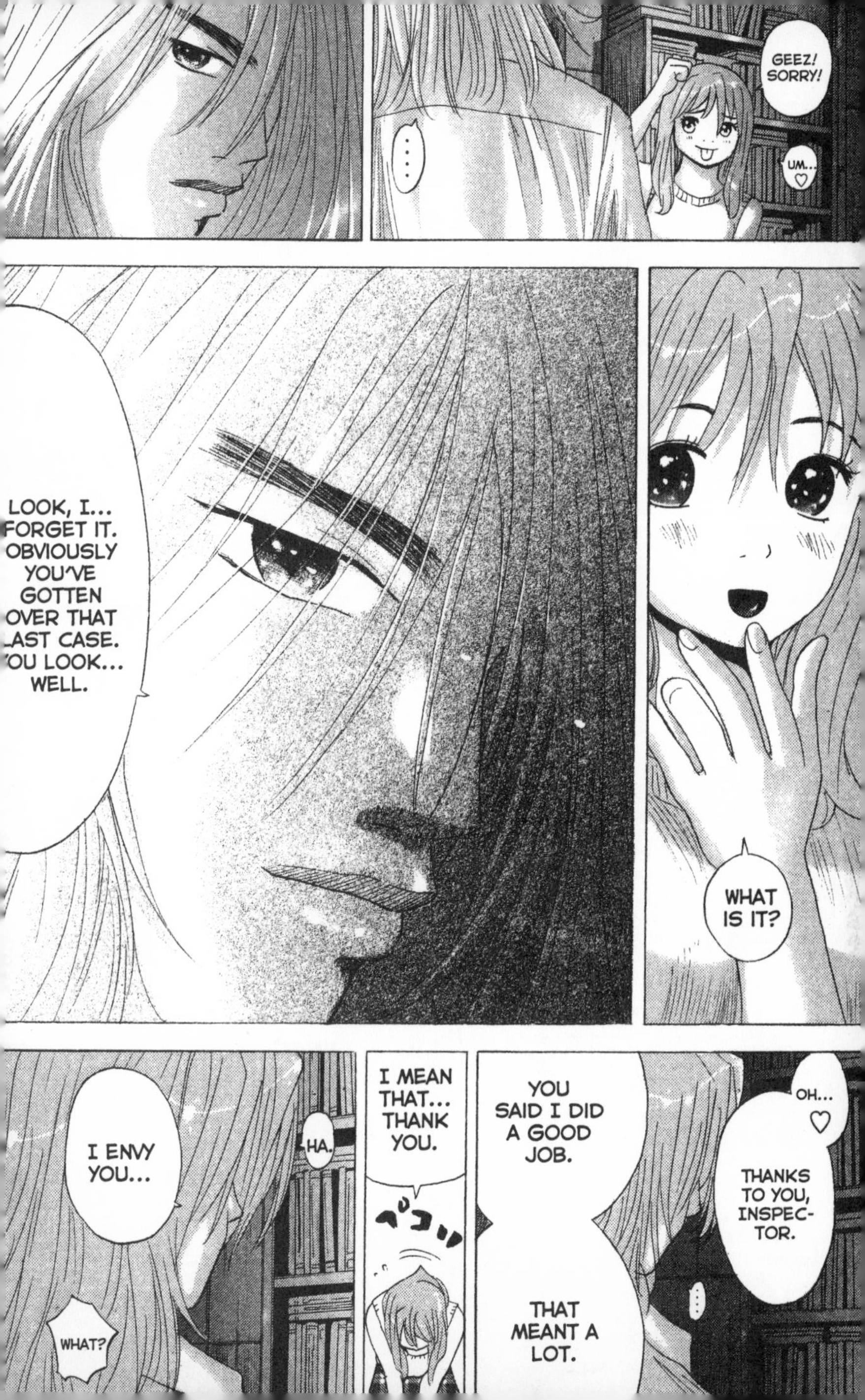

GEEZ! SORRY!
...
UM... ♡
WHAT IS IT?
LOOK, I... FORGET IT. OBVIOUSLY YOU'VE GOTTEN OVER THAT LAST CASE. YOU LOOK... WELL.
OH... ♡
THANKS TO YOU, INSPECTOR.
...
YOU SAID I DID A GOOD JOB.
THAT MEANT A LOT.
I MEAN THAT... THANK YOU.
ペコッ
HA.
I ENVY YOU...
WHAT?

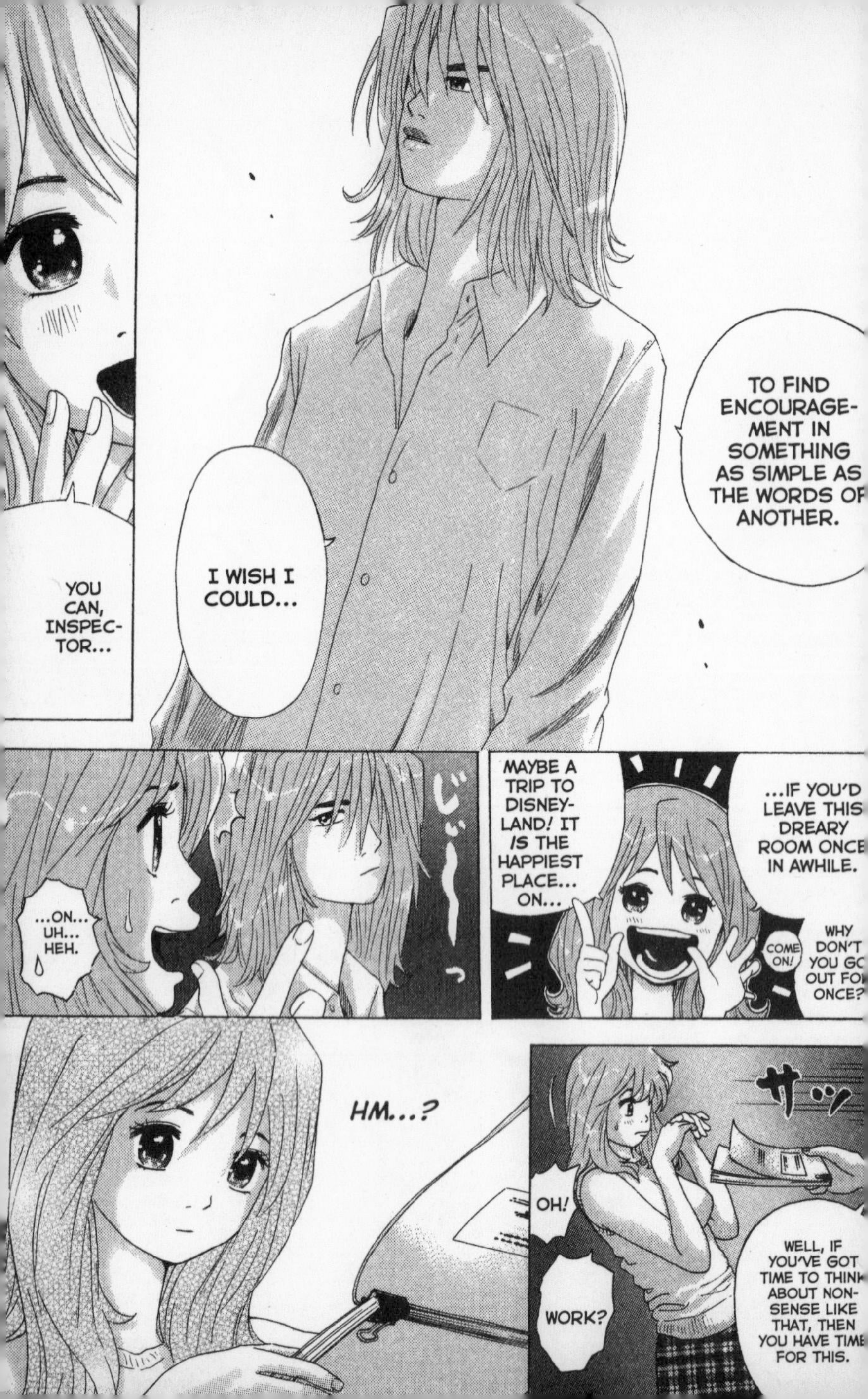
TO FIND ENCOURAGEMENT IN SOMETHING AS SIMPLE AS THE WORDS OF ANOTHER.
I WISH I COULD...
YOU CAN, INSPECTOR...
...IF YOU'D LEAVE THIS DREARY ROOM ONCE IN AWHILE.
WHY DON'T YOU GO OUT FOR ONCE?
COME ON!
MAYBE A TRIP TO DISNEYLAND! IT *IS* THE HAPPIEST PLACE... ON...
じーっ
...ON... UH... HEH.
サッ
WELL, IF YOU'VE GOT TIME TO THINK ABOUT NONSENSE LIKE THAT, THEN YOU HAVE TIME FOR THIS.
OH!
WORK?
HM...?

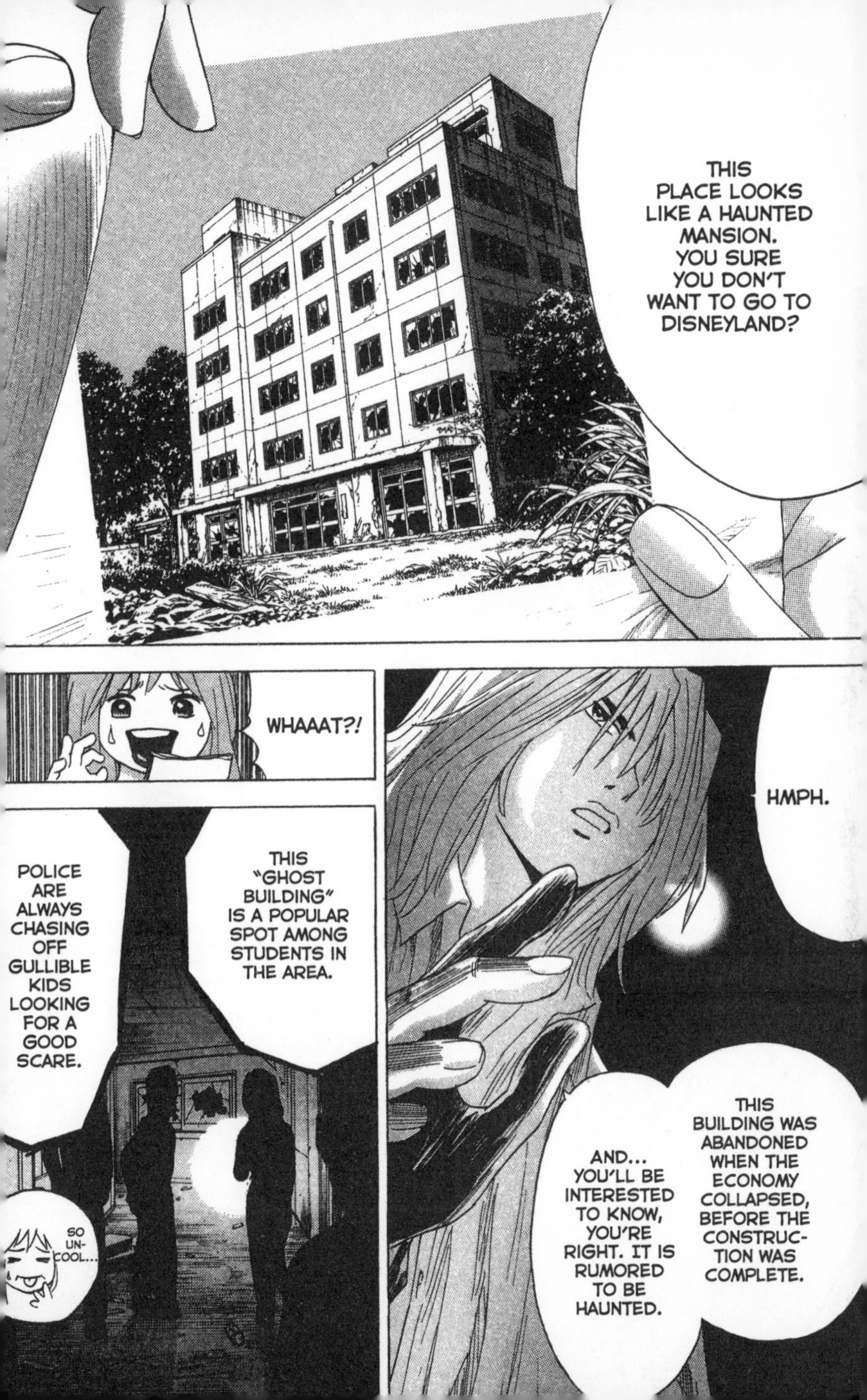
THIS PLACE LOOKS LIKE A HAUNTED MANSION. YOU SURE YOU DON'T WANT TO GO TO DISNEYLAND?
HMPH.
THIS BUILDING WAS ABANDONED WHEN THE ECONOMY COLLAPSED, BEFORE THE CONSTRUCTION WAS COMPLETE.
AND... YOU'LL BE INTERESTED TO KNOW, YOU'RE RIGHT. IT IS RUMORED TO BE HAUNTED.
WHAAAT?!
THIS "GHOST BUILDING" IS A POPULAR SPOT AMONG STUDENTS IN THE AREA.
POLICE ARE ALWAYS CHASING OFF GULLIBLE KIDS LOOKING FOR A GOOD SCARE.
SO UN-COOL...

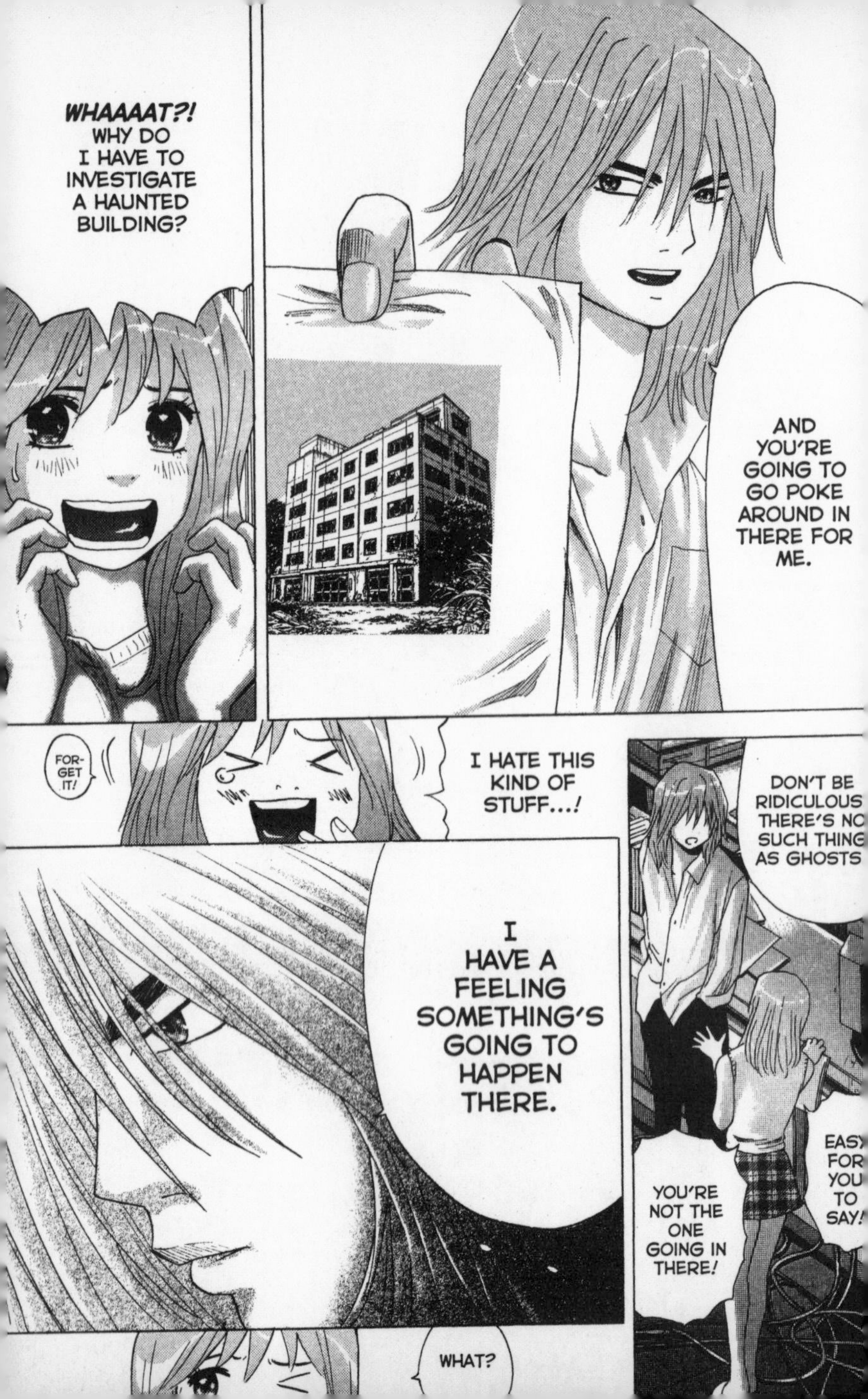
AND YOU'RE GOING TO GO POKE AROUND IN THERE FOR ME.
WHAAAAT?! WHY DO I HAVE TO INVESTIGATE A HAUNTED BUILDING?
DON'T BE RIDICULOUS THERE'S NO SUCH THING AS GHOSTS
EASY FOR YOU TO SAY!
YOU'RE NOT THE ONE GOING IN THERE!
I HATE THIS KIND OF STUFF...!
FOR-GET IT!
I HAVE A FEELING SOMETHING'S GOING TO HAPPEN THERE.
WHAT?

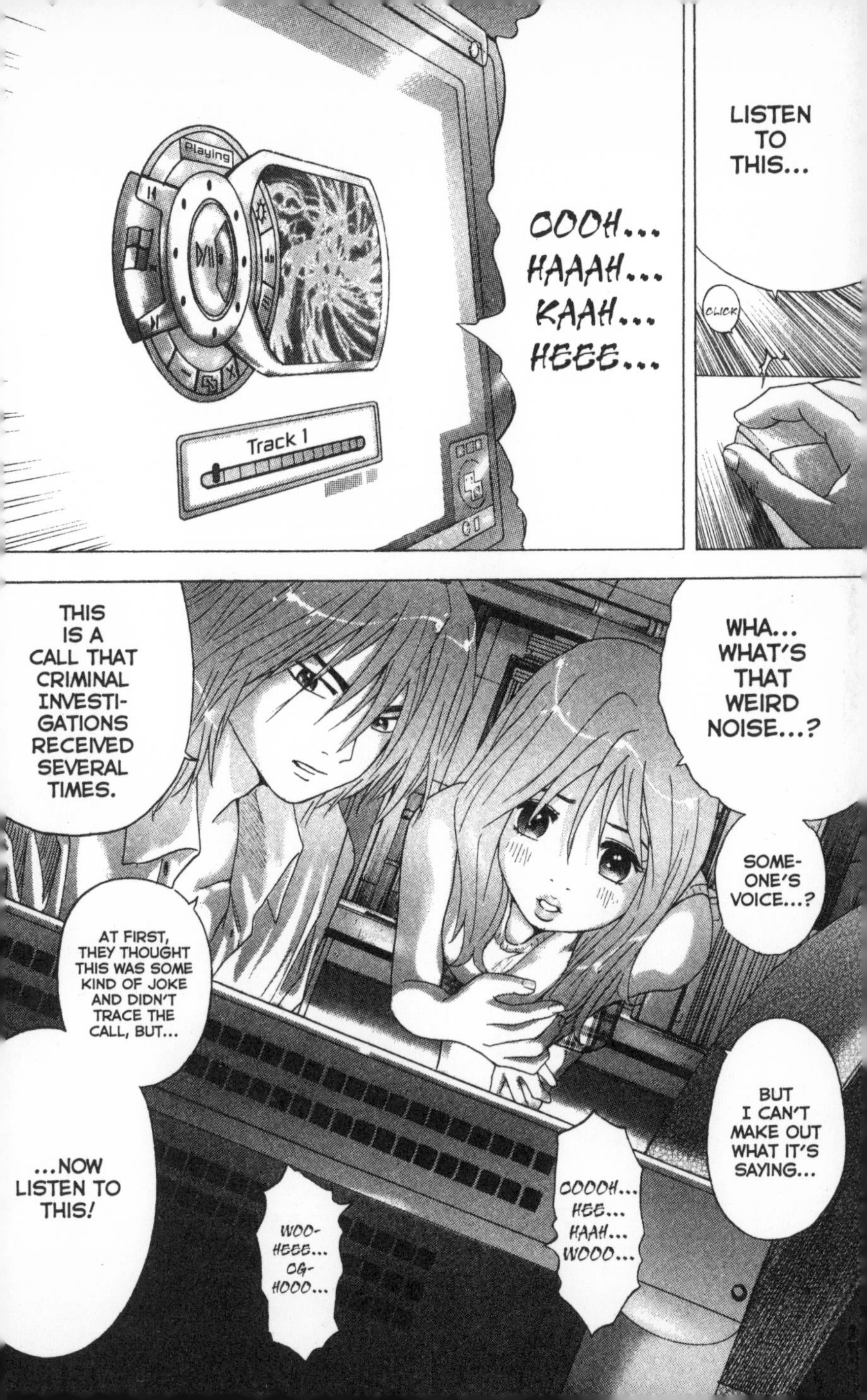
LISTEN TO THIS...
CLICK
OOOH... HAAAH... KAAH... HEEE...
Playing
Track 1
WHA... WHAT'S THAT WEIRD NOISE...?
THIS IS A CALL THAT CRIMINAL INVESTIGATIONS RECEIVED SEVERAL TIMES.
SOME-ONE'S VOICE...?
AT FIRST, THEY THOUGHT THIS WAS SOME KIND OF JOKE AND DIDN'T TRACE THE CALL, BUT...
BUT I CAN'T MAKE OUT WHAT IT'S SAYING...
OOOOH... HEE... HAAH... WOOO...
...NOW LISTEN TO THIS!
WOO-HEEE... OG-HOOO...

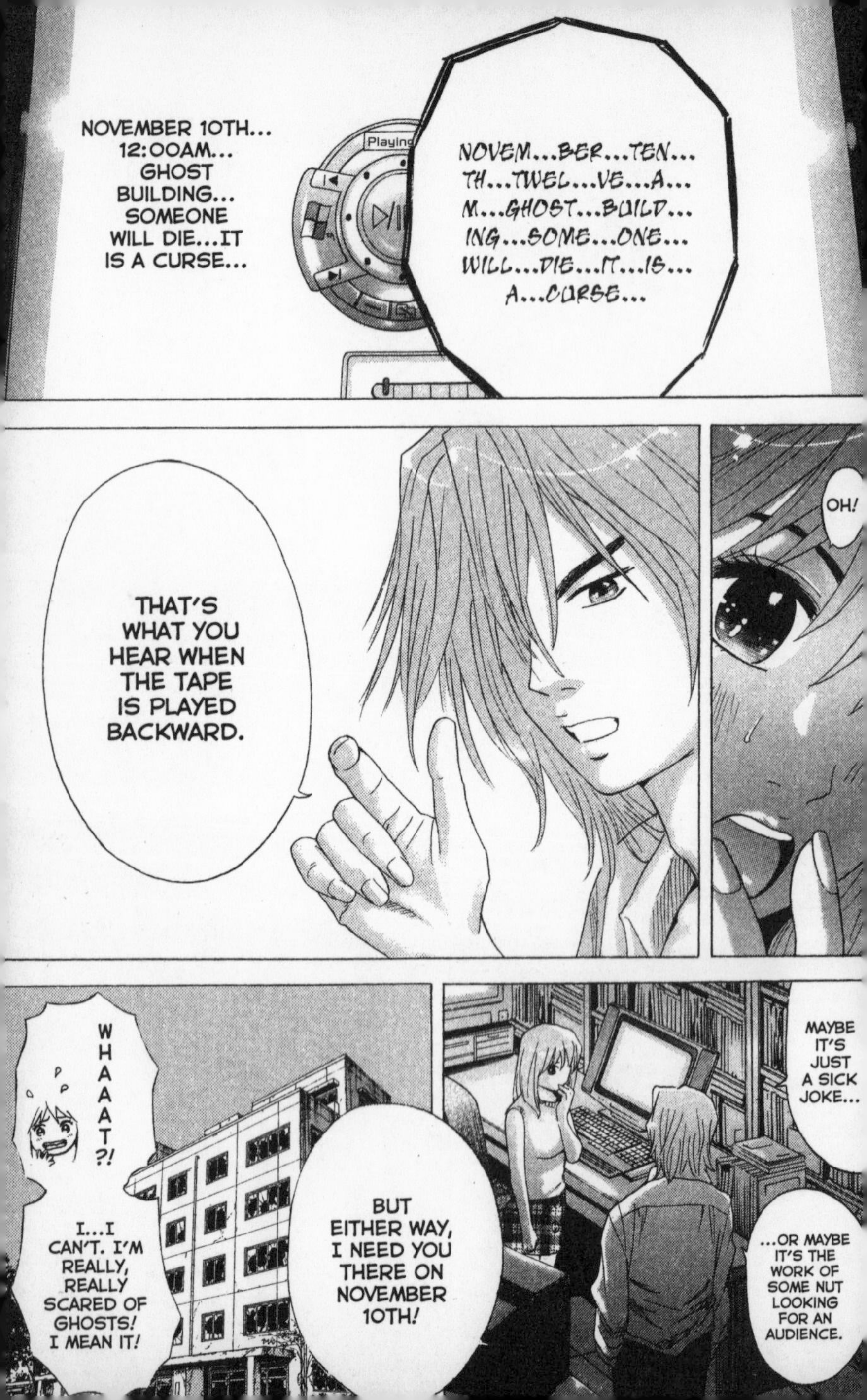
NOVEM...BER...TEN...TH...TWEL...VE...A...M...GHOST...BUILD...ING...SOME...ONE...WILL...DIE...IT...IS...A...CURSE...
NOVEMBER 10TH... 12:00AM... GHOST BUILDING... SOMEONE WILL DIE...IT IS A CURSE...
OH!
THAT'S WHAT YOU HEAR WHEN THE TAPE IS PLAYED BACKWARD.
MAYBE IT'S JUST A SICK JOKE...
...OR MAYBE IT'S THE WORK OF SOME NUT LOOKING FOR AN AUDIENCE.
BUT EITHER WAY, I NEED YOU THERE ON NOVEMBER 10TH!
WHAAAAT?!
I...I CAN'T. I'M REALLY, REALLY SCARED OF GHOSTS! I MEAN IT!

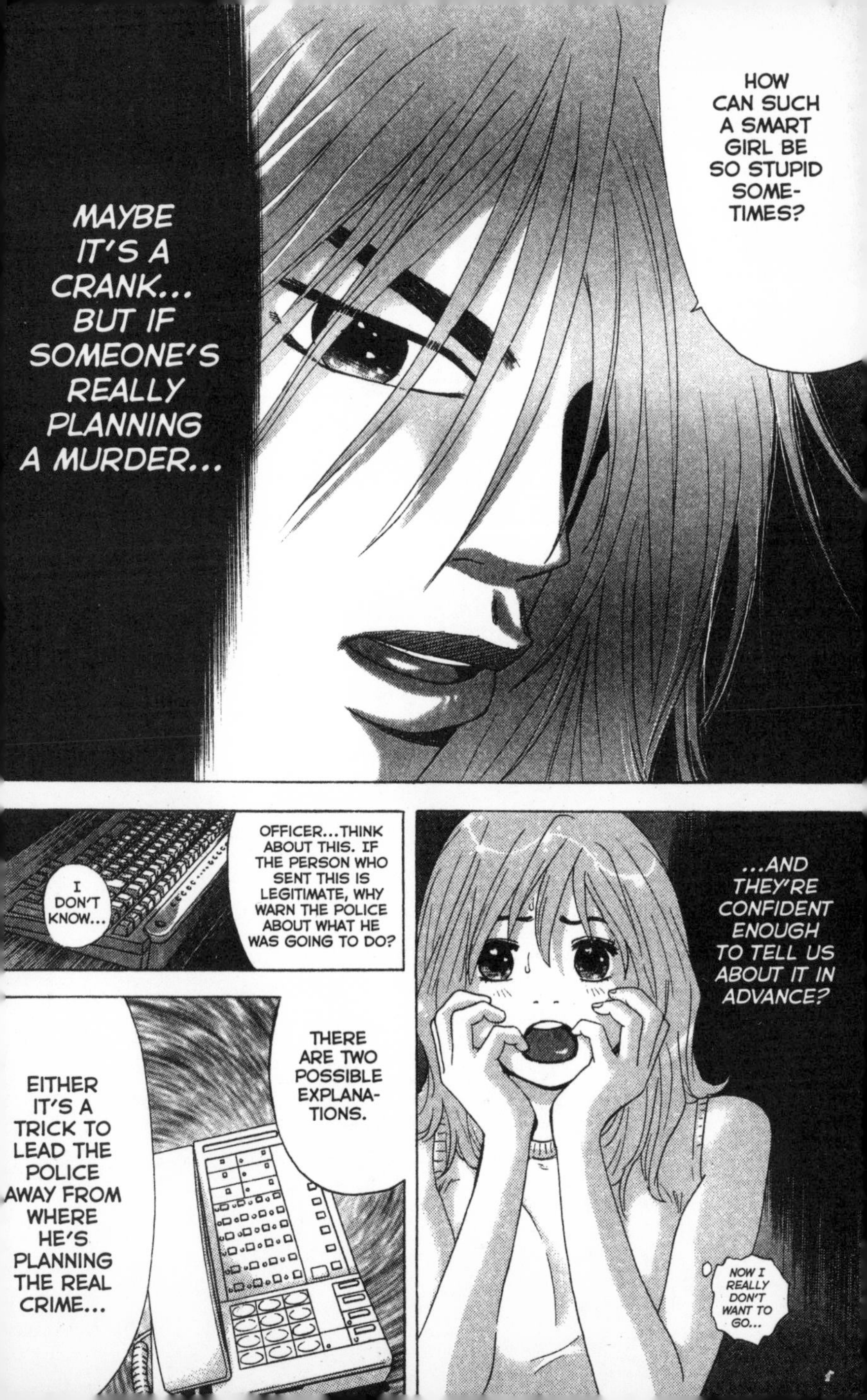
HOW CAN SUCH A SMART GIRL BE SO STUPID SOME-TIMES?
MAYBE IT'S A CRANK... BUT IF SOMEONE'S REALLY PLANNING A MURDER...
...AND THEY'RE CONFIDENT ENOUGH TO TELL US ABOUT IT IN ADVANCE?
NOW I REALLY DON'T WANT TO GO...
OFFICER...THINK ABOUT THIS. IF THE PERSON WHO SENT THIS IS LEGITIMATE, WHY WARN THE POLICE ABOUT WHAT HE WAS GOING TO DO?
I DON'T KNOW...
THERE ARE TWO POSSIBLE EXPLANA-TIONS.
EITHER IT'S A TRICK TO LEAD THE POLICE AWAY FROM WHERE HE'S PLANNING THE REAL CRIME...

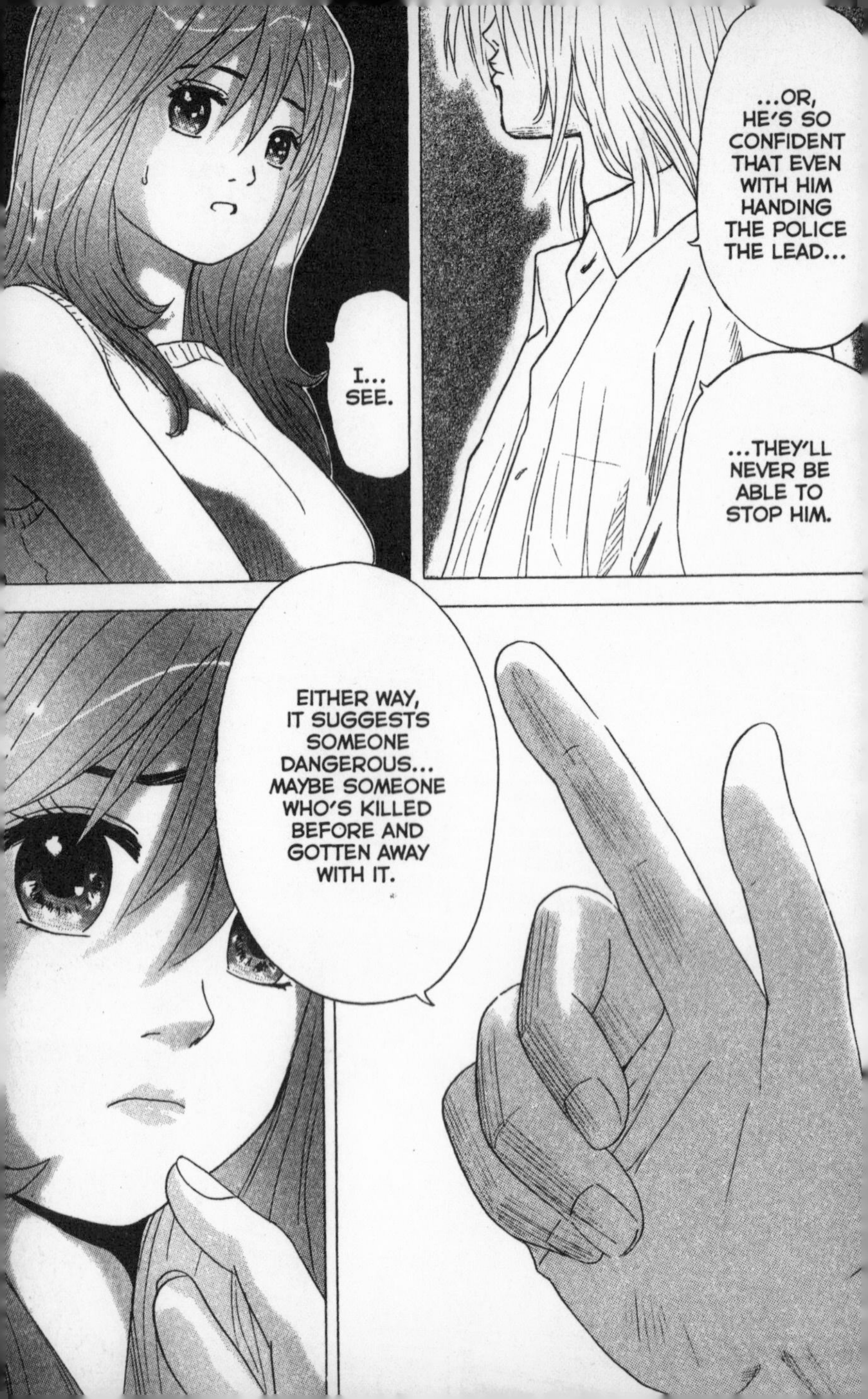
...OR, HE'S SO CONFIDENT THAT EVEN WITH HIM HANDING THE POLICE THE LEAD...
...THEY'LL NEVER BE ABLE TO STOP HIM.
I... SEE.
EITHER WAY, IT SUGGESTS SOMEONE DANGEROUS... MAYBE SOMEONE WHO'S KILLED BEFORE AND GOTTEN AWAY WITH IT.

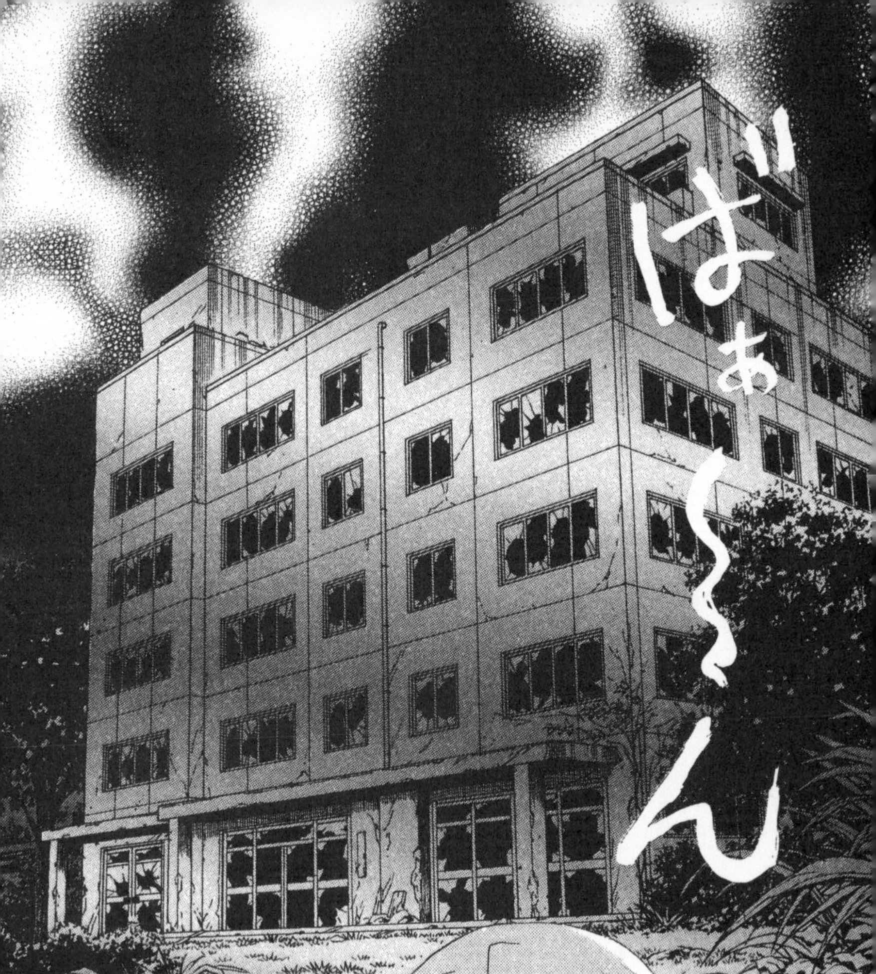
ばぁ〜〜ん

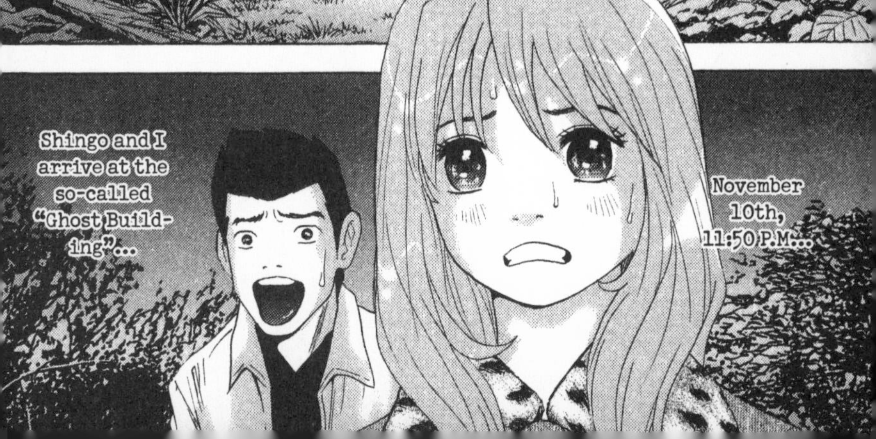
November 10th, 11:50 P.M...
Shingo and I arrive at the so-called "Ghost Build-ing"...

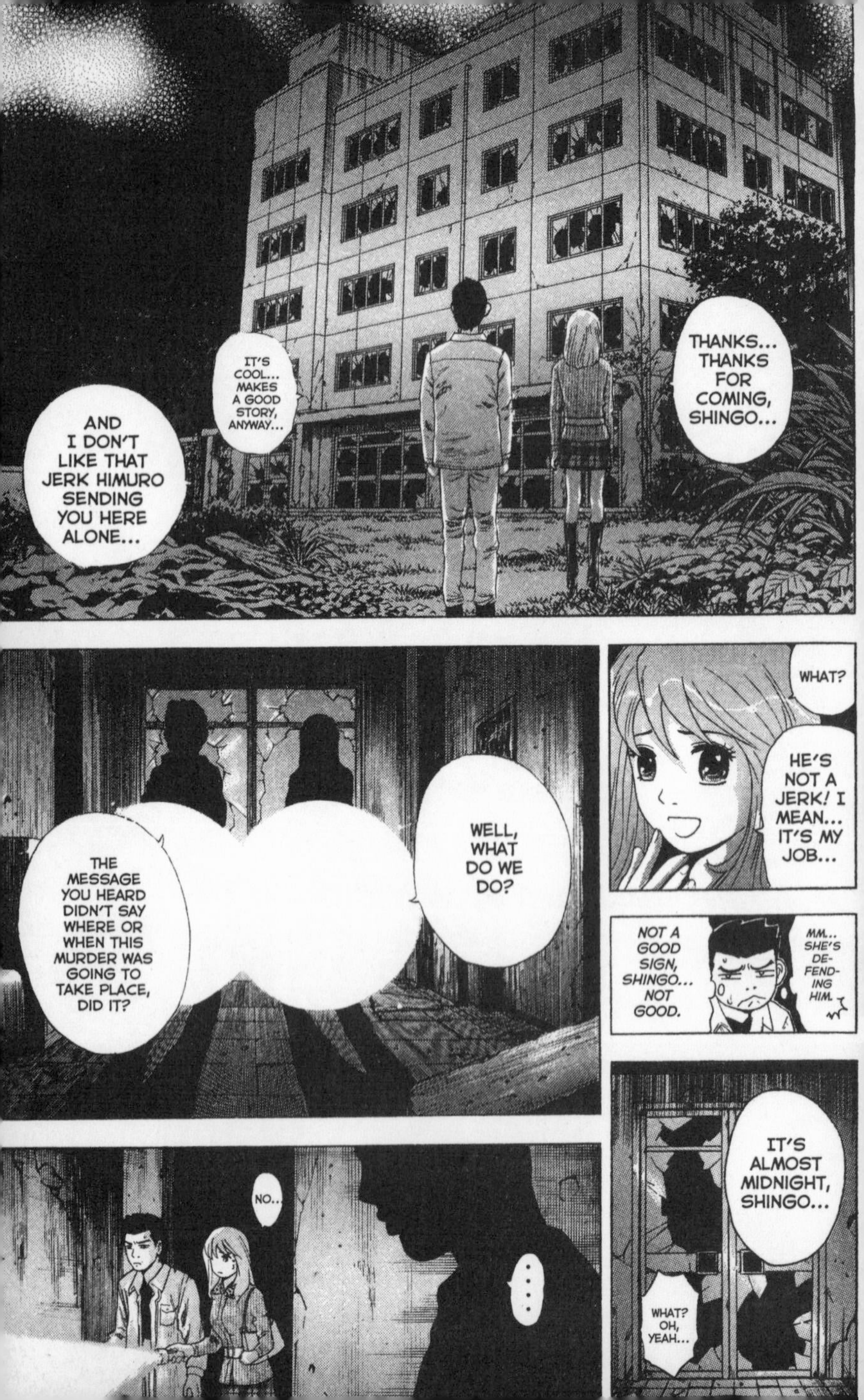
THANKS... THANKS FOR COMING, SHINGO...
IT'S COOL... MAKES A GOOD STORY, ANYWAY...
AND I DON'T LIKE THAT JERK HIMURO SENDING YOU HERE ALONE...
WHAT?
HE'S NOT A JERK! I MEAN... IT'S MY JOB...
MM... SHE'S DE-FENDING HIM.
NOT A GOOD SIGN, SHINGO... NOT GOOD.
WELL, WHAT DO WE DO?
THE MESSAGE YOU HEARD DIDN'T SAY WHERE OR WHEN THIS MURDER WAS GOING TO TAKE PLACE, DID IT?
IT'S ALMOST MIDNIGHT, SHINGO...
WHAT? OH, YEAH...
...
NO...

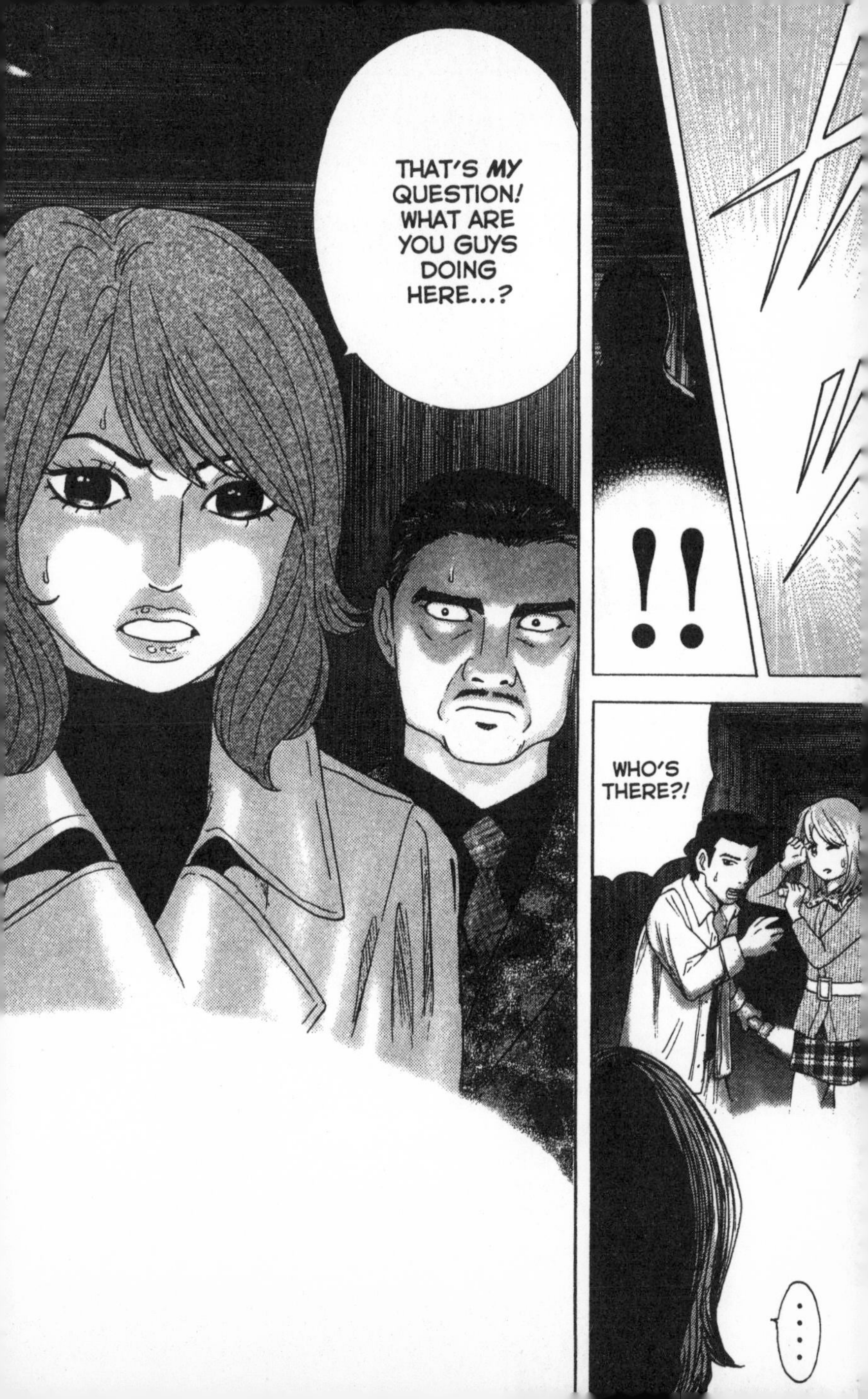
!!
WHO'S THERE?!
....
THAT'S *MY* QUESTION! WHAT ARE YOU GUYS DOING HERE...?

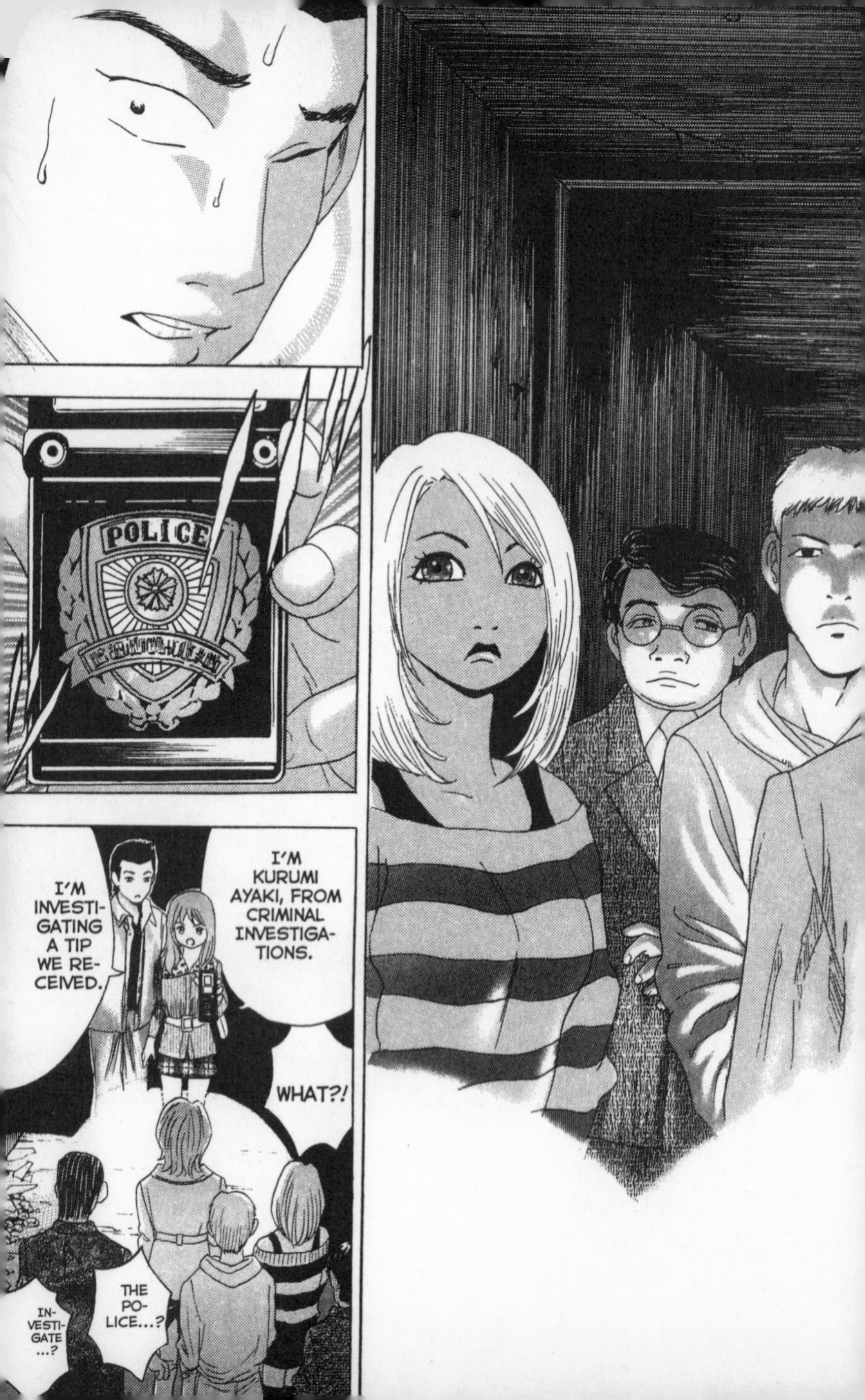
POLICE
I'M KURUMI AYAKI, FROM CRIMINAL INVESTIGATIONS.
I'M INVESTIGATING A TIP WE RECEIVED.
WHAT?!
THE POLICE...?
INVESTIGATE...?

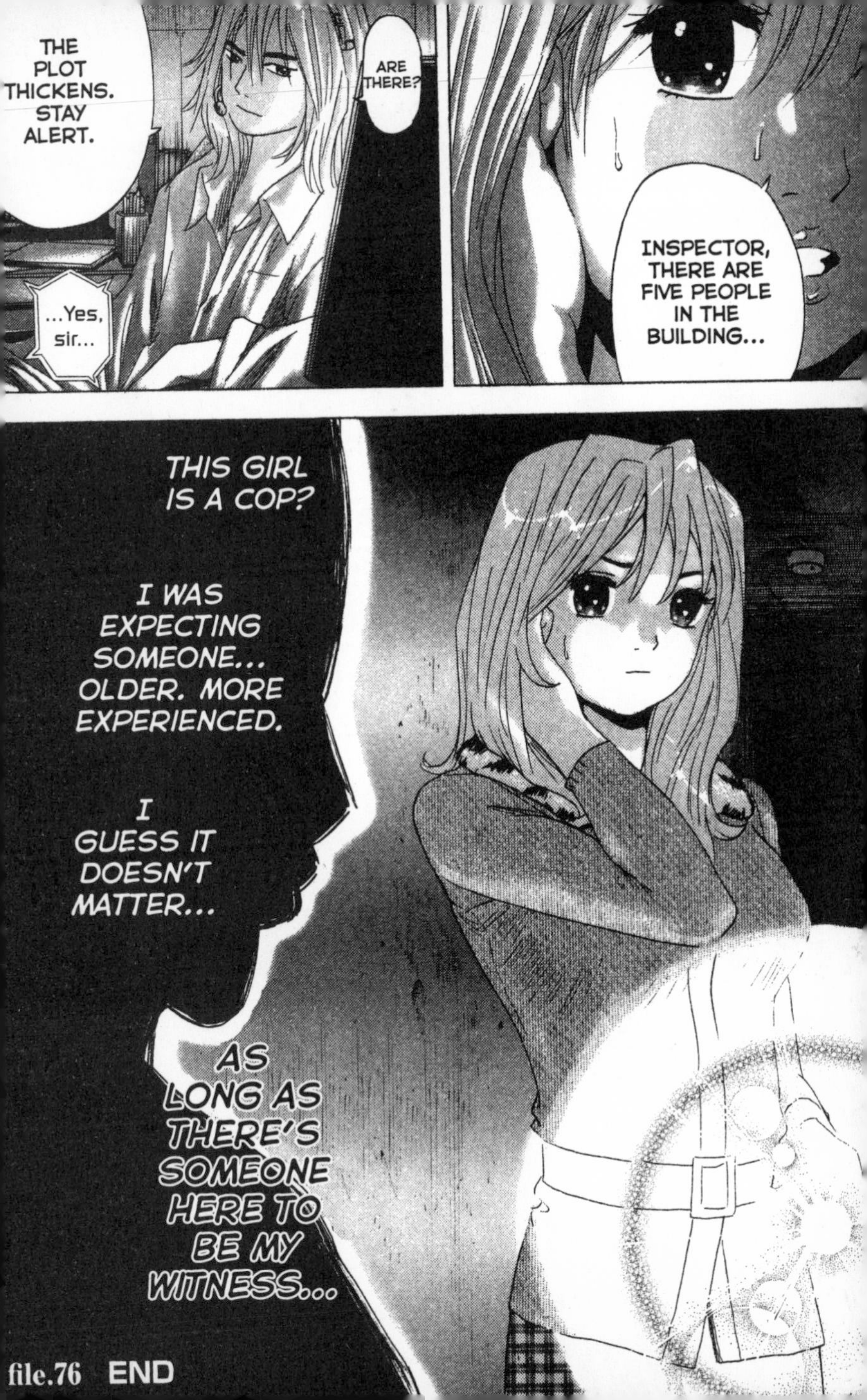
INSPECTOR, THERE ARE FIVE PEOPLE IN THE BUILDING...
ARE THERE?
THE PLOT THICKENS. STAY ALERT.
...Yes, sir...
THIS GIRL IS A COP?
I WAS EXPECTING SOMEONE... OLDER. MORE EXPERIENCED.
I GUESS IT DOESN'T MATTER...
AS LONG AS THERE'S SOMEONE HERE TO BE MY WITNESS...
file.76 END

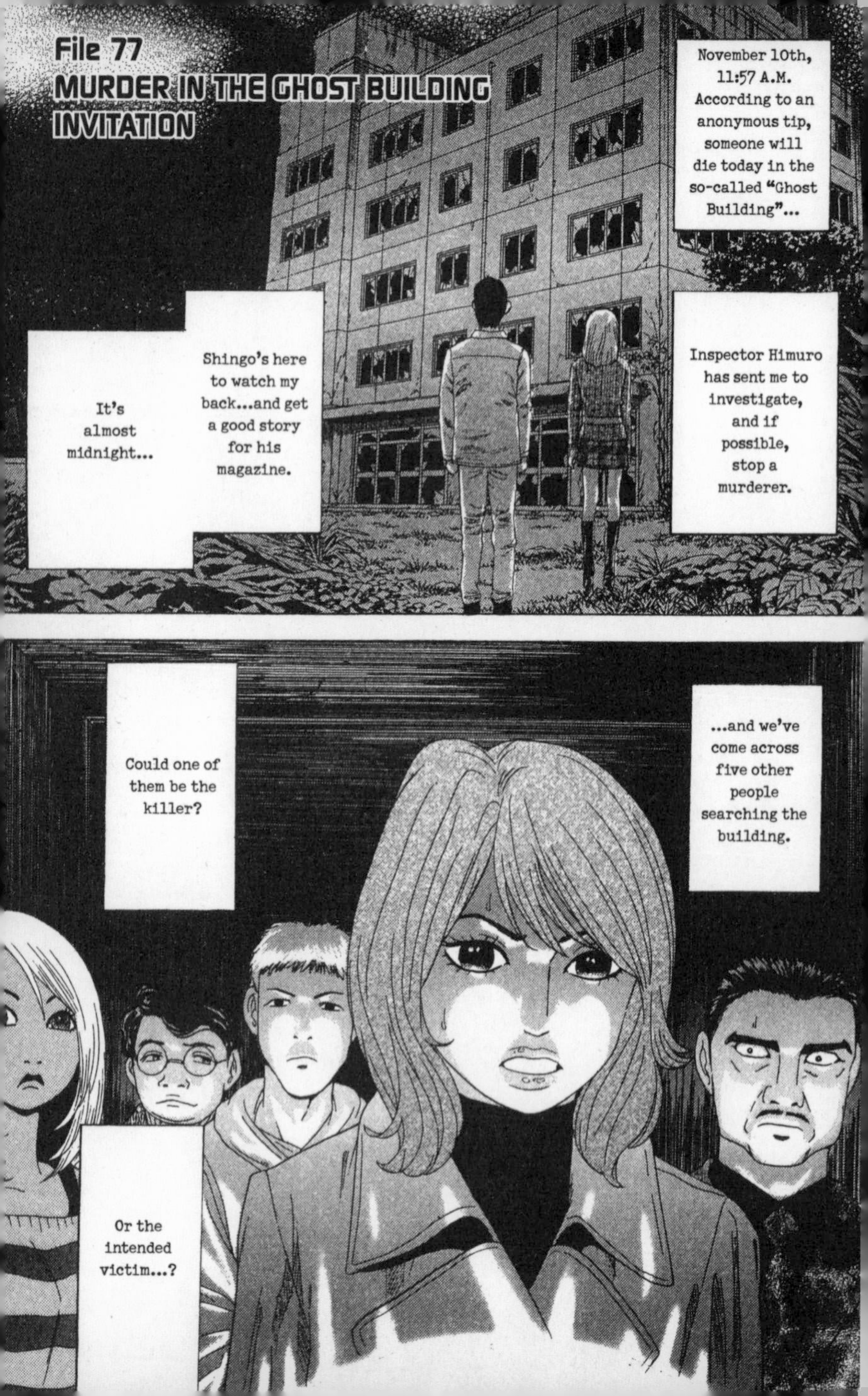
File 77
MURDER IN THE GHOST BUILDING
INVITATION
November 10th, 11:57 A.M. According to an anonymous tip, someone will die today in the so-called "Ghost Building"...
Inspector Himuro has sent me to investigate, and if possible, stop a murderer.
Shingo's here to watch my back...and get a good story for his magazine.
It's almost midnight...
...and we've come across five other people searching the building.
Could one of them be the killer?
Or the intended victim...?

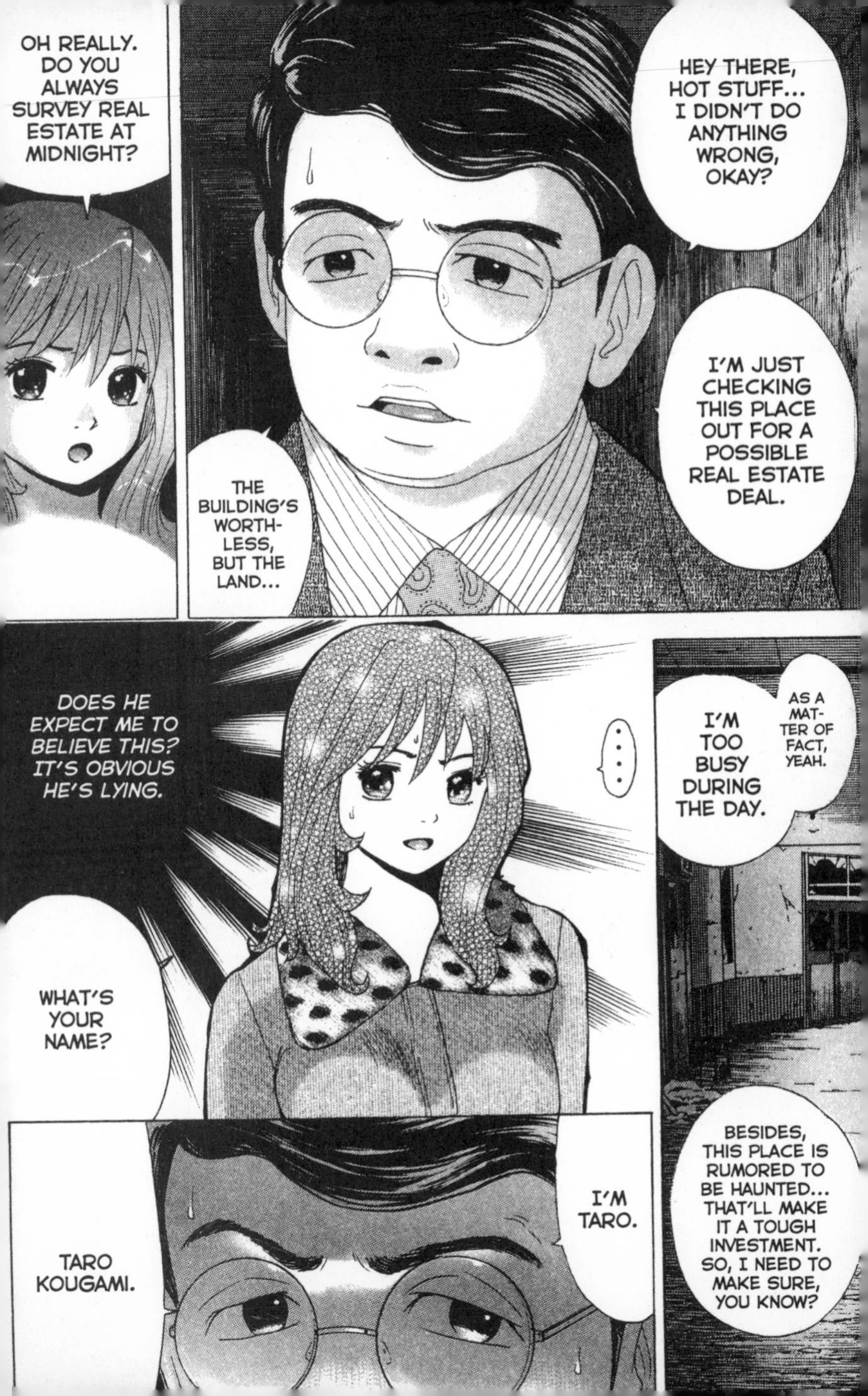
HEY THERE, HOT STUFF... I DIDN'T DO ANYTHING WRONG, OKAY?
I'M JUST CHECKING THIS PLACE OUT FOR A POSSIBLE REAL ESTATE DEAL.
THE BUILDING'S WORTH-LESS, BUT THE LAND...
OH REALLY. DO YOU ALWAYS SURVEY REAL ESTATE AT MIDNIGHT?
AS A MAT-TER OF FACT, YEAH.
I'M TOO BUSY DURING THE DAY.
BESIDES, THIS PLACE IS RUMORED TO BE HAUNTED... THAT'LL MAKE IT A TOUGH INVESTMENT. SO, I NEED TO MAKE SURE, YOU KNOW?
...
DOES HE EXPECT ME TO BELIEVE THIS? IT'S OBVIOUS HE'S LYING.
WHAT'S YOUR NAME?
I'M TARO.
TARO KOUGAMI.

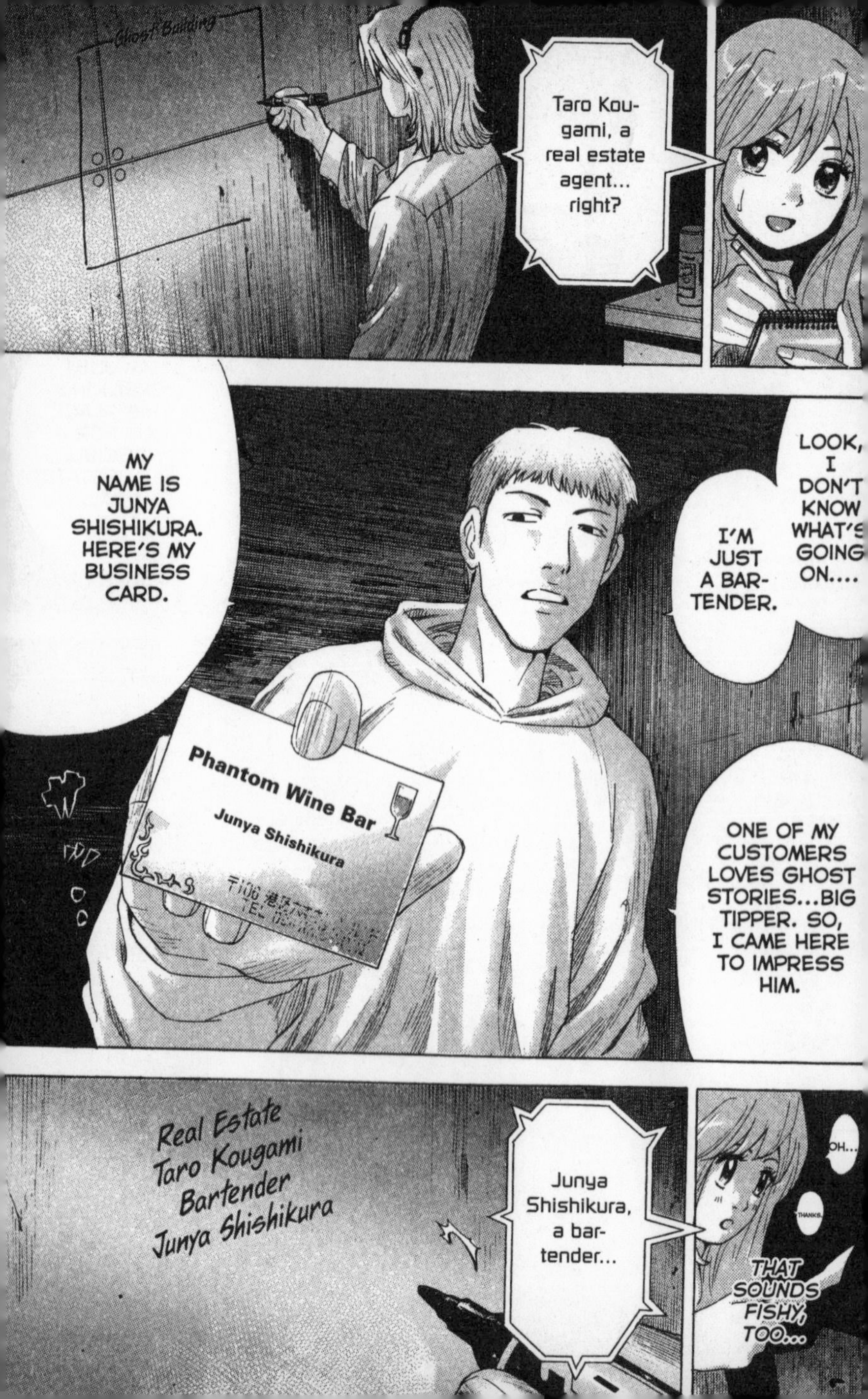
Taro Kougami, a real estate agent... right?
Ghost Building
LOOK, I DON'T KNOW WHAT'S GOING ON....
I'M JUST A BARTENDER.
MY NAME IS JUNYA SHISHIKURA. HERE'S MY BUSINESS CARD.
ONE OF MY CUSTOMERS LOVES GHOST STORIES...BIG TIPPER. SO, I CAME HERE TO IMPRESS HIM.
Phantom Wine Bar
Junya Shishikura
OH...
THANKS.
THAT SOUNDS FISHY, TOO...
Junya Shishikura, a bartender...
Real Estate
Taro Kougami
Bartender
Junya Shishikura

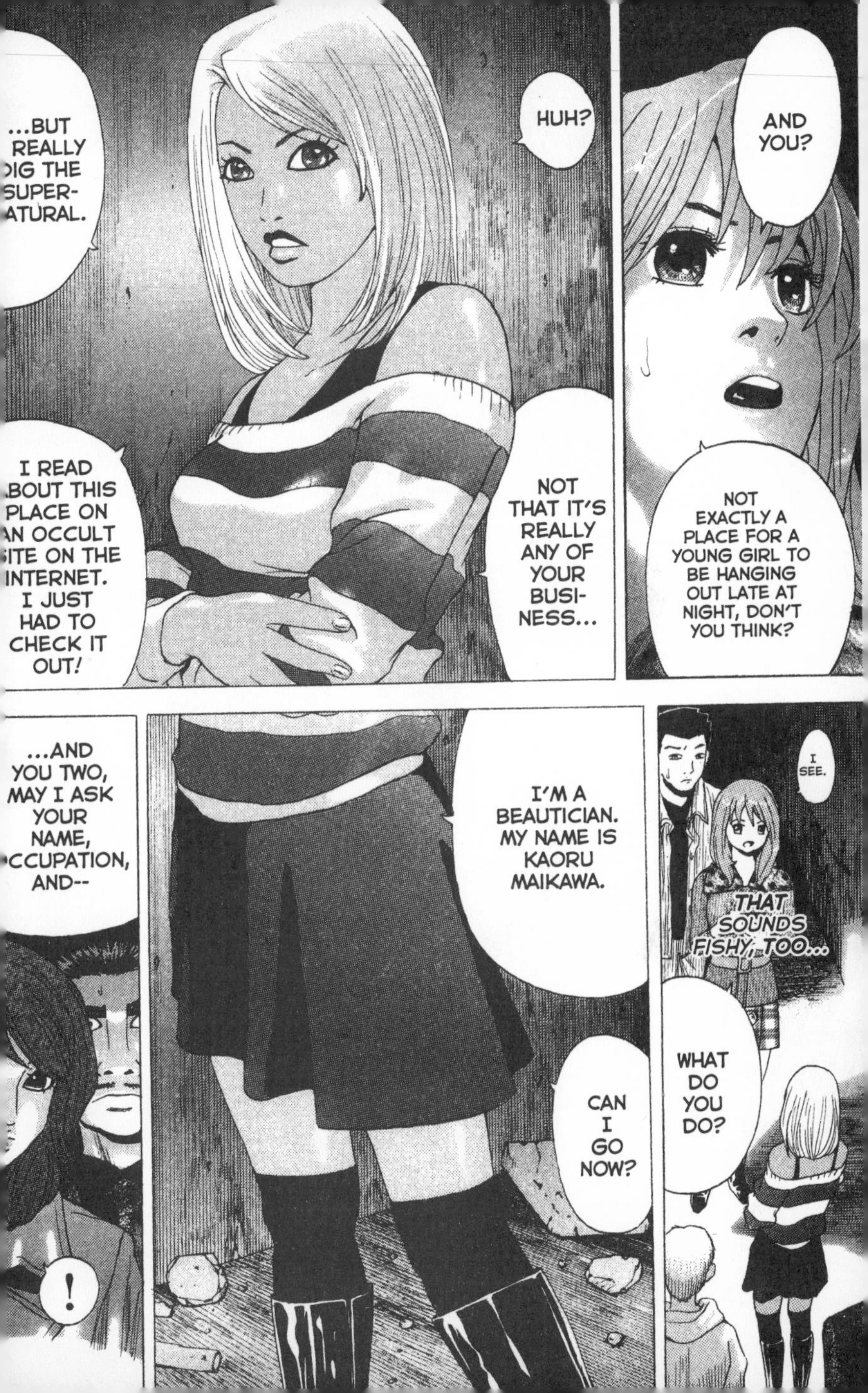
AND YOU?
NOT EXACTLY A PLACE FOR A YOUNG GIRL TO BE HANGING OUT LATE AT NIGHT, DON'T YOU THINK?
HUH?
...BUT REALLY IG THE SUPER- ATURAL.
NOT THAT IT'S REALLY ANY OF YOUR BUSI- NESS...
I READ BOUT THIS PLACE ON N OCCULT ITE ON THE INTERNET. I JUST HAD TO CHECK IT OUT!
I SEE.
THAT SOUNDS FISHY, TOO...
WHAT DO YOU DO?
I'M A BEAUTICIAN. MY NAME IS KAORU MAIKAWA.
CAN I GO NOW?
...AND YOU TWO, MAY I ASK YOUR NAME, CCUPATION, AND--
!

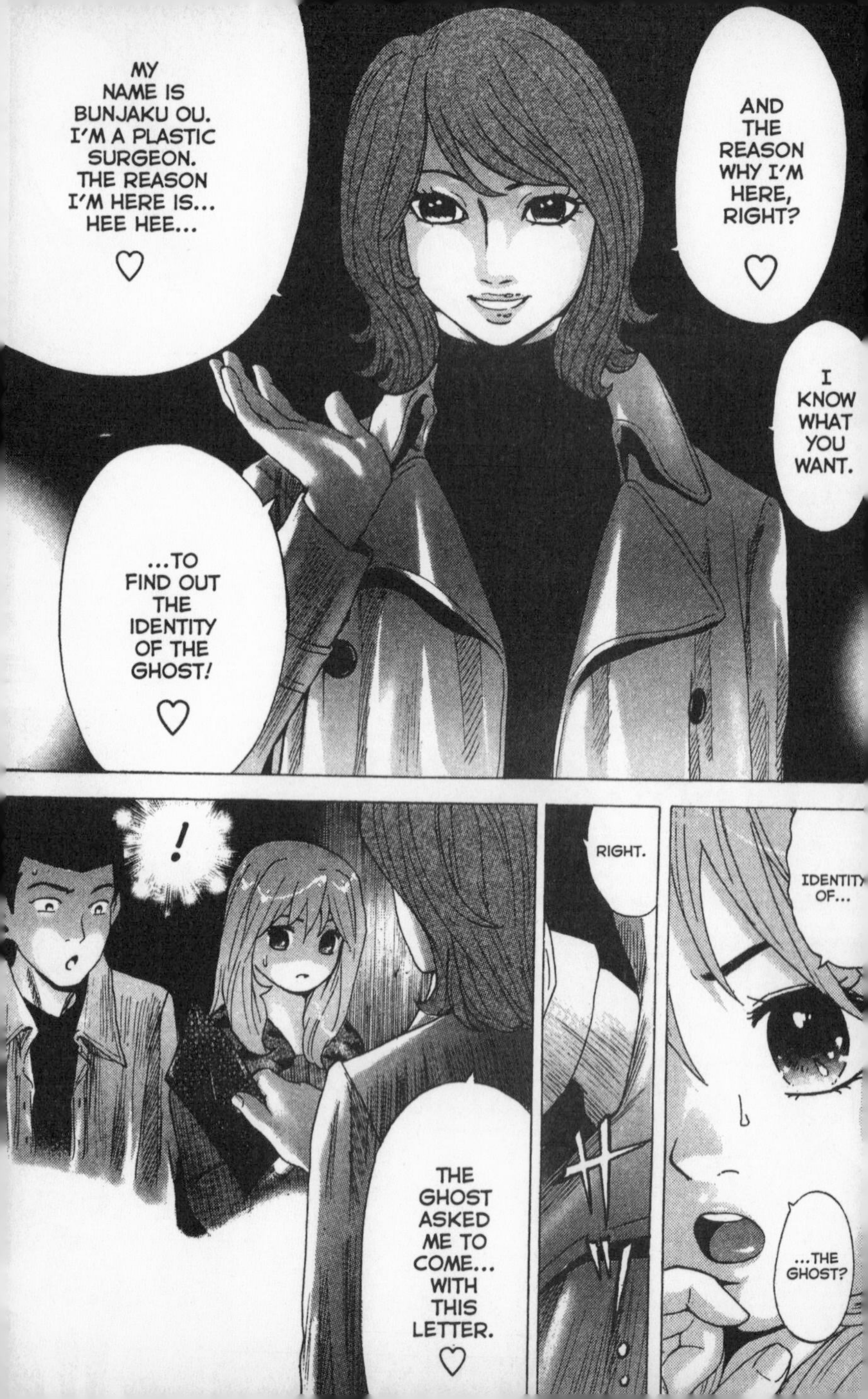
AND THE REASON WHY I'M HERE, RIGHT? ♡
I KNOW WHAT YOU WANT.
MY NAME IS BUNJAKU OU. I'M A PLASTIC SURGEON. THE REASON I'M HERE IS... HEE HEE... ♡
...TO FIND OUT THE IDENTITY OF THE GHOST! ♡
IDENTITY OF...
...THE GHOST?
RIGHT.
!
THE GHOST ASKED ME TO COME... WITH THIS LETTER. ♡

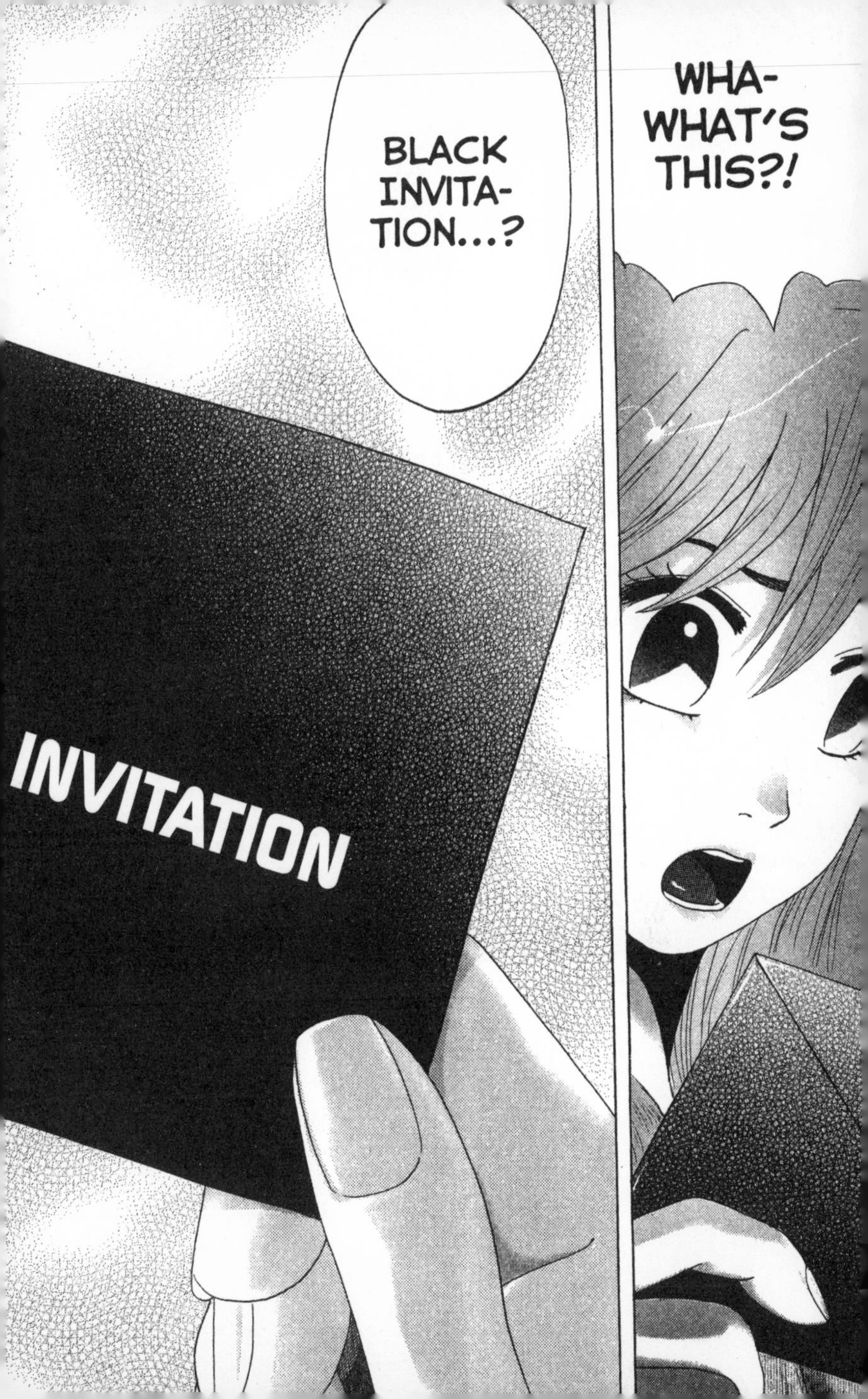
WHA-WHAT'S THIS?!
BLACK INVITA-TION...?
INVITATION

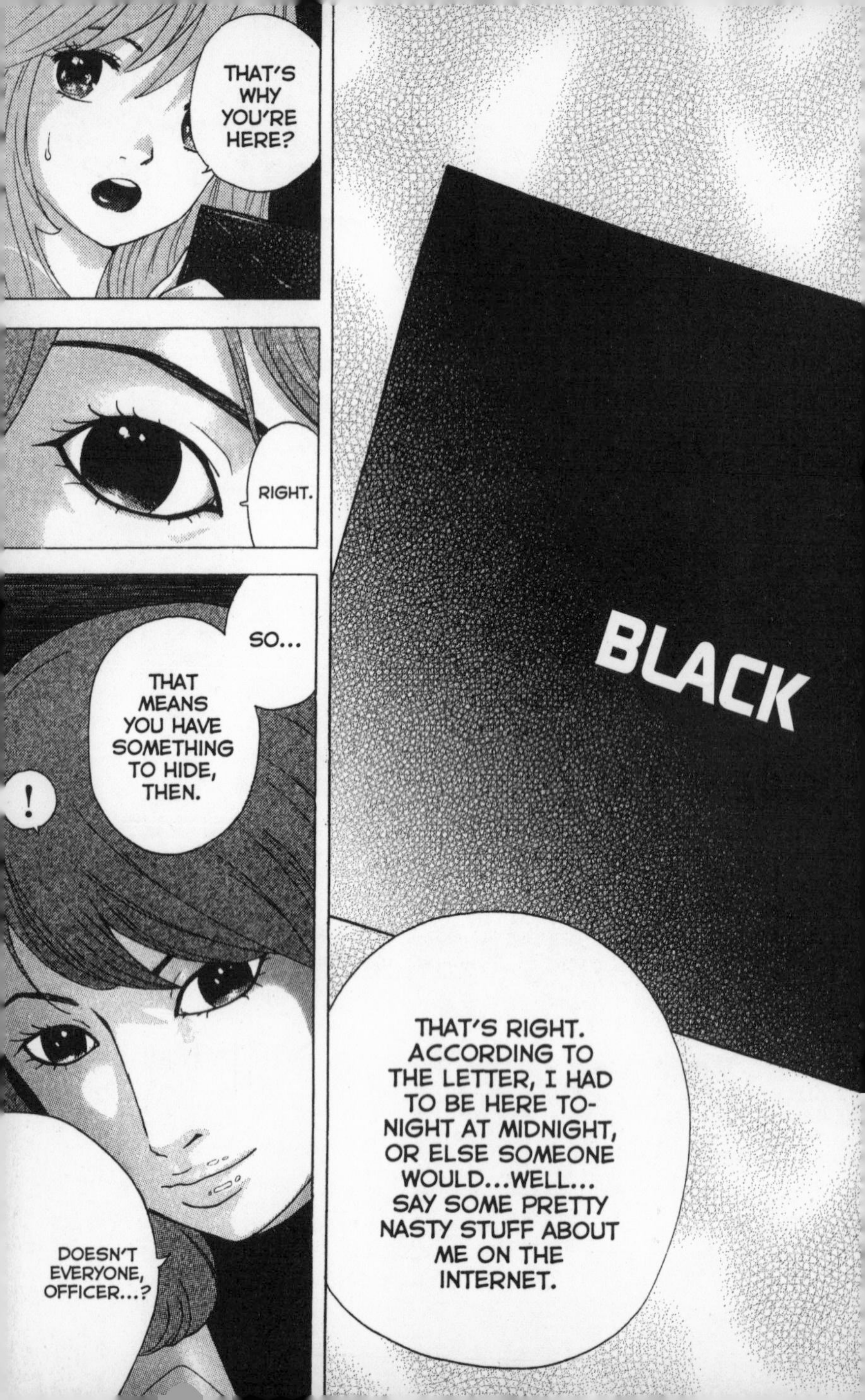
BLACK
THAT'S RIGHT. ACCORDING TO THE LETTER, I HAD TO BE HERE TO-NIGHT AT MIDNIGHT, OR ELSE SOMEONE WOULD...WELL... SAY SOME PRETTY NASTY STUFF ABOUT ME ON THE INTERNET.
THAT'S WHY YOU'RE HERE?
RIGHT.
SO...
THAT MEANS YOU HAVE SOMETHING TO HIDE, THEN.
!
DOESN'T EVERYONE, OFFICER...?

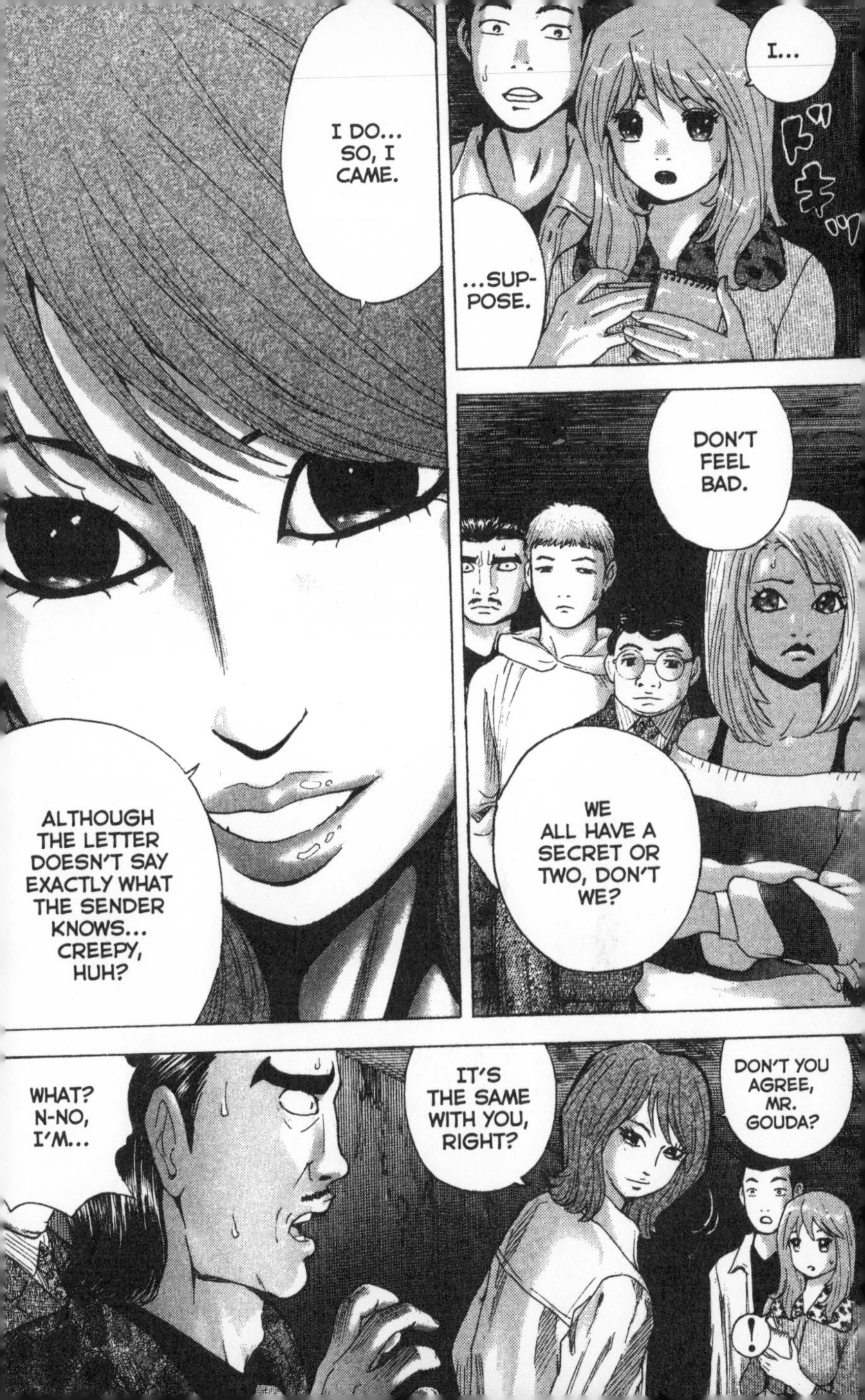
I...
ドキッ
...SUP-POSE.
DON'T FEEL BAD.
WE ALL HAVE A SECRET OR TWO, DON'T WE?
I DO... SO, I CAME.
ALTHOUGH THE LETTER DOESN'T SAY EXACTLY WHAT THE SENDER KNOWS... CREEPY, HUH?
DON'T YOU AGREE, MR. GOUDA?
!
IT'S THE SAME WITH YOU, RIGHT?
WHAT? N-NO, I'M...

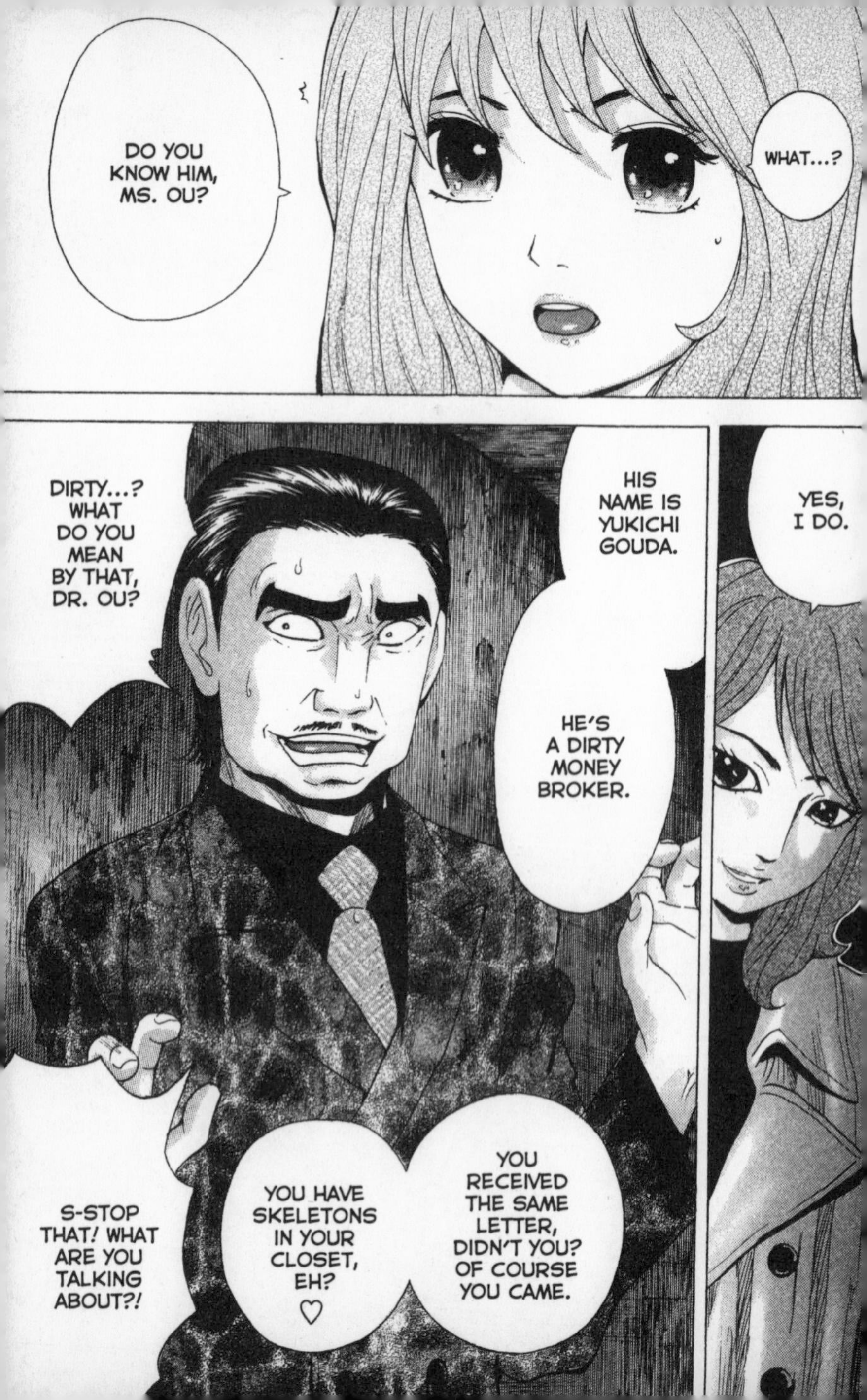
WHAT...?
DO YOU KNOW HIM, MS. OU?
YES, I DO.
HIS NAME IS YUKICHI GOUDA.
HE'S A DIRTY MONEY BROKER.
DIRTY...? WHAT DO YOU MEAN BY THAT, DR. OU?
YOU RECEIVED THE SAME LETTER, DIDN'T YOU? OF COURSE YOU CAME.
YOU HAVE SKELETONS IN YOUR CLOSET, EH? ♡
S-STOP THAT! WHAT ARE YOU TALKING ABOUT?!

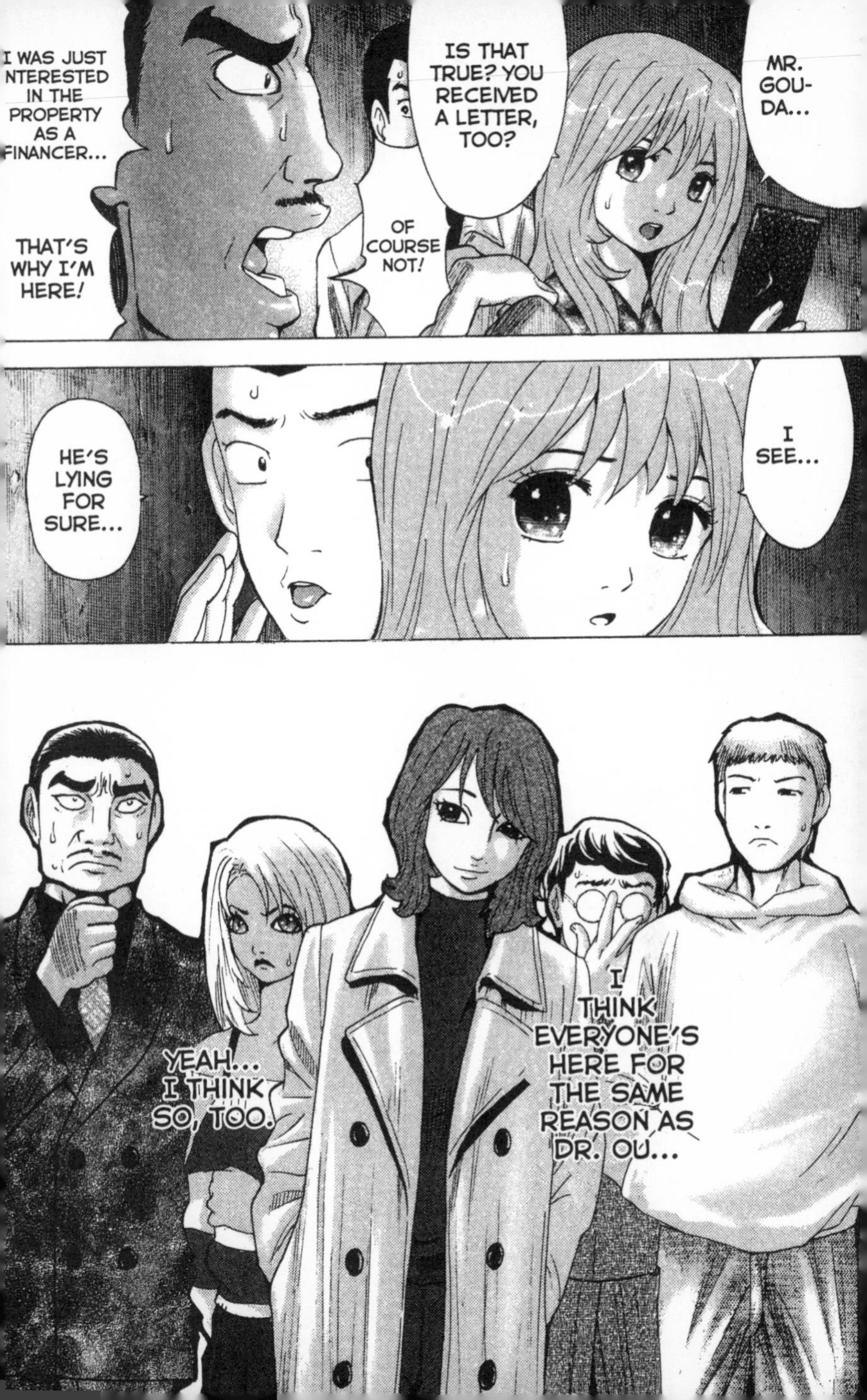
MR. GOUDA...
IS THAT TRUE? YOU RECEIVED A LETTER, TOO?
OF COURSE NOT!
I WAS JUST NTERESTED IN THE PROPERTY AS A FINANCER...
THAT'S WHY I'M HERE!
I SEE...
HE'S LYING FOR SURE...
I THINK EVERYONE'S HERE FOR THE SAME REASON AS DR. OU...
YEAH... I THINK SO, TOO.

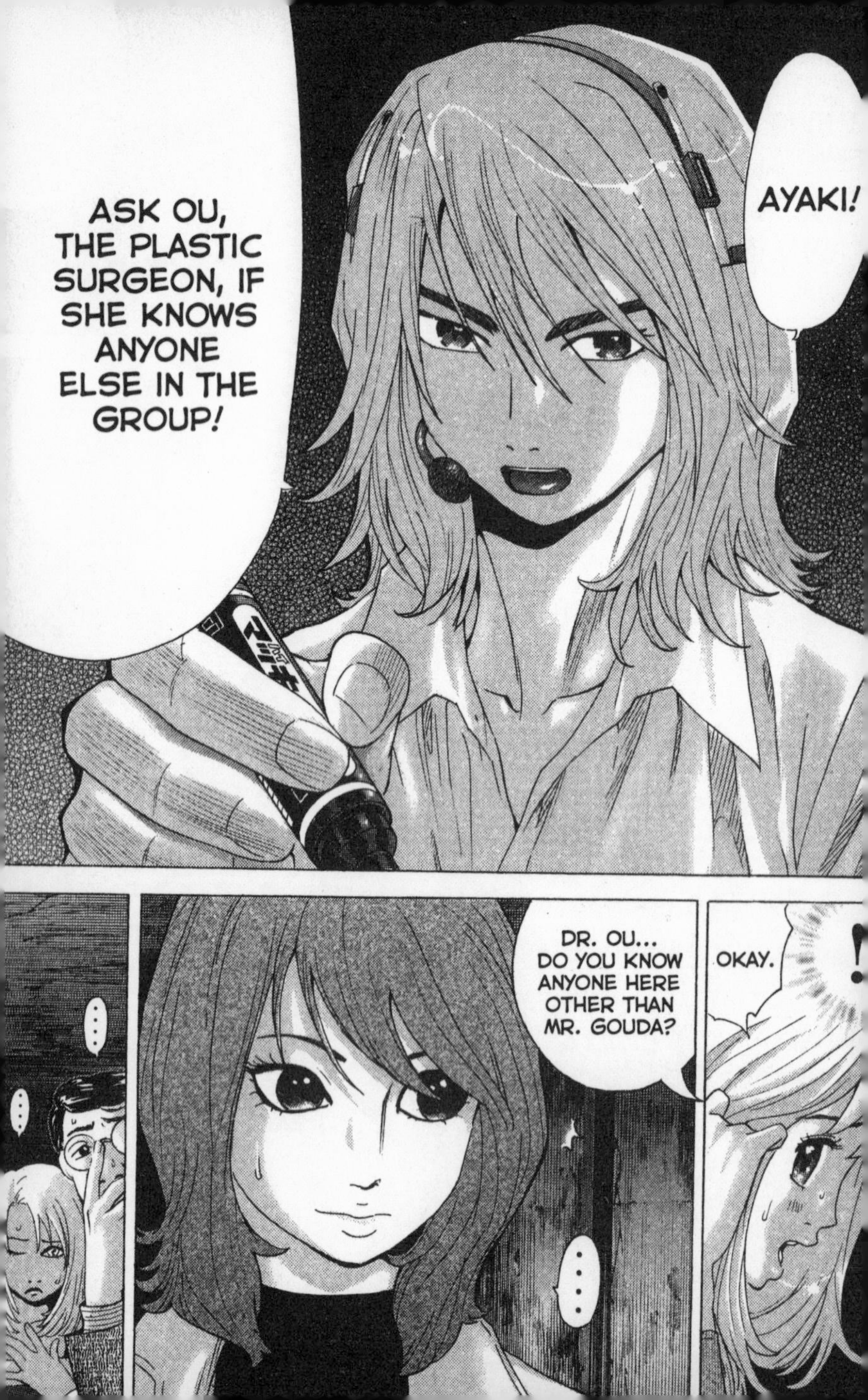
AYAKI!
ASK OU, THE PLASTIC SURGEON, IF SHE KNOWS ANYONE ELSE IN THE GROUP!
OKAY.
!
DR. OU... DO YOU KNOW ANYONE HERE OTHER THAN MR. GOUDA?
...
...
...

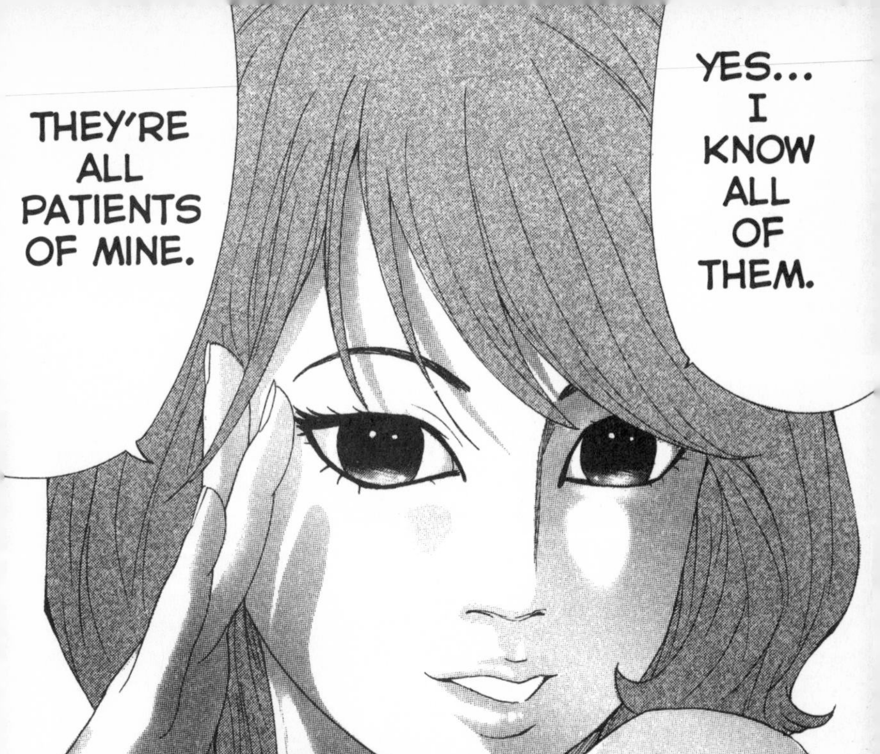
YES... I KNOW ALL OF THEM.
THEY'RE ALL PATIENTS OF MINE.
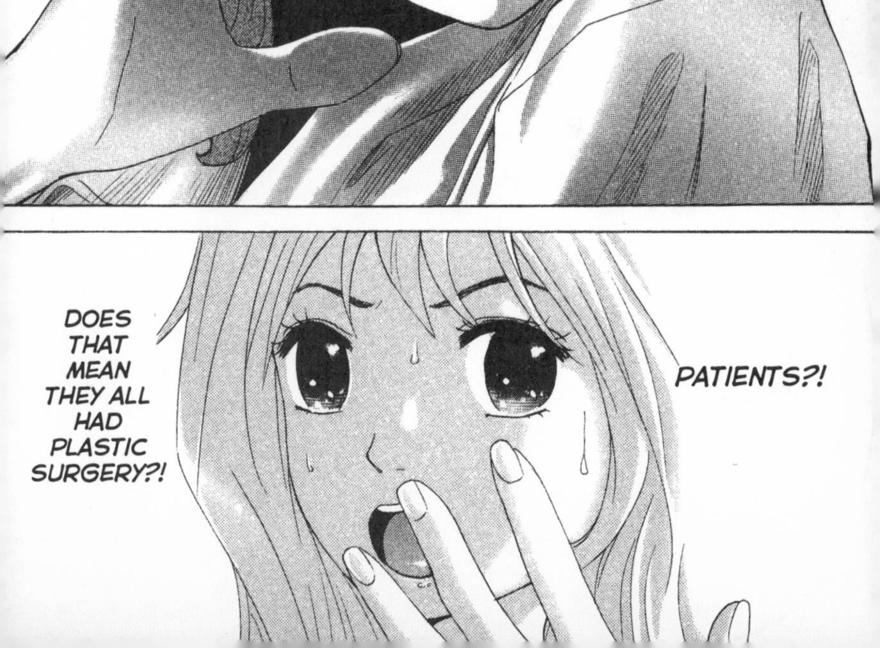
PATIENTS?!
DOES THAT MEAN THEY ALL HAD PLASTIC SURGERY?!

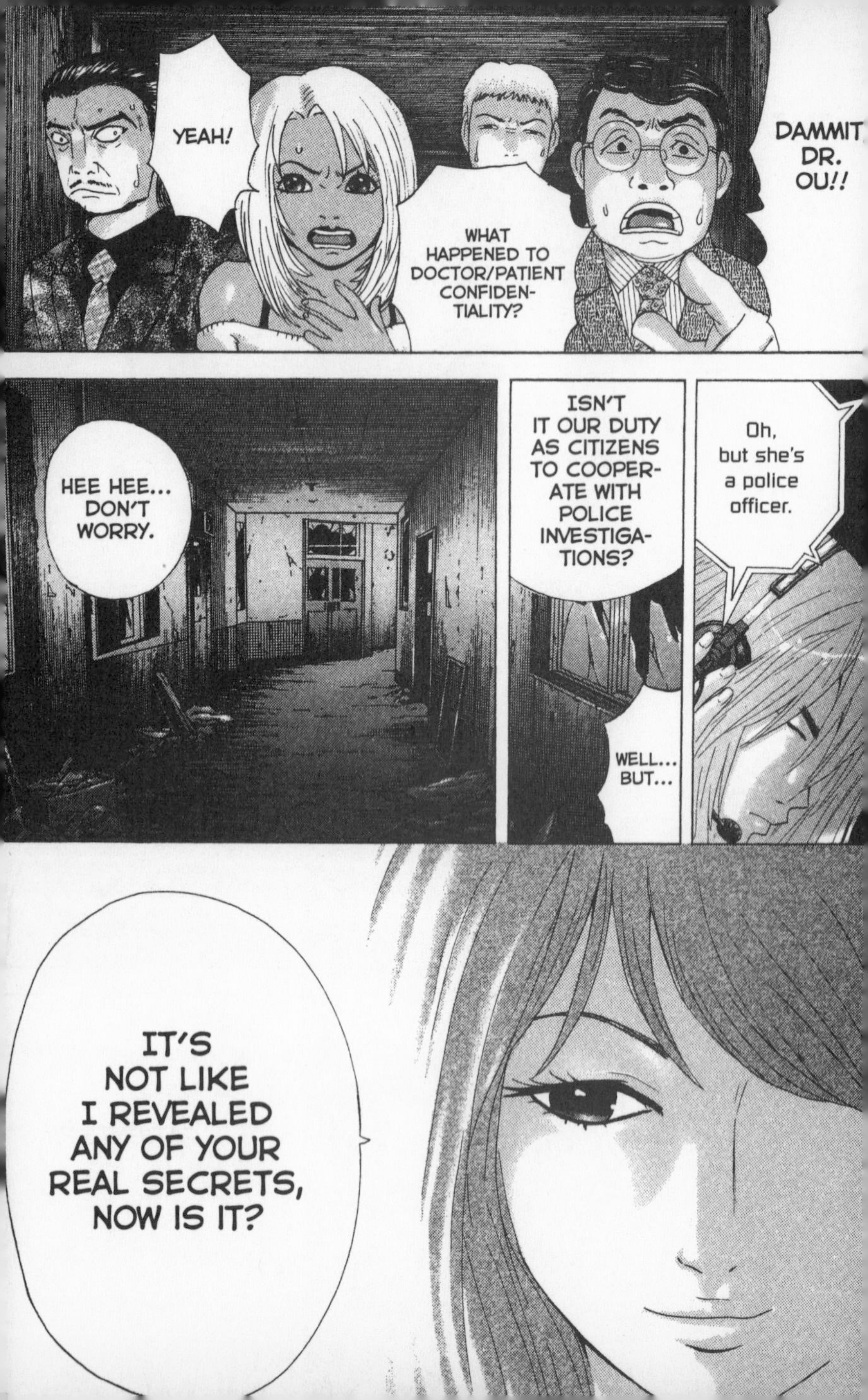
DAMMIT DR. OU!!
WHAT HAPPENED TO DOCTOR/PATIENT CONFIDENTIALITY?
YEAH!
Oh, but she's a police officer.
ISN'T IT OUR DUTY AS CITIZENS TO COOPERATE WITH POLICE INVESTIGATIONS?
WELL... BUT...
HEE HEE... DON'T WORRY.
IT'S NOT LIKE I REVEALED ANY OF YOUR REAL SECRETS, NOW IS IT?

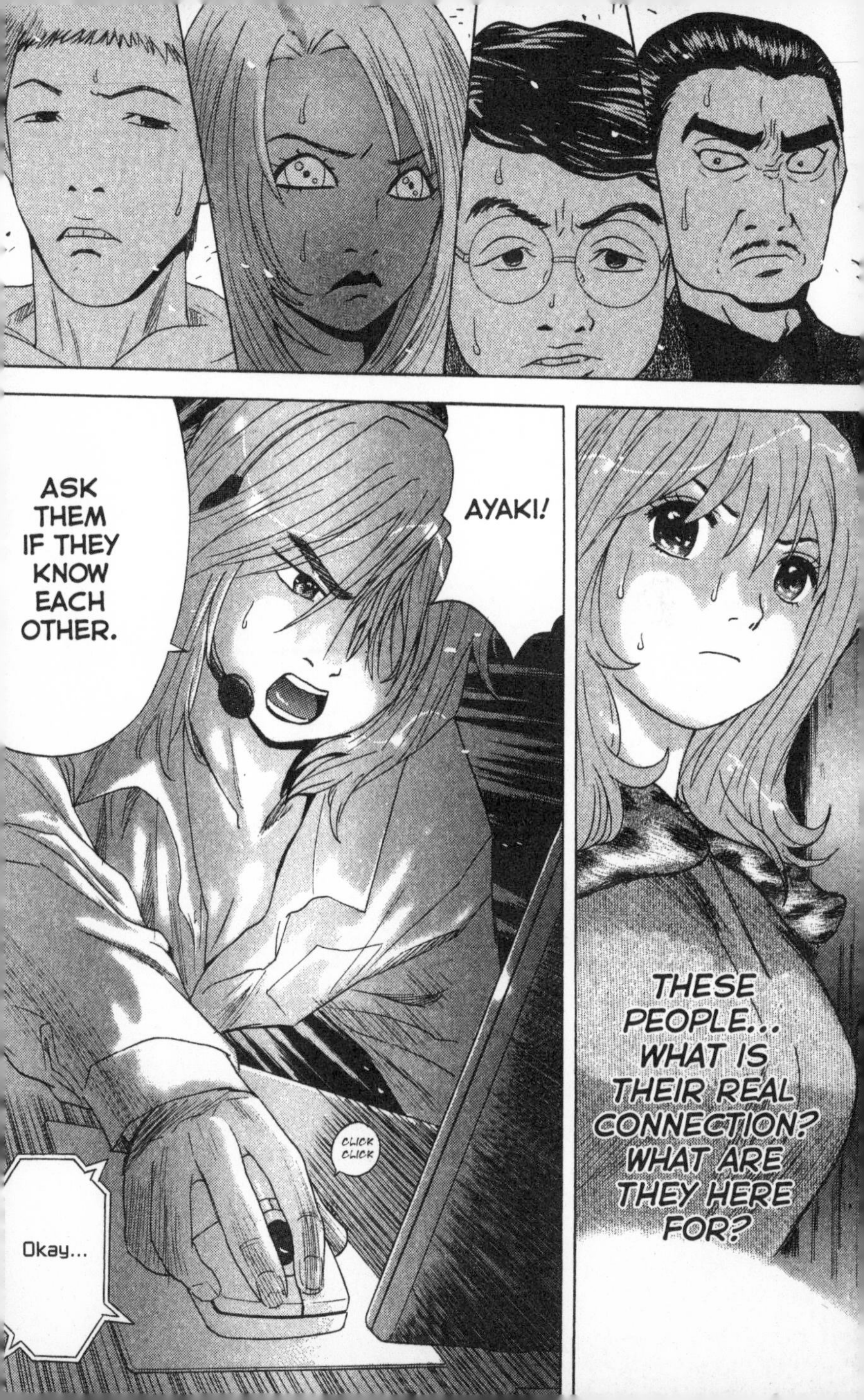
THESE PEOPLE... WHAT IS THEIR REAL CONNECTION? WHAT ARE THEY HERE FOR?
AYAKI!
ASK THEM IF THEY KNOW EACH OTHER.
CLICK CLICK
Okay...

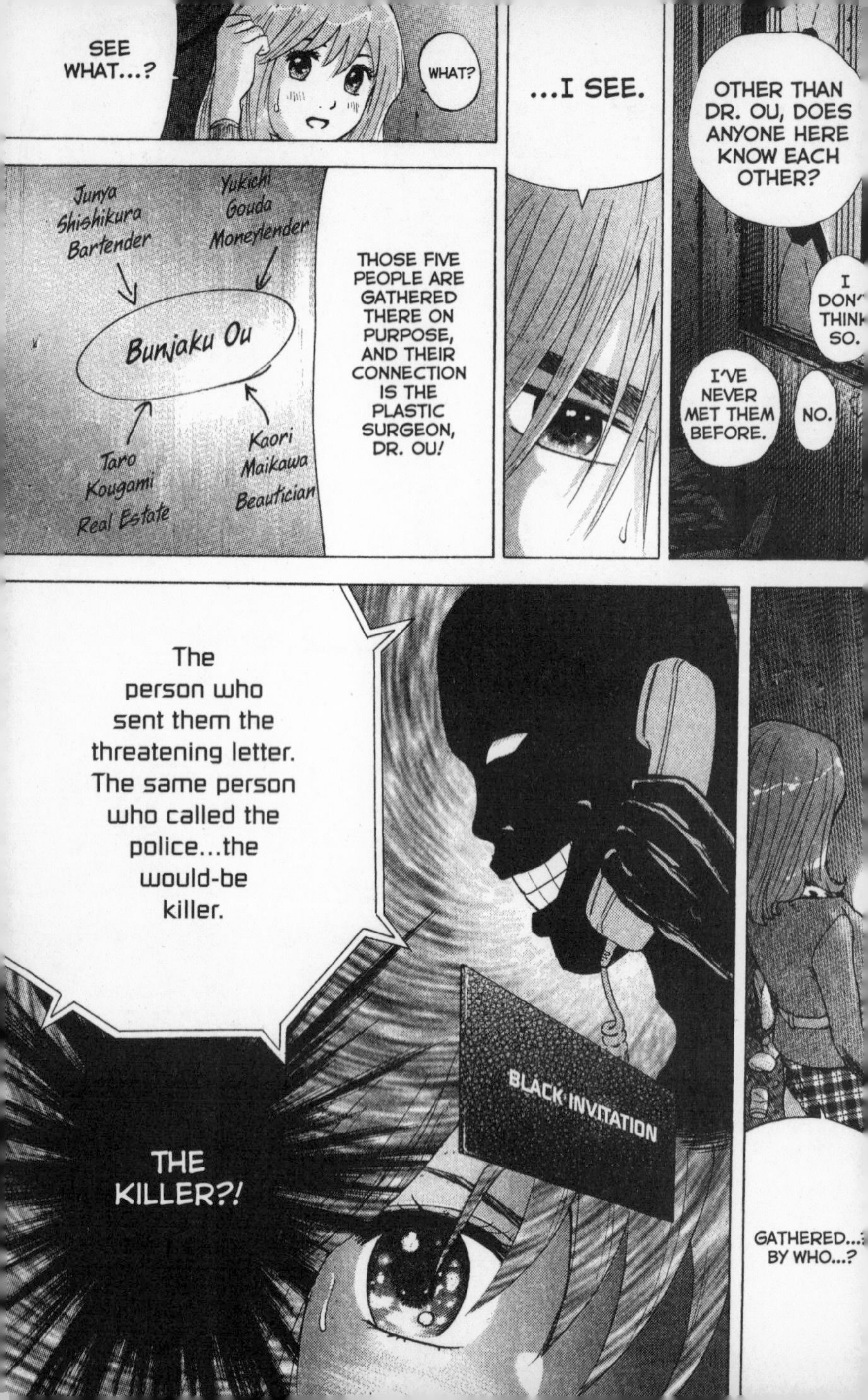

OTHER THAN DR. OU, DOES ANYONE HERE KNOW EACH OTHER?
I DON'T THINK SO.
NO.
I'VE NEVER MET THEM BEFORE.
...I SEE.
WHAT?
SEE WHAT...?
THOSE FIVE PEOPLE ARE GATHERED THERE ON PURPOSE, AND THEIR CONNECTION IS THE PLASTIC SURGEON, DR. OU!
Yukichi Gouda Moneylender
Junya Shishikura Bartender
Bunjaku Ou
Kaori Maikawa Beautician
Taro Kougami Real Estate
GATHERED... BY WHO...?
The person who sent them the threatening letter. The same person who called the police...the would-be killer.
BLACK INVITATION
THE KILLER?!

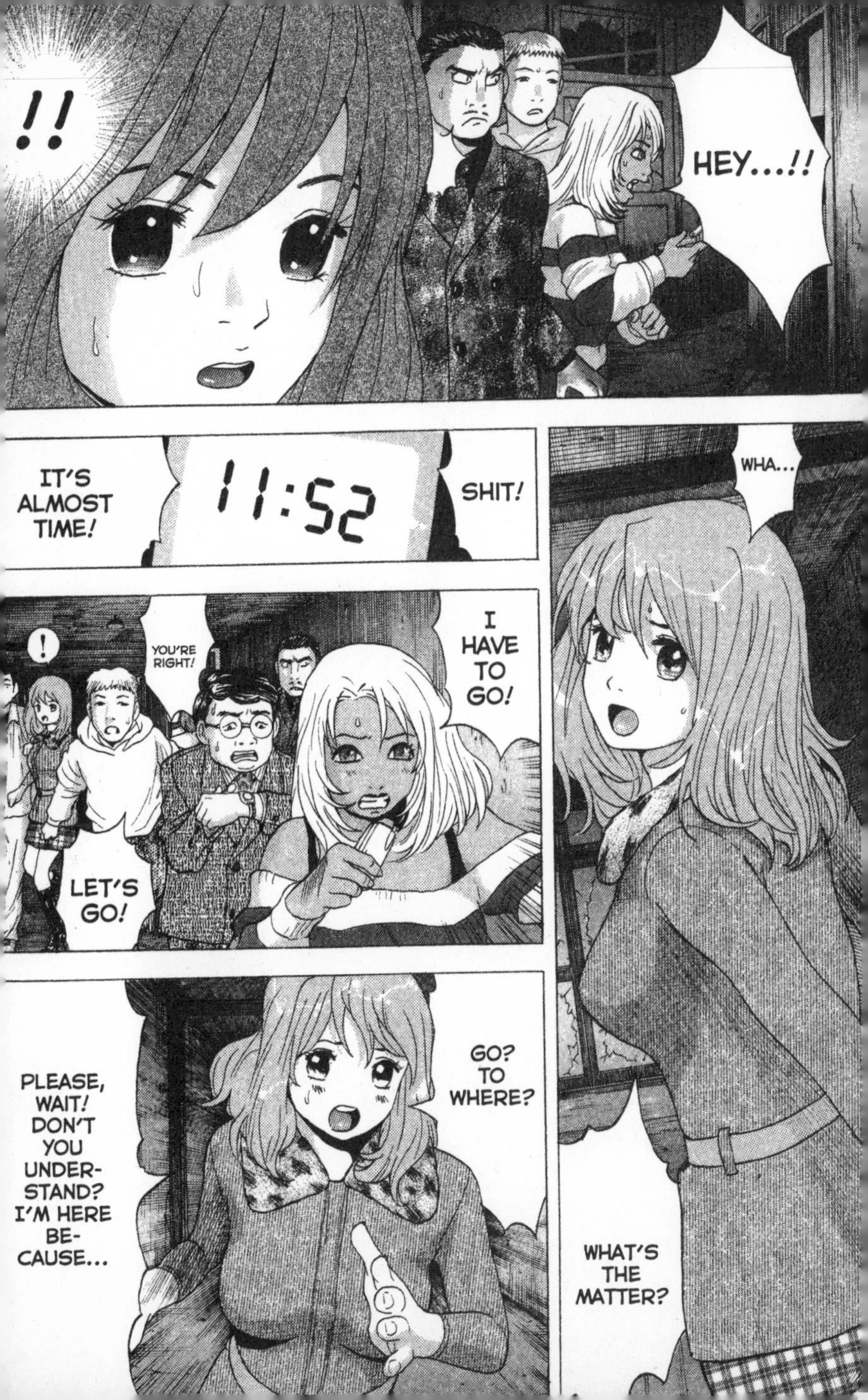
HEY...!!
!!
WHA...
WHAT'S THE MATTER?
SHIT!
11:52
IT'S ALMOST TIME!
I HAVE TO GO!
YOU'RE RIGHT!
!
LET'S GO!
GO? TO WHERE?
PLEASE, WAIT! DON'T YOU UNDER-STAND? I'M HERE BE-CAUSE...

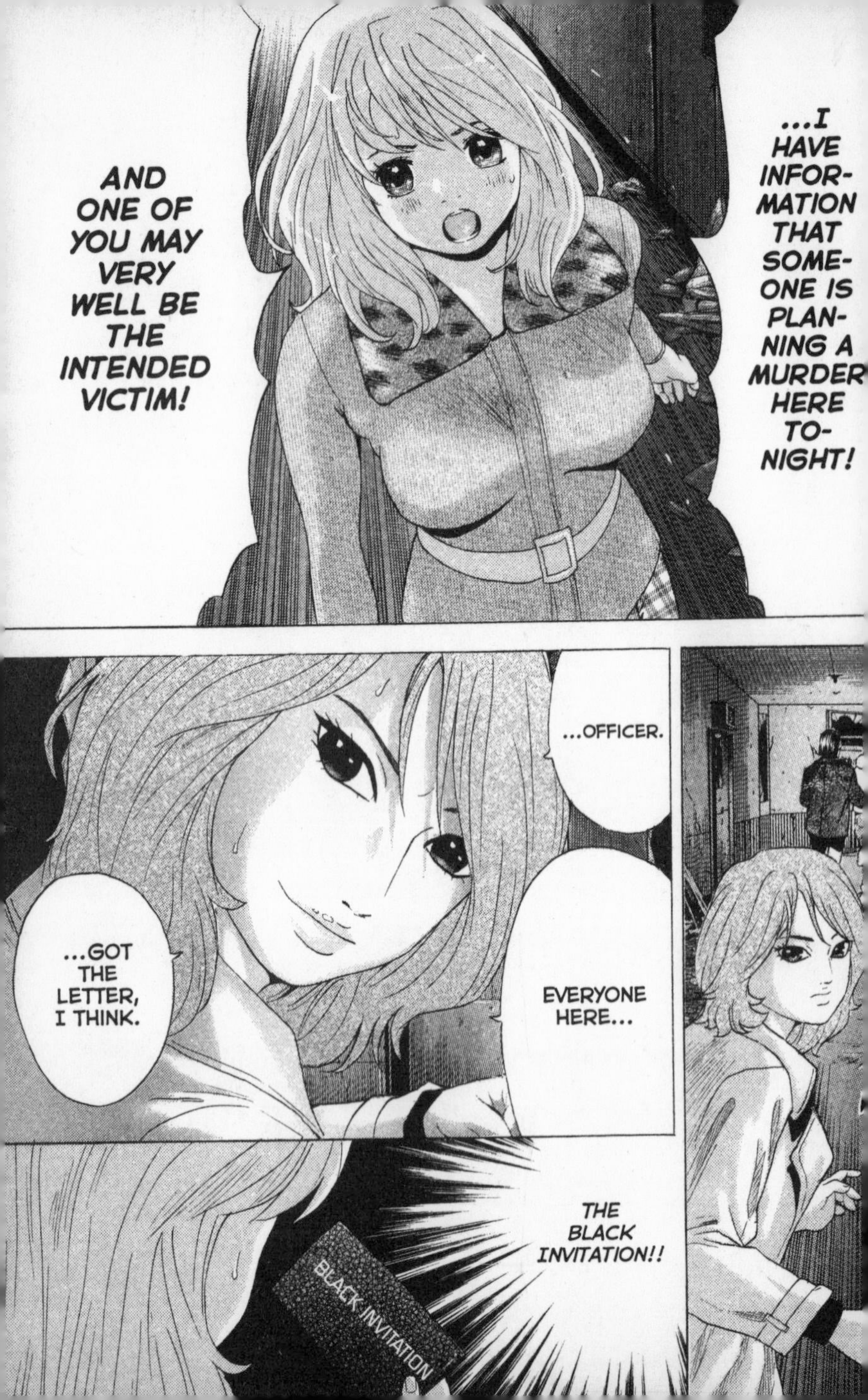
...I HAVE INFORMATION THAT SOMEONE IS PLANNING A MURDER HERE TONIGHT!
AND ONE OF YOU MAY VERY WELL BE THE INTENDED VICTIM!
...OFFICER.
EVERYONE HERE...
...GOT THE LETTER, I THINK.
THE BLACK INVITATION!!
BLACK INVITATION

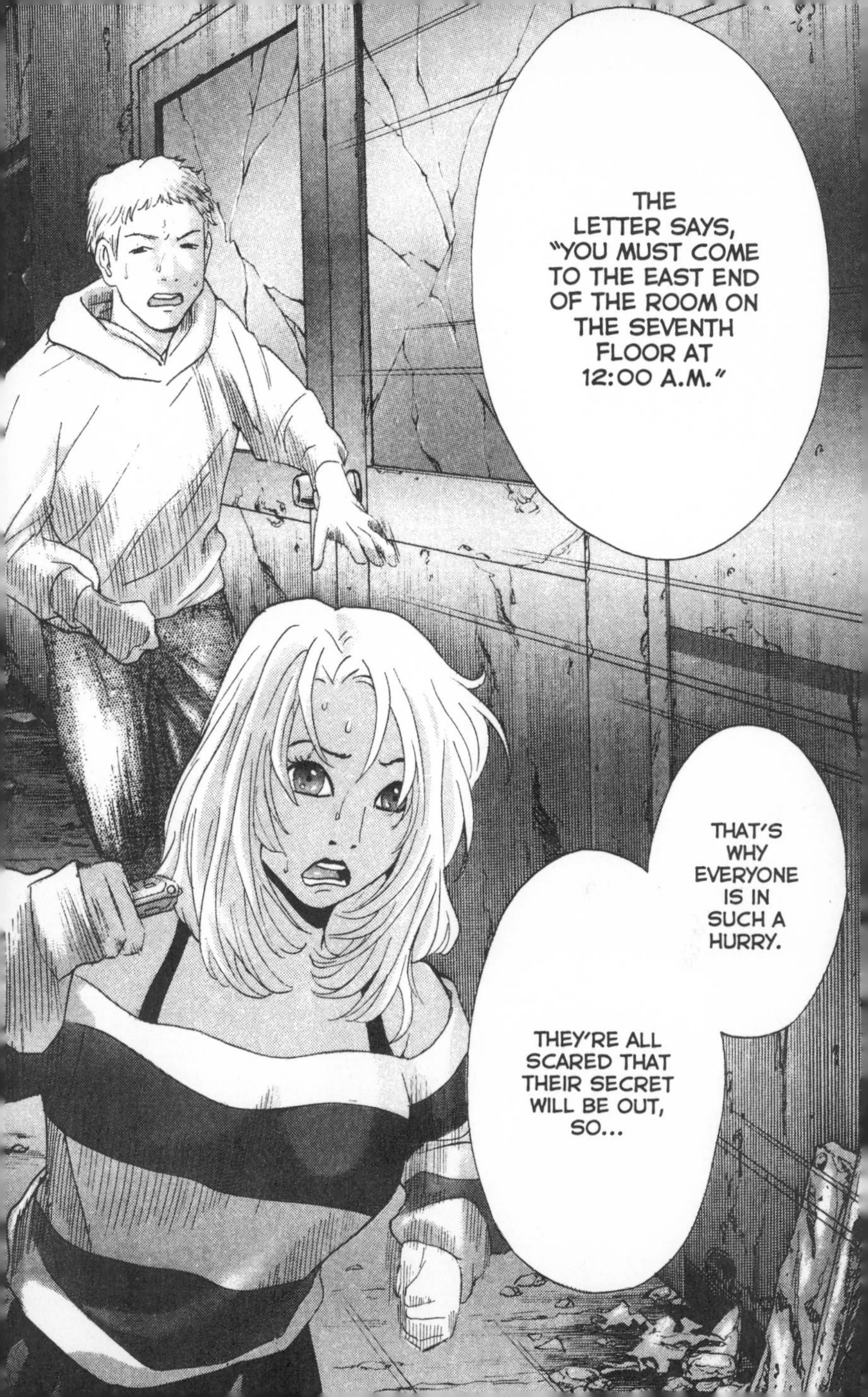
THE LETTER SAYS, "YOU MUST COME TO THE EAST END OF THE ROOM ON THE SEVENTH FLOOR AT 12:00 A.M."
THAT'S WHY EVERYONE IS IN SUCH A HURRY.
THEY'RE ALL SCARED THAT THEIR SECRET WILL BE OUT, SO...

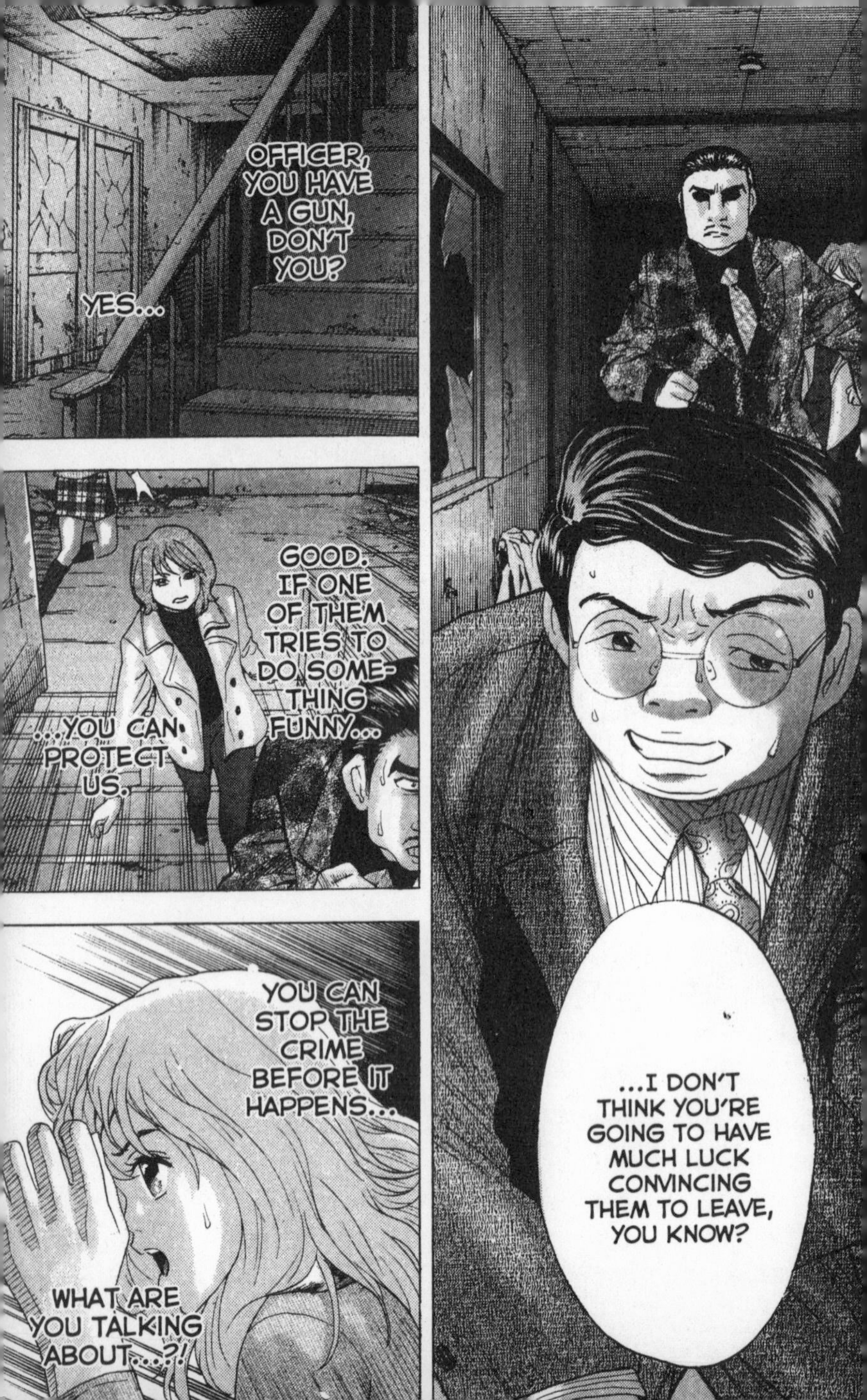
...I DON'T THINK YOU'RE GOING TO HAVE MUCH LUCK CONVINCING THEM TO LEAVE, YOU KNOW?
OFFICER, YOU HAVE A GUN, DON'T YOU?
YES...
GOOD. IF ONE OF THEM TRIES TO DO SOME-THING FUNNY...
...YOU CAN PROTECT US.
YOU CAN STOP THE CRIME BEFORE IT HAPPENS...
WHAT ARE YOU TALKING ABOUT...?!

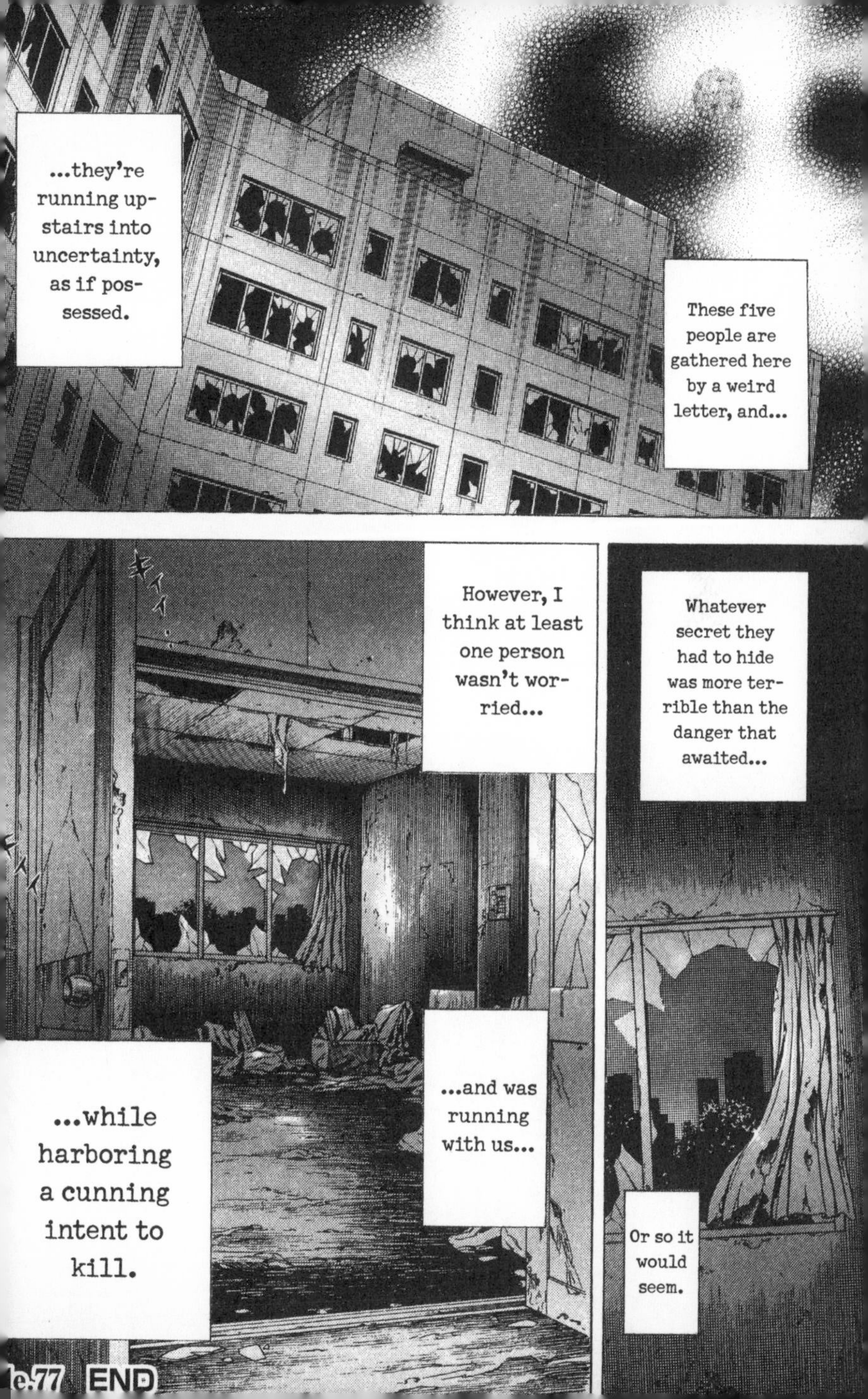
These five people are gathered here by a weird letter, and...
...they're running upstairs into uncertainty, as if possessed.
Whatever secret they had to hide was more terrible than the danger that awaited...
Or so it would seem.
However, I think at least one person wasn't worried...
...and was running with us...
...while harboring a cunning intent to kill.
e:77 END

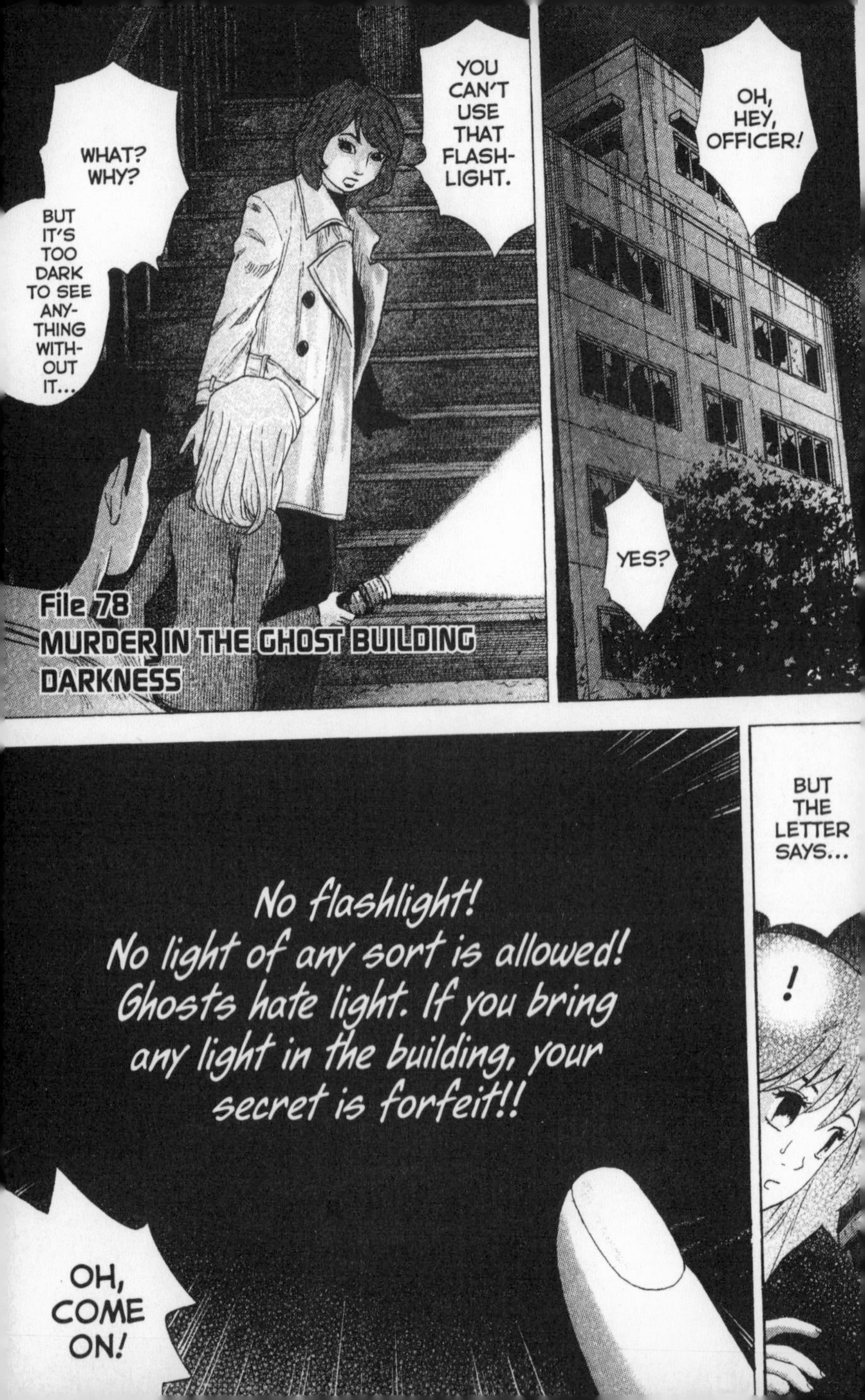
OH, HEY, OFFICER!
YES?
YOU CAN'T USE THAT FLASH-LIGHT.
WHAT? WHY?
BUT IT'S TOO DARK TO SEE ANY-THING WITH-OUT IT...
File 78
MURDER IN THE GHOST BUILDING
DARKNESS
BUT THE LETTER SAYS...
!
No flashlight! No light of any sort is allowed! Ghosts hate light. If you bring any light in the building, your secret is forfeit!!
OH, COME ON!

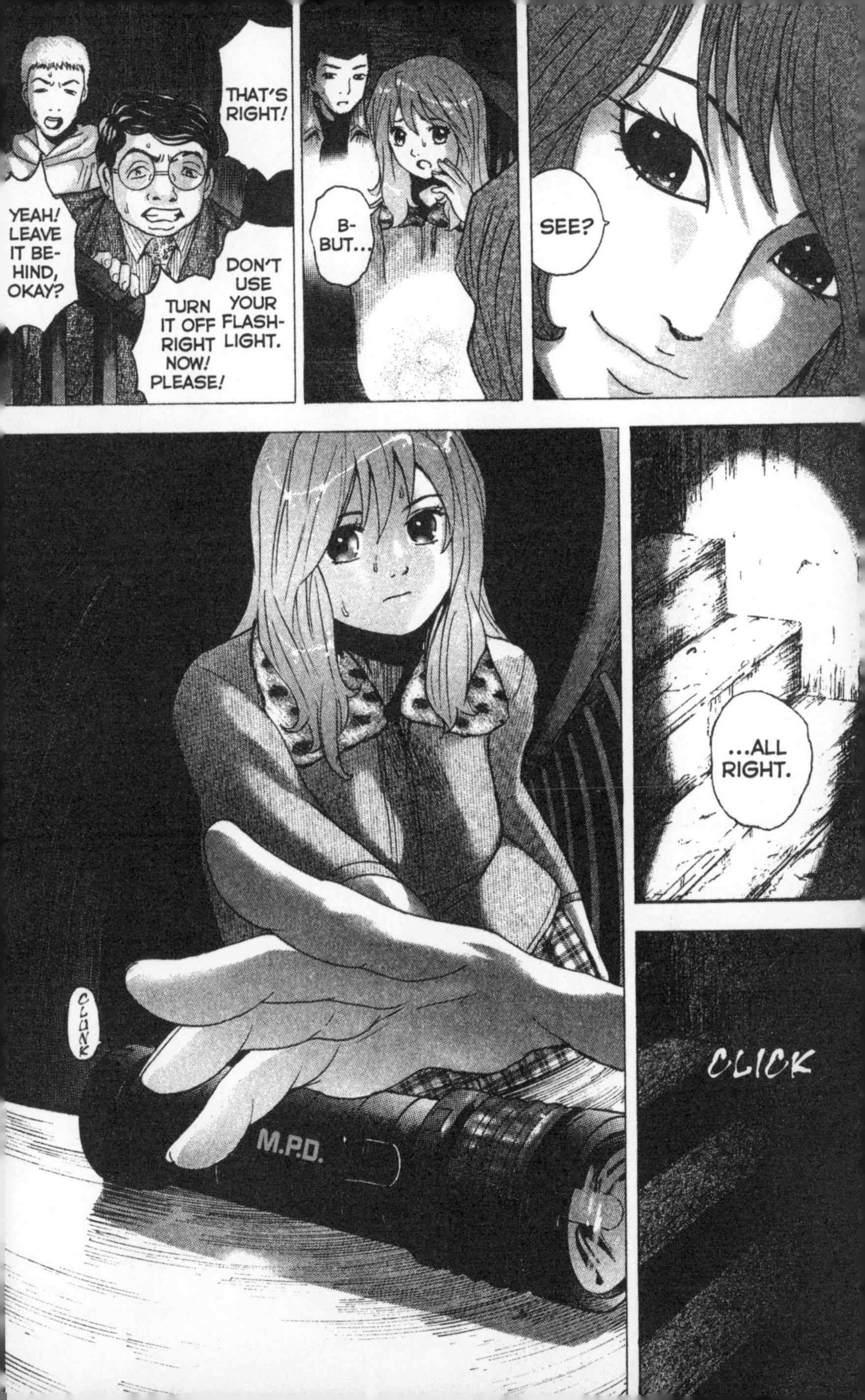
SEE?
B-BUT...
THAT'S RIGHT!
DON'T USE YOUR FLASHLIGHT.
TURN IT OFF RIGHT NOW! PLEASE!
YEAH! LEAVE IT BEHIND, OKAY?
...ALL RIGHT.
CLICK
CLUNK
M.P.D.

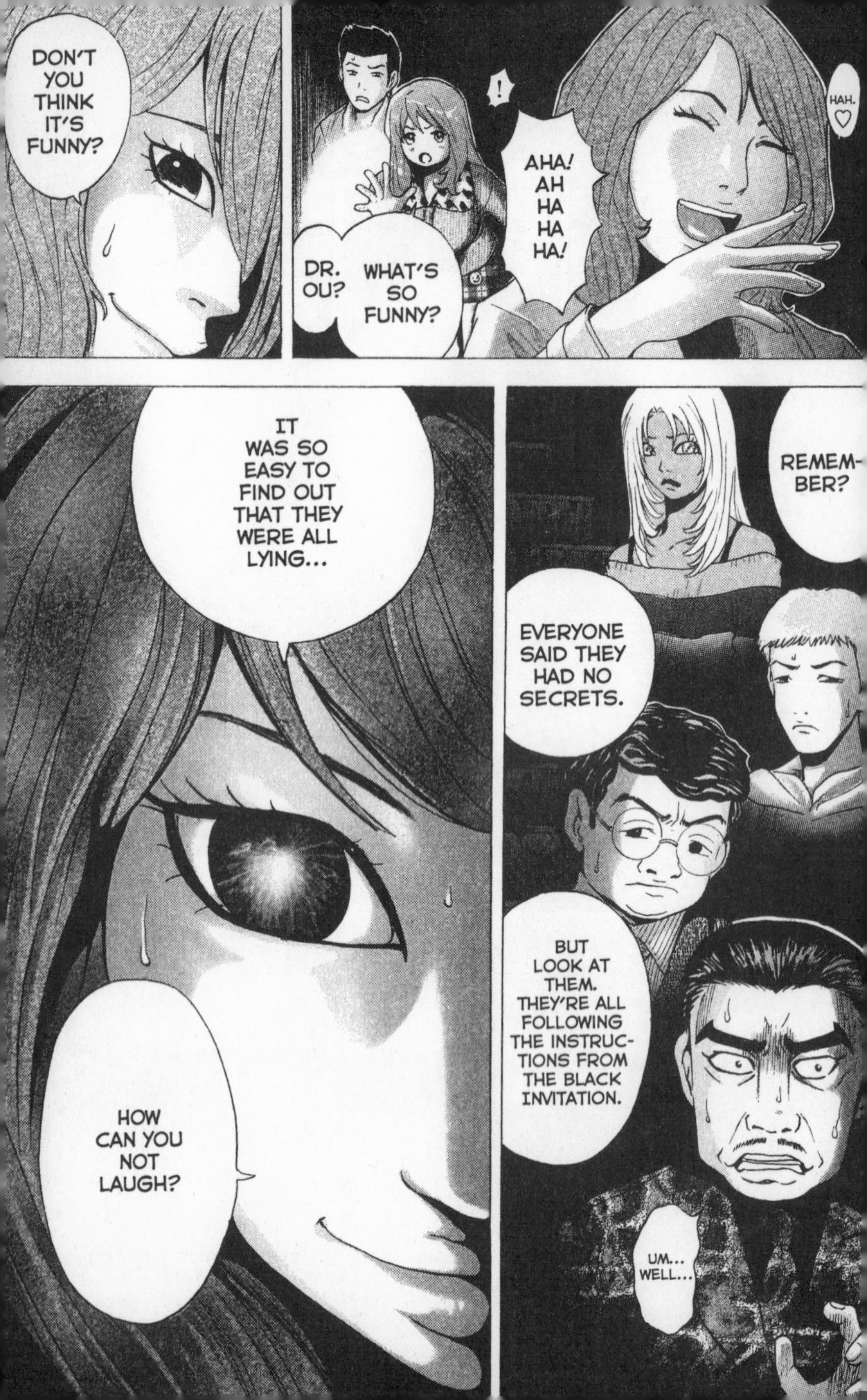
HAH. ♡
AHA! AH HA HA HA!
!
WHAT'S SO FUNNY?
DR. OU?
DON'T YOU THINK IT'S FUNNY?
REMEMBER?
EVERYONE SAID THEY HAD NO SECRETS.
BUT LOOK AT THEM. THEY'RE ALL FOLLOWING THE INSTRUCTIONS FROM THE BLACK INVITATION.
UM... WELL...
IT WAS SO EASY TO FIND OUT THAT THEY WERE ALL LYING...
HOW CAN YOU NOT LAUGH?

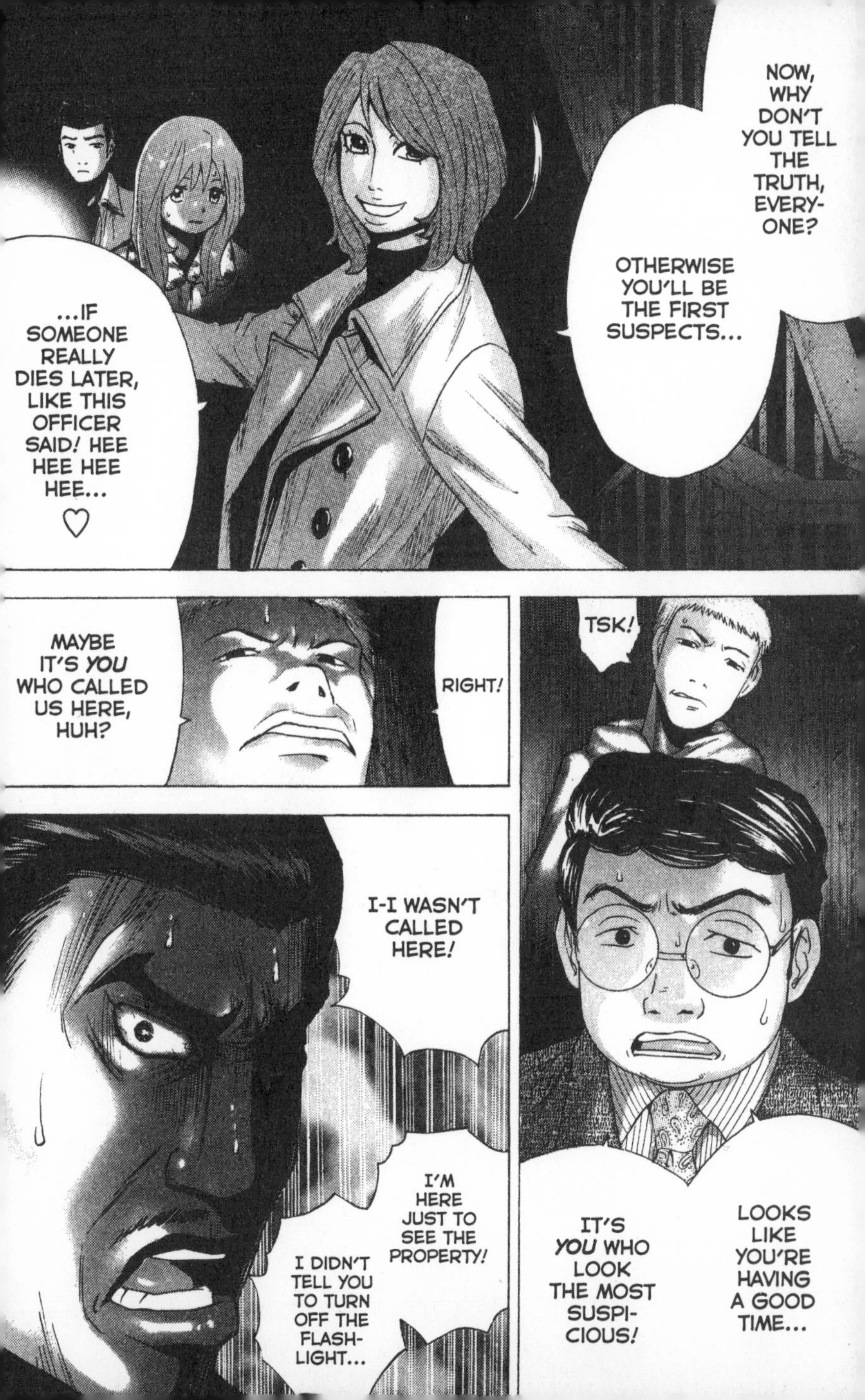
NOW, WHY DON'T YOU TELL THE TRUTH, EVERYONE?
OTHERWISE YOU'LL BE THE FIRST SUSPECTS...
...IF SOMEONE REALLY DIES LATER, LIKE THIS OFFICER SAID! HEE HEE HEE HEE... ♡
TSK!
LOOKS LIKE YOU'RE HAVING A GOOD TIME...
IT'S *YOU* WHO LOOK THE MOST SUSPICIOUS!
RIGHT!
MAYBE IT'S *YOU* WHO CALLED US HERE, HUH?
I-I WASN'T CALLED HERE!
I'M HERE JUST TO SEE THE PROPERTY!
I DIDN'T TELL YOU TO TURN OFF THE FLASHLIGHT...

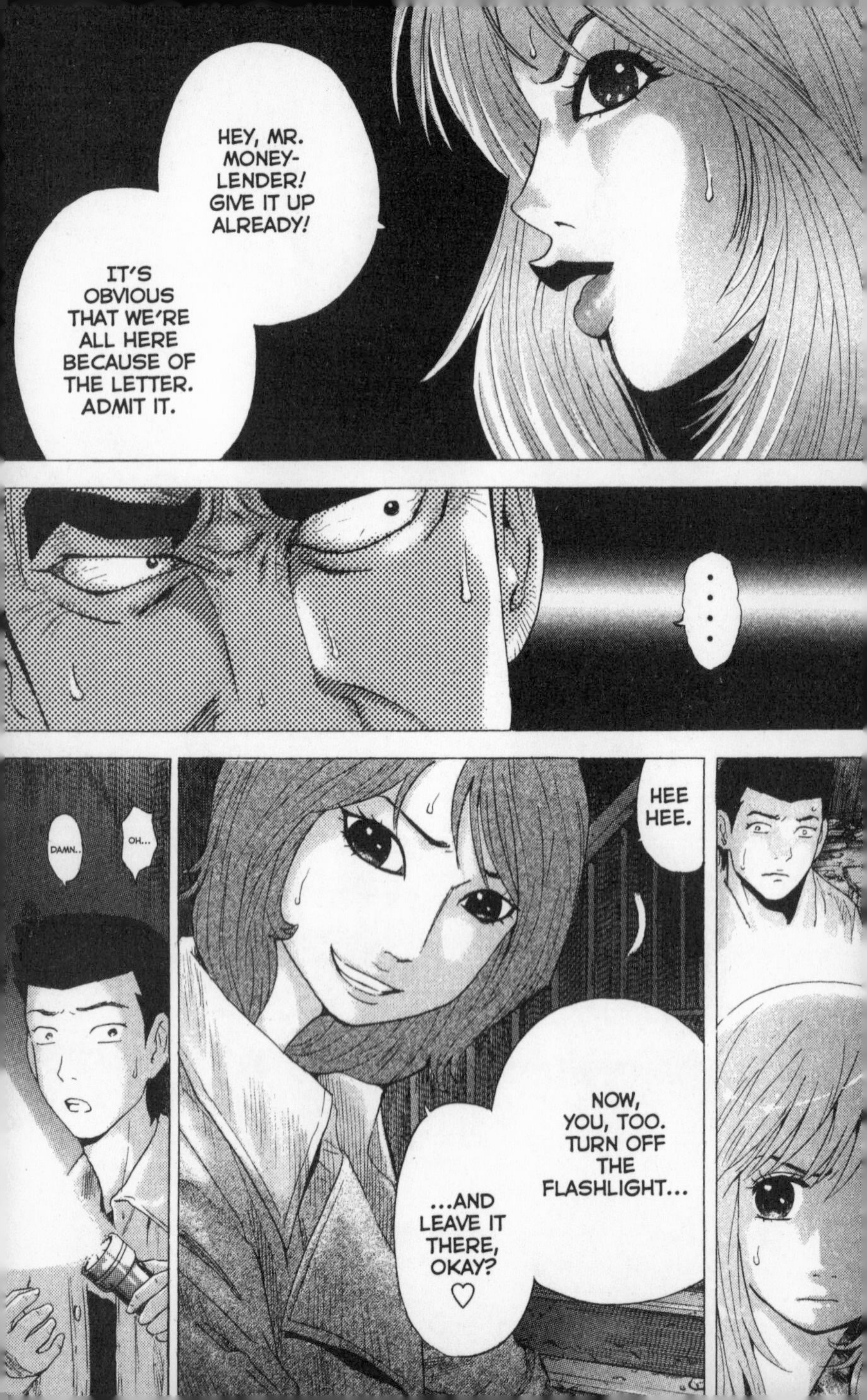
HEY, MR. MONEY-LENDER! GIVE IT UP ALREADY!
IT'S OBVIOUS THAT WE'RE ALL HERE BECAUSE OF THE LETTER. ADMIT IT.
....
HEE HEE.
NOW, YOU, TOO. TURN OFF THE FLASHLIGHT...
...AND LEAVE IT THERE, OKAY? ♡
OH...
DAMN..

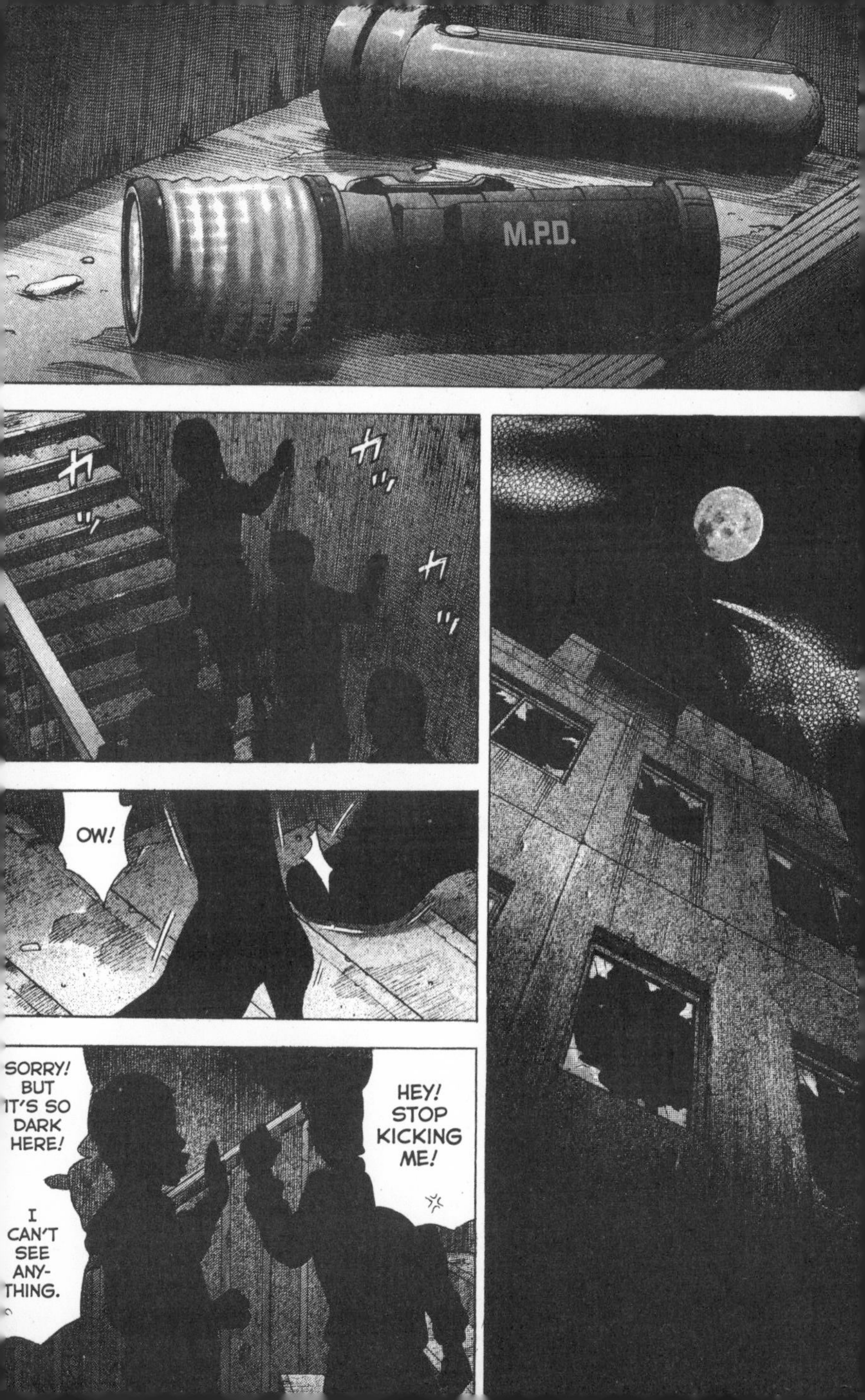
M.P.D.
カッ
カッ
OW!
HEY! STOP KICKING ME!
SORRY! BUT IT'S SO DARK HERE!
I CAN'T SEE ANY-THING.

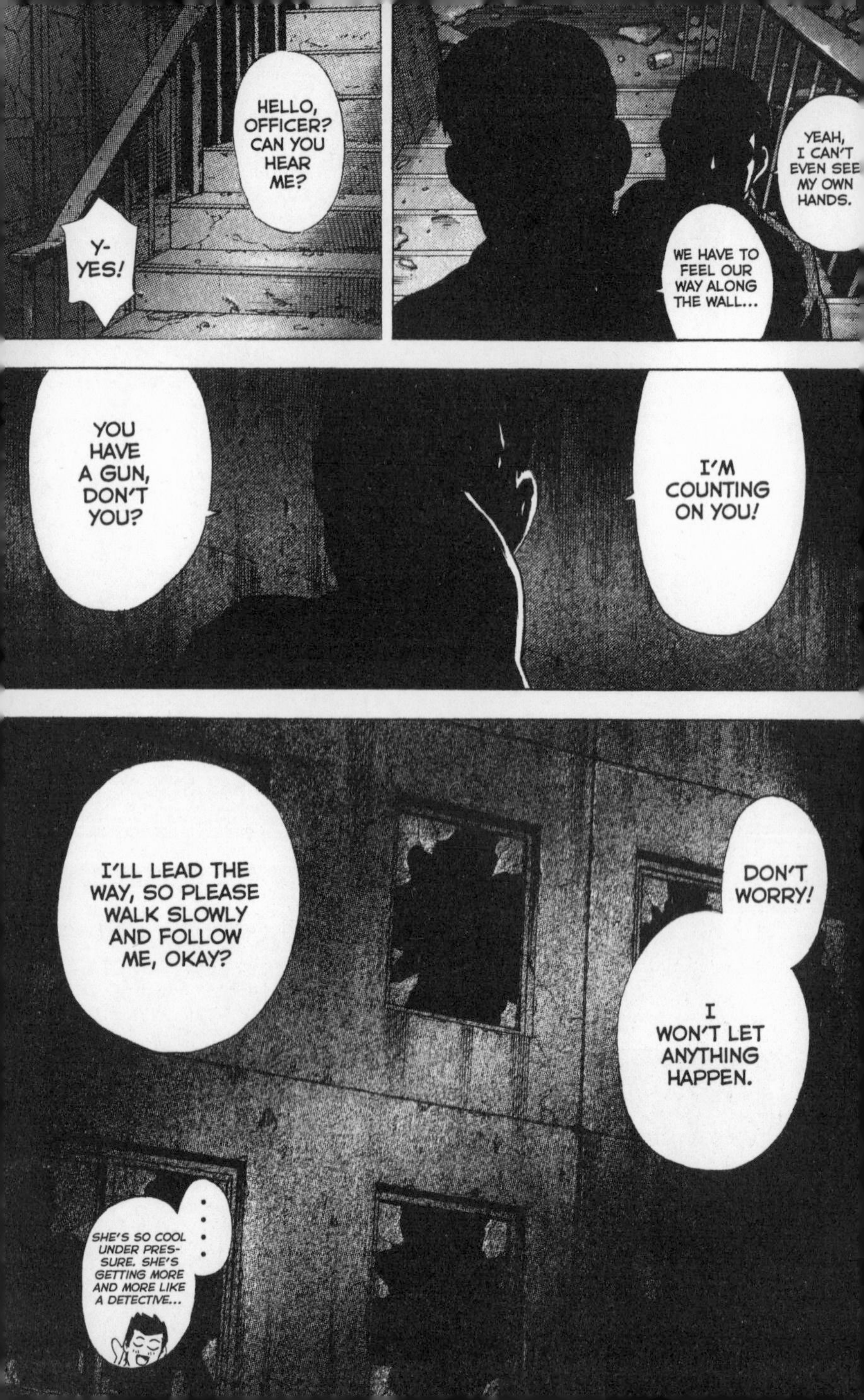
YEAH, I CAN'T EVEN SEE MY OWN HANDS.
WE HAVE TO FEEL OUR WAY ALONG THE WALL...
HELLO, OFFICER? CAN YOU HEAR ME?
Y- YES!
I'M COUNTING ON YOU!
YOU HAVE A GUN, DON'T YOU?
DON'T WORRY!
I WON'T LET ANYTHING HAPPEN.
I'LL LEAD THE WAY, SO PLEASE WALK SLOWLY AND FOLLOW ME, OKAY?
....
SHE'S SO COOL UNDER PRES-SURE. SHE'S GETTING MORE AND MORE LIKE A DETECTIVE...

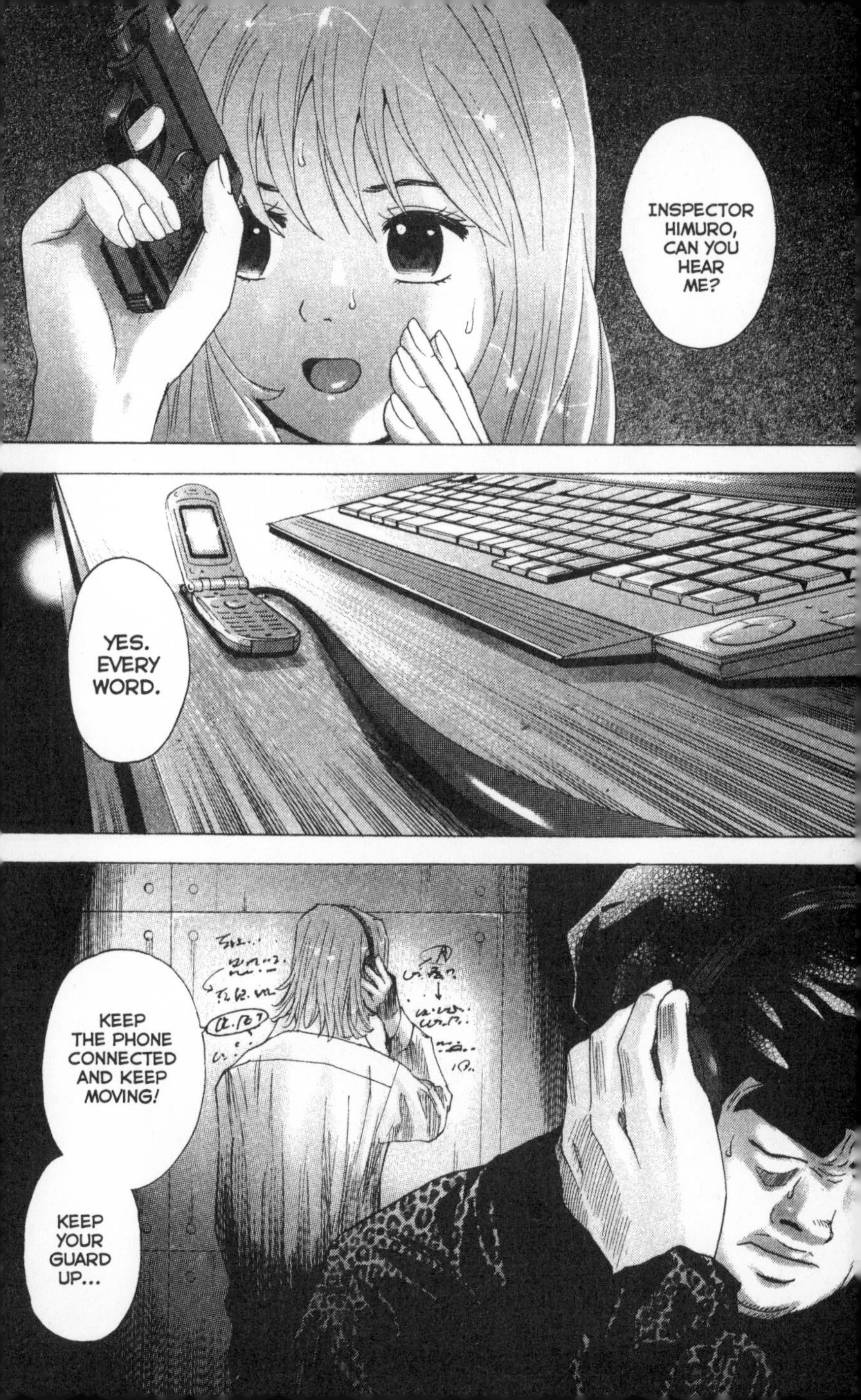
INSPECTOR HIMURO, CAN YOU HEAR ME?
YES. EVERY WORD.
KEEP THE PHONE CONNECTED AND KEEP MOVING!
KEEP YOUR GUARD UP...

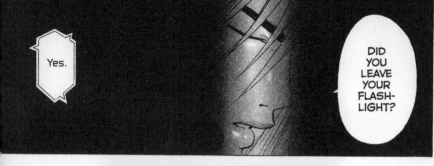

DID YOU LEAVE YOUR FLASHLIGHT?
Yes.
THEN BORROW A LIGHTER FROM YOUR FIANCÉ.
LIGHT IT WHEN I GIVE YOU THE SIGNAL.
All right?
RIGHT...
DO YOU HAVE A LIGHTER, SHINGO?
YEAH...
CAN I HAVE IT...?
SURE ...

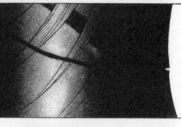

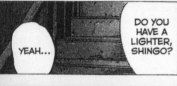

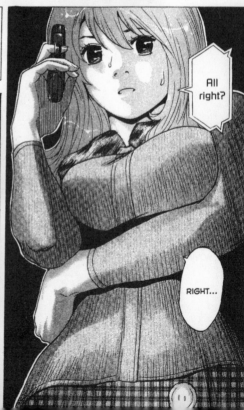

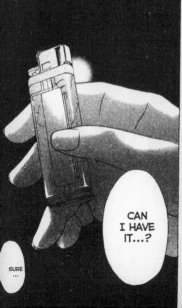

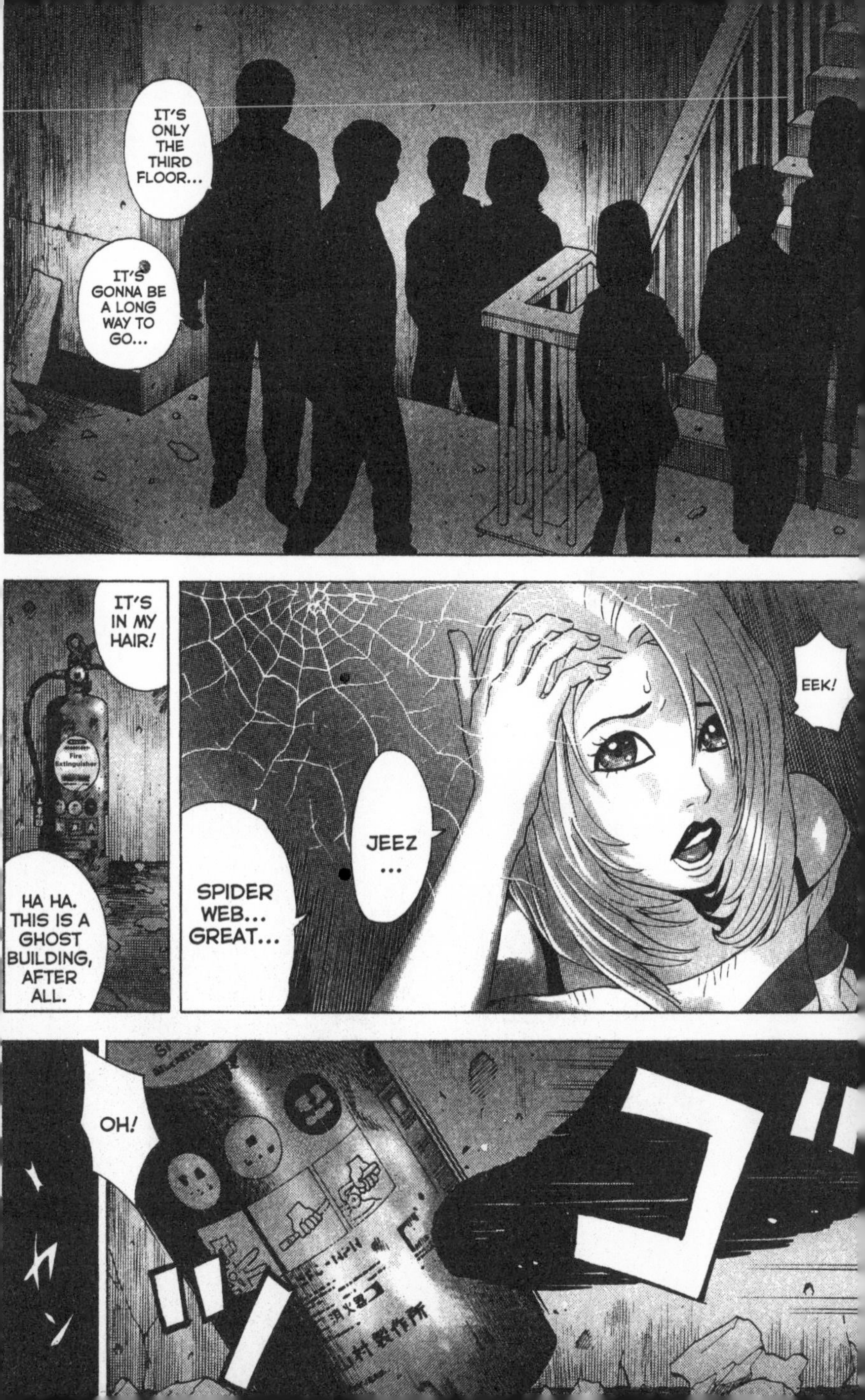
IT'S ONLY THE THIRD FLOOR...
IT'S GONNA BE A LONG WAY TO GO...
EEK!
JEEZ ...
SPIDER WEB... GREAT...
IT'S IN MY HAIR!
HA HA. THIS IS A GHOST BUILDING, AFTER ALL.
OH!

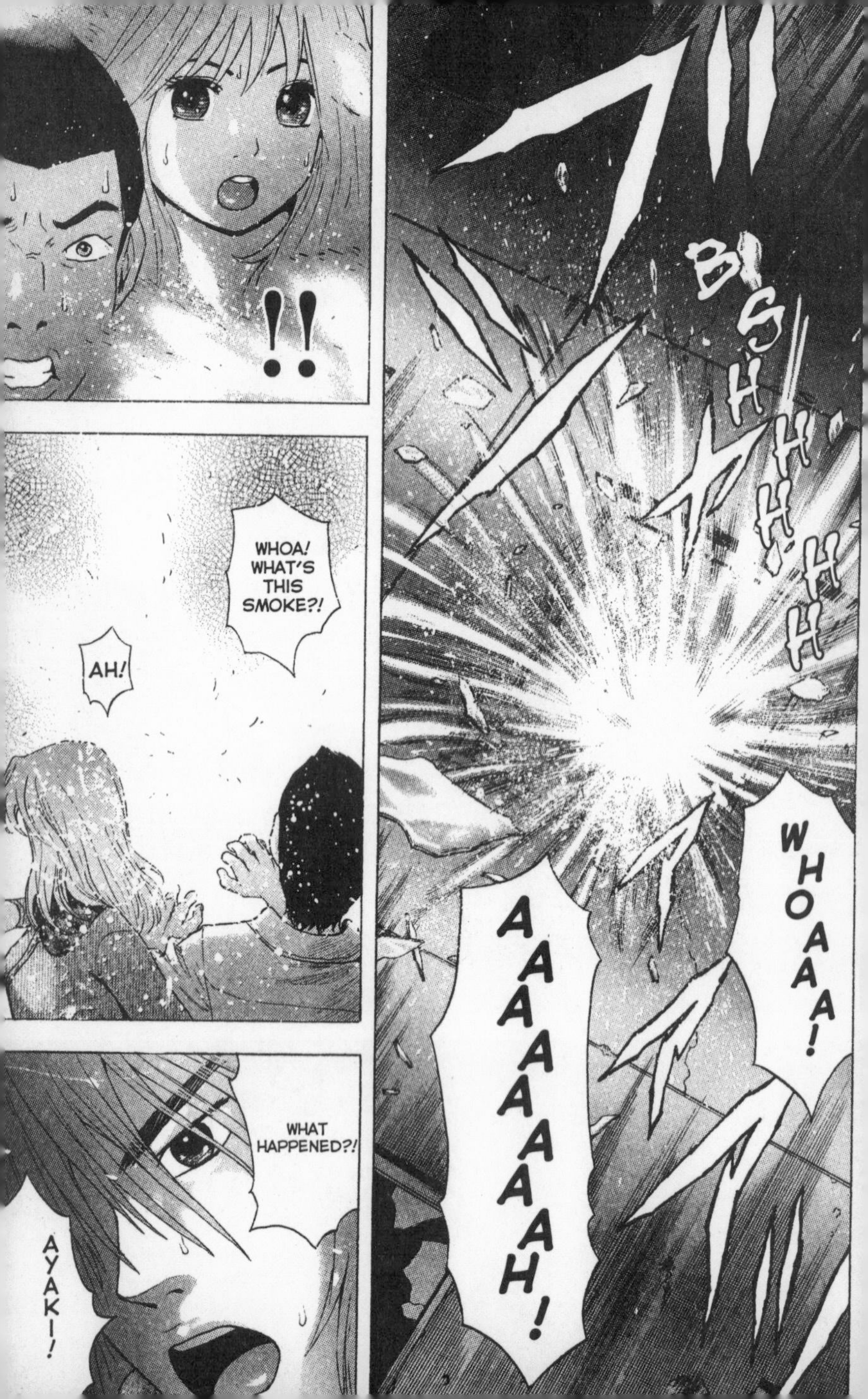
BSHHHHH
WHOAAAA!
AAAAAAAAH!
!!
WHOA! WHAT'S THIS SMOKE?!
AH!
WHAT HAPPENED?!
AYAKI!

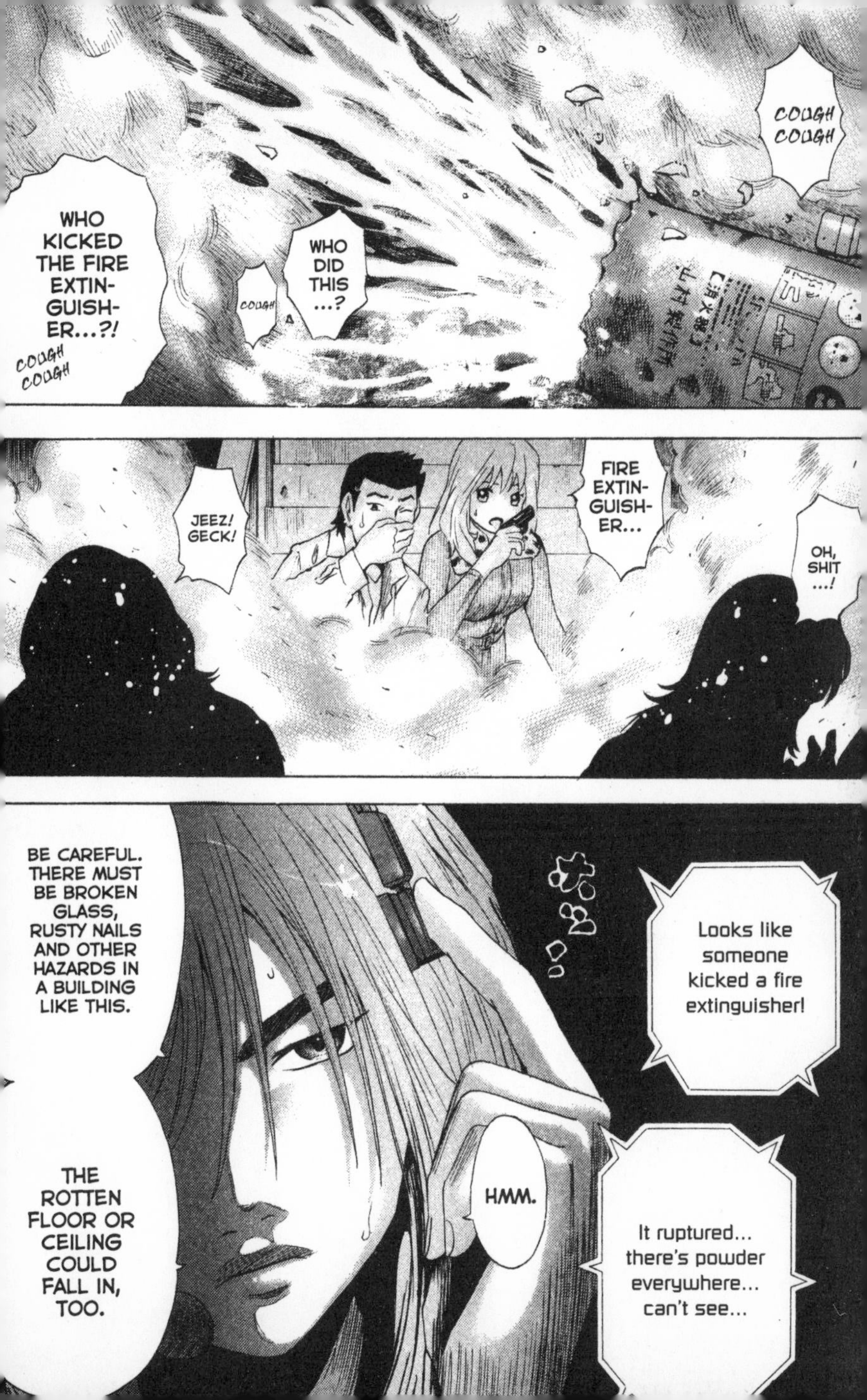
COUGH COUGH
WHO DID THIS ...?
COUGH
WHO KICKED THE FIRE EXTIN-GUISH-ER...?!
COUGH COUGH
OH, SHIT ...!
FIRE EXTIN-GUISH-ER...
JEEZ! GECK!
Looks like someone kicked a fire extinguisher!
It ruptured... there's powder everywhere... can't see...
HMM.
BE CAREFUL. THERE MUST BE BROKEN GLASS, RUSTY NAILS AND OTHER HAZARDS IN A BUILDING LIKE THIS.
THE ROTTEN FLOOR OR CEILING COULD FALL IN, TOO.

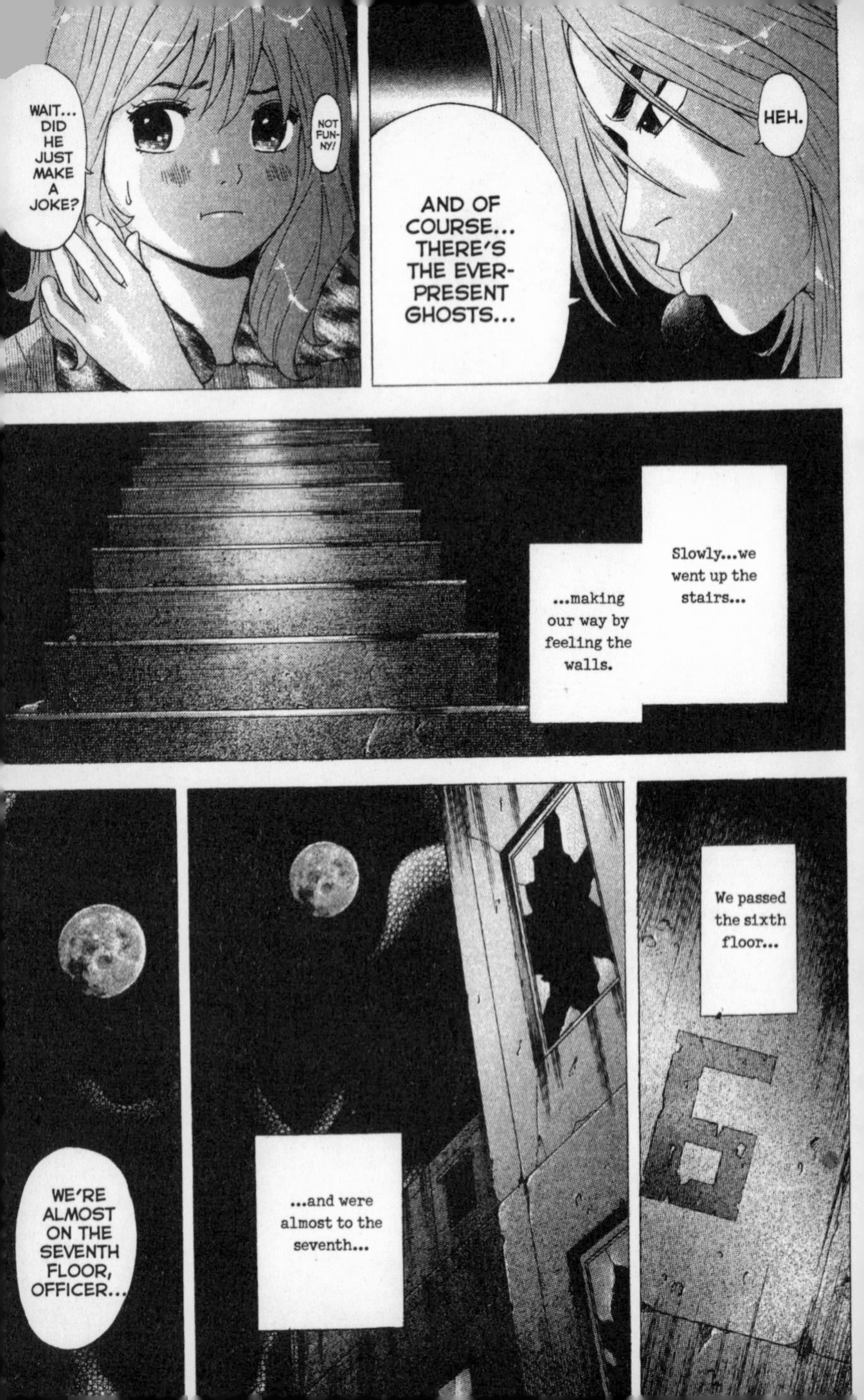
HEH.
AND OF COURSE... THERE'S THE EVER-PRESENT GHOSTS...
NOT FUNNY!
WAIT... DID HE JUST MAKE A JOKE?
Slowly...we went up the stairs...
...making our way by feeling the walls.
We passed the sixth floor...
...and were almost to the seventh...
WE'RE ALMOST ON THE SEVENTH FLOOR, OFFICER...

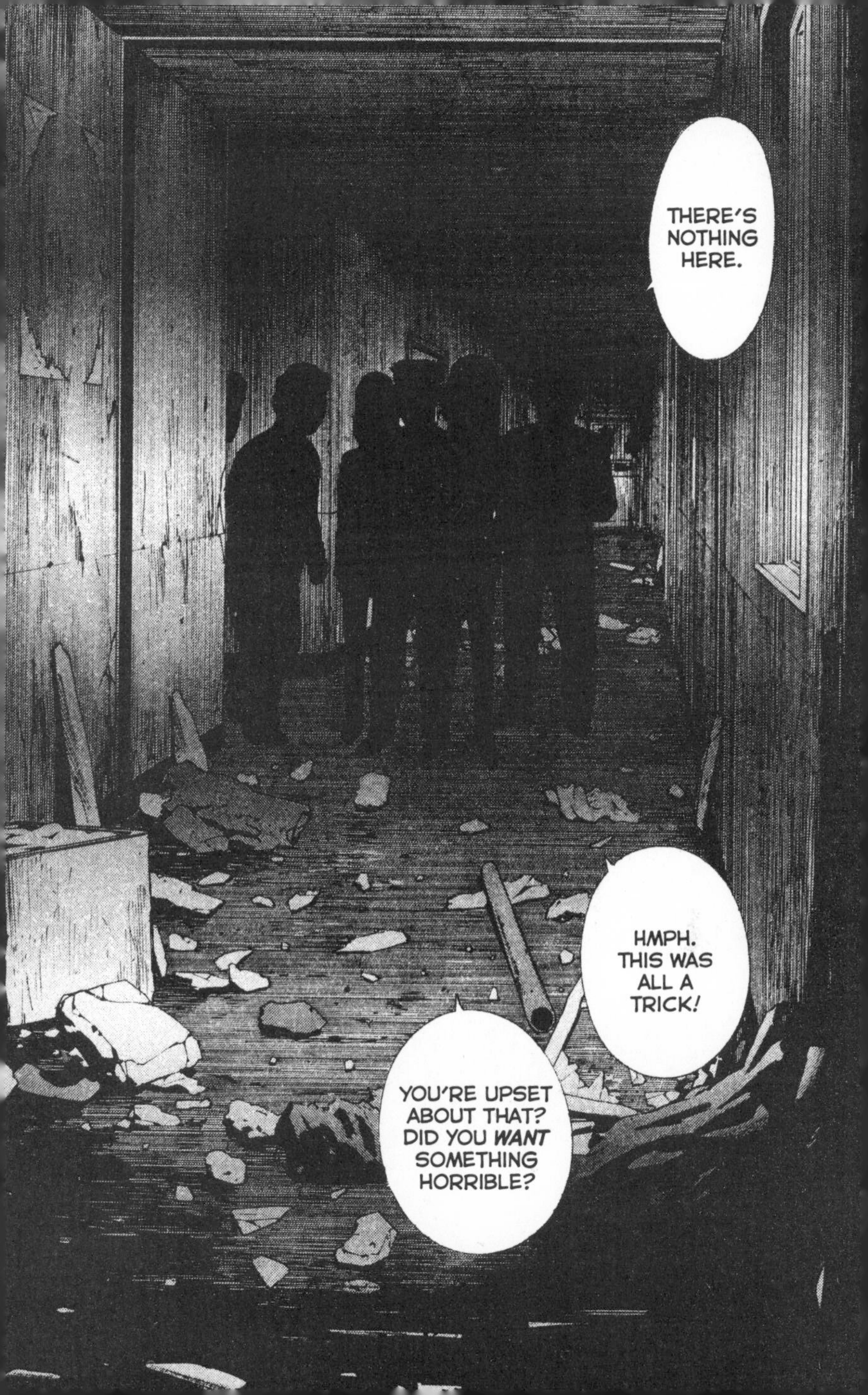
THERE'S NOTHING HERE.
HMPH. THIS WAS ALL A TRICK!
YOU'RE UPSET ABOUT THAT? DID YOU *WANT* SOMETHING HORRIBLE?

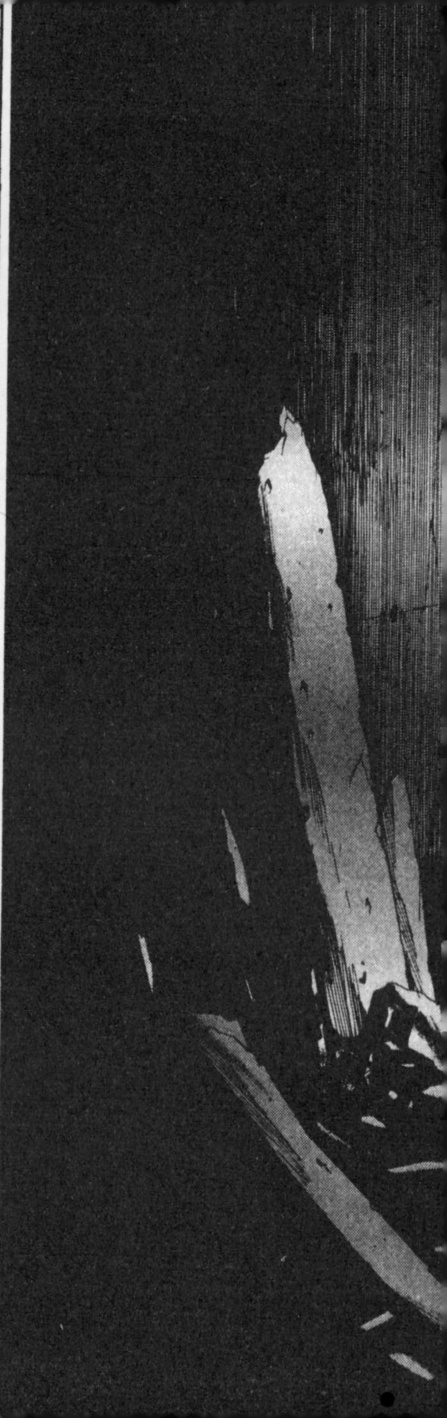
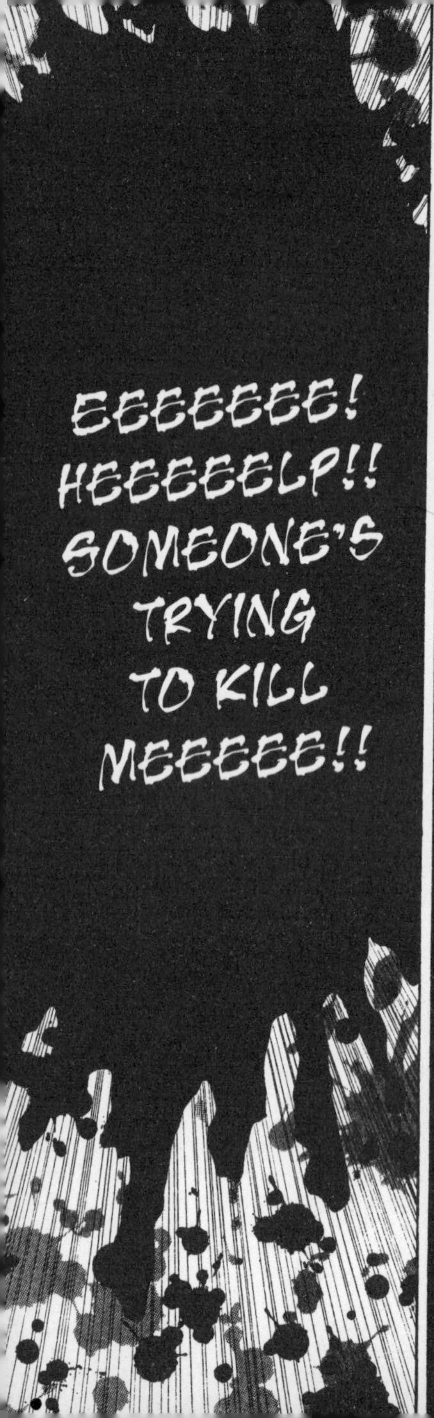
EEEEEEEE! HEEEEEELP!! SOMEONE'S TRYING TO KILL MEEEEEE!!

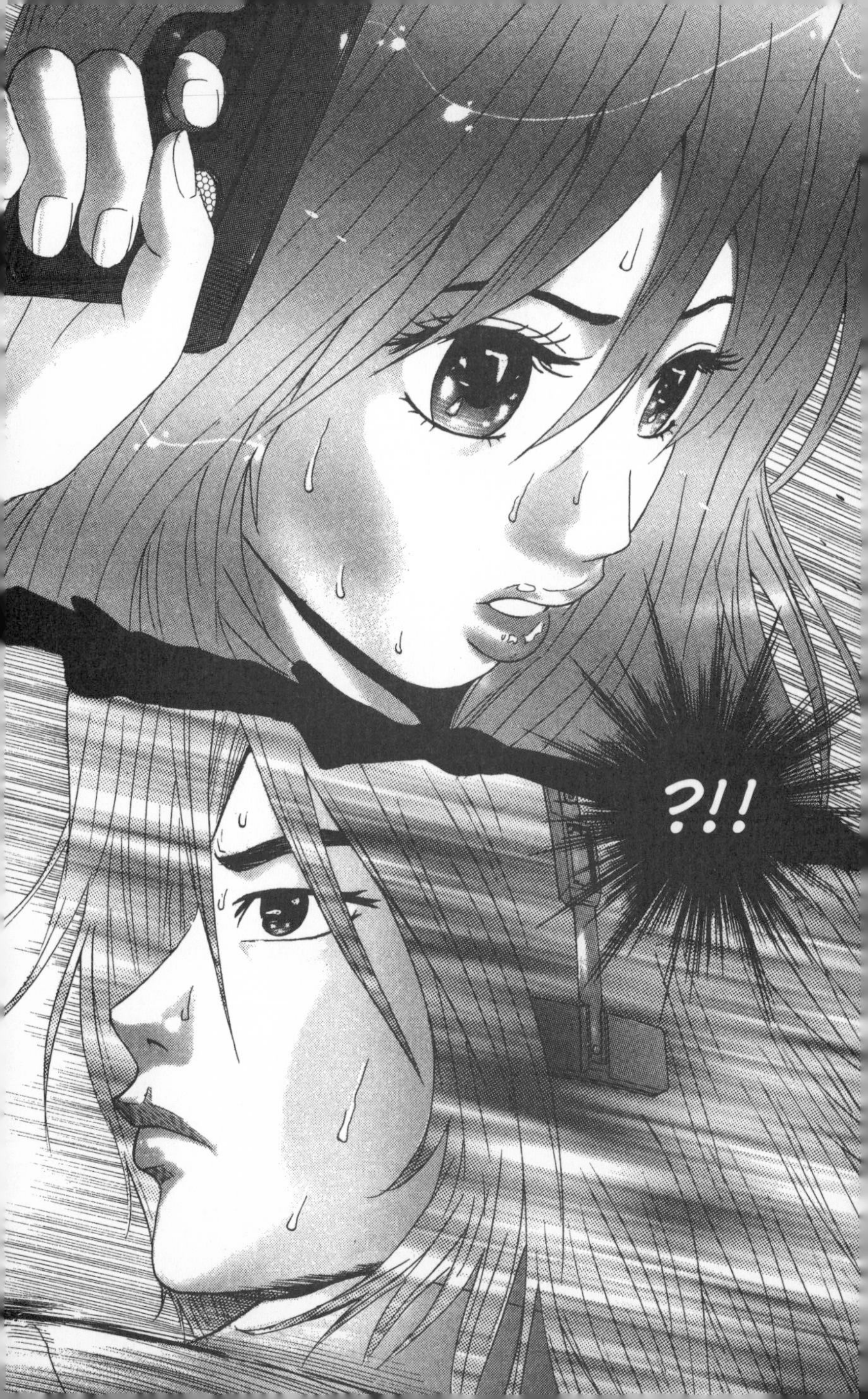
?!!

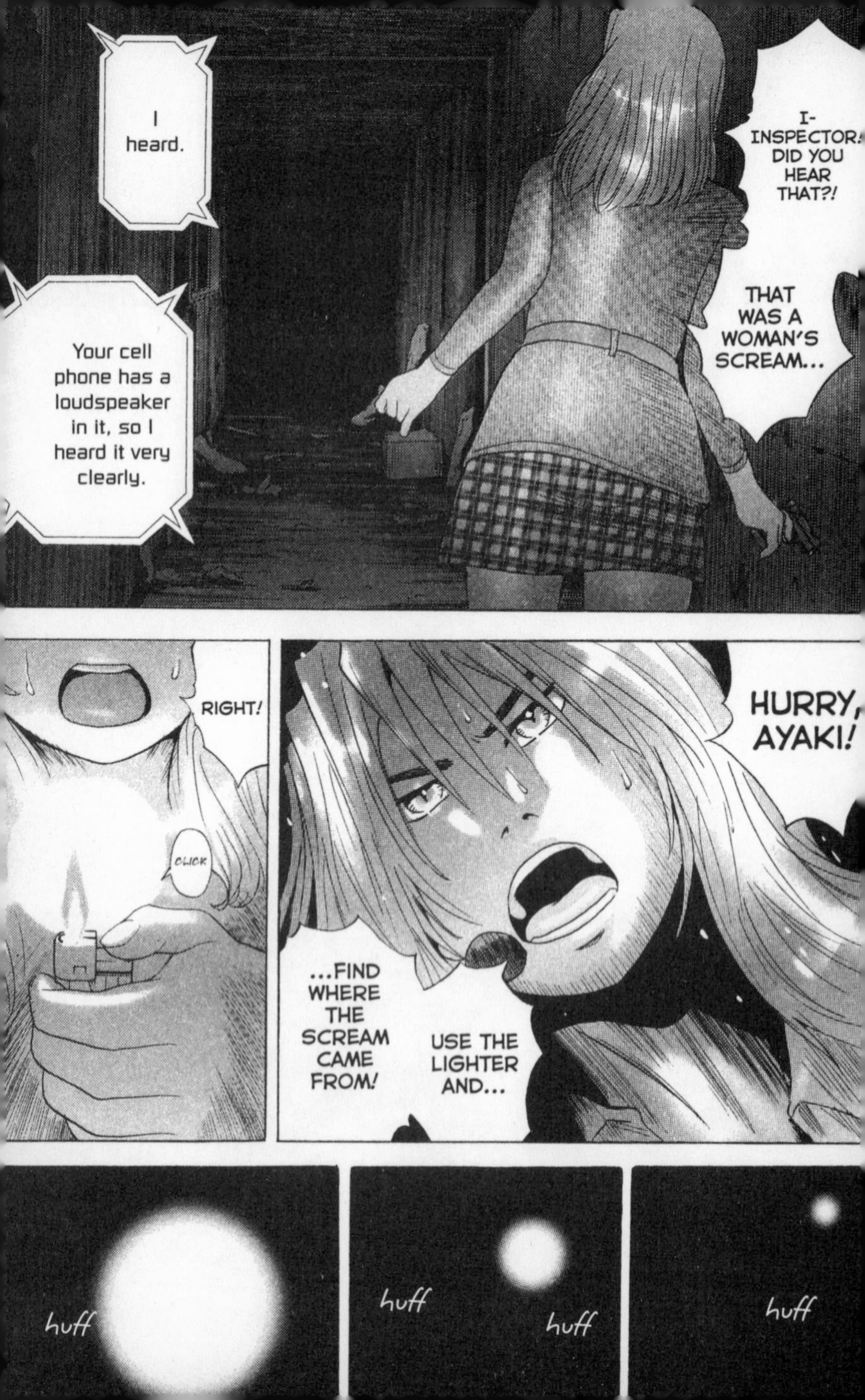
I- INSPECTOR! DID YOU HEAR THAT?!
THAT WAS A WOMAN'S SCREAM...
I heard.
Your cell phone has a loudspeaker in it, so I heard it very clearly.
HURRY, AYAKI!
USE THE LIGHTER AND...
...FIND WHERE THE SCREAM CAME FROM!
RIGHT!
CLICK
huff
huff
huff
huff

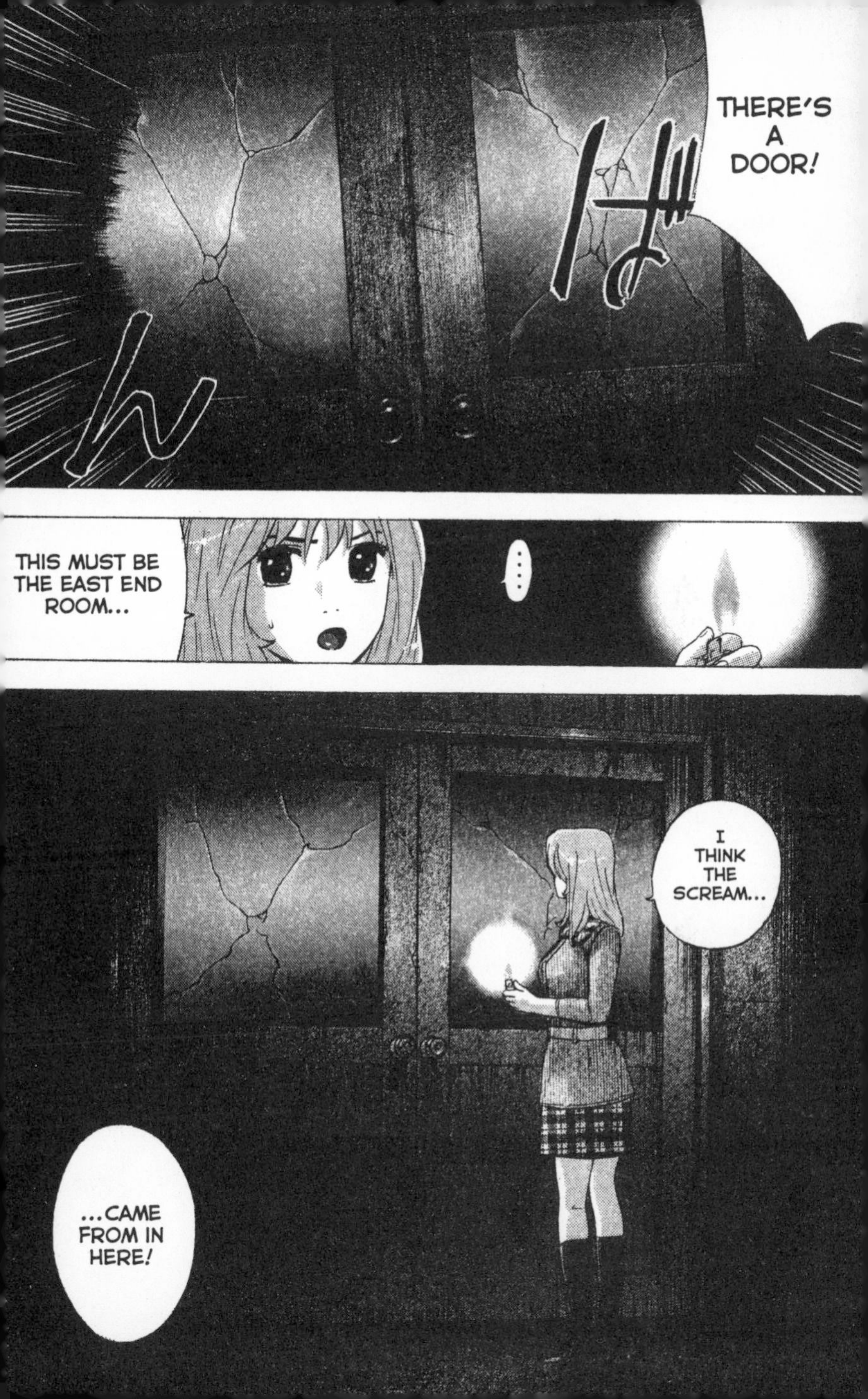
THERE'S A DOOR!
...
THIS MUST BE THE EAST END ROOM...
I THINK THE SCREAM...
...CAME FROM IN HERE!

OH...

KURUMI! I'LL OPEN THE DOOR!

ALL RIGHT!

GO FOR IT!

READY?

YOU STEP BACK...

...AND AIM THE GUN, OKAY?

OKAY!

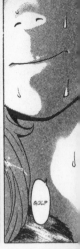

GULP

?!!!

HUH ...?

I CAN'T SEE...IT'S TOO DARK IN HERE.

USE THE LIGHTER, SHINGO...

OH! RIGHT!

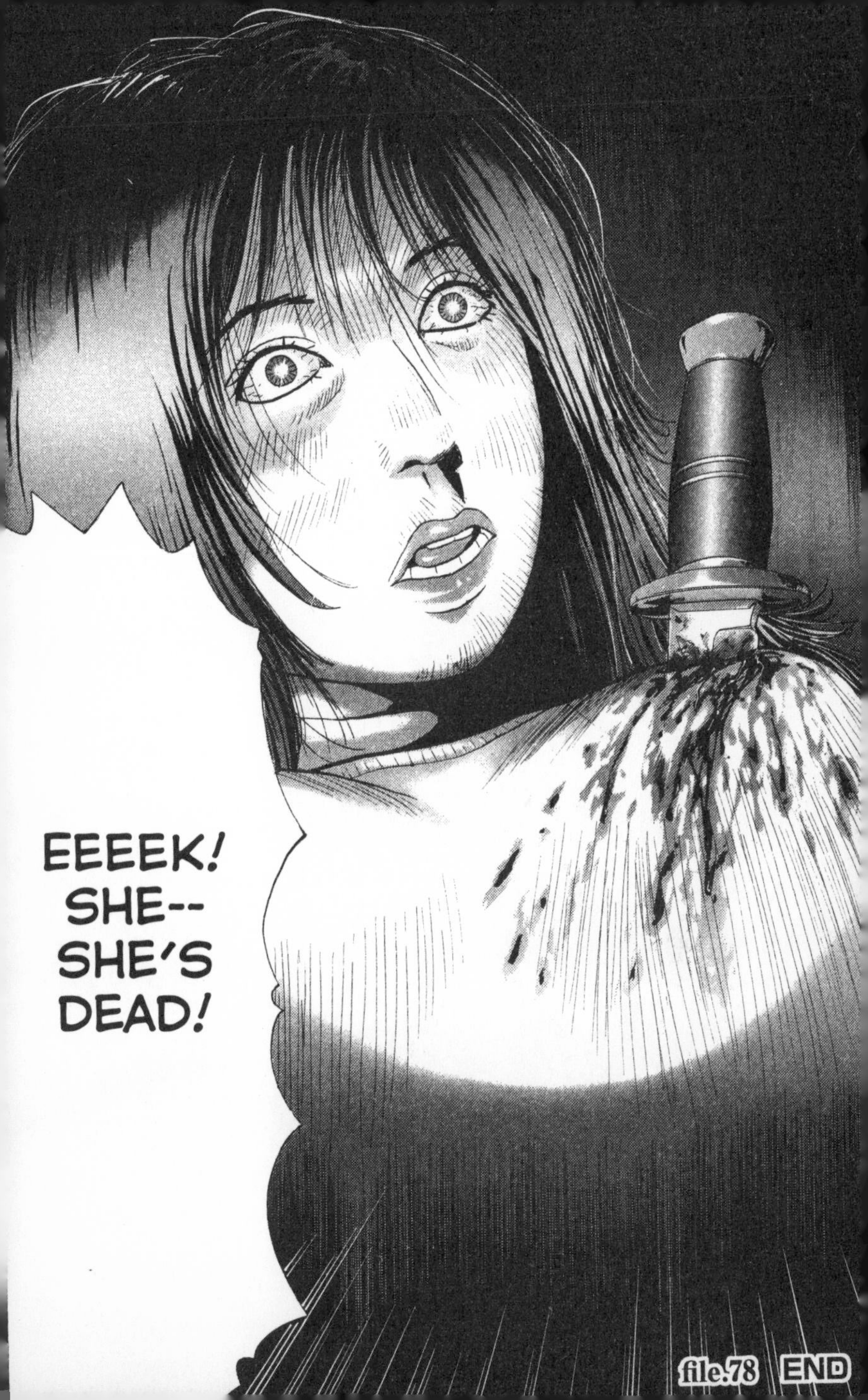
EEEEK! SHE-- SHE'S DEAD!
file.78 END

FROM THE JOURNALS OF Kozaburo Himuro:

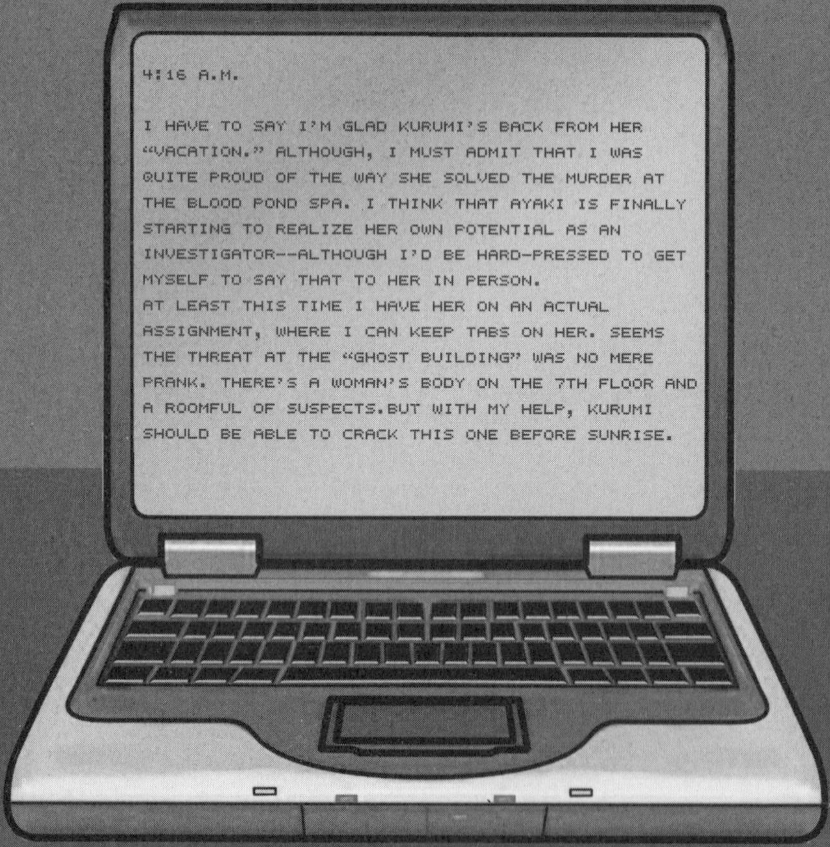
4:16 A.M.
I HAVE TO SAY I'M GLAD KURUMI'S BACK FROM HER "VACATION." ALTHOUGH, I MUST ADMIT THAT I WAS QUITE PROUD OF THE WAY SHE SOLVED THE MURDER AT THE BLOOD POND SPA. I THINK THAT AYAKI IS FINALLY STARTING TO REALIZE HER OWN POTENTIAL AS AN INVESTIGATOR--ALTHOUGH I'D BE HARD-PRESSED TO GET MYSELF TO SAY THAT TO HER IN PERSON.
AT LEAST THIS TIME I HAVE HER ON AN ACTUAL ASSIGNMENT, WHERE I CAN KEEP TABS ON HER. SEEMS THE THREAT AT THE "GHOST BUILDING" WAS NO MERE PRANK. THERE'S A WOMAN'S BODY ON THE 7TH FLOOR AND A ROOMFUL OF SUSPECTS.BUT WITH MY HELP, KURUMI SHOULD BE ABLE TO CRACK THIS ONE BEFORE SUNRISE.

HIMURO AND AYAKI
ARE BACK ON THE CASE IN...

.remote.

VOLUME 9

TOKYOPOP PRESENTS
MANGA 漫画
THE NEW SIZZLING HOT
FREE
MAGAZINE
ZELDA AND FRIEND FROM
WAR ON FLESH
© Justin Boring, Greg Hildebrandt and TOKYOPOP Inc.
SIGN UP FOR FREE WWW.TOKYOPOP.COM

TOKYOPOP SHOP

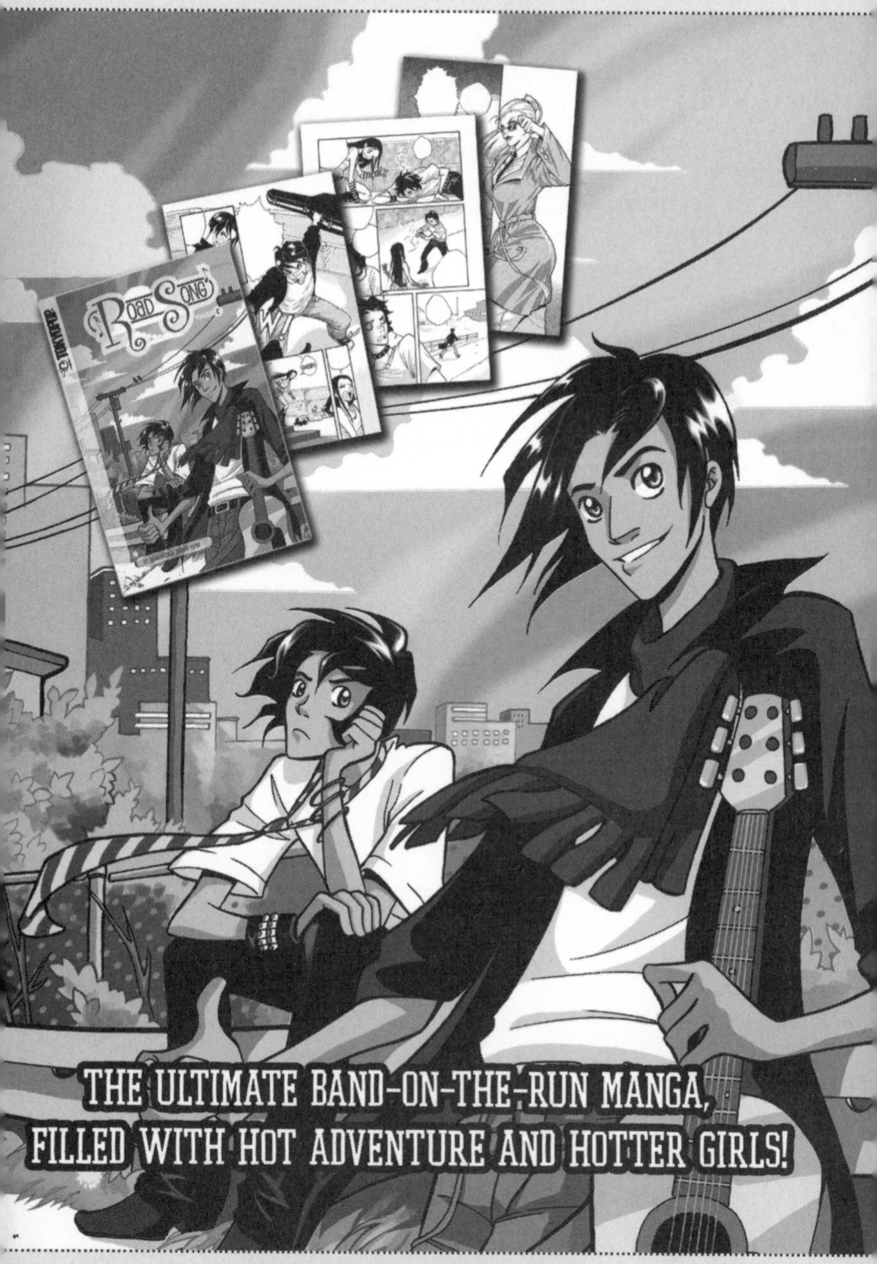

RoadSong
THE ULTIMATE BAND-ON-THE-RUN MANGA,
FILLED WITH HOT ADVENTURE AND HOTTER GIRLS!

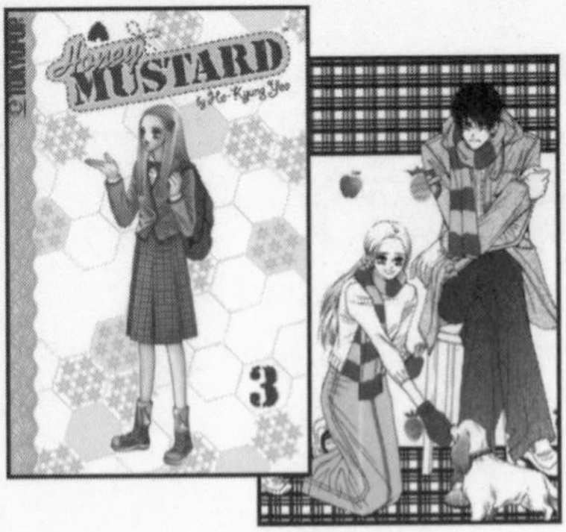
Honey
MUSTARD
by Ho-Kyung Yeo
3

BY HO-KYUNG YEO

HONEY MUSTARD

I'm often asked about the title of *Honey Mustard.* What does a condiment have to do with romance and teen angst? One might ask the same thing about a basket of fruits, but I digress. Honey mustard is sweet with a good dose of bite, and I'd say that sums up this series pretty darn well, too. Ho-Kyung Yeo does a marvelous job of balancing the painful situations of adolescence with plenty of whacked-out humor to keep the mood from getting *too* heavy. It's a good, solid romantic comedy...and come to think of it, it'd go great with that sandwich.

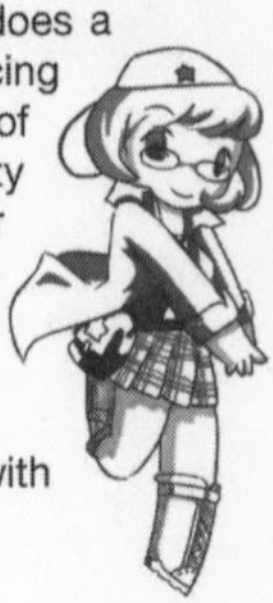

~Carol Fox, Editor

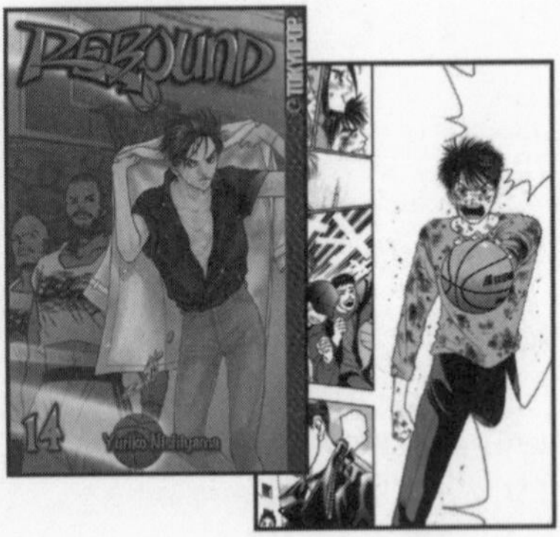
14

BY YURIKO NISHIYAMA

REBOUND

At first glance, *Rebound* may seem like a simple sports manga. But on closer inspection, you'll find that the real drama takes place off the court. While the kids of the Johnan basketball team play and grow as a team, they learn valuable life lessons as well. By fusing the raw energy of basketball with the apple pie earnestness of an afterschool special, Yuriko Nishiyama has created a unique and heartfelt manga that appeals to all readers, male and female.

~Troy Lewter, Editor

W9-CUP-003

STOP!

This is the back of the book.
You wouldn't want to spoil a great ending!

This book is printed "manga-style," in the authentic Japanese right-to-left format. Since none of the artwork has been flipped or altered, readers get to experience the story just as the creator intended. You've been asking for it, so TOKYOPOP® delivered: authentic, hot-off-the-press, and far more fun!

DIRECTIONS

If this is your first time reading manga-style, here's a quick guide to help you understand how it works.

It's easy... just start in the top right panel and follow the numbers. Have fun, and look for more 100% authentic manga from TOKYOPOP®!